GREAT ISSUES

Edited by Stuart Gerry Brown

GREAT ISSUES:
The Making of Current American Policy

NELSON M. BLAKE
W. FREEMAN GALPIN
HARRY SCHWARTZ
SIDNEY C. SUFRIN
PHILIP H. TAYLOR
WARREN B. WALSH

MAXWELL SCHOOL OF CITIZENSHIP AND PUBLIC
AFFAIRS, SYRACUSE UNIVERSITY

Essay Index Reprint Series

BOOKS FOR LIBRARIES PRESS
FREEPORT, NEW YORK

Framingham State College
Framingham, Massachusetts

INTERNATIONAL STANDARD BOOK NUMBER:
0-8369-2148-8

LIBRARY OF CONGRESS CATALOG CARD NUMBER:
70-134061

PRINTED IN THE UNITED STATES OF AMERICA

Contents

PREFACE   vii

I.   EVOLUTION OF SELF-GOVERNMENT IN
     AMERICA   1
     Nelson M. Blake

II. THE GROWTH OF AMERICAN DEMOCRACY   19
     Nelson M. Blake

III. THE AMERICAN PARTY SYSTEM   37
     Nelson M. Blake

IV. THE PRECONCEPTIONS OF ECONOMIC LIFE   55
     Sidney C. Sufrin

V.   ECONOMIC DEVELOPMENT   75
     Sidney C. Sufrin

VI. ECONOMIC DEVELOPMENT (Continued)   95
     Sidney C. Sufrin

VII. THE ONE-WORLD ARGUMENT   117
     Sidney C. Sufrin

VIII. THE SOVIET'S RUSSIAN HERITAGE   141
      Warren B. Walsh

IX. THE SOVIET'S MARXIST HERITAGE   161
     Warren B. Walsh

X.   THE SOVIET WAY: EARLY DEVELOPMENTS   181
     Warren B. Walsh

XI. THE SOVIET WAY: RECENT DEVELOPMENTS   202
     Warren B. Walsh

XII. THE DICTATORSHIP OF THE PROLETARIAT   228
     Warren B. Walsh

XIII. SOVIET FOREIGN POLICY FROM PETROGRAD
      TO YALTA   251
      Warren B. Walsh

v

XIV. DEVELOPMENT OF BRITISH LIBERALISM:
 BACKGROUNDS 277
 W. Freeman Galpin
XV. FROM LIBERALISM TO THE LABOUR PARTY 296
 W. Freeman Galpin
XVI. BRITISH DEMOCRACY GOES OVERSEAS 317
 W. Freeman Galpin
XVII. PATTERNS OF WESTERN EUROPE: GERMANY 334
 Nelson M. Blake
XVIII. PATTERNS OF WESTERN EUROPE: FRANCE 357
 Nelson M. Blake
XIX. PATTERNS OF WESTERN EUROPE: ITALY 376
 Nelson M. Blake
XX. CHINA: THE EVOLUTION OF SELF-
 GOVERNMENT 395
 Philip H. Taylor
XXI. MEETING OF EAST AND WEST 424
 Philip H. Taylor
XXII. NATIONAL SELF-DETERMINATION IN CHINA 449
 Philip H. Taylor
XXIII. THE BACKGROUND OF CONTEMPORARY
 AMERICAN FOREIGN POLICY 474
 Philip H. Taylor
XXIV. AMERICAN FOREIGN POLICY BEFORE
 WORLD WAR II 500
 Harry Schwartz
XXV. AMERICAN FOREIGN POLICY DURING
 WORLD WAR II 518
 Harry Schwartz
XXVI. AMERICAN FOREIGN POLICY SINCE
 WORLD WAR II 536
 Harry Schwartz
INDEX 563

Preface

I<small>T</small> <small>HAS</small> <small>BEEN</small> the purpose of the authors of this book to provide undergraduate college students with such information and interpretation as seems essential for understanding the great issues of the world in the mid-twentieth century, and, in particular, the transcendent issue of Communism, or the closed society, as against democracy, or the open society. The book treats variously of such issues as the reconstruction of Germany, France, and Italy; the civil war in China, and the tensions generally disturbing the Far East; but all these are seen in relation to the underlying mortal struggle between authoritarian and free societies. Thus considerable attention is given to the theoretical premises of Communism on the one hand and Western democracy (whether socialist or capitalist) on the other. At the same time it is hoped that sufficient factual information from the areas of politics, economics, geography, sociology, and history have been provided to facilitate the practical interpretation of the ideas sketched. The authors, it may be added, have come together in this collaboration from departments of history, political science, and economics.

At no time have the authors intended to emphasize the merely current. The original privately printed edition of this book was prepared in the fall of 1947. It was revised in the spring of 1949 and again in the summer of 1950 for the present publication, but the body of the text has remained throughout substantially unaltered except for what we hope are improvements in style and communication. The aim of the book is to explore the backgrounds of our world, and though it refers to events which took place in the early winter of 1950-1951, it is the earnest desire of the authors that the book not be mistaken for a discussion of contemporary events. The measure of its value will lie in such persisting usefulness as it may have whatever may be the events of the coming months and years.

The book was conceived originally as a group project and arose out of many long discussions among the contributors. The revisions also have been worked out on a coöperative basis, but the individual chapters are the work of the individual contributors as indicated in the table of contents. The editor's function has been largely that of coördinating discussion and planning.

The authors and editor wish to acknowledge with gratitude the many useful criticisms offered them by the staff members in the Citizenship Program of the Maxwell School at Syracuse University. The findings of these teachers, based on their classroom experience with the book, have been invaluable. The authors and editor wish also to express here their special thanks to Mrs. Virginia Marsden for her skill in handling technical details of production at all stages in the development of the book and their appreciation of her sorely tried patience.

S. G. B.

Maxwell School of Citizenship
Syracuse University
17 January 1951

GREAT ISSUES

CHAPTER I

Evolution of Self-Government in America

THE AMERICAN CITIZEN, reading his newspaper in these postwar days, often realizes for the first time that many of his basic assumptions about the nature and proper functions of government are not shared by many other peoples of the world. Russian leaders and publicists talk much of democracy, but they obviously place a very different meaning on the word from our own. English socialists come closer to us in their conception of democracy, but in carrying through the nationalization of large areas of the British economy they reveal assumptions about the proper function of government that are disturbing to many Americans.

Perceiving these things, the intelligent citizen finds that he needs to do some serious thinking. As to his own ideas of government, he is likely to ask: Where do these ideas come from? Why were they once assumed to be valid? Are they equally valid today? And then he will ask himself: Why have other people developed different ideas? Are these differences important? Which ideas seem likely to win the allegiance of people in parts of the world now hesitating in their choice? Can the United States live at peace with nations whose assumptions about government are fundamentally different from our own?

Obviously, the American's first responsibility is to understand better his own assumptions. He accepts as a matter of course the ideals of free speech, freedom of the press, freedom of religion, free elections, trial by jury, separation of powers, checks and balances, the supremacy of the Constitution, the rights of private property and private business. Why is it that Americans take these things for granted, when so many people in other countries do not even understand what we mean by the words?

When we attempt to trace these ideas back to their sources we find that many of them were brought to America from England. It was natural that this should be so. Although the present population of the United States probably derives more from non-English than from English stock, it was the English who came first. They set up the framework of government on the basis of their own experience, and later immigrants tended to accept and adapt themselves to this framework. Moreover, it should never be forgotten that the American colonies were a part of the British Empire for 169 years. During this period a great struggle between king and Parliament took place in the mother country. One result of the conflict was to focus attention on the whole problem of the nature of government, the powers which the state might rightfully exercise, and the rights of the individual which ought to be respected. The American colonists participated only indirectly in this great conflict, but they were nonetheless influenced by it. They digested the ideas of government developed in the English struggle and based on these their own arguments when they quarreled with the mother country and eventually declared their independence. Some of this tradition shared by both Americans and English will be discussed in a later chapter.

Much of the strength of English institutions derived from the fact that they were not first contrived by scholars and lawyers and then imposed as political blueprints upon the nation. Instead, the institutions evolved with very little conscious planning. They were adapted to the actual problems of English government as these arose over many centuries.

The same kind of evolutionary growth lies behind American institutions. To be sure, Americans are governed under the provisions of a specific document drafted in the year 1787. But there was little of mere theory in the Constitution. Behind it lay the lessons not only of centuries of English history but of 180 years of American political experience as well. Almost from the beginning, the colonists were given a share in the processes of government.

GOVERNMENT BY COMPACT OR CHARTER

Virginia, the first successful English colony in America, was founded and governed from 1607 to 1624 by the Virginia Company, an English trading corporation. Although the colonists had been promised that they would continue to enjoy the rights of Englishmen in the New World, the government was for several years an arbitrary one. All the inhabitants were regarded as servants of the corporation and were governed by rules and regulations made by the company in London, three thousand miles away. The company's authority in the colony itself was represented by a governor with practically unlimited powers.

This illiberal form of government had some excuse during the first years of settlement. The colonists included many unruly characters, and strict discipline was required until the colony gained self-sufficiency in its agriculture. But as conditions improved, the company itself recognized the desirability of giving the colonists an opportunity to express their views. In 1619 the Virginia House of Burgesses was created, composed of two representatives chosen from each of the eleven boroughs of the colony. Naturally, the company carefully limited the privileges of the new body. The ultimate lawmaking authority was retained by the London stockholders. But the colonists were allowed to make petitions to the company and even to enact laws which were binding upon the colony unless they were disallowed. The Virginia colonists were still far from having complete control over their own government, but at least they had been admitted to a share in that government. And they showed themselves true Englishmen by asserting as early as 1624 that no taxes ought to be laid on the land or commodities of the colony except with the consent of the assembly and that these revenues should be levied and employed as the assembly should direct. Already the colonial representatives were grasping at the power of the purse as a lever to extend their authority. In 1624 the Virginia Company lost its charter and the colony came under the direct rule of the king. But no attempt was made to deprive the Virginians of their recently acquired share in the colonial government.

Plymouth, the second successful colony, had an even more important political experience. It was settled by Separatists, radical Protestants who would not worship in the Church of England. When the first shipload of these Pilgrim Fathers arrived at the Massachusetts coast, they were confronted with serious problems. They had no real right to make a settlement in this area and there was no legal basis for government. To deal with this situation, the leading men in the enterprise met in the cabin of the ship and affixed their names to the famous Mayflower Compact. This read:

In the Name of God, Amen. We, whose names are underwritten, the Loyal Subjects of our dread Sovereign Lord King James, by the Grace of God, of Great Britain, France, and Ireland, King, Defender of the Faith, Etc. Having undertaken for the Glory of God, and Advancement of the Christian Faith, and the Honour of our King and Country, a Voyage to plant the first colony in the northern parts of Virginia; Do by these Presents, solemnly and mutually in the Presence of God and one another, covenant and combine ourselves together into a civil Body Politick, for our better Ordering and Preservation, and Furtherance of the Ends aforesaid; And by Virtue hereof do enact, constitute, and frame, such just and equal Laws, Ordinances, Acts, Constitutions, and Offices, from time to time, as shall be thought most meet and convenient for the general Good of the Colony; unto which we promise all due Submission and Obedience.

Where did these men get the idea that in the absence of government they could supply the need by simply agreeing to constitute themselves as a government and to abide by the laws thus enacted? It sounds like the social contract of John Locke, but John Locke was not yet born. The inspiration for the Mayflower Compact is to be found not in the realm of political philosophy but in the religious ideas of the Separatists. For a generation they had contended against the rule of bishops in religious matters. They had insisted that each individual Christian church should be based on the voluntary association of its members. The church came into existence when its members signed a solemn covenant, constituting themselves a Christian congregation with power to select its own ministers and officers, to establish its own creed, and to govern and discipline the individual members. Accustomed through long practice to govern themselves in religious matters, it was a natural step for the Separatists to extend the principle into the realm of civil government. On this simple basis and without any real constitution or framework of government, the Pilgrims proceeded to elect officials and make laws for many years.

Massachusetts Bay, to the north of Plymouth, was a very much larger and more powerful colony. For fifty years it governed itself as completely as Plymouth, but on a somewhat more secure legal basis. The Puritans who settled in Boston and surrounding territory were the proud possessors of a charter from Charles I. This document had a peculiar history. It had been originally granted to the Massachusetts Bay Company, a trading corporation similar to the Virginia Company. But instead of retaining its headquarters in London and maintaining long-distance control over its American colonists, the Massachusetts Bay Company itself moved to America; that is, the officers and most of the stockholders of the corporation moved and took their charter with them. This group, although composed of only about a dozen men, at first attempted to monopolize the entire government over some two thousand settlers. Criticism naturally arose and the original stockholders consented to admit other men to their ranks. These freemen, as they were called, elected the governor and his assistants and participated in voting taxes and making laws. When the freemen became too numerous and too widely dispersed to legislate directly, a representative system was devised. Thus out of a trading corporation an almost independent republic evolved. Let it be said at once, however, that a republic and a democracy are not necessarily the same thing. Not all the adults of Massachusetts were admitted to the ranks of freemen. On the contrary, none but members of the Congregational churches might be freemen, and only a minority of the colonists were able to pass the rigid requirements for church membership.

Massachusetts itself became the mother of other colonies. Rhode Island was settled by strong individualists who were expelled from Massachusetts because they criticized the political and religious system of that colony; Connecticut was settled by good Congregationalists who moved into the fertile Connecticut Valley for economic reasons. In both new colonies there was the problem of setting up a government, and in both colonies the problem was met as it had been at Plymouth by a covenant or agreement to establish a government and abide by the laws which were enacted. In the case of Connecticut, however, the process was taken a step further. In 1639 a document called the Fundamental Orders was adopted. This provided a complete framework of government and may be considered the first effort of Americans at drafting a constitution.

None of these New England colonies was on a secure legal basis from the English point of view. The Plymouth, Rhode Island, and Connecticut settlers had set up their governments entirely without permission from the king, and the Massachusetts settlers had done something perhaps even worse. They had carried the charter of an English trading corporation to the New World and had then stretched the document to the limit and beyond in setting up a government so contemptuous of the king's authority that it did not even permit the worship of the Church of England. After the English Restoration steps were taken to regularize the government of these colonies. Rhode Island and Connecticut were given unusually liberal royal charters, authorizing them to elect their own governors and to make their own laws through their elected assemblies, provided that such laws did not conflict with those of England. In 1684 Massachusetts was deprived of its charter and for a few years was subjected to arbitrary government. But in 1691 William and Mary, acting in the spirit of the Glorious Revolution, granted the Puritan colony a new charter. It was less liberal than that of Rhode Island or Connecticut, since the governor was to be appointed by the king, but in other particulars it gave the colonists an important share in the colonial government.

Although only the New England colonies had real charters, something equivalent obtained in several other areas. Maryland was a proprietary colony whose government had been entrusted to the descendants of Lord Baltimore, but the proprietor was required by the original grant to give the descendants a share in the making of laws. Pennsylvania and Delaware were similarly under the proprietorship of the Penn family, but in this case the rights of the colonists to participate in the government were recognized not alone in the royal grant but in a sort of charter which William Penn himself granted. The American colonists became accustomed at an early date to written documents in which the organization of government was detailed and the powers of each branch of the government were set forth.

POWERS OF THE COLONIAL LEGISLATURES

Although only Rhode Island and Connecticut enjoyed
permanently the privilege of electing their own governors,
all thirteen of the colonies had assemblies elected by the
property holders and participating actively in the government.

In theory, the powers of these colonial assemblies were
rigorously circumscribed. The upper house in each was
the so-called council and, except in New England, it was
an appointed and not an elected body, thus providing a
strongly conservative influence in the legislative process.
The royal governor, moreover, had an absolute veto over
bills passed by the colonial legislature. And finally, if a
colonial law cleared these two hurdles, it might still be
disallowed by the English Privy Council.

Despite all these handicaps, the colonial assemblies succeeded in making themselves extremely powerful bodies.
They did this exactly as the English Parliament had back
in the fourteenth and fifteenth centuries—through the
power of the purse. By refusing to vote the necessary taxes
for carrying on the government, they often compelled the
council and the governor to consent to laws which were
being proposed against the governor's opposition. They
learned to control the policies of the executive branch by
making specific appropriations for particular purposes.
Even the governor often found himself unable to secure
a salary unless he gave his assent to laws and policies which
the assembly demanded.

THE GREAT STRUGGLE WITH THE MOTHER COUNTRY

Between 1763 and 1775 the colonies and the mother
country were engaged in the great controversy that finally
resulted in the Revolutionary War. There were various
issues at stake, but the most important one was the power
of the English Parliament to tax the colonists. The mother
country based its policy on the contention that Parliament was the supreme legislature for the entire British

Empire and had the right to tax and legislate for the colonies in all matters whatsoever. But the Americans stubbornly denied this and asserted that they could be taxed only by their own colonial legislatures.

The colonists were consistent throughout the period in resisting the attempts of Parliament to tax them, but in choosing their arguments they shifted ground several times. The truth is that up to 1763 they had little occasion to ponder deeply over the general problem of government. Since in actual practice they had enjoyed a large measure of autonomy through their colonial legislatures, the abstract problem of where ultimate sovereignty lay had not worried them. But when they undertook to resist the imposition of new taxes, they found embarrassing problems. Parliament for many years had passed laws regulating the trade of the entire British Empire, and the colonists had acquiesced in these precedents. How could they now deny that Parliament had the power to legislate for them?

One of the early colonial contentions was that the issue at stake was that of internal taxation. They conceded that Parliament might lay an external tax like a customs duty, but not an internal tax such as the requirement that every legal paper must bear a revenue stamp. But a few years later when Parliament took this contention literally and sought to raise a revenue through new colonial customs duties, the colonists speedily objected to any taxation at all except through their own legislatures. Their argument was this: The British Constitution included the principle that a man's property was sacred; it could not be taken from him without his consent. As applied to taxation, this meant that no valid tax could be imposed unless it were voted by the representatives of those upon whom the burden would be laid. The colonists were not represented in Parliament, nor could they be because of the great distance between England and America. Therefore, they could be taxed only by their own legislatures. Since taxa-

tion of the colonists by Parliament violated the British
Constitution, it was void.

The principle that a law which violated the constitution
was void became basic to all American political thought
and remains so to this day. But it did not convince the
British government. After all, the British Constitution
was unwritten and men might argue about what it did and
did not include. The colonial case had weaknesses which
the British were not slow in pointing out. First, as regarded the principle of no taxation without representation,
the fact was that neither Britain nor the colonies had a
democratic franchise. Only property holders were allowed
to vote, but it had never been contended that those who
did not vote were exempt from the laws passed by Parliament or by the colonial legislatures. Moreover, there were
many centers of population in England that had grown
up since the parliamentary boroughs were designated;
these were not represented in Parliament, yet their inhabitants had to pay the taxes which Parliament imposed.
The British contention was that the members of Parliament acted in behalf of the whole nation, not just the
constituencies which had elected them. Even boroughs
which did not elect members to Parliament were therefore
"virtually represented" in the national legislature. The
colonies, it was contended, were likewise "virtually represented." Moreover, in an unwritten constitution, precedent was all-important, and precedent supported the
assertion that Parliament was the supreme legislature for
the whole British Empire with power to bind its subjects
in all matters whatsoever. Precedent likewise indicated
that the colonial assemblies were subordinate legislatures
whose powers were strictly limited.

Of course, the colonists denied the British interpretation of the constitution. They effectively demolished the
theory of virtual representation by pointing out that in
England both electors and nonelectors would be involved
in the same taxation. Therefore, the members of Parliament might be said to be representing both elements. But

in laying a tax on the colonists, the case would be quite different: no actual electors in England would be directly affected; indeed, they might be relieved of some of their own tax burden by taxing the colonists. The colonial interest could by no means be said to be represented under such circumstances.

But the actual precedents for parliamentary supremacy were harder to explain away. This was the great stumbling block to arguments based exclusively upon the rights of the colonists under the British Constitution. In this dilemma, the basis of the colonial argument underwent its final and most significant shift. The case was now appealed from the legal precedents to the court of right reason, to the natural rights which John Locke had set forth to justify the Glorious Revolution in England. What, asked James Wilson in 1774, is the ultimate end of the government? And he answered:

"All men are, by nature, equal and free: no one has a right to any authority over another without his consent: all lawful government is founded in the consent of those who are subject to it: such consent was given with a view to ensure and to increase the happiness of the governed, above what they would enjoy in an independent and unconnected state of nature. The consequence is, that the happiness of the society is the first law of every government."

Only the more radical of the colonial leaders at first adopted the argument of natural rights. The moderates were alarmed at its implications. Not only did it provide a basis for asserting that all the precedents of parliamentary legislation for the colonies were mere usurpations and that Parliament had absolutely no power to bind the colonists, but it might even be used to deny the authority of the king himself. As late as 1774 most of the colonial leaders not only acquiesced in the king's final veto power but even conceded that in the interests of practical necessity the British Parliament might be permitted to regulate the external trade of the Empire. But events overwhelmed the caution of the moderates. The outbreak of hostilities in 1775, the stern steps taken by the British king to suppress the rebellion, the need for foreign aid—all these things made it irrational for the colonists to continue to assert that all they wanted was to secure their right of self-government within the British Empire.

In 1776 the great decision was made. The Second Continental Congress asserted the independence of the United States and adopted an eloquent statement of the reasons for their action. The latter document, the Declaration of Independence, began as follows:

When in the Course of human events, it becomes necessary for one people to dissolve the political bands which have connected them with another, and to assume among the Powers of the earth, the separate and equal station to which the Laws of Nature and of Nature's God entitle them, a decent respect to the opinions of mankind requires that they should declare the causes which impel them to the separation.

We hold these truths to be self-evident, that all men are created equal, that they are endowed by their Creator with certain inalienable Rights, that among these are Life, Liberty, and the pursuit of Happiness. That to secure these rights, Governments are instituted among Men, deriving their just powers from the consent of the governed. That whenever any Form of Government becomes destructive of these ends, it is the Right of the People to alter or to abolish it, and to institute new Government, laying its foundation on such principles and organizing its powers in such form, as to them shall seem most likely to effect their Safety and Happiness. Prudence, indeed, will dictate that Governments long established should not be changed for light and transient causes; and accordingly all experience hath shown, that mankind are more disposed to suffer, while evils are sufferable, than to right themselves by abolishing the forms to which they are accustomed. But when a long train of abuses and usurpations, pursuing invariably the same Object evinces a design to reduce them under absolute Despotism, it is their right, it is their duty, to throw off such Government, and to provide new Guards for their future security. . . .

It will be seen that all bickering about the British Constitution is now abandoned. The claims of Parliament are
simply ignored with the clear implication that Parliament
never had possessed any powers over the colonists to which
the latter had consented. The whole argument is directed
to the reasons for the repudiation of the king's authority.
The king's tyranny threatens to destroy the ends for which
all government exists; therefore it is the right and duty of
the Americans to throw off his authority—to assume the
station to which the "Laws of Nature and of Nature's
God" entitle them.

The Declaration was largely the work of Thomas Jefferson. But he never claimed any credit for originality in
the philosophy on which it was based. The strength of
the document was in its bold assertion of a tradition that
was old both in England and in America. The doctrine
that governments derived their just powers from the consent of the governed was implicit in the establishment of
the Puritan Commonwealth in seventeenth-century England and in the Glorious Revolution; it was implicit in
the Mayflower Compact and the Fundamental Orders of
Connecticut. In the philosophy of John Locke it had been
made explicit and was familiar to every well-read Englishman and American. Involved in both Locke's and Jefferson's arguments are certain distortions of history. But
these do not invalidate their principal conclusions. Americans still believe that all governments *ought* to derive
their just powers from the consent of the governed and
that they *ought* to respect the fundamental liberties of
the individual. In its essence, Jefferson's philosophy is still
the American philosophy.

The Idea of Federalism

Having repudiated their allegiance to George III, the
Americans were free to construct their own institutions of
government. They did this first at the state level. While
the Revolutionary War was still in progress, the first state
constitutions were drafted. The procedure itself was com-

paratively novel, since precedents, like the framing of the
Fundamental Orders of Connecticut or similar documents
in England during the Commonwealth period, were rare.
These state constitutions were explicit in their assertion
of popular sovereignty; that of North Carolina, for example, said that "all political power is vested in and derived from the people only."

Like the burnt child who fears the fire, the typical
American of this generation showed a great distrust of
government. The New England towns sought to keep as
much government as possible on a purely local basis; the
states in turn were reluctant to surrender any part of their
power to a central authority. From 1776 to 1781 the
United States as a nation had as its sole central authority
the Continental Congress, an emergency agency which
waged war, made treaties, and raised money on behalf of
the United States without any constitutional basis at all.
In 1781 the thirteen states agreed to the Articles of Confederation, which formally lodged these and a few other
powers in a Congress composed of delegates appointed by
the state governments. But fear of central authority ran
through every part of this document. The sovereignty
and independence of the states was specifically reserved,
Congress was given no power to levy taxes or to regulate
commerce, and there was no adequate provision for a
central executive or judiciary.

Time soon proved that insufficient government may
bring evils almost as great as too much government. The
United States under the Articles of Confederation was so
hampered by lack of funds and authority that it could not
protect the frontiersmen against the Indians; it could not
secure for the early settlers in Kentucky the privilege of
sending their produce out through the Mississippi River
and New Orleans; it could not gain for eastern merchants
the opportunities which they needed to trade in foreign
ports; it could not provide the necessary conditions for
trade to flow unhampered from one state to another.
Despite the misgiving of those who feared central author-

ity, a stronger national government was obviously needed if the United States was to survive and prosper.

The answer was found in the Constitution, drafted in 1787 by a convention of state delegates meeting at Philadelphia, ratified by the states through specially elected conventions, and brought into operation in 1789. But the Constitution, like the Declaration of Independence, was not the inspiration of a moment. It was based on the political experience of the colonists in governing themselves under their charters, of the colonial legislatures in voting taxes and making laws, and more recently of the states in drafting their own constitutions and the Articles of Confederation.

The greatest success of the Philadelphia Convention was in its application of the principle of federalism—the creation of central authority with adequate powers to deal with national problems, while leaving to the states complete freedom to maintain their own elected governments and exercise all powers except those delegated to the national government. In this case, a new answer was found to an old problem—one which had frequently arisen before in American experience.

In 1643 the Puritan colonies of the Northeast had recognized the need for common action to defend themselves against the Indians, the Dutch, and the French. They had established a New England Confederation, which had operated with fair success for a generation and then failed for reasons that are significant to later American experience. Each of the four participating colonies had been given an equal voice in determining policies, yet one, Massachusetts, was so much larger than the others that it had a much greater obligation in case of war. The Confederation had received its greatest blow when Massachusetts refused to support a war against the Dutch which had been voted by the other three colonies over its objection.

The need for defense against the French and the Indians had continued for many generations, and in 1754 seven of the colonies had sent delegates to Albany to discuss the possibility of common action. The so-called Albany Plan, mostly the work of Benjamin Franklin, had resulted. This had proposed a central government composed of a President General to be appointed by the king and a Grand Council, composed of delegates chosen by the colonial assemblies; the larger colonies were to send more delegates than the smaller; the central government was to have authority to negotiate with the Indians, to maintain an army, and to make laws and impose taxes for specified purposes. The proposal had been rejected both by the English government and by the separate colonies, yet its influence on later events was considerable.

The Articles of Confederation of 1781, already described, had been in some particulars a backward step from Franklin's proposals of 1754. They had given the small states equal representation with the large—an obvious injustice to the latter—and they had given the central government no power to impose taxes—a fatal deficiency since the states had been unwilling to grant more than a portion of the funds which Congress had requested of them. But along other lines the Articles had demonstrated progress in American thinking, and many of its provisions were taken over almost directly into the Constitution. Such, for example, were provisions granting the people of each state free ingress and regress to and from any other state and the same rights of trade and commerce therein as the inhabitants of the state, requiring each of the states to give full faith and credit to the records, acts, and judicial proceedings of the courts and magistrates of every other state, and granting to Congress the sole and exclusive right of fixing the value of coins and the standard of weights and measures, and of establishing post offices.

What remained for the Constitution to do was to extend the authority of the central government sufficiently to make it adequate to deal with the demonstrated needs of the day. Vital new powers were granted to Congress— to levy taxes, to regulate foreign and interstate commerce, and to coin money. Provision was made for a President who should be commander in chief of the army and navy and have the power to negotiate treaties, to appoint ambassadors, judges, and other officers, and to recommend measures to Congress. Judicial power was vested in a Supreme Court and such inferior courts as Congress might establish. The states were prohibited from making treaties, coining money, or laying duties on imports or exports, and the Constitution, the laws of the United States, and the treaties made under authority of the United States were to be the supreme law of the land, binding upon state as well as federal judges.

Into the Constitution ran all the separate streams of political experience that we have been discussing. Proceeding directly out of the great English heritage were such principles as the bicameral legislature, frequent elections, freedom of debate, the right of the lower house to initiate all revenue legislation, and the principle that the privilege of the writ of habeas corpus should not be suspended except when the public safety might require it in cases of rebellion or invasion. Out of American experience came the principle of the explicit written document, defining the powers of each branch of the government. Out of the great tradition of John Locke and Thomas Jefferson came the simple but impressive preamble:

"We, the People of the United States, in Order to form a more perfect Union, establish Justice, insure domestic Tranquility, provide for the common defence, promote the general Welfare, and secure the Blessings of Liberty to ourselves and our Posterity, do ordain and establish this Constitution for the United States of America."

Another principle firmly entrenched in the Constitution was the separation of powers, the establishment of three distinct branches of government—legislative, executive, and judicial—with an ingenious set of checks and balances to prevent any one branch from dominating the entire government. Bills passed by Congress might be vetoed by the President, but his veto could be overridden by a two-thirds vote in the House and Senate. The President's power to negotiate treaties and appoint officers was checked by the need for Senate approval. The judges interpreted the laws, but their power was also limited since they were appointed by the President with the approval of the Senate and since they were dependent on the executive branch to carry out their decisions. Congress, moreover, had extensive powers to check the judiciary through increasing or diminishing the number of judges, establishing or abolishing inferior courts, and defining the jurisdiction of the courts. The framers of the Constitution had read of the importance of checks and balances in Montesquieu, a great French philosopher of the eighteenth century. He, in turn, believed that he had found the principle exemplified in the English government. But the American application of the principle was based as much upon American experience as on political theory, and nowhere else in the world were these ideas carried so far as here. The results have not always been happy, as frequent deadlocks between President and Congress illustrate, but most Americans still cherish the general principle of the separation of powers as a valuable safeguard against arbitrary government.

It was not easy to draft the Constitution. The Convention would have failed had not the members worked out first one compromise and then another. The so-called Great Compromise which underlay the whole document was that between the small states and the large whereby each state was given equal representation in the Senate whereas representation in the House of Representatives was apportioned according to population. Thus we may say that the experience of the Philadelphia Convention illustrates another American political conviction—the necessity of fair compromise to make government work.

CHAPTER II

The Growth of American Democracy

THE LOGICAL COROLLARY to the principle that all government ments derive their just powers from the consent of the governed would seem to be that all the governed should participate in the processes of government. But the Revolutionary generation shrank from following through to this conclusion. The federal government left the matter of the franchise strictly to the states and they continued to permit only male property owners to vote and hold public office. All the poor, all the women, and most of the Negroes were excluded from any participation in government. In some states, moreover, there were religious tests for officeholding. Most incongruous of all was the institution of slavery—a strange institution, indeed, for a nation that professed belief in the inalienable right of the individual to life, liberty, and the pursuit of happiness. Clearly, the establishment of republican institutions in the United States did not of itself make the nation a democracy. Many generations were required before this goal was even approximated.

THE FEDERAL BILL OF RIGHTS

American history demonstrates that a nation needs both radicals and conservatives. Leadership in the resistance to parliamentary taxation and in the assertion of American independence was taken by radicals. The Declaration of

Independence was a radical document, written by one of the greatest of American radicals, Thomas Jefferson. But the radicals of this generation went too far in their distrust of all government. It was the conservatives who saw the need for stronger central authority and who took the lead in the work of the Philadelphia Convention. The Constitution, as originally drafted, was a conservative document, showing distrust of democracy at many points—in providing that the President should be chosen by an electoral college instead of directly by the people, in providing that the senators should be chosen by the state legislatures instead of by the people, in providing that judges should hold office for life, and in restraining the states from issuing money or from making laws impairing the obligation of contract.

The survivors of the old radical party were very suspicious of the Philadelphia Convention. Such fine patriots as Patrick Henry, Richard Henry Lee, George Mason, and James Monroe organized a party to try to defeat the ratification of the Constitution by the states. They feared that in setting up a strong federal government all the liberties which had been fought for in the Revolutionary War might be jeopardized. Why, they asked, had no bill of rights been included as it had in most of the state constitutions? The conservative answer was not reassuring. The preamble of the Constitution, it was asserted, was "a better recognition of popular rights, than volumes of those aphorisms, which make the principal figure in several of our state bills of rights, and which would sound much better in a treatise of ethics, than in a constitution of government."

The battle over ratification was hard fought and extremely close. In Rhode Island and North Carolina the antifederalists were in a clear majority while in Massachusetts, New Hampshire, New York, and Virginia they were very nearly so. In order to carry these close states, the conservatives had to make a most important concession. They had to promise to support the addition of a bill of rights through amendments to the new Constitution. The outcome of the great contest was most fortunate for the future of the United States. It would have been a disaster if the new Constitution had been rejected, yet it was a very good thing that the radical party was strong enough to force the addition of a bill of rights. In a sense, it was another of the great compromises on which the nation was built.

The fulfillment of this pledge became one of the first matters of business taken up by Congress under the new Constitution in 1789. A great number of amendments had been proposed by the state ratifying conventions. These were studied and reworded by James Madison and other congressmen. Twelve were eventually passed by Congress, but only ten were ratified by the states. These, added to the Constitution in 1791, constitute the so-called federal Bill of Rights.

The most important parts are:

[First Amendment] Congress shall make no law respecting an establishment of religion, or prohibiting the free exercise thereof, or abridging the freedom of speech, or of the press; or the right of the people peaceably to assemble, and to petition the government for a redress of grievances.

[Fifth Amendment] No person shall be held to answer for a capital, or otherwise infamous crime, unless on a presentment or indictment of a Grand Jury, except in cases arising in the land or naval forces, or in the Militia, when in actual service in time of War or public danger; nor shall any person be subject for the same offence to be twice put in jeopardy of life or limb; nor shall be compelled in any criminal case to be a witness against himself, nor be deprived of life, liberty, or property, without due process of law; nor shall private property be taken for public use, without just compensation.

[Sixth Amendment] In all criminal prosecutions, the accused shall enjoy the right to a speedy and public trial, by an impartial jury of the State and district wherein the crime shall have been committed, which district shall have been previously ascertained by law, and to be informed of the nature

and cause of the accusation; to be confronted with the witnesses against him; to have compulsory process for obtaining
witnesses in his favor, and to have the Assistance of Counsel
for his defence.

[Eighth Amendment] Excessive bail shall not be required,
nor excessive fines imposed, nor cruel and unusual punishments inflicted.

At first reading, one is likely to be surprised that only
one amendment and less than fifty words are devoted to
such important freedoms as those of religion, speech, press,
assembly, and petition, whereas no fewer than five of the
amendments are devoted to the rights of individuals before the courts. But recent events in Europe have shown
the importance of these latter rights. They are the great
bulwark of the American citizen against secret political
police, special tribunals, and concentration camps—the
inevitable accompaniments of totalitarian government.

The federal Bill of Rights contains nothing that is new.
The development of its basic ideas may be traced in both
English and American political experience. But the addition of these ideas, in explicit terms, to the Constitution
was a great victory for the cause of democracy.

It should be noted that the first ten amendments are
limitations on the power of the federal government. Until
1868 protection of individual liberties from impairment by
the state government was dependent on the state constitution. But eventually the Federal Constitution was amended
to carry its protection into this area as well. The first
section of the Fourteenth Amendment reads:

All persons born or naturalized in the United States and
subject to the jurisdiction thereof, are citizens of the United
States and of the State wherein they reside. No State shall
make or enforce any law which shall abridge the privileges
or immunities of citizens of the United States; nor shall
any State deprive any person of life, liberty, or property, without due process of law; nor deny to any person within its
jurisdiction the equal protection of the laws.

EXTENSION OF THE FRANCHISE

The right of every man to vote was established by slow stages. The old theory, stubbornly clung to, was that only the man who owned property had the substantial interest in good government which entitled him to the franchise. Indeed, at the time of the Revolutionary War most states insisted that the possession of at least fifty acres of land was necessary. As more people began to live in towns and gain a living from commerce and industry, the qualifications were liberalized to permit owners of personal property or those who paid a specified amount in taxes to vote.

But this was not enough. The democratic right of every man to vote was vigorously asserted and had, in the end, to be conceded. Two great forces in American history hastened the victory of the democratic franchise. One was the frontier movement; the other was the growth of the cities. Life on the frontier was naturally democratic; inherited wealth and aristocratic background counted little in the new communities; a man earned the respect of his fellows only by his own qualities and accomplishments. When the frontier territories were ready to draft their own constitutions and secure admission to the Union as new states, they almost invariably rejected the old property-holding or taxpaying qualifications and bestowed the franchise on every white male citizen twenty-one years of age or over. Vermont, entering the Union in 1791, and Kentucky, admitted in 1792, set the new pattern, and most of the states subsequently organized followed their example.

Democracy on the frontier created a demand for democracy in the older states. New Hampshire responded by abolishing its taxpaying qualification in 1792; Maryland took the same step in 1809. But the battle was not so easily won in most of the eastern states despite the loud demands of the urban workers. The question was hotly debated in the politics of New York State. In words reminiscent of Thomas Jefferson the popular party demanded "the elective franchise—the birthright of every free citizen, to the enjoyment of which the law of nature and of nature's God entitles him." But when the proposal to liberalize the franchise was debated at the constitutional convention of 1821, some of the most respected leaders of the state opposed it. According to the great jurist, Chancellor Kent: "The apprehended danger from the experiment of universal suffrage . . . is no dream of the imagination. It is too mighty an experiment for the moral condition of men to endure. The tendency of universal suffrage is to jeopardize the rights of property and the principles of liberty." The conservatives were nevertheless defeated. The new constitution granted almost universal white male suffrage, and the few restrictions which were retained were swept away by a popular referendum in 1826. In other states the contest continued longer, but property and taxpaying qualifications were doomed by the rising democratic movement, and by the time of the Civil War all but a few states had recognized the right of all white adult males to vote.

The Rights of Negroes

Although a slaveowner himself, Thomas Jefferson saw clearly that Negro slavery was incompatible with the principles of the Declaration of Independence. He advocated the prohibition of slavery in the new frontier territories and pondered over the problem of how slavery might be gradually eliminated where it already existed. A minority of liberal Southerners during the late eighteenth century shared these convictions. But any hope for a peaceful solution to the slavery problem was dimmed by the invention of the cotton gin and the rapid spread of plantation agriculture through the deep South. Slavery seemed a necessary institution to the prosperity of the whole section and, since it was necessary, most Southerners convinced themselves that it was good. They resented deeply the activities of northern abolitionists who denounced all slaveowners as sinners and helped slaves to run away in defiance of the fugitive slave laws. The issue became so charged with emotionalism that a peaceful solution was impossible. Even though Lincoln was committed to take no step against slavery where it was already established, southern extremists regarded his election to the presidency as a threat to the institutions of the South and pushed through the secession of their states. The Civil War resulted, a long and bitterly fought contest. Lincoln's sole objective during the first two years of the war was to preserve the Union, but eventually he broadened his program to include the emancipation of the slaves. The great conflict ended in complete Union victory in 1865 and soon thereafter the Thirteenth Amendment was added to the Constitution reading: "Neither slavery nor involuntary servitude, except as a punishment for crime whereof the party shall have been duly convicted, shall exist within the United States or any place subject to their jurisdiction."

The abolition of slavery was a great democratic landmark, but the circumstances of its achievement were most unfortunate. The inability of American statesmen to formulate a program that might have brought about a peaceful, gradual termination of the old evil was the greatest failure in United States history. Not only did this failure result in a terrible war but it brought about Negro emancipation under circumstances which put the new freedmen under serious handicaps.

White men had been rationalizing the institution of slavery for many generations, and in the process they had developed assumptions about the racial inferiority of the Negroes that could not soon be eradicated. These prevailed in the North as well as in the South, and Negroes had been almost everywhere excluded from the franchise. Before the Civil War Negroes were permitted to vote in only six states—all located in the Northeast. When, after the war, the radical Republican faction insisted on the immediate enfranchisement of the Negroes as a condition to be met before the southern states could be readmitted to the Union, the idea came as a great shock.

Unfortunately most of the northern Republicans were interested in the Negro vote only as it might be manipulated for party advantage. The result was that ex-slaves—almost completely uneducated through no fault of their own—were given the franchise without any attempt to train them in the responsibilities of citizenship. Cynical white politicians organized the new voters and used them to establish corrupt "carpetbag" governments throughout the South. The result was tragic. The prejudice of southern whites against Negro suffrage was deepened until it became a violent phobia. Through intimidation and actual violence they tried to keep the colored voters from the polls. For a time the radical Republicans, still in control of the federal government, tried to oppose this. The Fourteenth Amendment, quoted above, was intended to grant Negroes citizenship and to guarantee their rights as citizens. The Fifteenth Amendment, adopted in 1870, declared: "The right of citizens of the United States to vote shall not be denied or abridged by the United States or by any State on account of race, color, or previous condition of servitude."

But northern opinion eventually turned against the continuance of federal intervention in the South. The evils of carpetbag government were so notorious and the continued use of troops was so contrary to American tradition that the federal government gave up its efforts and left the southern states to run their own affairs. White supremacy was immediately reasserted. At first indirectly through economic pressure, and then directly through legislation, the Fifteenth Amendment was circumvented. Negroes were deprived of their right to vote through literacy tests or poll-tax requirements. Since these standards were likely to disqualify poor whites as well as blacks, a favorite southern device became the white primary—that is, the exclusion of Negroes, not from the regular elections, but from the primaries where the party candidates were selected. Because the Democrats were the only party with any chance to win the regular election, to exclude the

Negroes from the Democratic primary was in effect to
exclude the Negroes from any influence over the choice of
public officials in the South. The United States Supreme
Court has now ruled that the Fifteenth Amendment may
not be circumvented in this way.

Even though poll tax and literacy tests, often unfairly
administered, still continue in many parts of the South,
Negroes who can jump these hurdles have a clear legal
right to the franchise. Most of them still do not vote for
fear of white resentment. But more Negroes have voted in
recent elections in the South than for many years in the
past, and the trend seems certain to continue—despite
the fulminations of men like Rankin of Mississippi or
Talmadge of Georgia. Meanwhile, more and more have
migrated to the North and West where their right to the
suffrage is not challenged and where the Negro vote is
eagerly courted by both parties.

But the issue of the franchise is only one of the battle-
grounds on which a struggle over the democratic rights of
the Negroes has been fought. Throughout the South
deprivation of colored citizens' right to due process of law
has been frequent. Lynchings are the most flagrant examples of this, but perhaps even more serious is the day-
by-day administration of two levels of justice. Negroes are
rarely to be found on southern juries, and the result is that
blacks accused of acts of violence against whites are almost
invariably convicted, while whites accused of similar acts
toward blacks are usually acquitted.

The equality of status to which Negroes are entitled
has often been denied in the North as well as in the South.
The state of New York is a pioneer in attempting to protect Negroes and other groups in their right to equality of
opportunity in securing jobs, but much remains to be
done in this field in the nation as a whole.

Thus, while it cannot be said that Negroes now possess
complete democratic rights, much progress toward this
goal has been made since 1865.

THE RIGHTS OF WOMEN

In 1848 a convention at Seneca Falls, New York, adopted a declaration that gave a new orientation to an old document. In part, it read:

When, in the course of human events, it becomes necessary for one portion of the family of man to assume among the people of the earth a position different from that which they have hitherto occupied, but one to which the laws of nature and of nature's God entitle them, a decent respect to the opinions of mankind requires that they should declare the causes that impel them to such a course.

We hold these truths to be self-evident: that all men and women are created equal, that they are endowed by their Creator with certain inalienable rights; . . .

The history of mankind is a history of repeated injuries and usurpations on the part of man toward woman, having in direct object the establishment of an absolute tyranny over her. To prove this, let facts be submitted to a candid world.

He has never permitted her to exercise her inalienable right to the elective franchise. . . .

He has made her, if married, in the eye of the law, civilly dead.

He has taken from her all right in property, even to the wages she earns. . . .

He has monopolized nearly all the profitable employments, and from those she is permitted to follow, she receives but a scanty remuneration. He closes against her all the avenues to wealth and distinction which he considers most honorable to himself. As a teacher of theology, medicine, or law, she is not known.

He has denied her the facilities for obtaining a thorough education, all colleges being closed against her.

Thus did a pioneer group of feminists raise their standard of revolt against the inferior status of women in the mid-nineteenth century. John Locke would have been profoundly shocked at this conclusion from his philosophy and even Thomas Jefferson would probably have been much surprised. Stubborn males quoted the Bible to prove that women should be under the authority of men; they asserted that women had a different sort of intelligence from men; they even resorted to flattery, by saying that women were by nature too fine and gentle for the hurly-burly of politics and business life.

But the feminists persisted in their offensive, and the males were driven out of one foxhole after another. The laws were amended to give property rights to married women. Women's colleges were established, and the principle of coeducation was gradually extended to the collegiate level. The medical schools fought hard to keep women out, since it was considered particularly unladylike for them to want to study anatomy, but eventually the feminists won this battle also.

Although women might become doctors, lawyers, and preachers, male conservatives were determined that they should never become voters. When the men ran out of other arguments, they even revived the theory of virtual representation that had been utilized in the eighteenth century to defend Parliament's right to tax communities which were not represented in that body. Women were represented in government, it was asserted, through the votes of their husbands, fathers, and brothers. But the women treated this argument with the contempt that it deserved and continued to demand the direct franchise.

Fortunately no civil war was necessary. One step at a time the men retreated. As in the achievement of manhood suffrage, it was the frontier areas that took the lead. Women were given full rights of suffrage in Wyoming territory in 1869, in Utah in 1870, and in Colorado and Idaho a few years later. In the older states the women had to be content for many years with partial suffrage. They were conceded the right to vote for school committees or other local officers, but denied the franchise in more important elections.

After 1900 the so-called progressive movement gave a new impetus to the extension of democracy. This resulted in several victories for women's suffrage on a state basis, and a growing demand for an amendment to the Federal Constitution to guarantee the right throughout the nation. Male resistance to the proposal was finally swept away by World War I. After a struggle to "make the world safe for democracy," it was obviously foolish to continue to deny women complete equality in suffrage. The Nineteenth Amendment, adopted in 1920, read: "The right of citizens of the United States to vote shall not be denied or abridged by the United States or by any State on account of sex."

SEPARATION OF CHURCH AND STATE

One of the greatest American problems has been the proper relationship of church and state. In seventeenth-century England, as almost everywhere else in Europe, it was taken for granted that there must be one national church which all persons should be required to attend and support. The first colonists who came to America acted as a matter of course on these assumptions. The Church of England was established by law in Virginia, and heavy penalties were prescribed against those who refused to attend its worship or support it through the payment of taxes. In Massachusetts the Puritans followed an even stricter policy. They organized Congregational churches, which were radically different in organization and worship from the Church of England, but they permitted no dissent from the new forms which they established. Those who sought to preach different doctrines were expelled, fined, whipped, and even—in the case of four persistent Quakers—hanged.

The first notable protest against the theory that it was the duty of the state to enforce religious uniformity came from Roger Williams. After his expulsion from Massachusetts for criticism of that colony's political and religious system, Williams engaged in a notable intellectual duel with the Reverend John Cotton of Boston on the important subject of the relations of church and state. In *The Bloudy Tenent of Persecution for Cause of Con-*

science (1644), the Rhode Island radical argued that churches were voluntary associations of men with like beliefs. If they were true churches, they had no need for worldly defenses since they were armed with "the breast-plate of salvation" and "the sword of the spirit." The state was necessary to protect the body and property of the individual, but it had no right to dictate in matters of conscience—to establish churches, to punish heretics, or to impose civil penalties or disabilities for any religious reason. The Quaker William Penn held very similar convictions.

But although Rhode Island and Pennsylvania practiced religious toleration in accordance with these principles, Williams and Penn were far in advance of their times. Prevailing opinion continued to hold that the preservation of religious uniformity was not only a permissible function of government but one of its most important duties. When religious toleration came gradually into practice, it was not because it was considered a good thing but because the enforcement of uniformity became impossible. Charles II, a bad Christian but a humane man, intervened to forbid the Massachusetts Congregationalists to hang any more Quakers. In time the Puritan colony grudgingly conceded the right of Baptists, Quakers, and Anglicans to worship in their own way. During the seventeenth century Maryland permitted religious toleration to all Christians who believed in the Trinity—as a matter of practical necessity since the proprietor was a Catholic and his colonists were partly Catholic and partly Protestant. But so far were the Marylanders from accepting religious toleration as a positively good thing that early in the eighteenth century, after the Catholic proprietorship was terminated, the colonial assembly passed religious laws which gave the Church of England the status of an established church and deprived Catholics of their right to public worship.

By the time the Declaration of Independence was signed, the practice of religious toleration had made substantial progress. Quakers, Baptists, Presbyterians, and Methodists had all encountered serious legal obstacles, but by now they had won in most areas the right to worship unmolested in their own churches. Catholics were not so fortunate; only in Pennsylvania and Rhode Island was public Catholic worship permitted. But the right to worship was only a first step toward genuine religious toleration. By no means had the colonial governments put all religious groups on a basis of equality. Instead certain denominations were highly favored by law. In the southern states from Maryland to Georgia the Anglican Church was still established. This meant that it was supported by public taxation; that nonconformers were forbidden to hold public office and, sometimes, to vote; and that in theory, if no longer in actual practice, men could be punished for refusing to attend Anglican services. The Congregational Church was in a similar position in most of the New England states.

The most dramatic struggle for the establishment of religious equality took place in Virginia. Step by step the special privileges of the Anglican Church were shorn away until in 1786 the famous Virginia Statute for Religious Freedom was enacted. Drafted by Thomas Jefferson, it states a great American democratic principle in memorable words. The preamble asserts that "Almighty God hath created the mind free," and that all attempts to influence it by temporal punishments are "a departure from the plan of the Holy author of our religion, who being Lord both of body and mind, yet chose not to propagate it by coercions on either." The argument broadens from an argument for merely religious freedom to an argument for freedom of opinion in every realm. The great force of Jefferson's words is still felt today. He said:

. . . to suffer the civil magistrate to intrude his powers into the field of opinion, and to restrain the profession or propagation of principles on supposition of their ill tendency, is a dangerous fallacy, which at once destroys all religious liberty, because he being of course judge of that tendency will make his opinions the rule of judgment, and approve or condemn the sentiments of others only as they shall square with or differ from his own; . . . it is time enough for the rightful purposes of civil government, for its officers to interfere when principles break out into overt acts against peace and good order; . . . truth is great and will prevail if left to herself; . . . she is the proper and sufficient antagonist to error, and has nothing to fear from the conflict, unless by human interposition disarmed of her natural weapons, free argument and debate, errors ceasing to be dangerous when it is permitted freely to contradict them.

Therefore it was enacted:

. . . that no man shall be compelled to frequent or support any religious worship, place or ministry whatsoever, nor shall be enforced, restrained, molested, or burthened in his body or goods, nor shall otherwise suffer on account of his religious opinions or belief; that all men shall be free to profess, and by argument to maintain, their opinion in matters of religion, and that the same shall in no wise diminish, enlarge or affect their civil capacities.

The separation of church and state was projected into the national field by the Federal Constitution, which forbade religious tests for federal officeholders and the establishment of any national church. At the state level there were still battles to be fought. Religious tests for officeholders were only gradually eliminated, and not until 1833 did Massachusetts abolish taxes for the support of the Congregational Church.

But a new and very troublesome problem in the relations of state and church had arisen. This was in the field of education. The extension of universal manhood suffrage had emphasized the need for universal education at least on the elementary level. The public school system—hitherto rare except in New England—was extended throughout the nation. In areas where there were already public schools some attempt had usually been made hitherto to include religious instruction. Such training had in truth been considered the principal business of the

New England public schools when they were first established in the seventeenth century. But Baptists, Methodists, Episcopalians, and Catholics all objected to sending their children to tax-supported schools where the religious education usually had a distinctly Congregational flavor. In 1827 a Massachusetts law prohibited the use of schoolbooks which were calculated to favor the tenets of any particular sect of Christians. Conservatives were shocked and raised a great clamor against what they called "Godless schools," but the Massachusetts authorities kept their heads and eliminated all religious instruction other than reading without comment from the Bible.

In New York State the issue took a different form. There public schools were less common at first and the state made a practice in some areas of granting financial aid to private schools maintained by charitable organizations. The question now arose as to whether state aid should be similarly extended to denominational schools. In 1820 a Baptist church in New York City made the first request for such funds. It received help for some years and was then cut off. A Catholic orphan asylum made a similar request which was granted, but the Methodists were denied. Obviously, it was a very delicate problem to decide which denominational schools should receive public funds and which should not. In the 1840's Catholics, Jews, and Scotch Presbyterians all began demanding public funds for the support of their separate schools. It was easy to see where the division of the school funds, once begun, would end, and in 1842 the New York legislature enacted a law prohibiting the allocation of any portion of the school funds to any school in which "any religious sectarian doctrine or tenet should be taught, inculcated, or practiced."

The same issue was raised in other states. Massachusetts had occasionally given support to Catholic parochial schools in local areas, but in 1855 a constitutional amendment forbade any such practice in the future. Most of the states now incorporated similar provisions in their state constitutions. It became a clearly formulated American principle that funds raised through taxes for education should not be diverted to private denominational schools.

No principle has been more important in the development of American education. Division of the school funds among Catholics, Methodists, Baptists, Presbyterians, and scores of other denominations would have been tragic; division among the three major religious groups—Catholics, Protestants, and Jews—would have been almost as bad. Instead of one public school system the taxpayers would be supporting three. Some suggestion of the handicap under which education would have operated is to be found in the experience of the South, where racial prejudice has led to the establishment of a dual system with separate public schools for the whites and the Negroes. So expensive is this wasteful duplication of facilities that all schools are below standard. The establishment of separate schools for the different religious communions would have been unfortunate for other reasons as well. For Catholic, Protestant, and Jewish children to study together in the same schools is a training in good citizenship; education carried on in an atmosphere of religious segregation would accentuate conflict of opinion, promote intolerance, and tend to involve religious issues in politics.

Democratic Adjustment to New Problems

As constitutions go, that of the United States is now an old document. Most of the other great powers of the world have changed their instruments of government not once but several times since 1789. An eighteenth-century document, drafted for the requirements of 4,000,000 people living in the age of the stagecoach, now serves the needs of 150,000,000 people entering the age of atomic power. How can this be?

The answer has been in American adaptability. As new problems—problems never visualized by the founding fathers—have arisen, Congress has legislated. Under the American system, Congress can exercise no powers except those granted in the Constitution. But fortunately, the Supreme Court has followed a policy of broad construction. Gradually the Constitution has been reinterpreted to permit Congress and the states to regulate the affairs of a more complex society. Sometimes, as in the case of the income tax, an amendment to the Constitution has been necessary.

The presidency has become a more powerful office than the founding fathers could ever have imagined. The rise of political parties, each nominating its own candidates for the presidency, has reduced the electoral college to a meaningless mechanism and, in effect, brought about the direct election of the President by the people. Men with a strong sense of leadership like Jackson, Lincoln, Wilson, and the two Roosevelts have brought the presidential office into direct contact with the people so that it is democratic in a sense never expected in 1789.

In other particulars, also, America has become increasingly democratic. The Seventeenth Amendment provides for the direct election of United States senators. Through devices like the primary election, the initiative, the referendum, and the recall, voters are given an opportunity to participate more directly in the governmental process. The slogan of the progressives who secured the adoption of these relatively new ideas is significant. "The cure for democracy," they confidently asserted, "is more democracy." Most Americans still believe this. They recognize that antidemocratic practices still persist in many areas of American life; they know that in actual operation democracy is sometimes ignorant, foolish, and corrupt. But these are areas for reform, not reasons for repudiating basic principles. Americans still passionately believe in democracy and their favorite definition is still that of Lincoln—"government of the people, by the people, for the people."

CHAPTER III

The American Party System

THE OPERATION of the American party system is a mystery almost inexplicable to foreigners and not much easier for native Americans to understand. Despite the fact that some nine parties nominated candidates for the presidency in 1948, Truman, the Democrat, and Dewey, the Republican, together received about 95 percent of the popular vote. Of 531 senators and representatives composing the 81st Congress, all but one were designated either Democrats or Republicans. In order to be elected to public office—at least at the federal level—it is obviously almost essential to wear one or the other of these magic labels.

But what do the labels mean? What are the Democratic party principles that bind the Negro congressman Adam C. Powell and the Negro-hating John E. Rankin to the same party organization? How does it happen that the pro-labor Senator Wagner and the antilabor Senator Eastland are both called Democrats? Nor it is easier to understand how the Republican label may be worn with equal aplomb by conservatives like Senator Wherry and Senator Bricker and liberals like Senator Morse and Senator Aiken.

An examination of certain episodes in American history may help to explain, if not to rationalize completely, the character of present-day political parties.

FEDERALISTS AND REPUBLICANS

Despite George Washington's repugnance for political parties, the first President's administration witnessed the emergence of two bitterly contending factions. Alexander Hamilton, the youthful and brilliant Secretary of the Treasury, was the first center of controversy. In a series of ably written reports Hamilton urged a bold attack upon the problems of debt and depression that had accumulated since the Revolutionary War. He proposed that the federal government should at once establish its credit by issuing new securities to the full value of the outstanding paper claims against the United States, that in addition the state debts incurred to support the Revolutionary War should be assumed by the federal government, that a great national bank should be established to facilitate the government's financial business, that a protective tariff should be levied not only to raise revenue but to encourage American manufacturing, and that for additional revenue there should be an excise tax on whiskey.

Hamilton's program was enacted almost intact and succeeded admirably in establishing the solvency of the new nation. But this was not its only purpose. More important even than saving the country from bankruptcy, it seemed to Hamilton, was to win the support of the prosperous, investing classes for the federal government. The public debt which Hamilton funded at one hundred cents on the dollar was mostly held by speculators, who had purchased it from the original holders at a fraction of its face value. Profiting by Hamilton's policy to the amount of some forty million dollars, this group had good reason to feel grateful to the new government. Since the same class now held federal securities from which they were deriving a steady 6 percent income, they wished with all their hearts for the success of the federal experiment. By his brilliant stroke Hamilton had transformed the national debt from an embarrassing encumbrance to a political asset. The assumption of the state debts intensified this result, transferring the material stake of the bondholders from the local to the national level, and the creation of the bank provided both an excellent investment and a useful mechanism for facilitating business. Merchants, bankers, and

speculators thus became warm admirers of Hamilton and
provided the leadership of the faction presently to be
known as the Federalist party. If this seems too narrow a
group to have maintained control of the federal government for twelve years and of many state governments much
longer, it must be remembered that property qualifications
for voting made the influence of the rich and the well born
much greater than later. Moreover, the Federalists secured
faithful followers from the lower ranks in society. The
manufacturers championed by Hamilton included thousands of independent artisans working in their own homes.
Grateful also to the Federalists were sea captains, fisher-
men, and shipwrights, who had benefited by the new
government's measures to encourage commerce. Even the
recently emancipated Negroes of New York tended to vote
for the party so highly esteemed by their former masters.

But Hamilton's program was by no means universally
popular. The same policy that to one man seemed com-
mendable as contributing to the establishment of the national credit was condemned by another as a scandalous
enrichment of speculators. To many of the Revolutionary
generation the whole tendency of Hamilton's activities
seemed wrong. Had America fought against the expansion
of British imperial control only to create a new central
government which would encroach upon the powers of
the states and the rights of the citizens? So strongly did the
frontiersmen of western Pennsylvania resent the imposition of the whiskey tax that they rose in the quickly sub-
dued but immensely significant Whiskey Rebellion. But
although Hamilton's opponents soon learned that they
might not safely resort to arms to oppose his policies, this
did not prevent the organization of a vast agitation against
them. The opposition was intensified by the outbreak of
war between England and France. The allegedly pro-
British policies of the Washington and Adams administrations led to a tumult of protest on the part of Americans who were warmly sympathetic to the French
Revolution. Antiadministration newspapers and political

clubs were the core around which the Republican party was formed.[1]

The Republicans found magnificent leadership in Thomas Jefferson, Secretary of State until differences with Hamilton brought about his resignation in 1793. Seeking to convince Washington that he should veto the bill creating the National Bank, Jefferson argued for a strict interpretation of the Constitution which would restrict the authority of Congress to that absolutely necessary for carrying out the specifically delegated powers. Since Hamilton defended the chartering of the bank under a broad interpretation of the Constitution, this difference in principle is sometimes assumed to have been the chief difference between the two political parties. But this supposition encounters difficulties when later developments are considered. Jefferson's most notable achievement as President was the purchase of Louisiana, which could only be defended under a broad interpretation of the Constitution. On this issue and on others like the embargo and the attempt at conscription during the War of 1812 the Jeffersonian party pursued nationalistic policies which were bitterly condemned by the Federalists, who were now advocating strict construction and states' rights.

These early examples of the inconsistency of American party politics become less bewildering if we ask the questions: Why were the Federalists broad constructionists on the National Bank and strict constructionists on the Louisiana Purchase? Why were the Republicans strict constructionists on the earlier issue and broad constructionists on the later?

Jefferson was a Virginia planter, highly suspicious of Hamilton's obvious intention of insuring the dominance of the eastern commercial classes. Since he regarded the National Bank as an institution designed to promote that

[1] Not to be confused with the present-day Republican party, organized in 1854. Terminology was loose in the early days and the Antifederalist party was occasionally—especially in the North—called the Democratic party.

dominance, he easily convinced himself that the proposal was unconstitutional. More important, he was able to build a great political party out of all other elements that feared the rule of the great merchants and the money-lenders. Some of this support came from the artisans of the towns, but the mass of the Jeffersonian strength was in the nation's farmers. Since the great plantation owners feared Hamilton's favoritism for commerce as much as the small farmers, the Republicans gained supporters from all the agrarian classes. So long as the Federalists controlled the national government, the opposition party naturally stressed state sovereignty and strict limitation of the powers of the federal establishment.

However brilliant Hamilton's achievements as a statesman, as a politician he was less astute than his great rival. The basis of the Federalist party was too narrow to begin with and became more so with each passing year. Jeffersonian agrarianism coincided with the economic interests of the great majority of the population and became irresistible with the growth of the West. Small wonder then that Jefferson as President regarded American control of the Mississippi as so vital to the interests of the frontier farmers that he quickly conquered any personal doubts regarding the constitutionality of the Louisiana Purchase. Nor were the Federalists, perceiving clearly that the influence of the commercial East would steadily diminish with the growth of the West, inconsistent in raising states' rights objections to expansion.

To emphasize the economic basis of American politics and to portray the Federalist-Republican struggle as one between two species of property interests rather than between two interpretations of the Constitution is not to impute selfish motives to the great party leaders. Hamilton sincerely believed that the control of government by the investing classes was for the benefit of the nation as a whole; he feared the rule of the ignorant many and trusted the rule of the talented few. Jefferson no less sincerely believed that the happiness and prosperity of the country as a whole depended on a government controlled by the rank and file of typical Americans—and in his view typical Americans were self-respecting citizens owning their own farms.

DEMOCRATS AND WHIGS

The War of 1812 completely disrupted the old party structure. Although fought ostensibly to defend American rights on the seas, the war was bitterly opposed by the very class which had the greatest stake in our shipping, while it was enthusiastically supported by western farmers hundreds of miles from the coast. To the Northeasterners war with England threatened to destroy completely a foreign trade which had been hugely profitable despite seizures and impressments. But to the Westerners war meant an opportunity for expansion, for the conquest of the rich farmlands of Canada, and for expelling the British, whom the frontiersmen suspected of stirring up the Indians against them. New England Federalists carried their opposition to the extent of refusing to coöperate in financing the war, obstructing the use of the militia outside their own states, and threatening disobedience in case conscription were attempted. This narrow sectionalism proved disastrous. At the close of the war the Federalists were so burdened by their reputation for disloyalty that they were finished as a national party. In the presidential election of 1816 the Federalist candidate received only 34 electoral votes to Monroe's 134. Four years later the demoralized Federalists did not even name a candidate and Monroe's reëlection was unopposed.

The disappearance of the Federalists resulted in eight years of one-party rule unique in American history. But the triumphant Republicans were not entirely the same party that Jefferson had led. A strong feeling of nationalism pervaded the country, and the Republican politicians adopted measures that once would have been anathema. A tariff more truly protective than any Hamilton had been able to secure was enacted, and a new National Bank was not only established but defended by reprinting Hamilton's arguments of 1791. It might be questioned whether the Republicans had not really absorbed the Federalists rather than killed them.

Although many Americans rejoiced at the recess on party politics, the abnormal situation did not long continue. In 1824 no less than five candidates—all labeled Republicans—sought the presidency. The election was so close that the final choice had to be made in the House of Representatives. When John Quincy Adams eventually secured the prize through the support of Henry Clay, whom he made his Secretary of State, the bitterness of those who had supported General Andrew Jackson laid the basis for a resumption of party warfare. Adams and Clay sought to win Congressional support for a program of tariff protection for American industries and federally financed roads and canals. But this program aroused hostility of two kinds: first, that of the Jacksonians, who were determined to oppose whatever the Adams-Clay faction proposed, and second, that of numerous elements in the population who disliked specific items in the presidential program. The Adams administration was one of furious political activity looking toward the election of 1828. In that contest both factions still claimed the old Republican label, but the Adams men differentiated themselves as National Republicans while the Jacksonians were called Democratic Republicans.

The Jackson party, which swept to victory and laid the basis for the Democratic party of the future, was a curious conglomeration. Most of the West voted for Jackson despite the fact that Adams and Clay had advocated federal roads and canals for the benefit of the section. The internal improvement program had little appeal for frontiersmen able to ship their products down the Ohio and Mississippi for sale to southern plantation owners, and they regarded the Adams men as primarily devoted to the interests of the East. They resented particularly Adams' policy of upholding Indian rights against the demands of

white settlers. Although Jackson was in fact a rich plantation owner rather than the coonskin-clad cabin dweller of
American tradition, the frontiersmen felt that he was essentially one of them. But the West alone could never have
given Jackson his great victory. He secured also the vote
of the South, whose lack of manufacturing and dependence on foreign markets had made it strongly antitariff.
Even in the Northeast Jackson made heavy inroads on the
Adams-Clay faction by securing the votes of thousands of
poor farmers, city laborers, and recent immigrants. The
broadened franchise of the twenties made possible a mass
democratic movement that would have been impossible
earlier.

In 1828 Jackson could profit by the unpopularity of the
Adams administration and enjoy the support of all the
"antis" even though they hardly agreed with each other,
since some of them were strong nationalists and some
states' rightists, some protariff and some antitariff, some
inflationists and some hard-money enthusiasts. As the
penalty of victory, Jackson now had to take the responsibility for policies likely to alienate certain sections of the
country. Thus his veto of an internal improvements bill
alienated a portion of the West, and his strong stand
against South Carolina's attempt to nullify the tariff lost
him the support of the planter aristocracy of the South.
But the old general had an instinct for political leadership
and gained more than he lost by his decisions. His fight to
the death against the second National Bank won him
thousands of new adherents, who exulted in the destruction of a corporation which they regarded as a privileged
monopoly inimical to democratic institutions. Jackson had,
moreover, the services of a shrewd group of practical politicians who capitalized on his popularity and built up a
vast political machine based upon the spoils system—a
system long operating at the local level of politics but only
now employed with real effectiveness on the national scale.
Thus was created the militant party, which carried Jackson
to triumphant reëlection in 1832 and elevated Jackson's

loyal lieutenant, Martin Van Buren, to the White House in 1836.

But Jackson was hated as vehemently as he was loved, and by 1836 a strong anti-Jackson party was in the field, calling itself Whig to symbolize its opposition to the tyranny of "King Andrew." The core of the party was the old National Republican group, led by Clay, Adams, and Webster, but practical politics required alliance with other groups in order to form a party with sufficient national strength to hope to win the presidency. Most of the more prosperous planters of the South aligned themselves with the Whigs. Few of them had any enthusiasm for the tariff, but they hated much more the threat to property which they associated with Jacksonian democracy. Substantial western farmers and merchants also affiliated with the Whig party, as did ambitious young professional men like Abraham Lincoln. Generally speaking, the Whigs were the party of the more prosperous and successful classes, but they succeeded better than the Federalists in gaining also the votes of many of the less privileged. A portion of the eastern workers were convinced by the arguments of Horace Greeley that they should vote for the high-tariff party, whereas in the election of 1840 the Whigs demonstrated that they could outdo the Democrats in demagogic appeals to popular prejudice. Taking a further lesson from their opponents, the Whig party twice rode to power on the popularity of military heroes.

Democrats and Republicans

The Democrats and Whigs were national parties, deriving their strength from all sections of the country. They maintained their national appeal by avoiding issues that ran violently against the interest or prejudice of any major section and by choosing their candidates in such a way as to appeal to as many voters as possible. Thus in 1844 the Democrats chose their candidates from Tennessee and Pennsylvania, while the Whigs named men from Kentucky and New Jersey. In 1848 the Democratic candidates were from Michigan and Kentucky, the Whigs from Kentucky and New York.

But an increasing number of voters became dissatisfied with the attempts of the old parties to straddle the slavery issue and attempted to organize movements like the Liberty party and the Free Soil party. So long as their support was drawn only from the abolitionists, the third parties were ineffective. The Liberty party polled only one-third of 1 percent of the vote in 1840 and less than 3 percent in 1844. But in 1848 things took a different turn. Many voters hitherto indifferent to the slavery issue were aroused by the Mexican War—a war which many Northerners believed to have been unnecessarily provoked by a proslavery Democratic administration. Thousands of dissident Democrats and Whigs joined forces with the Liberty party group to form the much more formidable Free Soil party. Demanding a prohibition upon the extension of slavery into the territories, the Free Soilers derived their strength as much from those who wanted to reserve the new agricultural lands for middle-class white farmers as from those who wanted to help the Negro. Nearly five times as many voters rallied around the slogan. "Free Soil, Free Speech, Free Labor, and Free Men" as had responded to the narrower appeal of the Liberty party four years before. The third-party vote was still less than 10 percent of the total, but it proved decisive. Their losses to the Free Soilers deprived the Democrats of the electoral vote of New York and hence of the election.

The Compromise of 1850 temporarily quieted the divisive slavery issue. Most of the rebellious Democrats and Whigs returned to their old party affiliations, and the vote of the Free Soil party was sharply reduced in the presidential election of 1852. But two years later the controversy was revived in more disruptive form than ever by the passage of the Kansas-Nebraska Act, repealing the Missouri Compromise and opening up new territories to squatter sovereignty. In the heat of sectionalism thereby aroused, the old Democratic-Whig party system that had dominated politics for thirty years disintegrated rapidly. The Whig party soon disappeared completely, and the Democratic party was seriously divided. New factions sprang up like mushrooms in the spring with no less than twenty-three presenting candidates in Connecticut in 1854 and 1855.

For a time it seemed that the chief beneficiary of this chaos might be the "Know-Nothings," a new party dedicated to curbing the naturalization of aliens and reserving public office for the native born. This crusade to "purify" politics attracted thousands of former Whigs both southern and northern, since it seemed to present an issue that might divert attention from the slavery controversy.

But even a campaign for 100 percent Americanism could not head off the growth of a great new party, committed to halting the further extension of slavery. The Republican party was born in the Middle West in 1854 and speedily gained support from many groups. Included in its ranks were the antislavery people from the old Liberty and Free Soil parties together with thousands of former Whigs and Democrats who were disgusted by events in Kansas. In the emotionalism of the fifties many northern farmers and workers, who cared little what became of the slaves in the South, voted Republican out of fear that the slavery system would be more and more extended until they were forced to compete with slave labor in their own communities. The movement grew so rapidly that the Republicans captured 42 percent of the ballots in the presidential election of 1856. Four years later the new party strengthened itself by a significant broadening of its program. Eastern industrialists were won to the party by its promise of a return to tariff protection, a protection which the Democrats dependent on the southern vote had denied. Also included in the Republican platform of 1860 was a pledge of free homesteads in the West. Thus was created the mighty alliance between eastern business interests and western farmers through which the Republicans carried fourteen out of the next eighteen presidential elections.

The new party carried enough states in 1860 to have won the election in any case, but its victory was made easier by dissension in the ranks of its rivals. Stephen A. Douglas fought valiantly to preserve the national character of the Democratic party during the fifties, advocating "squatter sovereignty" as a formula for solving the problem of slavery in the territories. But southern extremists, as unwilling as their northern counterparts to accept compromise, were now demanding federal protection for slavery throughout the territories. When Douglas was nominated for the presidency by the regular Democrats, the Southerners left the party and nominated a candidate of their own. The election was a curious affair. In the North it was a contest between the Republican Lincoln and the Democrat Douglas; in the South between the seceding Democrat Breckinridge and the "Constitutional Union" candidate Bell, a former Whig appealing for the votes of the moderates. The crisis that was driving the country toward bloodshed was clearly evident in the purely sectional character of the year's politics. When the Republicans carried the election, South Carolina promptly seceded from the Union in protest against what it described as a "sectional Combination—for the subversion of the Constitution." Other southern states followed and within five months the Civil War had begun.

The Republican party emerged from the war greatly strengthened. Just as Hamilton had bound the investing classes to the Federalist party through his financial policy, so Republican measures enacted during the war appealed strongly to northern businessmen. The protective tariff, railroad subsidies, federal charters for local national banks, and government war bonds created a material stake which insured that most northern capitalists would henceforth vote Republican. But to portray the post-Civil War Republican party as simply the party of big business is to miscalculate its voting strength. Many workers had been educated to regard the tariff as a prolabor policy, and farmers approved the open-handed land policies of the dominant party, which not only provided homesteads for settlers but aided the establishment of agricultural colleges and the building of railroads across the prairies. An incalculable advantage to the Republicans, moreover, was their reputation for loyalty to the Union in contrast to the Democrats, the party of secession and treason. The Grand Army of the Republic, composed of Union veterans, was a potent arm of the Republican party, and voters who had never seen the battlefield were almost equally susceptible to orators "waving the bloody shirt."

But the two-party system did not die. The Democrats soon revived, aided no little in their recovery by Republican abuse of power. Attempting to build up their party in the defeated South, the Republicans so mismanaged things as to bring about the opposite result. The disqualification of many ex-Confederates and the premature enfranchisement of the Negroes under the coercion of federal troops created such resentment that all but a small portion of the whites became permanently anti-Republican. The South, which in earlier American history had always divided its ballots between the major parties, now became the "solid South," delivering its electoral vote with monotonous regularity to the Democratic candidate. The numerous scandals of the Grant administration also aided Democratic recovery. Reform became a demand of the day, more profitable to the Democrats who were out of power than to the Republicans who were in. Adding these new supporters to their strength in the South and in certain areas of the North and West where they had always retained their popularity, the Democrats managed to regain the status of a formidable opposition party and to carry presidential elections in 1884, 1892, 1912, and 1916.

CHARACTERISTICS OF THE AMERICAN PARTY SYSTEM

Thus evolved the two great parties which still dominate American politics. Reflecting upon this history and upon more recent developments, we may hazard answers to some of the puzzling problems posed at the beginning of this chapter.

Why does one party never retain dominance? Washington deplored "faction" and invited all men of good will to support his administration. Monroe actually achieved a situation where his party was the only one operating at the national level of politics. Whig opposition to the Democrats disintegrated after 1852, while the Democrats were badly demoralized in 1924 and the Republicans in 1936. Yet in each of these cases, either the old opposition party revived or a new one formed. One reason is that the party in power must make decisions—must enact laws and administer them. These measures rarely please everyone, and the dissidents have a strong tendency to rebel against the dominant leadership and form an opposition party. Even if the party in power tries to play safe by doing nothing, opposition will develop from those who demand action. A second reason is that practical politics derives much of its dynamic character from the ambition of individuals for the power and prestige of public office. In a one-party situation there are always individuals dissatisfied with their position in the established regime and easily persuaded to join a new political grouping.

Why are there usually only two major political parties? The answer lies in part in the American constitutional system, which offers no consolation prizes. Since proportional representation is almost nowhere recognized in American government, the object of American politics must be to secure more votes than anyone else in some geographical area—whether it be city ward, Congressional district, state, or electoral college. Since most practical politicians aspire to office, they cling to the party designations that are most likely to bring them to power. If the case of Franklin D. Roosevelt, Jr., is cited as an exception, let it be noted that although he achieved the difficult feat of winning a seat in Congress without the backing of either major party, he at once announced his intention of associating himself with the Democrats in the House of

Representatives. This was elementary common sense under the American system because only within the ranks of one of the great parties can he expect to secure the committee assignments that will enable him to be an effective legislator. Moreover, if a congressman aspires to go farther in politics, he needs party backing for his future campaigns. Third parties are for enthusiastic amateurs; only rarely do they gain the support of men who make politics a profession.

Third parties are almost equally unpopular with the average voter, who usually argues that he should cast his ballot for candidates who have a chance to win. Even worse than wasting his ballot, it seems to him, is to use it in such a way that it actually assists the candidate whom he likes least. Thus the Progressives, mostly dissident Republicans, who voted for Roosevelt in 1912 contributed mightily to the election of the Democrat Wilson. So chagrined were they at this result that most of them returned to the Republican party in 1916. Those who voted for Wallace in 1948 were similarly helping Dewey, as may be seen by the vote in New York State, where Dewey's plurality of less than 50,000 could not have been achieved if 500,000 votes had not been cast for Wallace. If Wallace had won the same proportion of the ballots in such states as California, Illinois, and Ohio, Dewey would have won the presidency.

This is not to say that third parties serve no purpose under the American system, however. Often the independent voter actually has no preference between the major party candidates and therefore casts his vote in such a way as to call attention to some issue which is of supreme importance to him. Undoubtedly a large proportion of the ballots cast for Wallace in 1948 were protests against American foreign policy—a policy supported by both major parties but appearing to some voters as dangerously and unnecessarily belligerent toward Russia. The total Wallace vote was too small to affect that policy, but if it had been five million instead of one, the major party leaders might have been sufficiently impressed to change their tactics. Third parties thus have their greatest justification in educating the voters to new issues and inducing the old-line politicians to recognize these issues. It is a familiar fact that the platforms of the Populists, the Socialists, and the various "Progressive" parties have provided a preview of what was to become policy for the major parties a generation later. Indeed, the real weakness of American third parties lies exactly here. The reforms which they demand are usually those considered too extreme for practical politics at any particular time. As soon as the demand attains genuine popularity, the issue is usually appropriated by one or both of the major parties.

Why do people vote for a particular party? Tradition has always played an important part. Americans have a tendency to go to the same church and vote for the same party as their parents. No doubt there are thousands of families in which voting habits could be traced back for generations through Republicans to Whigs to Federalists or through Democrats to Jeffersonian Republicans. Even stronger than family influence is the tradition of the particular community or social group to which the individual belongs. If he is a small-town Southerner, he votes for the Democratic party as unquestioningly as he attends the Baptist Church. And, by a curious anomaly which has been true for a hundred years, if he is an Irish Catholic in some great northern city like New York or Boston, he also votes Democratic. But the same type of small-town Protestant in a northern or western state or an Irish Catholic in some other city may consider the Republican party the only respectable one.

But the proportion of American voters who show real independence is increasing, and it is to win these unattached ballots that the politicians exert their greatest efforts. The great depression apparently brought to an end one epoch of American politics and introduced another. For seventy years the Republicans had been the usually dominant party in national politics, but the economic debacle of 1929 destroyed the myth that they possessed a magic formula for maintaining prosperity. Franklin D. Roosevelt's New Deal revolutionized the political situation by adding to the Democratic ranks large groups that had been traditionally Republican. For a half-century after the death of Lincoln, the Negro vote was still being cast for the party of the Great Emancipator, but as a result of such benefits as work relief and slum clearance much of that vote was transferred to the Democrats during the thirties. Before 1932 the organized labor vote had been divided between the two parties, but the prolabor measures of the New Deal threw most of this vote to the Democrats. The most disastrous blow of all to the Republicans was the loss of much of the midwestern farm vote which had been theirs since 1854.

The year of real humiliation for the Republicans was not 1932 but 1936, when they carried only two states in the presidential election. But in accordance with a tendency of American politics which we have already noted, the Democratic predominance created its own reaction. Almost every New Deal measure displeased some voters while pleasing others, and the "antis" naturally gravitated to the opposition party. Many farmers, fearful that the New Deal had allowed the labor unions to become too powerful, returned to their Republican allegiance. On the other hand, certain labor leaders like John L. Lewis, disgruntled because they had too little influence at the White House, also deserted the Democrats. The same policies that won the Democrats votes among the Negroes aroused resentment in the South. Tradition was too strong for the southern rebels to vote Republican, but they opposed the New Deal in other ways. Allying themselves in Congress with the Republicans, they defeated many Roosevelt and Truman proposals, and by running the "Dixiecrat" Thurmond they attempted to bring about Truman's defeat for reëlection.

The words "Democratic" and "Republican" mean less and less in terms of a coherent philosophy of government.

Neither has a clear title to be considered the "liberal" or the "conservative" party. The party labels may perhaps best be thought of as two great magnets drawing into their respective fields the political particles of hundreds of local and sectional groups.

Irrational though they seem, American parties can be defended as effective democratic mechanisms. The essence of popular government is compromise. In terms of current issues, for example, America is confronted with the need to do justice to the demands of workers without sacrificing the legitimate rights of employers, to maintain the prosperity of agriculture without placing too great a burden upon consumers, to provide adequate medical care for the whole population without paralyzing medical progress. Politicians striving to hold the support of enough groups to insure the success of their respective parties must attempt to find common denominators of agreement. Their conduct often appears unheroic, but in the long run it tends to achieve what a majority of the voters have decided they want.

CHAPTER IV

The Preconceptions of Economic Life

IT MAY BE ARGUED that economic activity, which is only one of many kinds of human activity, is undertaken primarily to secure a living and protect oneself against the vicissitudes of the future. However, a less than complete logical defense can be made for the argument that people work only to secure food, shelter, clothing, and the luxuries of life, and to assure that in the future these things will be available to them and their families. Such a notion has its ideal, perhaps its only, value in analyzing certain aspects of social behavior. The abstraction of economic theory, that merely income considerations are the goals of mankind, must not be confused with the real substance of economic life, but on the other hand, the real substance is too complex to permit a direct attack. For our purposes "pure" political or "pure" economic analysis is only a first step toward fuller understanding.

The notion, then, that people work only for income is far too simple. A great deal of economic activity is undertaken because work itself has its satisfactions, satisfactions often clearly distinguishable from the more obvious economic satisfactions. For example, Thorstein Veblen, the great American social thinker, argued that there is an instinct of workmanship in people, an instinct which leads them to work and work well, quite apart from the money or income expectations of the job. In addition to this, the desire for prestige and preëminence, the desire to perform social services, the feeling that work is good for its own sake—all are elements which one must consider in analyzing or explaining human activity in the economic sphere.

This more realistic view of work or economic activity as inspired by a combination of desire for income and a drive to satisfy ends which are not purely economic takes on more meaning and form when placed in proper perspective and background. The perspective and background which add to the understanding of economic activity are, first of all, the political and social milieu in which the economic activity takes place. Securing and spending income is not in any sense a unique thing, but rather a complex of phenomena which differ in time and place. These phenomena are both socially and personally derived. An economic system based, let us say, on authoritarian controls, or upon a fear of and subservience to a churchly power, obviously would be different from an economic system in a political world of free democratic behavior. The economic system of a society in which family ties were very loose or nonexistent would be different from one which had a close, tight family structure. The role of inheritance, which varies widely in different cultures and in different periods, can scarcely be overestimated in considering such questions as distribution of national income or the economics of Continental European (and possibly American) agriculture. The way people behave or expect others to behave in the economic sphere affects every phase of our social life.

The world is a world of ideas. Thus, the existence of great corporations employing tens and hundreds of thousands of people, as is the case in the United States, depends upon certain ideas or concepts: the concepts of money, credit, prices, collective bargaining, scientific management, large-scale production, etc. All in all, these ideas or concepts exist in a political world in which certain modes of behavior are guaranteed by the political agency of society, namely, the state. These guarantees are conceptual rather than tangible things. The handicraft system of the Middle Ages, in which skilled artisans worked in their own small shops and employed very few persons, was in its turn based upon the political and economic ideas prevalent in that time. The examination of which came first, the economic changes or the political changes, which combine to make the modern economic and political world, is interesting but a little beside the point for present discussion. For our purposes, it may be assumed that economics reacts on politics and politics on economics. Both factors combine with each other and with still other elements of living to make our history.

Thus far, we have used the expressions "economic activity" and "economics" without having offered a definition of these terms. In its simplest form, economics, or economic activity, is the business of getting a living. To point up the future discussion, some of the special characteristics of the modern economic system of the United States may be indicated.

The system is capitalistic. That is to say, it is a system which depends upon great amounts of capital goods, i.e., goods which are not consumed in themselves but ultimately produce goods and services which are consumed. In our manufacturing industries the average investment per employed worker is probably somewhere in the neighborhood of six or seven thousand dollars. That means that someone, or some group, has invested capital for each employed worker in manufacturing amounting to much more than the average annual income of the employees in manufacturing. Compare this with the average Chinese farmer or Indian craftsman, who probably has an investment in tools worth a few dollars, and it readily becomes clear why industry in the United States is considered "capitalistic." Yet the mere existence of a great deal of capital or capital investment per employed worker is after all a technical consideration. Industry in the Soviet Union, or industry in Falangist Spain, if it is to enjoy the highest technical efficiency possible within the limits of technical knowledge, must also employ relatively great amounts of capital per unit of labor. Yet these states are not considered capitalistic.

Political and social considerations are of overwhelming importance in defining capitalism. The institutional structure of capitalism, in addition to its technical, physical structure includes:

1. Free enterprise.
2. The use of the corporate form in doing business.
3. Economic competition.
4. Freedom of contract (except the right to sell oneself into slavery).
5. Private property.
6. The price system.
7. The profit motive.
8. Freedom of labor to organize into associations.

These elements, in their turn, imply the existence and operation of a banking and monetary system, a system of commercial law, and a system of free markets.

We come to the conclusion, then, that economic activity is the getting and spending of income and the development of a technical and physical apparatus, in the setting of a system of institutions which tend to allow a certain degree of free choice to the individual.

The technical apparatus of American capitalism itself derives from an institutional complex, often called "technology." This institutional fabric has given us the knowledge of how to make goods on a large scale and how to use tools and implements of an ever-growing complexity, rather than forcing us to remain dependent upon only physical labor and simple tools. It has also given us the whole concept of using science as a means to the end of production of goods or services and of permitting experimentation and research to the same end.

Another type of institution is that which on the one hand lends stability and certainty to the system, namely, the legal and ideological assurances of protection and rights, and, on the other hand, opens the gates to initiative and new endeavor.

It would be futile and wrong to argue that the capitalism of the United States is the only system which can produce goods and assure people the freedom and liberties which they desire. Other conceivable, and possibly existing, systems permit this, but the capitalistic system is a combination of our political and our technical structure which gives us our own distinctively American economy and industrial culture.

In passing, it must be pointed out that probably no single attribute of American capitalism is peculiar to America. Other countries have similar ideas with respect to political structure, others with respect to certain phases of economic structure; still others have natural resources similar to ours. Yet the complex combination of the factors in the United States does provide an *entire* system which is *not* identical with any other on earth. Others may be better or worse; these are normative or moral questions. Logically, we can argue that our economic system is often related to but *different* in its organization, content, and workings from other systems.

Lest the importance of economic activity be overly stressed, we must bear in mind that leisure-time activities, family activities, artistic endeavor, going to school, reading books or writing them, and a host of other activities each take up part of our time and energies and, as a total, surely require more time and effort than do economic activities. Economic activity is merely the substructure which permits us to hold body and soul together at various levels of meanness or luxury, so as to permit the noneconomic activity.

The inquiring mind must sometime pose to itself the question, "How did the modern economic system get to be what it is?" The answer to this question has given rise to two quite distinct lines of thought. One way the answer may be sought is to trace the historical development of modern industry and modern economic organization. This might tend to neglect the role of ideas as determining economic life. Another approach would be to study the history and confluence of ideas while soft-pedaling the detailed brute facts of economic history. In the view of the present writer both approaches are fruitful. In the ensuing chapters we shall devote ourselves to sketching some of the economic history of the United States; in the present discussion we shall consider some of the *conceptual* or *ideological* elements in our economic structure.

The American tradition, or indeed any tradition, from this point of view, is made up of ideas and ideals. The ideas, or at least the economic and social ideas, of the American economic system were secured in the first instance from western Europe. "Ideas," as Ralph Barton Perry points out in his *Puritanism and Democracy*, "are objects of contemplation or intellectual affirmation. They are the basis on which conscious and willful action is based, and are the rationalizations of individual and social action about which we do not think but merely perform." In other words, the *ideas* of a monetary system, or of the corporation, or of wages are in themselves social institutions, or group modes of behavior, and they represent but one mode among many possible alternatives. Thus, paying people for work, or wages, is based upon the idea of using this particular institution, wages, to solve a particular set of social problems, i.e., securing work on the one hand and securing income on the other. The adding of the letter *l* to "idea" signifies "the idea's appeal to emotion and will." In other words, ideals are ideas or beliefs which involve "hope, desire, endeavor, emotion, and resolve."

With this background, let us examine some of the institutional elements of capitalism which were listed at the beginning of this chapter. That list included (1) free enterprise, (2) the use of the corporate form in doing business, (3) economic competition, (4) freedom of contract, (5) private property, (6) the price system, (7) the profit motive, (8) freedom of labor to organize into associations.

Most, if not all, of these ideas or ideals in the economic structure stress the individual and his freedom. That is to say, the concept of competition is the concept of one person or one group of people acting in the buying or selling of commodities or service relatively free from unknown or arbitrary restrictions imposed by the system (which is to say the government or monopolistic market) and within the framework of a social structure. This is a difficult concept, but nevertheless a useful one. Competition does not mean, and never has meant, the unabridgable right of any person or association of people to do whatever he or they wish to do. It merely means the right of a person or group of persons to act freely within the limitations known to everyone, and further, it implies, if it does not directly involve, the notion that the limitations are subject to change by some known, orderly process. Rules of behavior rather than authoritarian control are the keynote.

This concept of economic freedom is not an old one, even in the brief course of recorded human history. The freedom of a person to start a business, or to undersell his competitor, or to vary the nature of his product, or to hire whom he will is a distinctly modern notion—certainly a complex of ideas which came into the world as an ideal along with the development of modern capitalism. When the world was younger, and not any gayer, say in the thirteenth or fourteenth century, prices, quality of product, even nature of product in many instances, were regulated by custom, law, or arbitrary restraint of groups of business organizations; so that deviations, when discovered, meant economic death, and in many instances social ostracism, for the person or persons who deviated from the normal. Jobs and, more important, the training for jobs were similarly controlled. The guild system (and its variations in western Europe) was an economic system in which the control element—defining the control element as the arbitrary and traditional opposite of freedom—was stronger than the more personal elements of ingenuity and competition.

The breakdown of the guild ideology, a collapse which was never completely realized even in the modern world, occurred neither suddenly nor independently of major changes in the economic and social structure.

The Middle Ages, from our point of view, were relatively more static than the modern period which followed. One of the great static elements, or, properly speaking, one of the great conservative elements, of the period was the Catholic Church.

One cannot argue simply that capitalism and Protestantism or Puritanism go hand in hand. The city-states of Italy were ideologically capitalistic long before and after the Protestant revolution. On the other hand, the Boer Republic was excessively Puritan, while economically almost entirely devoted to agriculture or handicraft. Yet it is in the areas of Europe, where the Protestant Reformation was most successful, and indeed, where the Puritan revolution won the day, that modern capitalism developed.

In essence Puritanism, probably the most extreme form of Protestantism, is based upon the ideas that each person is the direct recipient of the word and direction of God and that each person must in the final analysis be responsible for his own activities, be they good or be they bad in the sight of God. This leads to the notion that success is a result both of work by the individual and of the willingness of God to permit, or even assure, this success. Without going into the theological ramifications of the Puritan ideology, I think it should be clear that such a theology is acceptable and, to use Professor Perry's word, "congenial" to capitalism. It is theological individualism with a vengeance, even if with some philosophical and sociological anguish.

Since capitalism is a social concept not limited to the individual, its justification must depend upon its general or social effects rather than merely upon its effects on the individual. The classical theoretical justification of capitalism is that its operation, employing private property, free enterprise, freedom of contract, etc., results in the production of more goods and in lower prices than would be the case if arbitrary restraints or strict institutional regulations were interposed between the individual and his aim to maximize his own gain. In the economic dogma used to justify private property, freedom of contract, and all the other ideas and ideals of capitalism, the defense of individualism is only secondary and derivative. The main defense of capitalism, in theory at least, is that it purports to secure the highest income at the lowest cost for the entire society. An integral part, but only a part, of this theoretical system is that the individual is free to contract, to work, to invest, and to make his own choices.

The congeniality, then, of capitalism and Puritanism is based upon the essential notions of individualism which are common to the theological system on the one hand and the economic system on the other. Taken together, both systems provide an apology or theory which purports to prove that the good of the individual *is* the good of the society. The converse, however, does not hold— namely, that what is good for society is necessarily good for the individual, if, in securing the optimum for the society, individuals are restricted and restrained from exercising their own choice and their own ingenuity. Individualism and free choice are in themselves social desiderata of such importance that limiting them makes any result at least somewhat bad.

This excursion into the theory, or more properly the apology, of Puritanism and capitalism must not be taken to mean that either system ever held that complete license was desirable or could be countenanced. The primary restraints, however, as conceived by both systems, were first and foremost the *internal* restraints of individuals on themselves. The individual must be allowed his own freedom of choice limited or restrained by his own conscience. Practically and realistically, however, these restraints were supplemented by restraints imposed by the state and by society. To draw the state into the essentially individualist pattern of capitalism or Puritanism implied that the state itself must be under the control of individuals, rather than an agency drawing its strength from its own sovereignty or caprice. Thus, we find that the very notion of a democratic state is the notion of a democracy in which individual wills are summated to discover the wishes of the group. This is, in itself, part and parcel of the same individualism, or individual philosophy, which makes up capitalism and Puritanism.

The preceding argument is not offered to convince the reader of the virtues of anything. It is merely offered as a statement of the essential philosophical assumptions of the three systems—Puritanism, democracy, and capitalism—which, in combination, provide the crude and rough blueprint of the American society, a blueprint which does not always explain the real structure, but without which the real structure is more confused and amorphous than it need be.

Error would be committed were the three props of the American economic structure, namely, private property or capitalism, the Puritan ethic, and democracy, viewed as extremely stable and unchanging. They are not. Different times, different conditions, different circumstances all have brought changes in the ideas associated with these three factors, and changes in the ideals associated with them. Furthermore, as time has passed, new ideological structures have developed, and branches have sprung from the three we have discussed. For example, the role of Puritan theology in modern life, as indeed the role of theology generally, has tended to diminish. The Wesleys, the Foxes, and the Penns of today find neither a world anxiously awaiting their views nor a world willing to use such views as a basis of action. Indeed, one might be tempted to say that much of the Puritan thought, with regard to individualism, has permeated the United States, Great Britain, and much of western Europe to the extent that virtually all religious sects and groups have made adjustments to the aspects of Puritan theology concerned with individualism, so that the question has ceased to be of overwhelming importance. Overt religious conflicts have been solved by the great changes which the world has experienced in the last two or three hundred years. It might very well be that one reason for the difficulty the Western world has in getting along with the Soviet-dominated world of eastern Europe arises in part from the lack of a common acceptance of the role of the individual in society, due to the historical and cultural differences of the two segments of the world.

The pure and naked concept of individual freedom in the economic sphere, we have pointed out, always has assumed that certain restrictions and limitations obtained on free enterprise of the individual or group of individuals. Indeed, the early political thinkers, whose economic theory was most congenial to private property and capitalism, developed various concepts of a social contract, or compacts, made among individuals or between subjects and the state. In a real sense, the Constitution of the United States represents an attempt at such a contract or convention. As time has elapsed and as the needs and ideals of Western civilization have changed, more and important limitations on the freedom of action have been instituted. Some, though by no means the majority, have come into being through the action of legislation. Less than a generation ago the U.S. Supreme Court held that legislatures could not restrict wages paid to women through the enactment of minimum wage laws (Adkins vs. Children's Hospital). Such legislation, the majority of the Court felt, restricted unduly the freedom of women seeking jobs. Yet, in this famous decision, the Court agreed that the limitation of the freedom of contract of women with respect to hours of work was justified on grounds of humanitarianism. Humanitarianism is, of course, a social restraint on the individual action of the employer in this case. The Fair Labor Standards Act and enactments of the several states since that time have sought to establish minimum wages, not for women or children alone—groups which along with idiots and Indians have long been considered, in a certain sense, wards of the state—but also for men. The Supreme Court has held such general minimum wage legislation to be quite constitutional.

This shift in attitude of the supreme judicial body of the United States can only be explained in terms of the changed view of the Court with respect to the propriety of limiting the freedom of contract of individuals for the ultimate benefit of those individuals through the betterment achieved by the whole society. In other words, the Court recognized that certain individuals, either businessmen or employees, might suffer economic harm through the introduction of minimum wage legislation. The costs of businessmen might have been increased, or certain people might lose their jobs. Yet the restraint on property, including labor's freedom to work, was permitted because the Supreme Court felt that the general welfare of the entire United States would benefit thereby.

Other examples might be given to show that the notion of property rights and freedom of enterprise for both capital and labor is not static but ever changing, which in turn would argue that the philosophic assumptions of the system are also undergoing changes, or at least are highly pliable. The examples which most readily come to mind are: laws respecting bankruptcy, by which individuals could escape the burden of their economic mistakes; laws respecting health and sanitation in factories, which buttressed the bargaining power of labor and restricted the bargaining power of management; laws respecting workmen's compensation, which require insurance protection for employees in certain circumstances; laws respecting the sale of securities, which are designed to protect the investor and the potential investor against the greater economic strength and knowledge of the person selling securities. Even regulations and city ordinances concerning traffic and building codes are indexes of the changing conceptions and ideals of the economic and social system.

Limiting ourselves more directly to the economic world, it appears that although the United States is a capitalistic state, and possibly the last of the important capitalist states, the conceptions of the present are markedly different from those of, say, a hundred or even fifty years ago. First and foremost, perhaps, one is struck by the great technological advance that has occurred in the last hundred years, which has virtually forced changes not only in the way of doing business but also in the very forms of business. It is almost inconceivable that a General Electric Company or a United States Rubber Company could exist as a family institution. More will be made of this point later. Let it suffice to say that the conception or idea of "person" in the United States of the twentieth century has an entirely different economic meaning from that which was held in the eighteenth or early nineteenth century. Economically and legally, as guaranteed by court interpretations of the Fourteenth Amendment, "person" is not limited to an individual but encompasses within its broad scope the corporation, which is a thing with life and a history all its own. Ideally, the corporation is an institution chartered or given being by the state at the request of a group of people who choose to invest their money, time, and effort in some particular business enterprise. Once the state has given its permission, the corporation becomes a legal "person," entitled to do business, make contracts, sue, etc. On the other hand, it may be sued, and must undergo the restrictions imposed not only by its charter but by legislation. The personality of the corporation is a very real thing in law and in economic life. For some years there has been a growing tendency on the part of courts and legislatures to attach this view of a legal "person" to institutions which have grown up without the specific charter permission granted by a state. The best example is that of a trade union. Few trade unions are corporations or have received charters for their being from the states or federal government. Yet many courts in the past have held that trade unions might be sued, as if they were legally chartered "persons." Indeed, the Taft-Hartley Act goes so far as to make trade unions specifically suable for certain actions which Congress considers improper.

The point is that the growing complexity of American economic society has tended to reduce the role and importance of individuals and has tended to give power to groups of individuals. Free enterprise and individualism in the modern complex world are, of necessity, different from the same institutions in a simple handicraft world or a world of small factories.

Thus far we have viewed what might be considered small groupings of people which occur to achieve certain economic ends, namely, the corporation and the trade union. The study of the economic activities of specific corporations or specific trade unions is undoubtedly rewarding. Of greater importance, however, in the discussion of the general economic life of the country is the fact that there have developed conscious or unconscious groupings of people along economic lines to advance their own purposes and industry. Sometimes these broad groupings develop an individual structure of their own; sometimes the development is less formal. Individual people are members, in most instances, of more than one economic grouping. The groupings use all sorts of techniques to further their interests, including political pressure, propaganda, restraints on their members, etc. The interests of the members of particular interest groups are not always consonant, and the internal conflicts may be of an enduring sort. The large vs. the small farmer, small business vs. large business, the competition within the railroad industry are examples of this inner conflict. But, on the whole, economic America can be divided into specific interest groups with fairly well-defined areas of mutual interest.

We all have heard of the "farm bloc" as a political entity. Yet the farm bloc is merely a political manifestation of the farmers or the agricultural interests in the United States seeking their own particular interests through legislation. Farmers, of course, frequently express their common interests by other means than politics. Industry, too, may be viewed as a special interest group, probably more complicated in its structure than agriculture, because the internal competition of industry is sharper than the internal competition of agriculture. Not only are manufacturers competing for the consumer's dollar, but particular restrictions of laws or custom bear with greater unevenness on businesses in accordance with their size, the products they make, their location, than is true for agriculture. The interest group of those concerned with trade, both wholesale and retail, also is a special interest group, again with important internal conflicts. The interest group of labor, which in the popular mind and legislation has often been confused with organized labor, is another important interest group. Attempts have been made in recent years to give voice to the special interest of the consumer. The success of this has been less than the success of the other interest groups, in part because consumers are so different and disparate in their interests and in part because the typical consumer is more interested in his role as income getter than as an income spender, so that most people have not lent themselves actively to the support of consumer groups.

In addition to these major groupings, particular segments, or combinations of segments of two or more groups, have also been effective as agencies pushing for restriction and regulation in the political, economic, or social sphere through propaganda. Banking houses have sought particular legislation as well as social acceptance after the great banking debacle of the last depression. Those engaged in foreign trade or domestic trade have offered legislative programs and propaganda fulminations with respect to tariffs. Even the people who abhor liquor and would save the lives and souls of others are a special interest group, and were at one time an important pressure group. They, however, fall outside economic consideration.

Above and beyond all these interest groups is the government. Responsible as it must be in a democratic state to pressure and propaganda, it has become an important agency of economic regulation and of direct intervention in the market place. The role of the government in modern economic life simply cannot be exaggerated for, in addition to administering the regulatory and restrictive laws, the restraints on unbridled enterprise and private property, the government itself has become the greatest competitive element in the economic system. Somewhere in the neighborhood of one-fourth or one-fifth of the national income, that is, the net production of the whole United States, passes through the government's hands or is created by direct government activity.

Such a world is different from the simple rationalization offered above of capitalism resting on the three bases of private property, free enterprise and democracy, and the Puritan ethic.

The institutional framework of American economics, or of the American scene generally, has become so broad and so deep that, obviously, it could not rest on three simple rationalizations. It rests primarily on its own capacity to supply to the people of America roughly what the people of America want. What they want, or better, perhaps, the ideals of what they want in our sphere of economics are economic freedom, i.e., the right to engage in economic activity (with a minimum of restraint), income, jobs, security, and an adjustment to the economic world which will relieve them of frustration while securing these other things.[1]

---

[1] Speaking for economic theory, it is clear to one who has worked in the field that modern economic theory has stepped way beyond the mere rationalization of capitalism as a system which supplies a bigger income with the same amount of effort and resources than would any other system. Occasionally, and more often in political than in economic discussion, such rationalization is resorted to, but factors in the determination of prices, employment, national income, under different assumptions of competition, have become the major subject of modern economic theory.

From the economic point of view, the conflict of interest groups arises from the attempt of each of the segments of economic society to better its own position. That is to say, each of the groups attempts to secure for its own members a bigger share of the national income and a stable position with respect to income and economic continuity. If a large share of the income and economic security and continuity can be achieved without injury to another interest group, or by positively assisting another interest group in its quest for income and security, there is no conflict, and there might arise either the mutual ignoring of one group by another or, in some instances, actual coöperation between or among the groups whose interests are coincident.

For example, two different groups, labor and agriculture, might contrive to secure advantages for both groups. This mutual attempt at coöperation, however, may have at least two results unhappy for its success. First of all, certain segments of the agricultural group and the labor group who feel that agricultural interest and labor's interests in the economic world are antagonistic to each other might attempt to drive a wedge between the groups. Such action would be positive action. Of equal importance, perhaps, is the negative action in which the segments of agriculture and labor who feel that their interests are not mutual simply refuse to participate in the mutual endeavor.

Specifically, at the present time, we have one wing of the C.I.O. joining with the National Farmers Union in an attempt to secure particular legislation designed to benefit agriculture and labor. On the other hand, we have such elements in the agricultural movement as the National Grange and such elements in the labor movement as parts of the A.F.L. and parts of the C.I.O. who, on the ground that it is not a reasonable coalition, do not lend the support of their time or energies to foster this mutual attempt.

Still other interest groups, with the National Association of Manufacturers and the United States Chamber of

Commerce as spokesmen, find in the coalition of agriculture and labor a threat which they can use as a talking point against the type of legislation being proposed. To this end, the interest groups who feel that their economic position would be hurt by the coalition seek to enlist the support of the population at large, usually considered as the "consumer group." This, of course, is really an attempt at securing political allies from many sources.

Another type of example should suffice. The manufacturing interests of the United States have traditionally supported the high protective tariff on the ground that low tariffs would permit the importation of European goods, which through competition would lower prices and hence the incomes of manufacturers. Without going into the soundness of the reasoning of these people, and on the whole it is sound from their own individual, or selfish, point of view, we know that this economic policy has reflected itself in the political attitudes of virtually all the great industrial areas of the United States. At present and for the past fifteen or twenty years, however, the attitudes of some of the elements in the manufacturing interest group have begun to change. The great expansion of American industry resulting from the institution of large-scale production has tended to lower costs, so that the fear of foreign competition has disappeared or diminished. The automobile industry, for example, certain elements in the farm equipment industry, and a number of other industries no longer fear competition of imports but, on the other hand, are themselves in a position profitably to invade foreign markets. To accomplish this, the ability of foreigners to buy American goods must be developed. One of the most direct methods of developing this is to reduce American tariffs. Consequently the solid front of industry in favor of a high tariff has begun to waver and break.

The economic and political repercussions of this are very great indeed, because if the two-party tradition is to obtain, either the Republican party must, if it is to hold

the allegiance of these groups, abandon its uncritical high-
tariff policy or the Democratic party must assimilate them
into its largely agricultural and labor ranks. The new
industrial segment, while supporting the traditionally low
tariff of the Democrats, might not be willing to support
the other traditional policies of the Democrats, e.g., "white
supremacy" in the southern wing of the party, civil rights
in the North. Nor can the older wings of the Democratic
party live in peace with the new converts.

It is apparent, then, that economic groups are static in
neither their structures nor their goals, and that economics,
as well as politics, make strange bedfellows. This shifting
and changing of economic interests has marked American
political history so deeply that we scarcely have in the
United States political parties with a given set of aims.
Rather we have sectional and economic interest groups
who are attached to loosely defined political parties
through history and expediency.

Some conclusions can be drawn from the foregoing.
When the American economic system or American capitalism was busily finding its place in the world, its ideological content in the sphere of ethics, politics, and economics was philosophically more marked and discernible
than at present. The philosophy of individualism, which
is often stated as essential to American industry, as we
have seen was always more than the philosophy of each
person using every and any means to secure his own ends.
It was a philosophy that argued that the economic ends
of the entire community were best secured by each person's seeking his own. It is a moot question whether history has justified that philosophical contention.

As the American economy has grown more complex and
as the social structure has undergone changes resulting
from the enormous growth of population, the great accumulation of capital, and its attendant growth of the
corporate form, the assumptions of competition and free
enterprise have not been realized. The role of the government in the economic life has become more emphasized

and, on the whole, the system has become more and more impersonal. Economic ends of individuals or of great interest groups often tend to conflict with the economic position of other individuals or other groups. In brief, we no longer have the ideological accord which existed in the simpler days of small-scale production, small agriculture, and local trading, nor the well-defined ideology which motivated men's behavior in the old days when the world was simpler and the magic of opportunity was available to all.

CHAPTER V

Economic Development

THE PRECEDING DISCUSSION was largely on the reflective level. No attempt was made to trace economic development in the United States in the light of the earlier, fairly well-defined ideology or more amorphous ideology of the present and the recent past. Nor was any attempt made to trace the actual facts of industrial development in the United States.

In the small space at our disposal we cannot do much more than offer a very brief sketch of the course of economic history in the United States. The purpose of offering such a sketch is to illustrate, by recourse to history, the changing ideologies and changing institutions of the United States, and also to provide the backdrop for the present economic scene.

The economic history of the United States has been the history of the development of a vast continent from an agricultural economy to a trading and manufacturing economy. That is not to say that trading and manufacturing were ever entirely absent. From the time of the Revolution the South was, from the point of view of production, agricultural. But in a broader sense, the South was concerned with selling its products, largely tobacco, rice, indigo, and naval stores, abroad or to the other sections of the nation. New England also, in spite of its early dependence on agriculture, was engaged in a flourishing foreign trade, a trade which worried the British trading fraternity and cost them heavily in competition. Indeed,

75

this competition, often illegal under British law, was an important factor in bringing about the Revolution. Not only was this competitive trade in fish and agricultural products, but some international and intercolonial trade in manufactured goods occurred. Nevertheless, in terms of numbers, most people made their livings in agriculture.

It is clear, then, that the enormous resources of the United States always comprehended more than mere agricultural capacities. The winning of independence left the United States with the task of organizing its economy. The victory in the Revolution may be viewed in part as a victory of the ideology of free trade over the ideology of mercantilism, a system which Great Britain unsuccessfully tried to impose on the colonists. Mercantilism is almost the antithesis of free trade. The mercantilistic policy of Great Britain, for example, insisted that goods traded with England move in British bottoms. It insisted upon direct restrictions on industrial activities in the colonies and levied taxes to restrict industrial activities and growth in the colonies. In brief, mercantilism represented authoritarian control by the mother country in the economic sphere, designed to maintain her manufacturing and trading preëminence. In this sense, mercantilism is akin to imperialism.

Even though the Constitution of the United States was an economic and political compromise, it was a compromise, in great part, *independent of the mercantilistic doctrine of the previous regime.* The Constitution guaranteed, for example, a free-trade area over the entire United States. It prohibited taxes on exports. It set the basis for a stable monetary system; at least it aimed to do this by giving Congress broad powers of monetary control. Furthermore, the Constitution provided for the sanctity of contracts and equality before the law—conditions essential to a free enterprise system.

The break with the past, however, was not complete because, as Professor Charles A. Beard and others have pointed out, property qualifications for state legislators and voters imposed important limitations on political freedom, and tariffs (import duties) and other politico-economic devices operating against the concepts of free economic behavior were allowed. The "police power" and "general welfare" provisions of the Constitution represent broad, ill-defined provinces in which the intervention of the federal government is permissible. That is not to say that such potential limitations are bad or restrictive on the individual; it is, however, to say that the reign of pure individualism was potentially curbed from the outset. State constitutions, too, had potential limitations on individual behavior.

The economic growth of special interest groups, as defined in the preceding chapter, depends on two related factors. First, economic growth depends upon a group's bettering its position vis-à-vis other groups competing for the same income and economic position. This, in a sense, is a static idea. The other way an economic group secures advantage is by partaking of the general growth of the economy, a growth which might be unrelated to any action of the group in question. This is a dynamic concept. For example, the opening of the West, the development of the gasoline engine, the use of electric power, knowledge of pricing and advertising are available to all rather than the secrets of a few. As the economy grows and develops, each group attempts to secure "its share," which is to say special advantage, in the growth. This in itself is a type of conflict, although the sharpness is often hidden because the very growth of the income of the community permits all to enjoy very real advantages.

In the light of this discussion, we shall very briefly sketch the history of agriculture, industry, and labor in the United States from the Revolution to the present.

AGRICULTURE

The point was made that at its inception the United States was primarily agricultural. The northern and eastern states engaged in trade and industry, but the backbone of their economies was agriculture.

The Louisiana Purchase in 1803 represented a sudden opportunity to agricultural interests. That the entire nation was behind Jefferson in his illegal, but wise, action is a myth which has developed through time, a myth which would not have been appreciated by the manufacturers and traders of the East at the turn of the nineteenth century. Jefferson, in his letters, clearly indicates that he was acting, first, to thwart a political threat to the United States, namely, to keep Napoleon I from entering via the back door of the Mississippi River, and second, to supply special advantages for growth to the agricultural interests, always so dear to the heart and thinking of Jefferson.

The War of 1812, too, was in great part an agricultural expansion, even though it did not quite come off. Josiah Quincy, the spokesman for the Federalists in Congress, said of the War of 1812 that it was a war "of Southern and Western policy, not the policy of the Commercial States." The acquisition of the West was a turning point in United States history in that it expanded the force of agriculture if by no other means than expanding its sheer size and potential.

The expansions of the United States, coming as they did in great bites which took time to digest, frequently left the groups moving to the West with immediate problems of settlement and defense, and thus tended possibly to minimize the more basic political and economic problems, which came to the fore only later as the digestion was more complete. Nevertheless, the expansion to the West did immediately create the question of how the land was to be disposed of. This political issue plagued America during the greater part of the nineteenth century and never was settled to the satisfaction of all interests, because the very distribution of the land created shifts in economic and political balance. The enormous growth of our population permitted a certain degree of prosperity to agriculture, which also acted to soften the economic conflicts. A ready market for the products of the western farm was provided after canals and roads opened the eastern seaboard to the western states and so eliminated the long trip down the Mississippi. In addition Europe, especially Great Britain, was always a steady customer.

The history of agricultural development in the United States is probably more nakedly economic than the history of most other interest groups, for unlike the urban groups, which seem more complex in their social motivations, agricultural groups have tended very often to support reform for purely economic reasons.

As the West developed, it nurtured a radical ideology, which is to say a more conscious individualism than was to be found in the East and South. Individualism in politics took the form of reduction in property qualifications for voters, the direct election of governors, and, on the whole, a political theory and system less encumbered by tradition and theorizing (rationalization) than was true in the South and East. Economically, too, individualism was strong in the West, because agriculture was developed on the family farm as opposed to the large-scale slave farm of the South or the relatively small intensively cultivated farm of the East.

In the Jacksonian era the individualism of the farmers found an ally in the growing class consciousness of the labor forces of the New England and Middle Atlantic states. This period is one of the more important turning points in American life because, had the agricultural West found it possible to ally itself politically with the agricultural South, two sections whose economic interests in many aspects were similar, the history of the United States might very well have been different, especially in that the Civil War might not have been fought. Such reflection, however, is idle, since one cannot roll back the course of history as one can snap up a window shade. Nevertheless, it does appear from the vantage point of the present that the tariff policy of the 1820's, a tariff policy which was directed in a mild way to protectionism, was neither to the advantage nor to the satisfaction of the agricultural South and West. The South talked of Nullification, too conscious of its own strength and without the political wisdom of seeking the support of the West. This in itself was sufficient to drive a wedge between those two sections, since the political attitude of the West was based upon a strong central government. The western states owed too much to the Union lightly to defy it. Furthermore, the question of the distribution of the public lands was, on the whole, badly handled by the South.

Senator Benton of Missouri, for example, tried hard to secure less federal control in the disposition of the public lands than the industrial East, especially the banking interests, desired. The southern group in the Congress were sympathetic, on the whole, to hastening the development of western agriculture, seeing in such development the creation of an ally. Daniel Webster, with consummate political skill, caused the entire discussion to be tabled, and so broke the engagement of the South to the West, forever keeping that marriage (or even liaison) from taking place. Had the southern politicians possessed greater political acumen and, possibly, greater political strength, they might have made an alliance of convenience which would have turned into a true marriage of mutual interests.

The question of development of the frontier was an important one to the immigrants settled along the eastern seaboard, for many of them desired to move west. The immigrants and artisans of the East, looking longingly to the West, felt a sympathy for the western farmer which provided a basis for the political and economic democracy of the Jacksonian era. It was by no mere chance that President Roosevelt, more than one hundred years later, used the name Jackson as the rallying cry rather than the name Jefferson, which was customary in the Democratic party. Jackson, more than any person up to Roosevelt, welded the small people, the farmer and the worker, into a political unity.

This is borne out in the banking and currency controversy of the Jacksonian era. The Bank of the United States was a private bank chartered by the federal government and performing many of the financial tasks of the government. It was, in effect, a governmentally sanctioned monopoly in banking. Its control rested largely in the hands of eastern capitalists, although many of its operations were in the West. Regardless of the truth or falsity of the charges of misfeasance and malfeasance made against the bank, it does appear that the bank was the symbol and engine of the manufacturing and trading elements of New England and the Middle Atlantic states. Jackson's attempt to destroy the bank through the refusal to renew its charter led to one of the sharpest and most vitriolic presidential campaigns the nation has ever seen—the campaign of 1832. Reading the history of the period, one cannot help feeling that the bank was more a symbol of wealth and power than an effective instrument of such wealth and power. This is a personal judgment on the part of the present author, but even the persuasiveness of a Schlesinger (Age of Jackson) cannot completely convince the reader of the opposite. The symbol, nevertheless, was sufficient to instigate a powerful political movement of farmers and labor against the merchants and manufacturers, and kept Old Hickory, old, asthmatic, and tubercular, in the White House.

The competitive banking system which followed Jackson's victory, in its very looseness, probably assisted the western farmers in securing cheap capital, but this seems to be more of a historical accident than a well-conceived plan. The point is that the economic interests of the farmers led them to what must be considered a political revolt, which, in turn, changed the alignment of political forces in the United States, since the West was now an area to be reckoned with.

The history of the western settlements in America is too well known to bear much repetition. Land had to be cleared, Indians beaten off or bought off, trading settlements established, and finally, roads (turnpikes) and canals built. Ultimately, by the end of the nineteenth century the development of transportation meant that the great agricultural West was firmly bound to its markets of sale and export.

This picture of the development of the West by itself, however, is badly out of focus. The development of western agriculture did not take place with static techniques of production. For example, the importance of Whitney's cotton gin (1792) cannot be overemphasized because it revived a declining agricultural system in the South, a decline brought about by impossibly ruinous farming methods plus low prices for tobacco, the staple crop. With the cotton gin, cheap clothing, that is to say clothing made of cotton, could profitably be made. The British and New England textile industries no longer had to depend upon wool or flax. Linsey-woolsey, the standard cloth for the poor, a coarse combination of linen and wool, was supplanted by cotton cloth, and the whole world benefited. Not the least to benefit was the South, which was converted within a few years to a great and prosperous agricultural area. For example, in 1800 the South produced around 35,000 bales of cotton a year; but by 1835 this had increased to more than a million bales.

Nor was the cotton gin the only important technical advance. Throughout the early years of the nineteenth century many persons concerned with agriculture, including such notable figures as Thomas Jefferson, George Washington, Daniel Webster, and a host of lesser-known but probably more successful inventors, worked on the question of improving the plow. The wooden plow was replaced as early as 1797 by a cast-iron plow which, unfortunately, did not work. However, fifteen years later Jethro Wood of Scipio, New York, patented an iron plow which did work, and which had replaceable parts. This made large-scale production possible and reduced the replacement cost to the farmer. By 1830 iron or steel plows were fairly common in the United States, Deere and Company being organized in 1858. Small tools used on the farm were also improved.

Harvesting, reaping, and threshing by hand are hard, thankless tasks. Farmers, especially on large farms, long had talked of doing these tasks mechanically. The Mc-Cormick reaper and the Hussey reaper, both invented in the 1830's, were the answer to farmers' long and often neither silent nor unblasphemous prayers. Large-scale agriculture in America, a land which was deficient in agricultural population in the nineteenth century, simply could not have developed without the mechanical reaper. The reaper was followed by various types of mowing machines and raking machines, so that by 1860 agriculture in America was well on the way to being mechanized. In the 1820's a hand-operated thresher was developed by one Jacob Pope, shortly followed by threshers driven by horsepower. The principle of the horse-drawn reaper became, in effect, the principle for other horse-drawn farm implements including rakes, hay balers, disks, disk harrows, etc.

The prime mover on the farm was the horse, and this remained true almost to the twentieth century, when the gasoline engine or electrically driven engine became cheap enough for general use. Attempts to use steam power were only moderately successful, in part because of the requirement of coal as a fuel, and because of the bulkiness of the machines.

It is not surprising to notice that the use of labor-saving agricultural machinery developed in the United States, Canada, and other countries where the agricultural population was slight as compared to the availability of land, so that the labor costs tended to be high. Economic necessity, that is, the necessity of efficiently exploiting the broad areas of the West, was the mother, or at least the wet nurse, of invention. European agriculture to the present day has not exploited power machinery nearly to the extent that the American farm has. In part this might be due to the greater wealth of the United States, and in part it might be due to the high cost of labor in the

United States. Whatever the reasons, the technical efficiency of agriculture expanded as a result of the extensive cultivation of the land and the intensive use of labor and capital.

The criticism made by European farmers and by some eastern American farmers of the western farmer, who seems to be rather unconcerned over the loss of a pig or two, or a calf, or who seems wasteful in his sowing and reaping methods, is largely beside the point. The eastern American farmer or the European farmer must, if he is to remain in business, intensively cultivate his acres and look after his cattle and crop with a most careful eye. Such care and attention would be too costly for the western farmer, whose attention must be spread over hundreds of acres of land and hundreds of heads of cattle. The nature of the two industries is economically different, the West developing on an extensive basis, the East (and Europe) on an intensive basis.

Implied in this discussion is the growth of scientific farming, which, perhaps, should be called economic farming. The debt of American agriculture and the world at large to the state universities and state agricultural schools of the West can scarcely be overestimated.

The development of agriculture, of course, was dependent upon agricultural markets both in the United States and abroad, because producing markets and consuming markets must be joined if goods are to move. The building of roads, railroads, and waterways permitted not only the growth of new industries in the West but the movement of agricultural products to the outside world. This development represented one of the important economic conflicts, a conflict which was equaled in sharpness only by the controversies which arose between agriculture and the groups defined by the farmers as "Wall Street and speculators." Indeed, the railroad controversy was really part of this "agriculture vs. the banks and the interests" fight, which has become a perennial conflict in United States political life.

In the period immediately following the Civil War the farmers of the Middle West began to recognize their economic dependence upon the railroad and also to see that this dependence could be limited through governmental regulation of rates. Farmers felt that the costs of the manufactured goods they used, as well as the prices they received for their products, were largely determined by the railroad charges levied. There was undoubtedly some truth in their contention, because the earliest history of American railways is in great part a history of stock manipulation rather than a history of the betterment of service and lower rates to railroad users. The farmers organized into Granges on the local, state, and national level. The purpose of the Grange was partially social and educational and partially economic. From the economic point of view, the Grange sought to better the farmer's relative position by undertaking coöperative buying and selling. On the whole, this was not successful, although in the twentieth century farmers' coöps did successfully emerge. The other economic function was to apply political pressure.

One such move was to strengthen the hand of the farmers vis-à-vis the railroads through state legislation. Legislation was passed in most of the middle western states providing for "just, reasonable and uniform rates." This began in Illinois and spread through the other grain states. In 1886, however, the United States Supreme Court held that such legislation interfered with the Congressional right to legislate on interstate commerce (Wabash, St. Louis and Pacific Railroad Company vs. Illinois).

The next year, the national Congress, ever sensitive to the pressure of the farmers, passed the Interstate Commerce Act, which provided for a federal commission to control maximum rates and differential rates. This problem of rate determination for public utilities, such as railroads, has been a bone of political and economic contention on both state and national levels since that time, and even at the present the railroad rate structure is undergoing both criticisms and adjustments.

Allied to the question of transportation costs has been the question of prices and price levels. Historically, with few years of exception, farmers have been a debtor group. That is to say, they are indebted to banks and mortgage companies for their mortgages, and to wholesalers and other business people for seed, tools, and, frequently, their very sustenance. The end of the crop year often sees the farmer paying his debts only to go into debt for the ensuing crop year.

As a debtor, the farmer is desirous of a public policy which provides cheap, or plentiful, money. During the period following the Civil War this attitude took the form of political pressure for the use of greenbacks, against the resumption of specie payment, and for the free coinage of silver. In this regard the farmers' interests are similar to those of labor, which, historically, has supported "cheap money" as a depression cure or vehicle for raising wages.

To criticize the farmers, or the labor groups, because of their uncritical support of a particular brand of monetary theory or fiscal policy is to miss the point of the agriculture-labor reaction against debt, unemployment, and economic insecurity. Criticism of the Populists—members of a movement of the 1890's which became politically extremely powerful and virtually captured the Democratic party—in terms of their theoretical ineptitude should not be taken as a defense of the more restrictive financial policy of the Republican party under a Mark Hanna. Sound money, or more properly a stable price level or even a slightly falling price level, is advantageous to investors and creditors; a rising price level is advantageous to debtors and low-income labor. It is true, there are dangers of inflation if the policy of rising prices is followed, but there are also dangers of deflation, with all its attendant economic woe, if the policy is too restrictive.

During the entire period, in spite of the periodic economic dislocations, from the opening of the West to the end of the First World War, agriculture enjoyed a successful history. Certain segments of the farm group, however, did not enjoy the new advantages, especially the one-crop sharecroppers of the South. Their lot was a hard one, as it is at the present. The economic power of these people and, consequently, their political power, is and has been slight, and it was not until the New Deal reached them a helping hand that they enjoyed even a slight advance in their position.

During the First World War American agriculture found itself in a preferred position. The demand for agricultural products rose after the first year of the European phase of the war, and during the war period wheat acreage increased by nearly twenty million acres, and rye by nearly five million acres. The total grain acreage increased by 12 percent between 1914 and 1919, or from 203 million acres to 227 million acres. Cattle and hog production increased by 20 percent. Exports increased by as much as 45 percent between 1914 and 1918, and in 1919 almost one-fifth of the agricultural production was for foreign sale. Prices rose during this period. Wheat which was selling for 97¢ a bushel in 1913 sold for $2.76 in 1919, and averaged about $2.20 during the entire war. Cotton which sold for 8¢ a pound in 1914 sold for 30¢ in 1919. Farmers were prosperous. Stimulated by the profits to be made, as well as by the pleas of the government, and with low interest rates and guaranteed loans, agriculture expanded mightily during World War I.

By 1920, however, Europe was again in agricultural production. The effect upon American agriculture was disastrous. Prices fell, and in order to maintain his income in the face of falling prices the individual farmer expanded his output. The generalized expansion of output, of course, reduced prices still further, and so the merry-go-round of increased output and lowered prices was set in motion. Agriculture was one of the few industries which did not enjoy the (so-called) Coolidge and Hoover prosperity.

The agricultural depression did not solve itself. Panaceas were considered, programs discussed, but nothing effective was done to solve the farmers' plight. In 1924 the Progres-

sive party, under the leadership of "fighting" Bob La
Follette, was revived but in the presidential election of
that year carried only the state of Wisconsin. "Revived"
is used advisedly, because the Progressives of 1924 were
the ideological inheritors of the Populists and the Jacksonians. La Follette and his followers tried very hard to
combine the urban labor groups with the farm groups in
a common political and economic attack on the industrial
and banking groups. Unfortunately for the Progressives,
the urban industrial groups were enjoying an unprecedented prosperity and so turned a deaf ear to the rallying
cries. Nevertheless, many of the trade-union leaders openly
supported the La Follette candidacy, even though the
labor groups officially either were nonpartisan or threw
their weight to one of the larger parties.

The farmers, however, were not ineffective in helping to
elect Franklin D. Roosevelt in 1932. The first three years
of the fourth decade were nightmare years for American
agriculture. Prices fell so low that it was frequently not
worth while to harvest crops. In Iowa, corn and wheat
were cheaper fuel than coal and were used to heat many
farmhouses. Prices received by farmers were in 1933 half
of what they were between 1910 and 1914. Forced sales
were almost the rule in many of the agricultural sections
of the country.

The depression, by this time, was not localized in agriculture but was generalized throughout the economy.
Urban labor and the agricultural interests joined, even
though the union was almost unpremeditated, in defeating the Republican party and bringing the Democrats into
power. The conditions of the Jacksonian era were repeat-
ing themselves in so far as the union of labor and agriculture was concerned.

The Roosevelt regime acted with vigor in assisting the
farmer.

The Agricultural Adjustment Act was passed in 1933
and provided that government bounties would be paid to

farmers who refrained from planting certain crops. For example, the cotton farmer received from three to eleven dollars for each acre of cotton he did not plant. Other basic crops were similarly aided. The price of hogs was steadied by government slaughtering of so-called surplus pigs.

This extensive program was very expensive, and some of its costs were met by a processing tax, which was an excise tax levied on manufacturers who were engaged in the business of converting agricultural products to ultimate use. It is difficult to assess the net effect of this program, because, although it was inflationary with respect to its expenditures to farmers, it was deflationary with respect to its taxing aspects. Ultimately, the act was thrown out as unconstitutional, when the Supreme Court held that the purpose of the tax was to benefit one segment of the economy at the expense of another.

In 1935 the Roosevelt administration again attempted to assist agriculture, by the passage of the Soil Erosion Act, an act designed to prevent erosion, control floods, and relieve unemployment by the use of federal funds. This act was followed, in 1936, by the Soil Conservation Act, which attempted to secure the same results as were outlawed by the AAA. The Soil Conservation Act provided that farmers who planted certain types of cover crops—clover, soy beans, etc.—in place of certain standing crops would receive payments for so doing. By such devices the federal government was successful in restricting the production of crops in surplus.

In 1938 another Agricultural Adjustment Act was passed, which more or less set a firm agricultural policy for the United States. One important provision of this act was the institution of storage loans to farmers. That is to say, the government stands ready to lend the farmer money on such crops as wheat, corn, tobacco, and rice when the price of these crops falls below parity. Parity is generally defined as a price for the agricultural commodity in question which will yield an income to farmers producing that crop equivalent to the proportion of the national income farmers producing such crops received during a base period, usually 1909-14.

On the whole, the period from 1932 to 1937 was one in which agriculture enjoyed some benefits. Cash farm income, for example, doubled in those five years, reaching 8.6 billion dollars. Parity loans meant, in effect, price fixing for agricultural products, so that fear of overproduction, that is, too large a production to be sold profitably, did not constantly stare the farmer in the face. On the other hand, the surpluses of stored commodities, by 1937, were becoming very great. This is reflected, for example, in the decline in the world price of wheat, which fell from 96¢ a bushel in 1937 to 50¢ a bushel in 1938. The parity price in 1938 was $1.12.

Although the situation was not so bad in corn, cattle, and tobacco as it was in wheat, these commodities, too, were beginning to experience a decline in price on the world market, even on the domestic market, by the end of 1937. It is interesting to note that farm income in 1938 was 12 percent less than in 1937, so that the gains of the New Deal were being lost.

The advent of the World War in 1939, of course, changed the whole outlook for agriculture and again threw it into prosperity, a prosperity never before envisaged.

World War II and its immediate aftermath saw American agriculture enjoy much higher incomes than before the war. Farmers enjoyed, it has been estimated, an income about three times their prewar income. High demand at home and abroad, price supports in the form of government loans led to enormous plantings. By 1948 and 1949 the situation began to show signs of changing. Reconsideration of parity prices to include labor costs, but also reconsideration of the government's lending policy to farmers began to receive more than the cursory interest of congressmen. An example will indicate the gravity of the problem. Potato loans kept the price of potatoes high for the consumer, yet government loans, which really were grants, amounted to nearly 240 million dollars in 1948-49. The same story was being repeated for other crops.

INDEX OF GROSS FARM PRODUCTION[1]
(1910-45)

Year	Production	Year	Production
1945	123	1927	100
1944	124	1926	101
1943	120	1925	99
1942	123	1924	97
1941	111	1923	98
1940	108	1922	97
1939	105	1921	91
1938	104	1920	101
1937	107	1919	96
1936	87	1918	95
1935	97	1917	90
1934	82	1916	92
1933	95	1915	98
1932	102	1914	93
1931	105	1913	91
1930	98	1912	90
1929	101	1911	88
1928	102	1910	85

Congress, if it desires to oppose a laissez-faire policy in agriculture, must devise some system of parity prices *plus* crop control. This point of restrictive crop control is the key to the problem in the eyes of many economists, yet politically it is difficult because farmers want to grow what yields profits, and parity prices are profitable prices. Furthermore, the policing, i.e., administrative, problems of crop control are difficult. However, regardless of the political or economic considerations one point stands out. The traditionally conservative farm group now, in their conservatism, accept, and indeed demand, government intervention on a very broad scale.

---

[1] U.S. Bureau of the Census, *Historical Statistics of the United States, 1789-1945*, Washington, D. C., 1949.

This discussion of agriculture in America does not pretend to be exhaustive or even moderately complete. Its purpose is to indicate the type and nature of the great conflicts between agriculture and the other segments of the economy.

In reading the agricultural history of the United States, one tends to find the farm group dubious as to the motives and often unsympathetic to the practices of the industrial East. Sometimes, but not often, the farmer has found an ally in the industrial workingman. On the whole, the antagonism of agriculture to other economic groups has been cultural as well as economic.

The expression, "farming is a way of life," in spite of the fact that it has been overworked by those seeking special advantages for agriculture, nevertheless has a great deal of truth in it. The family structure, the social attitudes, and the ideology of the farmer are different from those of the city-bred person.

To say that the farmer is an individualist in politics is not true. He has joined particular political movements with the same frequency that other groups have. To say that the farmer is an economic individualist is again not true. He has sought and received special aid from the government. He has engaged in coöperative adventures in the buying and selling of his products. To say that the farmer is on a lower cultural level is obvious nonsense, for there is no objective standard of culture levels. The truth of the matter is that the farmer is *different* because his culture, his economic circumstances, and his expectations are different from those of the urban population.

One interesting change has occurred in the ideology of the farm group which might have great significance for the future. To the city person, the farmer is at once conservative and radical. His support of prohibition, his attacks on social services undertaken by the state, and his general defense of what he considers "free enterprise" have been taken as marks of his conservatism. On the other hand, his support of cheap money in the last century and TVA-type experiments in the present century, and some of his great spokesmen in the Congress—Senators Norris and La Follette, for example—have marked him as a radical. This attempt at categorization, then, is not very helpful. However, it does seem that up until the great depression of 1932 the political manifestations of the agricultural interests usually, if not always, were directed against some competing interest group, e.g., the railroads, "Wall Street," or speculators. That tendency obtains today, but during the thirties farmers and farm interest groups began to broaden their horizons of criticism and look to changes in the economic and political structure to alleviate their situation. This shift from a personal to a general attack has not been complete, but its significance, should the tendency continue, will be enormous.

Objectively and socially viewed, the cultural life of farmers in America is intensely interesting. By the nature of their endeavor farmers tend to be physically isolated. This has led to the "farming as a way of life" view. The farmer *is* resourceful and self-sufficient. He has to be to live his days on the farm. Yet economically farmers are as dependent on the outside world as any other economic group—indeed, more frequently dependent because of the world-wide homogeneity of their products. Wheat of a certain grade is wheat of that grade the world over. Wheat or corn or hogs of a given farmer or a given state or even a given nation cannot be branded and trademarked as are sewing machines or automobiles. Therefore the competition usually found in the world markets is very stiff.

On the buying side the farmer is also the subject of economic weakness. The tractors and equipment he buys are subject to some sort of economic control, either administered prices or some other semimonopolistic control. That is to say, the farmer tends to buy in a noncompetitive market and sell in a highly competitive one. Hence his economic dependence.

Add to this the uncertainties of wind and weather and it will readily be seen that the farmer has no great degree of control over his economic destiny. Hence his insistence on government aid.

In spite of his economic reliance on the government in the realm of price controls and parity plans, the farmer, technologically, is growing more self-sufficient. The use of mechanized equipment has led to larger-size farms in America but has led also to a decline in the need for migratory labor. The American farm is typically a family farm with a few hired hands. This comment, of course, applies neither to the great ranches of the West nor to the "factory farms" growing produce and specialty crops in the East and Southwest. These farms are more like industrial undertakings than the more typical farms producing dairy products and the basic and stable standing crops.

From the point of view of equity—i.e., social justice or fairness—as well as from the point of view of economics—i.e., the best use of resources to secure social income—the farm subsidy policy, which has been an earmark of both the New Deal and the Fair Deal, is open to severe criticism. Often consumers have had to pay heavily (through high prices or taxes, or both) for farm products which could have been produced much more cheaply on a competitive basis. Furthermore, the political and economic systems have been distorted to take into account the political strength of the farmers, as a class. The political fact seems to be that, consciously or unconsciously, labor and agriculture have joined political hands, and the farmer has been helped beyond the wildest dreams of the Populists of half a century ago.

CHAPTER VI

Economic Development
(Continued)

THE INDUSTRIAL REVOLUTION and the preceding development of large-scale international trade made the large-
scale organization of business imperative. In great part
the economic history of the last three hundred years has
been the history of the development and growth of economic units. Large-scale production and large-scale trade
involve large-scale risks. A small businessman selling in a
relatively restricted market gets to know his buyers, what
they want and when they will want it. A local blacksmith,
for example, who knows the horse population of the area
he serves is in a good position to judge accurately the iron
he will need, the number of helpers he will need, and the
fuel he will need over a relatively long period of time.
On the other hand, an executive of a company making
parts for automobiles and selling in a national or world-
wide market cannot possibly have such information at his
finger tips. It is obvious, therefore, that risks of large-scale
enterprise may be very great. Two ways to minimize such
risks are relevant in this discussion. First, the businessman
can make intensive market surveys and thus get to know
the characteristics of his market; or he may attempt to
control the market through the growth of his own business,
or by acting in concert with firms who formerly were his
competitors.

Without going into the limitations of monopolistic activities, which have never been thoroughly effective in the United States, let it suffice to say that there have grown up certain legal protections to combat the risks in the elements of business.

The greatest of these legal protections is without doubt the legal sanction of the corporate-form business organization. In essence the corporate form implies that the original investors in a business turn over to the management of the business the sums of money which they desire to invest. The liability of the investor is then limited to his *actual investment*. Should the firm fail, the investor cannot be called upon to make good any debts of the company. The corporation is a legal "person" having the right to make contracts, to sue or be sued—indeed, to act by and large as if it were a real flesh-and-blood person. If the corporation fails, the owners of this legal person, that is, the shareholders, will not lose more than their original investment. If, on the other hand, the corporation makes money, that is, shows a profit over and above its costs, the profits are distributed to the shareholders in some proportion to their investments. It is axiomatic that large-scale production and large-scale distribution could not exist without some institution which limits the liability of the investors, for if an individual businessman who owns and operates his own plant (and has not sought the protection of forming a corporation or of limiting his liability) fails, the businessman is personally liable for all the debts he contracted.

From the economic point of view the corporate form means more than the mere limiting of the investor's liability. It also means that enormous accumulations of capital can be secured to finance enormously large-scale activities. Individuals or individual families could not supply the capital for such enterprises as the General Motors Corporation, the General Electric Company, the United States Steamship Lines, or the United States Rubber Company. These companies represent investments running into billions of dollars.

LABOR

The bargaining power of corporations is so great that the individual seeking work must take it on the terms and conditions offered to him by the corporation, unless he can find a bargaining agency to act for him. The trade union performs this function.

In spite of legal restriction on associations of workers in common law, restrictions on "combination and conspiracy," workers attempted overtly and covertly to form into groups and make group demands regarding hours, wages, and conditions of employment. For example, as early as 1786 the printers of Philadelphia tried to bargain collectively or as a unit with their employers to get higher wages and better hours. This example is given to show that even in the handicraft occupations, such as printing, the balance of bargaining power between employer and employee was weighted in favor of the employer.

In general it might be said that, *inter alia*, unions try to improve the economic conditions of their members through making more advantageous agreements with employers regarding wages, hours, and conditions of employment than would be attained if there were no unions. This probably is the major function of unions at the present time. Other functions include political reform, though some unions (few in the United States) eschew political reform and prefer political revolution. Other unions (e.g., the International Ladies Garment Workers) spend huge sums of money on education. This sort of function is especially important if a union has a large immigrant membership, so that the teaching of the English language and American ways of life is believed necessary. The uplift aspect of some unions has gone far beyond the teaching of the English language and American ways of life. It is not usually recognized that in many of the building and metal trades, for example, the unions spend relatively large sums of money and great amounts of time training apprentices, and a welfare concern for superannuated or sick members

is a big part of many union programs, e.g., the United
Mine Workers and the Needle Trades Unions. Thus, we
see that union functions are many and varied, but the core
function is concerned with wages, hours, and conditions
of employment.

The next question is that of the organization of the
unions to perform these functions. Here again there is no
single type of organization, just as there is no single function. The smallest unit of a trade union is usually a local;
that is, employees in a given trade, occupation, plant, or
industry in a given geographical unit, the locality, are organized into a group. By and large, democratic processes[1]
prevail within the group, and the officers are elected by
the local membership. Since in most instances in the
United States individual trade unions are organized on a
country-wide basis, the limits of activity of the locals are
usually defined by the national or international headquarters of the union. The word "international" is often applied because the unions frequently have member locals
in Canada and, in some cases, Mexico. In no case in
America do the nationals or internationals have local members in Europe, Asia, Africa, or Australia.

The problems faced by labor throughout the history of
the United States are, of course, particular aspects of the
problems faced by the entire economy. Generally speaking, a low national income reflects itself in low annual
earnings, that is, a low labor income, whereas a rapid
accumulation of capital reflects itself in high wages and
high employment. On the technical level the relationship
is also close between the state of the entire economy and
that of labor. When engineering knowledge in its several
aspects, the science of management, and the other industrial considerations of "know-how" were slight, the position of labor in the factory was generally neither so pleas-
ant nor so conducive to high labor productivity as when

---

[1] The problem of undemocratic or even racketeering behavior of
unions and unionists is interesting and important; however, such
problems must be left to more intensive studies of trade unionism.

the technical aspects of production were better developed. From this point of view, then, labor progress and problems are a segment of our national economy's progress and problems.

There is, however, another view to this matter. From the earliest days of our republic, not only has the stratification of society been of such a nature that it marked out a segment as "the labor class" or "labor," but working people themselves have, by one means or another, institutionalized their efforts through the organization of the trade union. Trade unions as institutions are extremely complex: a trade union is an economic institution in its bargaining function. Its organization and internal control mechanism is a political system with many ramifications. It undertakes education, political pressuring, insurance functions, technical training, and other social functions which make it a social institution of great significance. And above all it is a "movement"—an institution devoted to an ethical, perhaps almost mystical, ideal, which gives it religious overtones. Labor, of all the social groups in America, has developed a body of controls and an ideology which directly affects the behavior of great masses of men and women. Organized labor's strength is twofold. First, it has a positive ideology and a mechanism to effectuate its ideals; and second, its major antagonists, the owner-management class, lacking a similar institutional and ideological organization, is more often than not on the defensive. Defense rarely wins social disagreements.

The common law, which we inherited from Great Britain, did not look with great favor upon the organization of labor. But the facts of life and of social organization in a very real sense conquered the common law; thus after the 1830's the legal restraints on trade unions, while continuing to exist, did not reflect a firm national policy. In other words, trade unions, whose history is as old as the history of the United States, were, after the early years of the nineteenth century, on a fairly firm footing as a result of their acceptance by the courts and to a greater or lesser degree by the legislatures and general public. Their persistent state of being led to their acceptance.

As we have seen, Jacksonian democracy was the child of the marriage of agrarian and labor interests. Indeed, it was during this period that local trade unions, first in Philadelphia and later elsewhere, organized into unions of unions, and so developed into inter-industrial organizations. It is especially interesting to note that during the Jacksonian era the ideals of the trade unions were not merely the securing of better wages and better hours but also the limitation on child labor, the extension of the system of free education, the institution of the workingman's lien, the abolition of poll taxes and other restrictions on the vote. *These ideals were sought not through collective bargaining but rather through political action.*

Thus, from the historical point of view the interest of organized working groups in politics has a long tradition in American life. American unions never were merely economic organizations. Their social and political aspects were always important and vital.

The role of American trade unions in our national life did not achieve great proportions until the development after the Civil War of the Knights of Labor (organized in 1869). Structurally, the Knights of Labor was an organization which individuals, professional groups, or trade unions could join. (Bankers and lawyers, the Levites and priests of modern society, were suspect, interestingly enough.) Ideologically, the Knights had no distinct, well-defined program but sought better wages, hours, and working conditions through collective bargaining, and through propaganda and political pressure sought to develop a system of producers' coöperatives which would supplant private enterprise. It cannot be considered successful in its positive contributions to collective bargaining or political thought, although in its time it achieved a position somewhat similar to that held by the Communist party today. That is to say it was an almost mystical organization, feared and condemned, but not well known, by the more conservative classes in society. It was supplanted, after a brief tussle, in 1886 by the American Federation of Labor. The new organization officially condemned the policy of intervention in the political arena and sought to secure its end through collective bargaining. In passing it should be remarked that the American Federation of Labor is, itself, a loose association of trade unions. Although from its inception until the 1930's it preached the gospel of collective bargaining as the way to salvation, both officially and unofficially the A.F.L. and its constituent members intervened in local, state, and national elections and so in spite of its protestations to the contrary did engage in political activity on a grand scale. Next to the farm pressure groups, it is often said that the labor pressure groups are the most powerful in American legislation. In many states and clearly in all cities the labor bloc surpasses the political power of the farm groups.

By the time the New Deal came into power, the A.F.L. as an effective organization consisted of the hard core of building tradesmen and metal tradesmen which altogether included about a million persons, although the membership of the A.F.L. at that time was somewhere near three million. The New Deal, with its obvious interest in the underdogs of society and its particular philosophy of securing prosperity by increasing "purchasing power," gave an enormous impetus to the whole doctrine of trade unionism. It can be truthfully said that President Roosevelt was more influential in the trade-union movement than any of its own chosen leaders. Nor is this truth changed, except to be strengthened, when one considers the organization of the Congress of Industrial Organizations, an offshoot of the A.F.L.

The C.I.O. was organized by dissident A.F.L. unions when the latter refused to implement its policy of organizing the mass production industries. This refusal was based upon the long tradition of the A.F.L. to respect craft lines. Union leaders like Sidney Hillman of the Amalgamated Clothing Workers and John L. Lewis of the United Mine

Workers realized that mass production industries represent a new departure in technical developments which virtually obliterates historical craft lines. Finally, after two years of argument, they simply withdrew from the A.F.L., taking with them some fourteen national unions to form the C.I.O. in 1935.

Since that time the growth of the union movement has been enormous, so that in the neighborhood of fifteen million individuals are organized into A.F.L., C.I.O., and independent unions. This growth is not merely due to the split in the union movement, although the competition between the two rival bodies has undoubtedly resulted in their securing more members. Other reasons for the growth of the union movement are the favorable political climate and favorable economic circumstances of the Roosevelt regime. For example, the National Industrial Recovery Act provided that each code of fair competition have a provision assuring workers of the right to join unions of their own choosing. Later the National Labor Relations Act (Wagner Act) was passed, providing a federal board for determining the bargaining agent as well as bargaining unit of employees through the process of governmentally supervised elections. That is to say, the National Labor Relations Board was set up to conduct elections upon the petition of a union to determine whether that union was in a majority in a given plant or unit of the plant, and to insure, under pain of legal punishment, that management bargain collectively and in good faith with the union or unions in its establishment. The Taft-Hartley Act of 1947 did not entirely destroy the governmental mechanism of protection to trade unions. It did broaden the scope of governmental intervention and coverage, so that industry, as well as labor, could seek elections to determine bargaining agencies of labor. In doing this it also placed limitations on trade union activity which in the Roosevelt New Deal period had actually been fostered.

The rapid growth of the trade union movement in the last decade or two has placed great responsibilities on the unions. Sheer size represents power in politics, so that politicians tend to woo both labor leaders and those whose interests are contrary to labor. This means that labor issues are live ones. The postwar inflation reflected itself in wage increases as it did in price increases. This has led many people, not excluding ordinary politicians and extraordinary ones seeking the presidency, to point to wage in-·creases as the cause of high prices, while their opponents, with equally bad insight and logic, thump the tubs and assert that it is the price advance which necessitates the wage increases. That wages and prices are both part of the entire price-cost structure, and so are both interrelated and conditioned by such other elements as the fiscal policy of the government, bank policy, and general postwar economic imbalance, is of course recognized only by the thoughtful. Such an analytical approach, however, is perhaps too dull or difficult to inflame the minds of men.

The trade unions are undoubtedly in politics to stay. Many leaders of unions are anxious to join politically with agriculture. Others in the union movement and in agriculture feel that such joint political action is neither possible nor mutually desirable at this time. Jackson and Roosevelt, during their respective careers, joined these groups when both were weak and poor. Now that both are strong and rich their aggressiveness seeks new outlets.

In the very recent past the union movement in America has not spent its energies entirely in pushing for higher wages. Welfare funds, i.e., sickness funds and pension funds, conditions of work, paid holidays, overtime conditions, and a host of other fringe items are on the labor-management agenda. Nor is collective bargaining the only avenue for seeking these gains. In the election of 1948, when Mr. Truman surprised even his most ardent supporters by defeating Mr. Dewey, the trade-union movement was the loyal right arm of the Democratic party. Labor's support of Mr. Roosevelt was well known, but the New Deal leader's popularity was so great that the labor vote was but one segment among the victorious many. In the Fair Deal organized labor stands out as possibly *the* important segment. Labor leaders have not been slow to recognize this and, in spite of their early failure to secure the repeal of the Taft-Hartley Act, are still active on the political front. It might very well be that legislation will be used to secure the so-called fringe demands, e.g., sickness and pension benefits, rather than collective bargaining. The proposal of Mr. Truman for a state-subsidized medical plan is more than a straw in the wind. Labor, feeling its political power, will undoubtedly use it.

Some economists are fearful of the monopolistic nature of the trade movement. Businessmen, while fearful of this new power, can sympathize with it and possibly will find ways to "make a deal," since they too have a fondness for, or at least sympathetic understanding of, the security of monopoly.

The unanswered questions of the future of a powerful union movement in America, of capitalism, and of American democracy are great and perplexing. It should be an exciting, if not particularly peaceful or well-chartered, future.

INDUSTRY

The economy of the United States, in very large part, is an industrial economy. From the early days of the republic when industry, as we have seen, was small as compared to agriculture it has grown until now it is the dominating type of economic activity in the United States. If we included in industry manufacturing, the distributive trades, banking and finance, and the other economic activities which are adjuncts of industry, it would be clear that ours is primarily a business economy in terms of employment, investment, income, and general power.

Our discussion of agriculture and trade unions shows that their actions on the economic scene were always against the backdrop of business generally. Business is not only the setting of the scene but also the commanding figure of the scene. This growing importance of business in America dates back to our early colonial life and clearly emanates from the attitude represented by Alexander Hamilton and the Federalists. To the western European not unfamiliar with business organization and business practices American culture, agriculture, social movements, and ideology all seem subordinate to the institution of business as exemplified not only by our tariff policy and our own peculiar concept of free enterprise but by such firms as the General Electric Company, United States Steel Corporation, Chase National Bank and such individual spokesmen for big business as Commodore Vanderbilt, Jay Gould, John D. Rockefeller, Philip D. Armour, and Andrew Carnegie. Even so sophisticated a writer as Anatole France saw the American Congress as a sort of super-board of directors of American industry, declaring war on such enemies as the world oil industry or the world grain markets and concerned with virtually nothing else. Of course, this is not a true picture.

The dominance of business has never been complete. As we have seen, coalitions of agriculture and labor have, on occasion, been politically superior to business. Nor is there a single interest group acting in unison called "business." For example, in America we are developing the cult of small business, a cult which insists that special privilege be given by law to small business, a class often undefined, and that small business, like agriculture, represents a "good way of life." Much of this is sentimentalism, covering an economic conflict between enterprises of various sizes. Furthermore, when a few firms dominate a given field, as in the oil industry or cigarette industry, there is no assurance that the interests of these firms are perpetually congruent. Gasoline wars are too well known to confirm that thesis. The competition of oligopolies, i.e., a few business firms dealing in the same commodity, can become much sharper and more devastating than the competition of a vast number of small firms.

In addition to competition within any market, the political manifestations of the economic interest of different types of industry have been, and will probably continue to be in the future, sources of struggle. It is often asserted, for example, that American industry is sympathetic to a high protective tariff. Yet such industries as the automobile and agricultural machinery industries which have secured a competitive place in world markets find the protective tariff unnecessary and even a hindrance to their development and an embarrassment in their dealings both at home and abroad.

American industry has grown at a faster rate than the economy generally. That is to say, a constantly greater proportion of the economic wealth of the United States and the population of the United States is concerned with the fabrication and distribution of goods than with the growing of agriculture or forestry products.

This growth of industry, or business, has been effected by at least three major elements. First, the development of the United States with its growth of population has tended to force the development of industry to meet the needs of the population. (See the table on page 107.) As the farmers and frontiersmen moved west, sawmills, iron foundries, and other necessary industries found fertile land for the seeds of their investment. It was only in the very early period of American history (if ever) that farmers were completely self-sufficient. The great migration to the West never could have occurred without the Conestoga wagon or the Kentucky rifle. These were the products of industry. The traveling merchant, with his pots and pans, condiments, yard goods, family remedies, and other household necessities, was more than the advance agent of American industry; he was an integral part of the growing industrial system.

The second important factor in the growth of American industry was the great inventions which occurred during the nineteenth century. The internal-combustion engine, mechanical farm implements, the sewing machine, the harnessing of steam power for boats and trains, the technique of building relatively weatherproof roads, the

POPULATION OF THE UNITED STATES[2]

Year	Urban	Rural	Percent of Total Population	
			Urban	Rural
1790	201,655	3,727,559	5.1	94.9
1800	322,371	4,986,112	6.1	93.9
1810	525,459	6,714,422	7.3	92.7
1820	693,255	8,945,198	7.2	92.8
1830	1,127,247	11,738,773	8.8	91.2
1840	1,845,055	15,224,398	10.8	89.2
1850	3,543,716	19,648,160	15.3	84.7
1860	6,216,518	25,226,803	19.8	80.2
1870	9,902,361	28,656,010	25.7	74.3
1880	14,129,735	36,026,048	28.2	71.8
1890	22,106,265	40,841,449	35.1	64.9
1900	30,159,921	45,834,654	39.7	60.3
1910	41,998,932	49,973,334	45.7	54.3
1920	54,157,973	51,552,647	51.2	48.8
1930	68,954,823	53,820,223	56.2	43.8
1940	74,423,702	57,245,573	56.5	43.5

Estimates of internal migration were disbanded during the war years owing to the constant shifting. However, the Department of Agriculture did attempt such with the use of war ration books.

Urban: Areas with population of 2500 or more and incorporated (generally).

1945 marked the first year since the end of World War I when the farm population showed an absolute increase. In both instances this was due to the return of the servicemen. There was a small return during 1933 but this was of less than a year's duration.

[2] Years 1790-1940: *Sixteenth Census of the United States, 1940, Population*, vol. 1, p. 20. Farm population changes: U.S. Department of Agriculture, Series BAE no. 7; P-S no. 5; P-S no. 6.

development of high-grade precision instruments which made possible large-scale manufacturing, and the evolution of a fairly efficient banking structure were among the inventions which not only gave tone to the economy but were the very basis of economic development.

Last of the three important factors is that of financial and technical combination. Most large firms in America did not grow large as a result of their own internal expansion. It is true that some did—Atlantic and Pacific Stores and Ford Motor Company are two leading examples, but they tend to exemplify a relatively small fraction of American business activity. Most firms grew large through combining with their competitors, or through purchase, or through amalgamation. The United States Steel Corporation, the great rubber companies, the great railroads—indeed, virtually all the great industrial concentrations—are truly concentrations and combinations of firms which once were competitive.

Other factors are important in an understanding of American economic growth, but the three mentioned—natural growth, invention and innovation, and industrial and financial combination—are peculiarly American in their nature.

Like agriculture, business, in the course of its history, was several times at great historical turning points. The first was probably that of the Jeffersonian period. Jefferson, it will be recalled, believed in agriculture as the good life, regardless of whether the income of the entire economy would be greater or less under an agricultural system than under an industrial system. Jefferson's Louisiana Purchase was, from the economic point of view, an overt attempt to throw the balance of power, both political and economic, to the agricultural interests. For a time the maneuver was successful, in that the industrial East of the United States enjoyed less political power than the agricultural West and South. This carried almost up to the Civil War. The Civil War, like other great wars America has fought, was a victory of industry as well as a victory of arms. Realizing that hindsight is almost always correct, we nevertheless feel that it should have been apparent to economically minded people of the 1860's that the southern states after the first impact of the war simply never had a chance. The economic potential of the Union so overshadowed that of the Confederacy that war should have been unthinkable to even the most rabid Southerner. In the view of the present writer, political and emotional sentiments in the South conquered the economic understanding of life, *the result being that business interests of the North, after the war, argued that their peculiar self-interest coincided with the self-interest of the United States.* The Jeffersonian ideal was not accomplished; indeed, its converse won the day!

Economic activity tends to feed on economic activity. That is to say, large investments create income, job opportunities, a rosy expectation for the future, all of which are inducements for further investments, further job opportunities, better expectations, and so on. This almost endless chain of business activity feeding on business activity knew almost no bounds during the latter part of the nineteenth and early part of the twentieth centuries, with an open frontier in the West and an economic adolescence which could digest virtually any amount of new investment and new population.

The notion that the open West provided unending job opportunities for the immigrants from Europe is well known. What is less often recognized is that the development of the West, and with it the growth of great industrial and financial centers along the entire seaboard as well as in the West, provided an investment outlet for enormous quantities of European capital. The railroads, the canals, the New York subway system, part of the steel industry, and other manufacturing industries all were the recipients of European capital. The extent of this investment was such that virtually up until the First World War the export trade of America was just about equal to the payments required of American industry by European

investors. Industry and investment the world over benefited by the opening of the West. That is not to say that
American industry was controlled by foreigners; it is to say
that the borrowings and the financial obligations of American industry to foreign investors were extremely large.

This relationship, however, almost never implied any
subservience of American industry to European interests,
or attempts of European investors to dictate economic
policies within the United States. The United States was
developing internally; it was exploiting its own markets
with only minor excursions into Mexico, Latin America,
Europe, and the Pacific areas.

The course of economic activity was not a smooth one,
but we came out of each depression with at least a slightly
higher level of output and employment than we went in,
so that the secular trend was upward. Depression was
felt, for example, from 1802-04; 1807 was a panic year; the
War of 1812 was fought in a depressed period; 1842 and
1843 were years of depression; the panic of 1873 is notorious, although it probably was not so severe as the panic of
1893; 1907 and 1913-14 were bad years from the point of
view of production and employment. These depressions,
however, were merely the minor stumblings of a man running a very successful foot race.

Probably of greater significance than the depressions in
the development of industry were the political attempts
by nonbusiness groups to restrain business, either on the
basis of ideological differences with the business community or on the basis that the interests of the business community were running counter to and adversely affecting
the interests of other economic groups.

As was pointed out, agriculture and labor demanded
and secured some reforms, reforms whose importance we
have often tended to forget. The Interstate Commerce
Act of 1886, the institution of a public school system,
health and sanitation laws, as well as other public services,
all represent encroachments or limitations upon the complete freedom of free enterprise. In 1890 the Sherman

Antitrust Act was passed, as a result of public agitation from many interest groups including some segments of business, to restrain the growth and power of the giant combinations in American industry. Restraints of trade or commerce were made illegal, but the act was not sufficiently implemented so as to be readily enforceable, or so that the area of its coverage was beyond question. Some successful prosecutions were brought under the act, but on the whole, the net effects of the early antitrust suits did not do much to destroy monopoly. More important than the prosecutions is the fact that the Sherman Act represents a new political point of view. In the language of this discussion it was a possible turning point which was not quite effective.

The accession of Theodore Roosevelt to the presidency upon the assassination of President William McKinley caused a revitalization in the antitrust attitude of the United States government. Roosevelt, in a sense, was a figure similar to Jackson and Franklin Roosevelt, in that he sought to force an alliance of groups which by themselves were ineffectual but in combination could be powerful. The great trusts were feared by agriculture, small business, and labor, so three groups were available to Roosevelt for his alliance. The line of attack was defined in the Sherman Act, and Roosevelt pushed that line of attack as hard as he could. Indeed, in his administration more antitrust suits were brought (forty-eight) than in the combined presidencies of Benjamin Harrison (seven), Grover Cleveland (eight), and William McKinley (three). The exuberance and drive of Theodore Roosevelt did lead to some successful prosecutions under the act, but in the Standard Oil case (1911), a case which had lingered in the courts for more than five years, the Supreme Court held that the application of antitrust status must be "determined by light of reason." This may be viewed as a statement by the Supreme Court that the Sherman Act was only as effective as the several personalities of the Supreme Court thought proper. The Supreme Court was

criticized as an agency which raised itself by its own boot-
straps above the policy set by the Congress. Whether or
not such criticism is justified, the decision is important
in that it represents the blocking of an economic and
political philosophy. From our point of view, it was not
the Supreme Court which became ascendant, it was big
business which maintained its ascendancy.

It was not until 1914 that an act (the Clayton Act)
was passed designed to strengthen the obvious weaknesses
of the Sherman Act. Although President Wilson, in whose
term of office the act was passed, was viewed by many
business interests as a radical, his administration did not
attempt a frontal attack upon trusts and monopolies but
rather tried to restrain what his administration considered
"improper or evil economic effects" of monopolies and
corporations. It was more a philosophy of control of evil
than a philosophy of the extirpation of an economic and
social institution—to wit, monopolies.

On the whole, the economic policy set by the Wilson
administration has continued through to the present, so
that the government sets itself up as a watchdog over
monopolistic activity rather than as destroyer of monopolies. *The rule of reason has triumphed*, although reasonable men have never yet been able to define reason. Prag-
matism has become our state philosophy in this regard
rather than a clean-cut position against all private economic monopolies.

One important consideration of the Clayton Act was
to exclude farm coöperatives and trade unions from the
antitrust laws. In part this was an obvious political play by
the Democratic party for farmer-labor support; in part it
represented a policy which we have more or less adhered
to—a strengthening of the underdog vis-à-vis the top dog.
In a sense, this represents government by equalizing or
balancing economic forces rather than government by setting the ideological norm and trying to enforce it.

The period following the First World War was one of
great prosperity in American industry. Outside of the

minor depression of 1921, the postwar years up to 1929 were bountiful. The tendency to industrial combination increased, and even permeated the banking field and the distribution field. A peculiar economic phenomenon occurred, in that the price level during the period was slightly downward, although profits, employment, and wages moved upward. This was brought about, probably, by the great increases in industrial efficiency which occurred during the period. It is estimated that labor productivity went up by as much as 2 percent to 3 percent a year, so that profits were safe in spite of gently falling prices. Incidentally, this situation tended to soften the antagonisms between labor and capital, with the result that the trade union movement deteriorated. Only three major segments of the economy did not enjoy the prosperity. They were agriculture, coal mining, and textiles.

The depression which began sometime in the middle of 1929, as was pointed out before, hit all economic activity indiscriminately. Its impact on the social thinking of people was probably greater than the impact of World War II. Industrial production fell by as much as 50 percent; employment fell by as much as eleven million out of a working population of about fifty million. Ruin stared everyone in the face.

The economic policies of the F. D. Roosevelt administration, in addition to its agricultural policies of raising farm prices and attempting to curtail production, included the fixing of minimum wages, first through the NRA codes of fair competition and later through the Fair Labor Standards Act, public works and public relief on an unprecedented scale, and restrictions on financial operations in both public utilities and the banking and investment trades. On the whole, it may be said that the theory, if not the practice, of the Roosevelt administration was "reflationary." That is to say, the government's policy was to raise the price level and so make business profitable.

Outside of the brief NRA experiment, in which price fixing and other monopolistic practices were permitted,

the Roosevelt administration offered no specific program
or policy for business, as it did for labor and agriculture.
This, of course, is in line with the general interests of
business, but the attempts to strengthen the hands of
agriculture and labor and to meet their immediate and
long-run needs caused business to view the administration
as antibusiness. This in itself is an indication that business generally saw in the Roosevelt administration a political turning point which, if successfully carried through,
would have reduced the economic ascendancy of business,
if it did not completely destroy that ascendancy. That
general attitude continued up to and, to a certain extent,
through World War II.

The post-World War II period has, thus far, been one
of unprecedented prosperity through 1950. Employment
and production have exceeded the fondest hopes of America. The little depression of 1949 saw some unemployment, but that figure never exceeded five million, while
employment hovered near the sixty-million mark. Prices,
which rose so rapidly after the abolition of OPA in 1946-
47, began to fall, but national income reached a high in
1948 (nearly 225 billions of dollars). In real terms, i.e., in
goods and services, national income far exceeded the prewar levels.

In spite of the fortunate economic circumstances, the
postwar period has been a troubled one. As was pointed
out above, the great depression made a deep mark on
people's minds, so that businessmen are often fearful of
the economic future. We have not enjoyed our prosperity.
We have acted as though it were a chance occurrence
which time would reverse and replace by unemployment
and misery. We have almost the subconscious attitude of
fearing the future. Whether or not there is theoretical or
scientific justification for this cannot be discussed here,
except to point out that *if the belief in the inevitability of
depression is general enough it will be realized.*

Wartime savings, wartime shortages, a going and un
injured economic system, a high European demand, only

in part supported by United States government funds, a
large public expenditure, all have joined in maintaining a
very respectable degree of economic prosperity. The first
and second rounds of economic adjustment to peacetime
conditions have been successfully met.

NATIONAL INCOME BY DISTRIBUTIVE SHARES[3]
(1929-45)
(in billions of dollars)

Year	National Income	Compensation of Employees	Proprietors' and Rental Income	Corporate Profits and Inventory Valuation Adjustment	Net Int.
1945	182.8	122.9	30.2	19.7	3.1
1944	182.3	121.2	27.7	23.5	3.2
1943	168.3	109.1	26.0	23.7	3.4
1942	136.5	84.7	22.7	19.8	3.9
1941	103.8	64.3	16.5	14.6	4.1
1940	81.3	51.8	12.7	9.2	4.1
1939	72.5	47.8	11.3	5.8	4.2
1938	67.4	44.7	10.8	4.3	4.3
1937	73.6	47.7	12.2	6.2	4.4
1936	64.7	42.7	9.9	4.9	4.5
1935	56.8	37.1	9.9	3.0	4.5
1934	48.6	34.1	6.6	1.1	4.8
1933	39.6	29.3	5.2	− 2.0	5.0
1932	41.7	30.8	4.9	− 2.0	5.4
1931	58.9	39.5	8.2	1.6	5.9
1930	75.0	46.5	11.0	6.6	6.2
1929	87.4	50.8	13.9	10.3	6.5

NOTE: Because of rounding, detail will not add to totals.

One important novel element in postwar economics is
the sheer size of the federal budget. The government is
spending something near fifty billion dollars a year to
carry out all its social, political, military, and economic

[3] U.S. Bureau of Census, *Historical Statistics of the United States,*
1789-1945, Washington, D.C., 1949.

commitments. This is about one-fifth of the national income. The effect of such expenditure, even when met in greatest part by taxation, on employment and production is tremendous. Furthermore, the administration, whether it be Republican or Democratic, has been trained by the experience of the 1930's, so that the counterdepression activities of the federal government, in the event of a depression, may be taken almost for granted.

CHAPTER VII

The One-World Argument

FROM THE ECONOMIC point of view, America's entry into the Second World War occurred in late 1938 or early 1939. It was during these years that the United States began to develop its own armament and war industries, and also began to supply (sell) the countries later to become its allies the means of waging war.

Unemployment in the United States was high at the beginning of this period, probably amounting to between nine and eleven million persons. In a sense this was fortunate because it permitted rapid expansion of employment and scarcity of labor did not become a factor limiting production. Indeed, if one leaves out of account the wartime entry into the labor market of persons not normally seeking employment, a number somewhere in excess of two million, the total membership in the armed forces, approximately eleven million during the war period, just about equaled the unemployed and persons potentially employable during the period just preceding the war.

Had we entered the war with full employment, the dislocations to industry would have been greater than they actually were. Of course, this is not a defense of maintaining unemployment as an economic reservoir in the event of war. The statement is made simply to indicate that from the point of view of labor supply we began the war in a relatively fortunate position.

In addition to unemployment of labor, we were suffering from unemployment (underutilization) of capital at the beginning of the war period. This, too, permitted rapid increase of production without putting as great a burden on the investment industries as would otherwise have been the case. The rosy picture, however, is not complete. Putting people to work in the manufacture of the material of war meant retraining labor for new types of jobs and also converting industry and supplying new investment for the war industries. This was a most formidable task.

From 1940 until the end of 1945 unemployment fell sharply, reaching a low of less than a million in the first part of the latter year. This million of unemployed people consisted largely of frictionally unemployed, i.e., people unemployed for a short period while moving from one job to the next. An industrial working population of fifty-five million, it might be expected, will have a frictional unemployment of somewhere between three and five million, so that the less than a million reported as unemployed represents what might be considered negative unemployment. This means, of course, that the techniques to attract people into the labor market were, on the whole, very successful. During the war, exclusive of prisoners of war and Italian service units, the only forced labor in the United States was labor in the armed services. The young men drafted into the army and navy had no choice of job. Indeed, early in the war the uncertain policy of enlistment was abandoned in favor of the more certain method of the draft. For persons not covered by the draft, inducements were the principal means of allocating labor. Wages, in spite of the attempts of the government to maintain a wage policy, rose rather sharply; in 1939 average weekly earnings were $27.04, whereas in 1944 they had risen to $48.83. Hourly earnings in this period increased from an average of 72¢ to $1.067. Average hours per week for employed persons increased from 37.6 in 1939 to 45.6 hours in 1944. The latter figure indicates that the forty-eight-hour week was prevalent in 1944.

The great increase in production during the war period

is one of the most startling and gratifying experiences of that period. Yet labor productivity increased but slightly. It is estimated that approximately half of the increase and output between 1940 and 1944, an increase approximating 70 or 80 percent, was due about 50 percent to the increased hours of work, about 25 percent to the absorption of the unemployed, and somewhere in the neighborhood of 13 percent was the normal increment in the working force. *Only about 5 or 6 percent is attributed to increased productivity.* This is small when one considers that the normal rate of increased productivity per man-hour has historically been about 2 percent, and should have been larger in the development of new (war) industries, where productivity increases are large until the tempo of plant and worker production becomes constant.

On the whole, the labor controls exercised by the government during the war were of a voluntary nature. The War Manpower Commission was set up as the agency to assure the appropriate distribution of labor. A system of labor priorities was established so that employers could not hire labor without the approval of the Commission. Although this system was abused, it should be noted that the concentration of employment in the war industries and the proportion of the total population employed in the United States compare favorably with German, Russian, and British experiences, each of which used somewhat more compulsion than did the United States.

The government also instituted the National War Labor Board to exercise a tripartite control over wages. This Board, representing management, labor, and the public, was responsible for the wage policy and disputes (strike) policy of the government. The voluntary settlement of strikes without recourse to the Board was always permitted and encouraged. If, however, wage adjustments were involved, or if disputes on non-wage questions occurred, the Board attempted a settlement. In its strike program it was successful, the coal industry being the only major industry to suffer from a prolonged strike during the war. Other strikes occurred, to be sure, but on the whole, their effects were not very serious in impeding the war effort. With regard to wage policy, the Board was statistically less successful, although the runaway inflation of wages that many had expected did not occur.

The pressure on wages was bound to be very great, as more and more people were employed in war and other investment goods industries which did not produce consumers' goods to offset the wages paid. Thus prices tended to rise, making further wage demands inevitable. The sheer shortage of labor, too, led businessmen to compete for labor through higher wage offerings, and labor was not slow to recognize its scarcity value.

One way to look at this is to examine the size of the national income during the war period as measured in dollars. In 1940 the total national product, i.e., all the products of the United States including income, investment, depreciation, etc., was 100.4 billion dollars; in 1941 it had risen to 125.2 billion; in 1942 it was nearly 160 billion; in 1943 it rose to nearly 193 billion; in 1944 it approximated 211 billion; in 1945 it reached 213 billion. The real income and product comparisons, that is, the actual goods and services available during these years, are difficult to make because the nature of the output changed during the war period and the prices of specialized wartime goods were appreciably higher. Nevertheless, in the net, production rose sharply. In 1939 about 1.3 billion dollars was consumed in war expenditures. In 1945 war expenditure was still as high as 76.1 billion dollars, whereas in 1943 and 1944 this amount had been considerably exceeded (80 billion in 1943 and nearly 89 billion in 1944).

The war, then, in addition to causing national output to increase, also swallowed up a large proportion of that output in war activities. With many incomes rising, prices rose very sharply, and probably would have risen even more sharply had not a system of rationing and price fixing been introduced. Several specific formulas were worked out by the Office of Price Administration for the control of specific prices, and later a General Maximum Price Control was instituted. Appropriate markups and specific prices were fixed on virtually all items of trade. Rationing was also undertaken for many types of consumers' goods, including food, shoes, and gasoline. Probably more important, from the point of view of the functioning war economy, than rationing of consumers' goods was the rationing undertaken by the War Production Board of raw materials and semimanufactured products. Priorities with varying degrees of claim were allowed manufacturers by this agency, so that the nature of the goods produced was under the control of the government.

The operation of such agencies as the War Manpower Commission, the Office of Price Administration, and the War Production Board clearly required coördination. This was supplied by the Office of War Mobilization and the Office of Economic Stabilization.

This brief sketch indicates the degrees of control, positive control, exercised by the federal government during the war. The policy here was not to equalize relative economic power of the competing groups, nor to sanction good actions of monopolies and control bad actions. The program was positive. The constant threat of government seizure, which power the federal government had under the several war powers acts, undoubtedly was influential in directing the economy to the end of winning the war.

One must add to this sheer political and economic control the ideological elements. During the war period, businessmen, labor leaders, and farmers were all willing to give up some of their rights and privileges to assist in winning the war. The diverse and often conflicting ideologies of the prewar period were channeled and directed by the fact of war itself. When the war was over, and the end came more suddenly than many in positions of power expected, the federal government debated how reconversion and decontrol were to take place. Underlying much of the discussion was the feeling that the end of the war would see a sharp depression in prices and an unemployment of fairly great magnitude. To this end, many of the more restrictive controls on industry and labor were dropped rather quickly, including many price controls, wage controls, and priority controls. By two years after the war, the controls were virtually nonexistent. Yet the expected depression did not occur. Employment actually rose to an excess of sixty million, even though the labor force was expanded by the returning service people and by unemployment in the war industries.

The question was not one of depression policy or unemployment, but rather one of full employment and inflation. In the two years after the war, prices rose, but the national production or gross national output rose to the rate of nearly 225 billion dollars a year. Shortages almost as great as wartime shortages continued or affected many goods.

During the war the employed worker was on the whole better off than the employed worker before the war. True, he could not buy an automobile or a radio, but the typical wage goods, that is to say the food, clothing, and minor comforts of life of the wage worker, were more plentiful during the war than ever before. The high rate of money income, sustained by the wartime savings of the working group, reflected itself in an insistent demand for items in short supply such as housing, white shirts, radios, meat, etc. The changes in eating habits are important. Before the war, meat was eaten two or possibly three times a week by a large proportion of the people. During the war the increase in money income and the rationing made meat available to the whole of the people. In the postwar period this led to changes in the demand for meat, even though production was at record levels.

This leads us to a consideration of the economic status of the farmer. In 1940 group farm income was in the neighborhood of eleven billion dollars; in 1945 it approached twenty-five billion dollars. The demand for agricultural products, not only at home but to help feed our allies, put farmers in an extremely favorable position vis-à-vis the other groups in society. The postwar years saw no change in this situation, and the share of the national income going to agriculture continued to increase.

This great prosperity was not without its problems. First and foremost, probably, was the underlying fear that "what goes up must come down." Labor leaders, business leaders, and farm leaders all felt that a depression, or at least a recession, was, if not imminent, at least a likely chance. Secondly, the economic need of Europe and Asia was extremely great and entailed consistent expenditures by the United States. During the war, "Lend-Lease" had been the vehicle of supplying our allies with needed goods. Lend-Lease was discontinued at the war's end, but the needs of not only our allies but also the conquered nations continued as a moral, if not a legal, claim against us.

The end of the war, then, found the United States in an extremely prosperous circumstance—a prosperity, however, which was marked by fairly acute shortages of some classes of goods and moderate shortages of many others. By the summer of 1947 it was pretty clear that the recession or depression which many expected was not an immediate likelihood. Employment was high—so high that the slogan of Henry Wallace and his followers that "the United States must plan for sixty million jobs" because almost meaningless, as employment for the first time in the history of the country actually passed the sixty-million mark. Agriculture was enjoying a prosperity that it had never dreamed of, with corn and wheat, cattle and hogs at record highs. Yet, shot through this level of production and consumption was the fear of a depression.

In 1945 and 1946, with prices rising, there was the inevitable clamor for higher wages, a clamor which was not always acceded to by industry, so that strikes were resorted to by labor with great frequency. The growth of nation-wide collective bargaining meant that in some industrial areas strikes brought virtually nation-wide stoppages. Coal is an example. In other instances, where the union was successful in securing a company-wide agreement, and the company was a large one with shops and factories in many areas, the strikes had more of the applications of a nation-wide strike. The strikes against General Motors and General Electric in 1946 are examples of this.

The postwar strike situation, plus a certain amount of unreasoned antagonism against trade unions because of labor practices which arose during the acute labor shortage during the war, caused some elements in industry to seek political protection against strong trade unions.

After much debate, the Taft-Hartley Bill was enacted in 1947. Without attempting to be specific, and to analyze the many intricacies of the act, it will suffice, for our purposes, to point out that it outlawed the closed shop and placed restrictions on the union shop and maintenance of membership; it denied supervisors, i.e., foremen, the protection of the National Labor Relations Board; it provided that unions may be sued for breach of contract and, further, that third parties who are injured by jurisdictional strikes or secondary boycotts may sue the union; a cooling-off period of sixty days was instituted so that the *status quo ante* under a contract could not be disturbed for sixty days after a union had voted to strike; unions are required to supply to the government certain information about their financial situation and the salaries of officials; and union officials must sign an affidavit that they are not Communists, if the union is to enjoy the privileges of the National Labor Relations Board. The cooling-off provision requires emphasis, because it was taken from the "War Labor Disputes Act" (Smith-Connally Act), whose cooling-off provision had virtually no effect on strikes. This is the merest summary of some of the more important provisions of the act. Attempts to repeal the act in 1949, after the Democrats secured control of both houses of the Congress as well as the presidency, failed. Nor did the Congressional election of 1950 indicate that the country at large considered the Taft-Hartley Act an important political issue.

From the point of view of ideas, the act represents a

possible turning point in government policy with respect to unions. No longer does the policy of the government seem pointed in the direction of strengthening unions as a means of equalizing their bargaining strength; rather, the act has been widely interpreted as a means of limiting the activity of unions and, by implication, strengthening the hands of management. It is probably significant that immediately after the passage of the act many large companies indicated that their past relations with union labor would not be affected by the act. If this is to be taken seriously, it means that, in some instances, mass capital and mass labor had accommodated each other, so that a *modus vivendi* had been found.

In 1951, as the economy was moving toward another era of controls very similar to those of World War II, employment actually exceeded 62 million jobs. Again, however, shortages were beginning to be felt because of both the high flow of money income and the growing demands of the "mobilized" economy.

During World War II many political leaders publicly announced that United States policy would be to weaken Germany in the postwar period so that she could never fight another war. As laudable (if impracticable) as these intentions were, they did not take into account the importance of Germany as a raw-material and manufacturing center for the rest of the world. Nor did these lofty sentiments take into account the political and economic dislocations which postwar Europe would experience, or the foreign policy of the Soviet Union.

All things considered, western Europe made a fairly good reconversion after the war. But this is not saying very much, because the devastation of the war, a devastation which was not only economic but also political and social, was enormous. Fortunately, all of western Europe looked to the United States for assistance, and found that assistance, originally, in UNRRA. UNRRA aid, however, was not sufficient to rebuild economies. Great Britain, shouldering a fantastically large burden of debt, has tried hard to develop her export trades and has succeeded; but even though her exports exceed those of the prewar period, her imports and her debts are too heavy. Rising prices in America, plus an underestimate of her internal needs, tended to cause Britain's United States loan of about four billion dollars to be used up three or four times as fast as she expected. France, on the verge of revolution, with her trade union movement in many instances led by Communists, has found neither political nor economic stability. Italy, with the largest Communist party in Western Europe (in 1948), a party probably numbering over two million, is torn by internal dissensions among Communists, Socialists, Neo-Fascists, and other political groupings which almost defy definition. The successful revolt of the Indies, resulting in their dominion status, is in the process of removing Holland from the rank of even second-class powers. And so on for the other European countries.

To complicate the matter further, the USSR, through political and extra-political means, has virtually captured all of eastern Europe and China, and is making headway in Asia. This troubled world situation of course affects the political and economic behavior of the United States.

Implied in our foreign policy for the past several years is the idea that democracy, by which it may be presumed that we mean some sort of political and economic system not too distasteful to the United States, must be secured in western Europe, if only as a defense against the encroachments of Russia. In addition to this political consideration, there is the sentimental one that the United States, as a prosperous nation, has the responsibility for assisting other nations, at least free nations, in their recovery. And last, there is the underlying belief that the economic prosperity of the United States depends in great part upon the economic prosperity of western Europe, for without trade with these nations world trade will be reduced and the standard of living in America will fall.

It was inevitable that political leaders of the United

States should think in terms of some program or plan to help restore a degree of stability to Europe.

The European Recovery Program, or Marshall Plan, had its inception in June of 1947 when the Secretary of State George C. Marshall, addressing the graduating class at Harvard, suggested that the nations of Europe draft a program by which America might help Europe help itself. The second step was a report, compiled in Paris in September, in which sixteen western European nations complied with Mr. Marshall's suggestion. The third step was a report on October 18 by a committee on American resources, headed by the Secretary of the Interior (Julius A. Krug), which asserted that a large program of European aid would not unduly strain American resources. The fourth step was a report by the President's Council of Economic Advisors, which said that the program would not injure the American economy, provided measures were taken to stem inflation. The fifth step was a report by a citizens' committee of nineteen, headed by the Secretary of Commerce (W. Averell Harriman), which correlated all the other reports and charted a program for action.

THE PARIS CONFERENCE ON THE MARSHALL PLAN

The Paris conference was called to take an inventory of the European nations. All the nations of Europe were invited, but only sixteen attended, namely, Great Britain, France, Holland, the Netherlands, Sweden, Denmark, Ireland (Eire), Belgium, Luxembourg, Switzerland, Italy, Austria, Greece, Turkey, and Portugal. The USSR and the nations under her influence (Rumania, Czechoslovakia, Bulgaria, Yugoslavia) were conspicuous by their absence. (Yugoslavia after a falling out with Moscow indicated a desire to partake of the western bounty. This represents a crack in the iron curtain.)

The report made as a result of the meeting is designed primarily as an analysis of the maladjustments which have resulted from the war and an examination of what the participating countries can do for themselves and for each other to work toward a lasting solution.

The scale of the destruction and dislocation of World War II was greater than that of World War I. Agricultural and industrial production was severely reduced, traditional sources of food and raw material supply were cut off, so that when the war was over the devastated countries had frightful burdens to assume. Through the efforts of the European countries themselves and of the United States, other countries, and UNRRA, recovery proceeded fast. But it was not maintained in the winter of 1946-47, and the European economy suffered a serious setback. Coal continued in short supply, and the lack of it curtailed industrial production. Food and other commodities remained scarce, and the prices of food and primary products rose. The foreign exchange resources of the participating countries had, therefore, to be drawn upon heavily. An exceptionally severe winter was followed by a long drought and intensified these difficulties, so that by the summer of 1947 the earlier hope of a quick recovery had receded.

The report assumes a high degree of self-help by the countries concerned and mutual help among them. In order to ascertain what could be achieved, technical committees were set up to make special examinations of agriculture, fuel and power, steel, timber, and transport, together with such related industries as agricultural and mining machinery, and the general problem of manpower. The recovery program is designed to achieve the following results by 1951:

1. Restoration of prewar bread, grain, and other cereal production, with large increases above prewar in sugar and potatoes, some increases in oils and fats, and as fast an expansion in livestock products as supplies of feeding stuffs will allow.

2. Increase of coal output to 584 million tons, i.e., 145 million tons above the 1947 level (an increase of one-third) and 30 million tons above the 1938 level.

3. Expansion of electricity output by nearly 70 million kilowatt hours, or 40 percent above the 1947 level, and a growth of generating capacity by 25 billion kw. or two-thirds above prewar.
4. Development of oil-refining capacity in terms of crude oil throughout by 17 million tons to two and a half times the prewar level.
5. Increase of crude steel production by 80 percent above 1947 to a level of 55 million tons, or 10 million tons (20 percent) above 1938.
6. Expansion of inland transport facilities to carry a 25 percent greater load in 1951 than in 1938.
7. Restoration of prewar merchant fleets in the participating countries by 1951.
8. Supply from European production of most of the capital equipment needed for these expansions.

In figuring the cost of this program, the European nations feel that they will need twenty-two billion dollars from outside sources (approximately twenty billion from the United States), over a four-year period. The breakdown of the figures shows a need for 8.04 billion dollars in 1948, 7.35 in 1949, 4.65 in 1950, 3.40 in 1951, for a total of 22.44 billion dollars.

THE KRUG REPORT

In October 1947, the Secretary of the Interior sent his committee's report to the President. This report contained detailed physical assessments of our national resources. The report did not deal with the economic (per se) and fiscal problems of foreign aid. It stated that American resources can support a considerable program of foreign aid. Shortages of wheat, steel, coal, nitrogen, fertilizers, and some industrial equipment would be intensified, but they would be of short-run nature and would "taper off" as the aid program progressed.

Some of the highlights of the report are as follows:

U.S. Employment and Foreign Aid. About one million jobs would be created to produce goods for the five-billion-dollar-a-year aid program. Employment now ranges between fifty-five million and sixty million persons. Between 1947 and 1952, the labor force in the United States will increase by another 2,500,000 simply as a result of natural population growth. If necessary, the work week could be increased from forty to forty-four hours a week.

Wheat. Wheat is by far the most important item of American food in relation to foreign needs because of its high caloric value. Whether the United States meets the President's goal of exporting 570 million bushels of wheat in the next crop year, compared with 400 million bushels this year, depends on the success of the voluntary conservation program and the weather.

Steel. Steel in many ways presents the most troublesome problem of all. Meeting substantial European demands for American steel will aggravate a serious domestic supply situation.

Coal. The amount of coal which may be exported to Europe during the 1947-52 period is insignificant in terms of United States resources. U.S. coal production is only limited by the supply of coal cars. To meet this shortage, pooling arrangements must be adapted, coal car production must be increased, and coal should be purchased by domestic and foreign users during off-season months.

Fuels. An "acute" problem exists in petroleum. The nation now produces enough petroleum only for its own use; it undoubtedly will have to depend upon imports to meet future demands. One-fourth of the annual consumption of natural gas is lost or wasted. Conservation practices are called for in all the fuel industries.

Land. Still greater increases in high-grade farming lands are possible under irrigation and drainage programs. Attention should be given to the lower Mississippi and Gulf coast regions.

Nonferriferous Metals. Physical reserves of copper, lead, and zinc ores appear to be inadequate to meet long-run domestic needs. Imports must be increased and substitutes developed.

Krug defended the aid program on a moral basis. The report advocates a foreign-aid program not only because its figures indicate the country has the resources to aid Europe but on three other grounds: It will prevent hardship and starvation for millions of people; it provides the basis for getting world economy off dead center; and it creates circumstances favorable to full production throughout the world, and to expanded world trade.

THE REPORT OF THE PRESIDENT'S COUNCIL OF ECONOMIC ADVISORS

In their report the Council advised the President to seek renewal of some wartime powers to deal with a threatened inflation of industrial prices under the combined impact of heavy domestic demand and a twenty-billion-dollar European recovery program.

The Council warned that serious inflation already existed in prices of food and steel. They said the nation's ability to support a European recovery program of the proportions contemplated already had been demonstrated but warned of serious trouble ahead unless firm measures were taken to counteract current trends.

Although the Council's report dealt mainly with the impact of a foreign-aid program on the domestic economy, it also warned that without such aid western Europe faced bankruptcy and chaos and that in those circumstances continued prosperity in the United States was impossible.

In order to prevent the combined impact of domestic and foreign demand from furthering the growing inflation in this country, the Council suggested the following governmental controls:

1. Allocation of scarce materials for domestic use.
2. Continued use and strengthening of export controls.
3. Penalties or premiums to discourage hoarding of scarce materials or their misuse for purposes inconsistent with balanced national and international needs.
4. Restrictive measures against speculation in any commodities in short supply because it does not serve an economically useful function.
5. Maintenance of tax revenues at existing high levels, reduction of government expenditures, and encouragement of individual savings.
6. Enlargement and aggressive use of the power to control the expansion of credits.

These measures when used in proper combination could help directly to reduce the impact of any given level of foreign aid on the domestic economy, the report said. However, if they proved inadequate for any reason, the presidential advisers recommended using "at least the minimum powers necessary for a more frontal attack upon these price increases."

The report also noted that, while the restoration of Europe's industries would provide customers for American products, it inevitably would create competitors since such countries could repay the aid only with the products of their revived industries. Thus, it was to be expected that American war-born industries would receive a test of their efficiency when European products again appeared in the market. But the report suggested in this connection that orderly competition was a healthy condition and that in the long run the United States had to become a large importing nation if it wanted to continue exporting in large volume.

THE HARRIMAN REPORT

In the most exhaustive report on the European Recovery Program, President Truman's Committee, headed by

Secretary of Commerce Harriman, proposed a program costing up to seventeen billion dollars and aimed at "the prevention of World War III."

This semiofficial report said that the American way of life and the heritage of free peoples everywhere were threatened by a ruthless and determined drive by Soviet Russia and its satellites to achieve world domination; that the "first major battle" for survival of individual liberty is now being fought in western Europe; and that aid is imperative.

Estimating the cost of the four-year program at between twelve billion and seventeen billion dollars after a drastic scaling down of European demands, the report placed the cost to the United States Treasury in the first year at $5,750,000,000 and proposed that $3,000,000,000 be provided as grants-in-aid for food, fuel, and fertilizer.

The Committee further recommended that a new federal agency be set up to administer the program. It proposed that full powers of decision be vested in a strong executive as chairman of a board of directors of members of the President's cabinet most directly concerned.

The Committee proposed the following:

1. Stabilization of currencies of the sixteen European nations participating in the recovery program as "an essential immediate step without which further aid from this country will be wasteful and ineffective."
2. Cutting off of further loans and grants if any participating nation failed to meet production or other goals scheduled by such country. Also provision for thorough inspection of program progress.
3. Use of funds obtained by a participating government from sale of food, fuel, and fertilizer shipments only to reduce or avoid inflationary borrowings from banks, or for productive purposes. Local currencies thus realized should not be used for general budget spending by the government.

4. Immediate statutory increase in the lending power of the World Bank, if necessary to start a program of international reconstruction loans.

5. A new two-billion-dollar lending program by the (U.S.) Export-Import Bank, a semigovernmental bank, to finance essential raw material purchases in categories unsuited for World Bank loans and ineligible for grants-in-aid, the bank loans to be made by direction of the European recovery administrator.

6. Immediate partial restoration of the President's limited war powers to direct channeling of goods overseas and to soften the impact on the economy of the United States.

7. Extension of export controls including a system of priorities to insure delivery of goods for export; conservation orders limiting domestic use of critical materials; and set-aside orders on food and other items in short supply.

The report called for a "radical reform" of this country's policy of holding down the level of German industry. Although there was no thought of re-creating Germany's war potential, the Committee said revival of German industry and of Ruhr coal production was "indispensable" to the recovery of Europe.

As the Marshall Plan evolves into the European Recovery Program it becomes the blueprint for an economic partnership without precedent in international relationships. The European Recovery Program was something new in the world. It is a bi-continental venture in coöperation of a kind never heretofore attempted, the invention of necessity and therefore vital. If it is made successful, it is bound to develop a life and power of its own which might change the economic and ideological structure of the future.

President Truman formally presented this program to Congress in November and December of 1947. Whether or not one agrees with his argument, history will probably view it as a forthright and courageous statement and analysis. President Truman argued that assistance for Europe and inflation control within the United States are two faces of the same coin. He asked for the allocation of scarce materials for domestic use; for the development of export controls; for restraint on various types of industrial hoarding and speculation; for maintenance of high taxes; for control of credit; and for the right to impose price and wage ceilings where necessary. In addition, he asked Congress immediately to vote interim aid amounting to a sum of nearly 600 million dollars to assist Italy, France, and Austria over the economic quagmire of the next few months. The total recovery program for Europe would probably amount to some twenty billion dollars, with an additional program to help China and Korea.

The immediate reactions to President Truman's introductory speech before Congress were mixed. However, the speech did, in a sense, draw the lines between those who feel that political and economic assistance to Europe implies the institution of economic controls within the United States and those who feel that the social costs of economic controls within the United States are too great in terms of their restrictions on freedom of enterprise and private property. Senator Taft, probably the most articulate spokesman for the latter view, seemed to grant the argument that large-scale help to Europe implies controls within the United States, and after weighing the pros and cons preferred less help to Europe and less controls within the United States.

Events showed the Marshall Plan to be a success. Western Europe, by 1950, was a going concern. Rationing and shortages existed in spots, but outside of a few countries the lot of the ordinary people was far better than in 1946. Furthermore, the threat of communism in western Europe clearly lessened after the French and Italian Communists staged unsuccessful political strikes in 1948. How stable the upswing in employment and production is cannot be foretold, but economic analysts are, in the main, fairly sanguine about the European economic situation. Great Britain is still in a difficult position. Depending as she does on foreign trade for her prosperity, she suffered in 1946 to 1948 because her purchases in America were very costly. However, when in 1948-49 prices in America began to decline Great Britain suffered again because competition forced her to sell goods in the United States too cheaply. The social experiments too, like socialized medicine, rigid control over investments, and nationalization of certain industries, have tended to induce economic uncertainty and possibly to increase costs of production. The net result is that Great Britain, long the greatest economic power in western Europe, is in an unhappy and difficult position. Yet her prosperity is just as important to the well-being of the Western world as is the utilization of German resources. The devaluation of virtually all the currencies of the world in 1949 (except in the USSR and the USA) has acted to assist the foreign trade of the European nations, and to reduce the blocked currency debt burden of Great Britain by making it worth while for the "sterling area" creditors to buy in Great Britain and so reduce their nation's credit position. By January 1951, Great Britain was able to "get along" without any further Marshall Plan aid. Britain and Sweden especially, together with other countries, began to find exports profitable because of the great increase in American and other imports to supply the new war economies which were developing after the outbreak of the Korean war. In part, the work of the Marshall Plan is being continued by the funds supplied by the United States and other countries for the rearming of the western European powers.

That the economy of the West is a single economy is being discovered again and again as defense and general economic problems are considered on an international basis. The big problem facing the administration of such an undertaking is whether or not economic nationalism, so

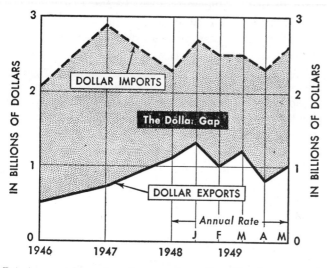

Britain must have American goods to live. She does not sell enough to America to pay for imports. The dollar gap from 1945 to 1948 totaled $7.6 billion.

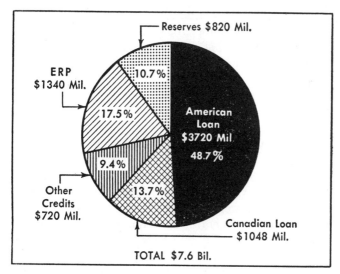

The dollar gap over the 1945-1948 period was made up by credits and by withdrawals from British reserves.

often desired by the little men of politics, will be conquered by economic internationalism, so sorely needed
by the world. Great Britain, strangely enough, often
seems inclined to throw its weight in the direction of nationalism in economic matters, whereas France, traditionally nationalistic, often counters the British attitude. If
economic nationalism wins, it seems to this observer, all
the hopes of international economic success are lost; if
internationalism wins, on the other hand, the West may
enjoy a reasonable and secure economic future.

These great issues are formally argued out in the
Organization for European Economic Cooperation, the
committee of the countries participating in the Marshall
Plan. The committee's main function is to allocate Marshall Plan assistance and advise the member countries and
the United States on programs and policy.

Of growing importance is the European Consultative
Assembly. This body, composed of representatives of the
legislatures of all the western European countries, although as yet a mere debating society, has official standing and might very well be a necessary step in organizing
a United States of Europe. Its possible importance in making Europe a legal or administrative unit, as it is a cultural
and economic unit, exceeds the bounds of present imagination.

From the point of view of the general discussion of the
past three chapters, the Marshall Plan was more than a recovery program for Europe; it was an exaggerated test of
public policy. Should the fact and fiction of free enterprise, price prosperity, and general economic freedom be
continued? Or, indeed, can these be continued in the
present complex world? Or should governmental intervention in economic matters, which in a sense means a greater
degree of political control of economic life, be instituted
in the hope that such control will provide a smoother-
running, more efficient, and "fairer" economic system?

This, it would seem, is a basic political and economic
question facing the United States. Freedom has always

implied freedom to make mistakes, and possibly even freedom to do wrong. But the question is whether the test of
individual freedom as envisaged by the founding fathers of
our economic and political system is the same as the test of
the freedom of action for large corporations, large trade
unions, and large pressure groups. If our preconceptions of
freedom do not apply, surely others must be introduced.

Among the freedoms which presumably make up a free
economy is the freedom to enter business, the freedom to
take a job, and the freedom to buy in the lowest market.
Does freedom to enter into a business exist in a world
marked by monopoly? Does the freedom to get a job exist
in a world of large trade unions, often with arbitrary restrictions, or where industry is so large that a worker must
take a job without bargaining? Does the freedom to buy
a house or take a job or go into business exist in a world
marked by racial and religious discrimination? Does freedom to buy in the lowest market mean anything in a world
of administered prices and price agreements?

These are serious and important questions, and they
cannot be answered by recourse to philosophical ideals
which are nonexistent in the real world.

On the other hand, restraints on unions, restraints on
business, restraints on hiring whom one will, raise the
awful question of *"quis custodiet ipsos custodes?"* Is our
political democracy so sensitive to right and wrong and
to the public opinion of the highest-minded citizens that
it will always act in the proper manner—proper, of course,
being defined by each person for himself? Are government
administrators and politicians omniscient so that the economic decisions will always be correct and lead to fuller
employment and bigger output?

In the last few paragraphs we have posed a dilemma.
The solution of this dilemma will determine the actual
turn made at this turning point of American political and
economic history. The dilemma is a difficult one, in part
because we cannot solve it at our leisure and through experiment. European requirements, both political and eco-

nomic, and the great fear of communization of Europe are forcing our hand. We need leisure to act and debate, and that leisure does not seem to be forthcoming. Not only are European and Asiatic uncertainties forcing our hand, but the Russian threat is overwhelming. Furthermore, there seems to be no generally accepted ideology or even ideological framework in American industry, labor, and agriculture. As we have seen, individualism, in its historical sense, is not a great prop to the present system in America, nor has it been replaced by a sharp, well-defined class consciousness or set of class consciousness which the more orthodox Marxists claim to find in America. This observer is inclined to find no ideological unity, except of a most primitive personal sort, i.e., the agreement that more income is better than less income. Our great political competitor, the USSR, however, has an imposed ideology from which deviation means sudden death to the deviator. That is undoubtedly an advantage in the political and economic arena, but a disadvantage to people as people. The British experiment in middle-of-the-road socialism avoids the forced feeding of its people with ideas but gains ground only very slowly because of profound economic weaknesses. A general world war, or even a good-sized limited war involving major powers, probably would provoke restraints on people, markets, institutions, and ideas so that our very concepts of freedom and justice would be changed. The Western world's economic recovery from World War II and its social future hangs in the balance for as long a period as the threat of war is felt in the world.

An assessment of the Russian and British attempts to meet the crises of the mid-twentieth century is made in the following chapters.

CHAPTER VIII

The Soviet's Russian Heritage

It is an odd and disquieting paradox that the European power which is geographically closest to the United States of America is in many other respects the farthest removed. The straits which separate Soviet Siberia from American Alaska are narrow. The gulf which lies between "the American way" and "the Soviet way" is so wide that many thoughtful observers doubt if it can be bridged. This chasm is not the creation of recent years, although it has been greatly widened and deepened during the last generation. Some of the sharpest differences between us and the USSR are indeed due to the philosophy, policies, and actions of the Communists; others spring from the differences in our pasts. We share with Great Britain, for example, certain heritages. The Magna Charta—both myth and fact—is as much a part of the American as of the British background. So are the evolution of Parliament and the development of civil liberties. Even though the average American student may not recall having heard of John Locke, and certainly is not likely to be familiar in detail with Locke's theories, these theories are nonetheless vaguely familiar to him. But the *Ulozhenie of 1649, the Charter of the Gentry, the Nicholas System,* and *Pobiedonostsev* are just meaningless words, two of which the average student can't even pronounce. Americans have heard of Perry's "opening of Japan" (although they may confuse him with Peary), but what do they know of Muraviev-Amurski, who planted the Russian eagle on the

Asiatic mainland opposite Japan? Virtually everything about the USSR (and its predecessor, the Empire of Russia) is utterly foreign to us. Historical contacts between us and the Russians were very few and relatively unimportant. We do not share the same cultural, political, or social heritage. We have literally lived in a world apart, until within the last generation events in Russia have forced themselves increasingly upon us. Because "the Russian problem" is a new one for us, it is no wonder that we assume it is altogether novel.

This mistake may be natural enough, but it increases our difficulties by misleading us. "The Russian problem" did not begin when we first happened to notice it any more than Russian history began with the Bolshevik Revolution. There had been more than a thousand years of recorded Russian history before anyone heard of the Bolsheviks. The first Muscovite dynasty began in 1113; and the Romanov dynasty, which came to an inglorious end in 1917, was started seven years before the *Mayflower* anchored off Cape Cod. Moscow, capital alike of medieval Russia and of the Union of Soviet Socialist Republics, was founded at a time when only the Norsemen knew of a New World to the west. There had been states and empires on the Russian plains before there was a Moscow, and there had been tribes long before there were states. The history of Russia is a long one, and the Bolsheviks did not and could not wipe it out. What the USSR is today is due partly to what it was before the old regime fell. The Soviets are partial prisoners of Russian history as well as of their own dogmas. Moreover, Soviet life and Russian life alike have been conditioned by the lands in which those lives have been spent.

Geographically almost everything about the Russian land must be said in superlatives. In the first place, the USSR is big (and the USSR is a little smaller than the Czarist empire was in 1914). Roughly 15 percent of all the land area of the world lies within the Soviet borders.

This vast and sprawling state is nearly three times as large as our United States. Compared to European states, it is a tremendous giant—40 times the size of France or Germany; 180 times the size of England. The summer sun never sets on the USSR. When the twilight of evening falls on Leningrad, the dawnlight of the next day is touching Kamchatka on the Pacific. This is partly because of its great size. It takes the sun eleven hours to cross the Soviet Union (and less than four to cross the United States). It is also due in part to the northerly location of the USSR. Sevastopol, on the southern shore of the Crimean Peninsula, is considerably farther north than Chicago. Moscow is in the same latitude as central Labrador, and Leningrad lies close to the parallel which touches the southern tip of Greenland. The shortest day of the year in Leningrad lasts less than six hours; the longest, almost nineteen.

As one would expect in such a northern land, the dominant season is winter. Frost and snow come early and stay late. The Siberian arctic has less than two months of frost-free days a year, and even the Ukraine can count on having only 120 to 180 such days. The snowfall is not as heavy as one might guess because the climate is relatively dry. But the cold is usually unrelenting, so that little of the snow melts until spring. Bitter winds from the arctic push the dry snow across the wide, flat plains, piling up huge drifts. Soviet peoples have to spend a good deal of time and effort to keep warm during the winters. They know this, of course, and plan their houses and their clothing with the winter needs in mind. No generalization about so large an expanse of land is likely to be wholly valid, and the climate in certain sections of the Soviet Union is subtropical, rather than subarctic. Crops are grown the year around in some of the Transcaucasian valleys, and rice is raised around Vladivostok. But, by and large, the Soviet lands are cold and dry. The annual average rainfall in the western USSR is twenty inches; in the central Asian deserts, three; but the Sayan mountains, farther east, get as much as forty-seven inches of rain a year.

Similar contrasts and exceptions to generalizations make it difficult to describe the topography of the Soviet Union in a few words. There are below-sea-level depressions, plateaus, hills, and mountains. There are swamps and marshes, and there are deserts. There are glacial moraines and active volcanoes. Obviously there is no single characteristic common to all the land. Fortunately for those who would describe it, the life of Russia and the USSR has been mainly concentrated within what is sometimes called the fertile triangle. The western leg of this triangle runs from Leningrad to the Black Sea. The northern and southern legs go, respectively, from Leningrad and the Black Sea to Lake Baikal in Siberia. Currently and historically this has been the center of Russian life and action. Here are the most fertile soils, the most favorable climates for agriculture, the most available (if not the richest) subsurface resources, the highest concentration of water-ways, and so on. Regions beyond this triangle have sometimes been important and new ones are being made so. Subject to these exceptions, when we talk of Russia or the Soviet Union we are generally referring to the fertile triangle.

Most of the land within this segment is level or rolling. There are some hills but no true mountains. The Urals are large wooded hills like the Appalachians. Their label of "mountains" is more a matter of tradition than the fact. They do not actually divide Europe from Asia except by a man-made decision and tradition. Animals, plants, and weather go readily across them. The real mountains lie along the southern and eastern borders of the state, outside of the triangle.

There are six clearly defined vegetation belts within the USSR, but only three within the triangle. These are the coniferous forest belt, the mixed and deciduous forest belt, and the steppes. The coniferous forests, which build acid podzol soils, are found in the north; the mixed and deciduous, which build brown soils, in the center; and the steppes, with their very fertile chernozem or black soil, in the south. The richest farm lands are, of course, in the black-soil belt.

The USSR is second only to the USA in mineral wealth. Some of the richest deposits lie outside the triangle, in Siberia; but the triangle itself has large supplies of coal, iron, oil, copper, gold, aluminum, potash, and so on. It may also be of interest and importance to note that the USSR has quantities of both uranium and thorium. Some of the Soviet claims to mineral wealth may be exaggerated, and some of the deposits are costly and difficult to exploit, but the fact remains that the USSR is very rich in natural resources.

The rivers of the USSR are historically and currently important. Here again one finds the contrasts which mark so much of the Russian story. The western rivers include the Volga, largest in Europe. The Siberian rivers are among the world's largest. But all the rivers flow either into land-locked seas or icelocked oceans. The general direction of their flow is up and down rather than across the nation (i.e., north-south rather than east-west). However, the headwaters of the main western rivers and their tributaries are mostly close together, forming a network of water roads which have been linked by portages and canals. These water roads have been and still are of great importance to the peoples of Russia. They formed the best and often the only ways of travel. Migrations moved along them. Settlements grew up beside them. Trade, to a considerable measure, depended on them. They linked the great Russian plain together and so facilitated the development of a centralized state. The Soviets, incidentally, have been active in improving the water roads by means of canals, most of them built with forced labor. Both in canal building and in the use of forced labor, as in many other things, Lenin and Stalin have followed a direction first pointed out by the czars.

Geography has played an important, though not always

a decisive, part in Russian development. The landlocked character of the state has been a determining force. It is possible to tell much of Russia's history in terms of her search for a satisfactory sea road to the world. This led her rulers to the Baltic and to the Black Sea. It helped lead them across the vastness of Siberia to the Pacific. It brought her into conflict with Great Britain and with Japan. Twice in recent wars lack of a satisfactory oceanic port has seriously hampered the Russians. German naval power closed the Baltic to Russia in 1914 and again in 1941. Turkish action blocked the Black Sea-Mediterranean water route in 1914, and German actions closed it in 1941. Vladivostok, the USSR's main Pacific port, was at the mercy of Japan, although it was not shut off until August, 1945. The urge to the open oceans has had great force throughout all of Russian history and remains a major consideration today. The USSR is the only great power without free access to the world's oceans. It is not to be expected that she will permanently and meekly acquiesce in this situation. The drive to the sea is now complicated by certain aspirations of the Communist party, but it is basically Russian and nationalistic rather than Communist and ideological in nature.

Other geographical features have also affected Russian development. The states erected on the great Russian plains, from the days of the Great Principality of Kiev (which ended in the twelfth century) to the present, have lacked any naturally defensible frontiers. The steppe lands of the South were from immemorial times the highways of Asiatic conquerors. The broad, flat lands of western Russia have been the roads of invasion from the west. Teutonic tribes, Lithuanians, Poles, modern Germans, and others have from time to time streamed across these lands into the heart of western Russia. Repeated invasions, two of the greatest of them coming within the lifetimes of men who are still not middle-aged, have made the Russians very security-conscious. It is probable that autocratic government within Russia originated and has been con-

tinuously maintained partly because of the fact and threat
of invasions from abroad.

The existence of a frontier, with its promise of opportunity, has also played an important part in Russian history, just as it did in American history, except for the important fact that most of the subjects of the czars were not
free to go to the frontiers at will. Siberia is today the great
frontier land of the USSR, and Stalin regards it as the
Soviet land of the future. His government has made increasingly strenuous efforts to develop Siberia both through
free settlers and through the extensive use of forced labor.

These examples of the geographic influence must serve
as illustrations, since a full catalogue would take too long.
It should be noted, however, that there is a striking con-
tra-indication of the power of geography as a determinant.
General lack of rainfall, short growing seasons, and the
relative infertility of much of the soil make farming a particularly difficult and hazardous way of life, but Russia has
always been primarily an agricultural society, in spite of
nature rather than because of it.

Before we leave the subject of Russian geography to
talk about the peoples, it might be well to straighten out
the matter of names. To be quite literally accurate, the
names "Russia" and "Russian" should be applied only to
the lands and peoples of the Russian Soviet Federated
Socialist Republic. This is one of the sixteen member or
constituent republics which form the federal union known
as the Union of Soviet Socialist Republics. But the RSFSR
is the largest and most powerful of the sixteen. It has 66
percent of the population and 75 percent of the land area
of the USSR. Its capital, Moscow, is also the capital of the
federal union. This might in itself be enough to excuse the
interchangeable use of "Russian" and "Soviet," or of
"Russia" and the "USSR" or the "Soviet Union." We
have, however, excellent native precedent for such inter-
changing. Like us, the peoples of the USSR find it easier
to speak of their federal union as Russia and of themselves
as Russians, and to use the longer and proper forms only

when it is necessary to make some distinction. There is no reason why we should be more insistent upon technical exactness than they are.

The number of Soviet citizens and the extreme variations among them make it as difficult to generalize accurately about the people as about the physical geography. Since no census was taken between 1939 and 1950, and since the war caused tremendous changes in population during those years, there is no precise demographic information available for the latter date. It appears that the terrific losses in population due to the war more than offset any gains made through natural increase and through annexations. Since the end of the war in 1945, however, the population has increased in size. Calculations based on data published by the Soviet government in connection with their 1950 elections indicated a total population at that time of about 201 million persons. No brief description can adequately depict so vast a number of people, nor can it take into account the differences which obviously exist between a Great Russian bureaucrat who lives in Moscow and a Chukchi hunter who lives in Far Eastern Siberia.

Partly for factual reasons and partly for propagandistic reasons undue emphasis has often been laid upon variations. There are a large number of linguistic and national groups within the Soviet Union. That is the factual aspect. But the exaggerated attention often given to the number and diversity of the groups sometimes makes it seem as if there were no homogeneity at all among the Soviet peoples. This is quite the reverse of the facts. Approximately seven out of every ten Soviet citizens are Slavs; and about five out of every ten are Great Russians. This represents a rather high degree of homogeneity. The emphasis on heterogeneity has sometimes been for the purpose of playing up claims about the Soviet policy toward national and linguistic minorities.

All Slavs are historically kin in the sense that they had a

common origin more than a thousand years ago. That is too long ago to have much significance now except as a propaganda device. The various Slavic groups, dispersed by migrations early in the medieval period, subsequently developed under circumstances sufficiently different to give each its own cultural characteristics. The western Slavs (Czechs, Poles, and Slovaks) came under Roman, German, and, later, west European influences so that they are culturally closer in many respects to western Europe than to Russia—an orientation which the Soviets are currently doing their best to reverse. The southern Slavs (Serbs, Croats, and Slovenes) fell under Byzantine and Turkish influences. And the eastern Slavs, with whom we are most concerned, lived on a battleground between Europe and Asia.

The Great Russians, historically a mixture of Slavs and Mongoloid peoples, were dominated for two centuries by the Asiatic Tatars with very important consequences which will be referred to later. Other Oriental influences also played upon them, but there were contacts with Scandinavia and the West too. The Great Russian heritage is Eurasian. The next largest group are the Ukrainians, who used to be called Little Russians and who account for approximately 20 percent of the total Soviet population. The Ukrainians, like the Great Russians, were also very strongly influenced by Byzantine and other Oriental ways. But they came under strong Polish influences for a time, which somewhat modified their culture. The Byelorussians, who are the smallest and least important of these three eastern Slavic peoples, are geographically and culturally the transition between the other two. Differences among the three have persisted despite the dominance (which still continues) of the Great Russians over the other two. It is the view of some competent, non-Slavic specialists that all three groups are equally "Russian." This is hotly disputed, and it may be noted that there have been and still are strong nationalist feelings among some Ukrainians. By and large, however, each of the three is closer to the other two than it is to any other group, including the western or southern Slavs.

Two major population shifts have taken place during the Soviet regime. One is the movement from the rural areas to the cities; the other is an eastward migration. In 1926 there were only a dozen Soviet cities with populations over 200,000; in 1939 there were thirty-nine cities above that size. There were eleven cities in 1939 with populations of 500,000 or more; in 1950 there were fifteen or sixteen. Moscow, which gained almost a million inhabitants between 1939 and 1950, is still the largest Soviet city. Its population in 1950 was about 5,100,000. Leningrad was in second place with about 3,300,000 inhabitants. No other Soviet city had more than a million residents in 1950; but many towns and cities had grown greatly since the 1939 census. The majority of the Soviet people, however, were still rural. The eastward migration may be measured by noting two points. First, the population of Siberia grew from about seven million in 1926 to about twenty-two million in 1939. Second, the biggest urban growth between 1939 and 1950 took place in the Urals and Siberia. This reflects the fact that uncounted millions of people were sent to these areas during or after the war. The majority of Soviet citizens, however, still live west of the Urals.

What are these people like? One might as well ask, What are the American people like? There are many variations among groups, to say nothing of the almost infinite differences among individuals. Bear in mind, then, that to each of these statements there must be very numerous exceptions.

The Slavic groups—if you look at them from far enough away so that individual characteristics are invisible—do seem to have certain likenesses. They are a great family people. The family has traditionally been the very foundation of Russian life, the social and economic unit of society. The Communists sought for some years to change this, but they found that it was too deeply rooted to be extirpated. Accordingly they changed their tactics and re-stored the family to its honored place. Foreign observers from earliest times have commented upon the hardihood and capacity for endurance displayed by the Russian people. This has repeatedly been demonstrated in our own time. The Russians bear cold, hunger, and deprivations with a patience and durability that is amazing. Perhaps only the tough have survived the centuries of hardship. Observers have also long been in agreement about the general inefficiency and low output of Russian workers. Their leaders have persistently sought to change this, but their success has apparently been distinctly limited. It has been plausibly suggested that this characteristic is a heritage from the forced labor of serfdom. After all, the only way in which a man under forced labor can escape being worked to death is to learn to evade. Open rebellion or sabotage is a guarantee of disaster. To manage to look busy without actually being very busy and without working too hard is virtually the only way out. Current reports indicate that this technique has not been forgotten.

Many writers have stressed the resemblances between the American and the Russian peoples. It is of course true that we are alike physiologically. It is also true that many Russians have their American counterparts—and vice versa. But it should not be forgotten that Americans and Russians are heirs to very different traditions. Our heritage is primarily derived from England and western Europe; theirs, from eastern Europe and Asia. They are the legatees of Oriental empires and customs; we, of Western empires and customs. At a time when our ancestors were slowly and painfully developing the individualistic doctrines of the right of free inquiry and of the priesthood of all believers, theirs were accepting the collectivist doctrines of state service and state ownership. There is nothing in their past to compare with the Renaissance, the Protestant revolutions, or the French Revolution—all of which contributed to the growth of individualism. Roughly a century before the Renaissance nearly all of the Russian lands were conquered by the Tatars and remained a part of the Tatar dominions for more than two centuries.

One of the foundations of this vast Tatar empire was the principle that state service was the inescapable obligation of every person within the bounds and power of the state. The worth of an individual was measured in terms of this service. Those who did the most for the state were held to be the most valuable and were given special rights and privileges as well as powers. Those who did not serve the state were deemed worthless and were denied rights. This doctrine and its relatively efficient practice were thoroughly established in medieval Russia during the centuries of Tatar control. When the Muscovite princes finally took over from the Tatar khans they accepted the principle that the individual existed for the state.

This doctrine and its practice were extended as the Muscovite princes expanded their power. The obligation to serve the state was held to be universal. The nobility (whose original name in Russia meant "serving-people") served the prince (the personification of the state) directly. Commoners served the prince indirectly. The peasants, for example, were valued only because they were the literal support of the nobility who served the state. But the peasant service was indirect and less, individually, than that of the nobility. Hence it was held that the individual peasant was comparatively of very little importance. This, then, was a doctrine of inequality among men.

It was, moreover, a concept which agreed well with another Tatar principle which the Muscovite rulers also adopted. This was the claim that all the land, all the people, and all the other resources were the exclusive property of the sovereign. In order to enable nobles to serve him, or to reward them for service, the prince loaned estates, and peasants to work the estates, to the nobles. At first these were really loans which were revocable at the will of the prince if the noble did not give satisfactory service in return. This condition gradually disappeared and, in time, the grants became permanent. The theory that landownership was for the purpose of state service lasted, legally, however, until late in the eighteenth century.

Very large areas of land were never so distributed but remained the possession of the prince or the state. As a matter of fact, the state and its institutions remained a very important landowner as long as the Russian Empire lasted. Down to 1917, well over a third of all the land in European Russia and a very much higher percentage of the land in Siberia remained the property of the czar, the imperial family, and the state. It may also be noted that, in addition to the land, certain important natural resources, some kinds of mines, factories, and mills, and most railroads were state owned under the czars. State banks were the chief financial agencies of the Empire.

Knowledge of these facts helps in understanding both the old and the new Russia. Under Soviet law, the land and the natural resources, along with the "tools of production" are state owned. This is alien to our way and to our tradition. It is not alien to the Russian tradition. Baron Haxthausen, a German agrarian expert who made a meticulously careful survey of Russia for Nicholas I in 1843, reported: "The Russians say . . . that the country now called Russia . . . has thus by the providence of God become their property. The disposal of it, as in a family, belongs to the father, the head of the race, the Czar. An individual has a right to share in it only so long as he lives in unity with the Czar and his people. The soil is the joint property of the national family and the father, or Czar, has the sole disposal of it. . . ." Forty-five years later another careful student of Russian ways wrote: ". . . The power of the Tsar and the ownership of land in common are the two fundamental principles which distinguish the Russian people from all others. . . . At the present time, in the whole of Greater (sic) Russia, ninety-eight percent of all the peasant farm lands are owned in common."

Farm lands in European Russia were not usually owned by individuals until the agrarian reforms which followed the 1905 Revolution. Even after those reforms made such personal ownership possible, most of the lands continued to be held by a sort of corporation (the mir) within each village. The mir, which was made up of peasants, owned the lands jointly and allocated sections to individual families for their use. Pasture lands, woodlots, ponds, and streams were held and used in common. The origins of this mir are lost in the mists of the long ago. The institution existed all through the period of serfdom (when it acted as the intermediary between the individual peasants and the landlord) and it persisted long after serfdom was abolished (serving then as the responsible intermediary between the peasants and the government).

These historical facts do not wholly explain state ownership today, but they show why it was easier for Lenin and his associates to establish state ownership than would otherwise have been the case. The Russian peasant, to speak only of the land, was more familiar with the practice of individual use under collective ownership than with full private ownership. This was what led the late Sir Bernard Pares, one of the leading Western authorities on Russia, to say: "If the Russian peasant is collectively minded today, it's because he always was." It would be quite wrong, however, to interpret current Soviet practices in ownership, government, and other matters merely as natural extensions of traditional Russian practices.

Take the matter of landownership as a first example. The statement made above that most of the farm lands were jointly owned even after the agrarian reforms is accurate. But it omits something important, namely, that a strong trend toward the extension of full private ownership—something long desired by many peasants—set in immediately after the reforms made it possible. Within a space of seven years after the reforms, almost six and a half million peasants took advantage of the new law to become private proprietors of their farms. The orderly course of this was interrupted by the 1914-18 war and the revolutions, but the movement continued until the Soviets put a forcible end to it.

Government offers a second example. The government of the USSR is an absolute autocracy, dominated and personified at this moment by Stalin. (See Chapter XII.) This is a form of government historically familiar to the Russian people. In fact, it is almost the only form they have ever known. The power of the rulers of Kievan Rus, the first Russian state, was autocratic or, when the autocracy was sometimes curbed, oligarchic. The government of the so-called Free Commonwealth of Novgorod, which flourished in the thirteenth and fourteenth centuries, was dominated by oligarchs of land and wealth. The princedom of Muscovy, from which grew the czardom of Russia, very early became and remained an absolute autocracy. Read the lists of the Russian czars. All of them were autocrats. To the last day of the Empire, the Fundamental Laws (constitution) maintained that the power of the autocratic czar was supreme, under God. Even the weak little Nicholas II, last of the czars, sought to live up to this pattern. This is continuity.

On the other hand, the pattern was being shattered during the last years of the Empire. Here is change which is as much a part of history as continuity. A revolution in 1905 forced the reluctant Nicholas to share a part of his power with a national assembly whose lower house was elective. The sharing was inequitable. He retained more than he gave away. The elected lower house (the Duma) was never fully representative of the people, nor was it ever the dominant institution of the government. Little by little, however, the Duma learned how best to employ its limited authority and it was on the way to making a real place for itself when war and revolution supervened. The Duma did not survive, but for eight months after the first 1917 Revolution the Russian people had a taste of free self-government. Conditions were unbelievably adverse, and the Provisional Government went down in defeat, but this does not prove either that the Russian people are incapable of self-government or that they have never desired it. The only true democratic national election Russia has ever seen was held in this period, and despite the great difficulties and extreme confusion of those days 80 percent of those entitled to vote did so. This is a better record than people long accustomed to free elections usually make, and it demonstrated neither apathy nor ineptness but the reverse.

This new line of development was brutally and suddenly cut short by Lenin. The assembly which had been chosen by the freely expressed will of the majority of the Russian people was anti-Bolshevik, so Lenin forcibly dissolved it. The historical tradition of authoritarianism was much closer to the plans and needs of the Bolsheviks, and to its framework they forced a return. Government was again seized and held by an elite. This fits both the party doctrine and the pre-1905 historical pattern of Russia. Except very briefly there has never been an equality of all men in Russia. What has been and still exists is a minority of privilege to whom the usual rules do not apply and a majority of the underprivileged among whom a sort of equality is to be found.

The general patterns of absolutism and the attempted justifications of it have been essentially the same in all ages and among all peoples. The basic assumption is always that the people are too stupid, or too greedy, or too selfish, or too inefficient, or too unenlightened to protect or to govern themselves. Therefore, so the excuses run, it is absolutely necessary for "enlightened" and "advanced" persons to assume the task of protecting and governing the herd for the promotion of the common good. This seems to many an entirely logical and a not unattractive proposition, particularly in times of stress, danger, and confusion when the very possession of power and the willingness to accept responsibility appear as *prima-facie* evidence of good intentions and adequate ability. Most absolute governments have come into being in times of upheavals, and most of them have established and have maintained themselves partly by use of force. One arm of all such governments has always been some form of secret police. The tasks of this police may be broad and varied, but always the primary one is the preservation of the rulers, who never dare trust themselves to an open expression of majority will. The Bolsheviks established such a police force within a month after they had seized power in Petrograd. They have kept it ever since. Its name and its organization have several times been changed, but its substance and function have remained the same. Said one authority: "The form of government in Russia is not now of the kind to give free scope for any sort of originality. . . . Independent thought in political affairs is not allowed any outlet. . . ."

The comment is currently valid. It was made, however, with reference not to the Soviet regime but to the czar's government in 1887 and it is a striking illustration of the continuity of this aspect of Russian and Soviet history. Russian governments have made use of secret, political police at least since the days of Ivan the Terrible. The czarist secret police, like the Soviet's, underwent reorganization and renamings. It was more active in some periods than in others. It did not approach the current police in efficiency or ubiquitousness. But it was the historical forerunner of the present form. The point is that although the Soviet people did not previously know so large and so effective a secret police, they have only very briefly lived under a government which was not a police state. No one is likely to pretend that the people enjoy this, or to suppose that they do not grumble about it (safely under their breath). We do not enjoy a common cold, and we grumble when we have one, but we are habituated to accept it because we know no way to avoid it.

Another instance in which a Russian heritage and a Communist doctrine coincided is in the feeling for universal brotherhood among men. The old Russian peasant believed very deeply in this. His traditional greeting was,

"Brother." Marx and Engels, who, to judge from their correspondence which the Soviets have published, scorned and despised the workers, nonetheless prated in their writings about the international brotherhood of the proletariat. This became one of their most appealing propaganda slogans, and it has been fully exploited by their followers. It was close enough to the concept of the Russian peasants to be intelligible and attractive to them.

Still another curious resemblance is in the field of religion, or of religion and quasi religion. There was developed in medieval Russia a legend which had wide popularity and great persistence. This was the "Theory of the Third Rome," which, in outline, was as follows: The First Rome (on the Tiber) fell into error and supported a heresy in the great schism which divided the Eastern and Western Catholic Churches. This cost the First Rome its leadership because it no longer served the Truth. A Second Rome then developed (Constantinople), but this, too, fell by the wayside and paid for its deviation from Truth by becoming the prey of the infidel Turk. Only Moscow maintained the ancient faith pure, whole, and unsullied, and therefore to Moscow, the Third Rome, passed the torch of Truth and the obligation to carry that Truth to the benighted nations beyond its borders. The legend was reborn in somewhat different form among the Slavophiles and the Russian Pan-Slavists of the nineteenth century. Sincerely, or sometimes with tongue in cheek, these people argued that Russia had a monopoly upon "the good, the true, and the beautiful," and that this laid upon Holy Russia a divine obligation to solve the world's problems in the Russian manner by sharing the Truth which Holy Russia alone possessed.

Today the Communists believe that they alone know the causes of and have the cure for all the world's ills. Once again, the Party (church) in Russia is the repository of the Truth. Once again, there is an obligation to spread this Truth and to share it. Once again, Moscow contains the greatest shrine of the believers (Lenin's body). This is not fanciful. The step from a religious Messianism to a quasi-religious Messianism, from the Holy Russia of the Orthodox Christian to the Holy Russia of the Communist, is not a long one for many people.

One reason, perhaps the main reason, that such doctrines can flourish is ignorance. If you know little of the world at most and nothing of the world at all except what your masters permit you to hear, it is hard to avoid smug complacency. Both the czars and the Politburo have seen to it that their people have not had free access to the world and vice versa. Refusal to admit foreigners, limitation of free travel within the country, and prohibition against emigration or travel abroad by their own people have been characteristics of Russian governments for centuries. Sometimes the restrictions have been very much loosened, but they have never been abolished. Printed or written materials have fared no better. The free importation, publication, or circulation of books, papers, magazines, etc., has sometimes been a privilege. It has never been a right. Censorship, border control, and "security" are more widespread and more efficient today than they were under the czars, but they are not otherwise different. From the earliest times, Western ambassadors complained that they were allowed no freedom of movement. The complaint is still heard. Moreover, the fear of infection by ideas was not born with the Bolsheviks. No Communist functionary of today can possibly be more apprehensive concerning this than was Czar Nicholas I (1825-55). Nicholas, like Stalin and his associates, counted the ignorance of the Russian people about the rest of the world as a vital safeguard to the regime. Here, as in the cases of landownership and government, the Soviets have reverted to an earlier period rather than simply continuing an existing situation. Contacts between Russia and the West were very much greater under the last czar than they are now.

A similar combination of continuity and change is observable in foreign affairs. Russian expansion at the expense of the Chinese began in the seventeenth century and was carried on with vigor during the latter nineteenth century. Czarist generals (and others) annexed central Asiatic lands to the Russian Empire, and the secret reports of the Russian General staff reflected a considerable interest in India. The Russian drive against Persia had its first major successes in the early nineteenth century, and Russo-British rivalry in Persia (as well as elsewhere) was a factor in nineteenth- and early twentieth-century diplomacy. Russian interest in the Balkans is not new either. It was a Russian Pan-Slavist of the 1860's who laid down the dictum that Russia must either establish her frontier on the Adriatic or else withdraw behind the Dnieper. And the quarrel between Russians and Poles is almost a thousand years old.

It is relatively easy to point out elements of continuity, but to try to interpret Soviet expansion as nothing more than a continuation of czarist expansion is to overlook the extremely important element of change. No Russian czar, no matter how ambitious he may have been to expand his power over Poles or Persians or Chinese or others, ever thought of himself as the leader of a world movement. Czarist foreign policies did not constitute a *Weltpolitik* in the way the Soviet foreign policy does. No czar dreamed of a Russian world empire. But the Soviet rulers of Russia have dreamed of and worked toward a World Soviet Socialist Republic since before they came to power. Something new has been added, and it is traceable to two men who were not Russians at all. They were Prussians, and their names were Marx and Engels.

CHAPTER IX

The Soviet's Marxist Heritage

KARL HEINRICH MARX AND FRIEDRICH ENGELS have proved
to be among the most influential men in human history.
As in the case of all such personages, there has grown up
around them such a tissue of myths and legends that the
truth is often forgotten. Marx, particularly, is frequently
depicted as a paragon among geniuses to whom no normal
tests of judgment ought to be applied. The theories which
these men promoted have been sanctified as a "science of
society." The publication of their personal letters and
other papers by the Marx-Engels-Lenin Institute of Moscow makes it possible to strip away some of the screen of
myths and so to get a little closer to the truth.

Marx was born in the then recently Prussianized town
of Trier (or Treves). His father, a prosperous but undis-
tinguished lawyer, had been overjoyed when the town
became a part of the rising kingdom of Prussia, whose
ways and leaders he idolized. Some of this reverence for
the Prussian tradition of autocratic arrogance was passed
along to the son. Karl, completing the lower schools with
a brilliant record, became a university student in 1835
and technically remained one until 1841. His undoubted
talents were little devoted to regular university work,
however, and his record was not distinguished. He finally
took a doctoral degree, not from the university where he
had been studying but from another—a sort of mail-order
affair. He had high hopes of a teaching job, and legend
says that he was denied an opportunity to teach because

he would not conform to the reactionary pattern required. The legend is wholly inaccurate. Marx didn't get the teaching post he wanted, not because he was radical but because his sponsor was. As a matter of fact, Marx never did manage to earn his own living for any length of time nor did he ever adequately support his wife and children. Throughout his life, Karl Marx was a parasite upon the the charity and generosity of others, especially of Engels.

Friedrich Engels was very unlike Marx in many ways. He was the son of a wealthy textile manufacturer and early took his place in the family business. Businessmen in those days did not usually have a university education and Engels was no exception. But he was blessed with an extremely strong urge to learn, and he read and studied voraciously throughout his life. His learning eventually surpassed that of most university-trained people. Unlike Marx, Engels earned his own way and more, proving himself to be an industrious and successful businessman. Typical of his versatility was his record in Manchester (England), where as a young man he was sent by his father's firm. His ability and hard work won the respect of the business community. His social graces made him a very welcome guest in Manchester society. And, at the same time, he began his study of the working class by intimate association with them.

Engels first heard of Marx from some of the latter's one-time cronies in Berlin and was so interested by what he heard that he sought Marx out. Their first meeting was not propitious. Marx was then editor of a small newspaper (a job he held for three months before being fired) and, full of his own business and importance, had little time for this unknown admirer who sought an interview. In short, he gave Engels a quick brushoff. But the two met again, this time in Paris, where Marx had secured another job (which he also soon lost). By then both Marx and Engels had been converted to the somewhat vague, rather kindly, and wholly irrational communism of Moses Hess. They soon moved away from Hess's humanitarianism, but it originally gave them a point of contact and led to their subsequent collaboration.

Finding that they perfectly complemented each other, they decided, in Marx's words, to engage in a joint business and their partnership was one of the closest on record. Engels supplied ideas, literary talents, funds, and a boundless, selfless devotion to Marx. It is more difficult to catalogue Marx's contributions. He, too, had ideas and a capacity to set up finely drawn and closely reasoned formulas. He was perhaps tougher, more vigorous, and more ruthless than Engels and he certainly shared in the admiration of Marx. The two men grew to think so much alike, to talk and to write so much alike that they became intellectually as one. The writings and the doctrines which are popularly referred to only by the name of Marx were actually the joint product of both minds. It is too much to say, "No Engels, no Marx," but either without the other would have been very much less than he was.

These two men, starting from an assumption which they were never able to prove, concocted a doctrine which has affected the thinking and the lives of millions of people. The basic assumption, which time and men alike have repeatedly shown to be utterly false, is that the capitalist system must, because of its inherent evils, inevitably hurtle to destruction. Marx first formulated that dogma in these words: "The system of trade and money-making, of property and the exploitation of human beings, leads to a breach in extant society which the old system is powerless to heal." He had no proof of this. Economic theory and economic history were both completely unknown to him. No matter. He simply asserted it and there it was. This assumption is the basis for what is almost everywhere called "scientific socialism." The label is a monstrous misnomer. One does not create a science by claiming to state a "law" and then ignoring or denying all facts which do not fit it. If the Marxist dogma had been forced to depend upon its inherent reasonableness, it would have got nowhere.

But there was in the dogma a flaming promise, not well defined or described but enormously appealing. This was the promise that the inevitable revolution would usher in a day of gladness when men would be freed from evils and from coercions. It was a dream shared by millions who were in no sense Marxians. It was a vision of a better world. The lure of Marxism would seem to rest partly upon the sectarian ecstasy with which this promise is reiterated and partly upon the fanatical scourging of acknowledged evils. About half of *Capital,* Marx's and Engels' largest and most elaborate work, is devoted to illustrations of injustices in capitalist society. No reasonable man denies that such wrongs have existed and still exist. The Marx-Engels thesis, however, was not that such faults exist but that they are bound to get progressively worse until mass human misery brings the revolution.

Marx-Engels claimed that they had uncovered the secret of society, that they had found out what makes individuals and groups tick. With this secret, they said, they could unravel the story of the past, understand the present, foresee and predict the future. Their followers have faithfully accepted this unproved and unprovable revelation. Said the authoritative Soviet journal, *Bolshevik,* in January, 1945: "Our [Communist] Party . . . leans on the Marxist-Leninist theory and masters the knowledge of the laws of social development. [This] theory . . . gives the Party the ability of adjusting itself correctly in any situation, of foreseeing the course of events, of understanding . . . current developments; and of recognizing not only how and in what ways events are now developing, but also how and in what ways they must develop in the future." The unanimity with which all Communists accept these dicta may be illustrated by the following quotation from *Political Affairs* (May, 1946), official magazine of the American Communist party: ". . . Marxism, the science which explains the laws of social developments, class relations, and the ultimate, Socialist, outcome of the class struggle in modern capitalist society. . . ." What are the major claims of this "science"?

Marx-Engels claimed that labor was the sole source of value, and that the worth of any item was determined exclusively by the number of hours of manual labor which went into its production. Profit is also value and therefore all profits are created by labor in the following way: A worker is paid one dollar an hour. In half an hour he produces goods having the value of one dollar. So far it has been an even swap—his labor equals the value of his output. But during the second half-hour he also makes goods having the value of a dollar. This dollar is "surplus value" and was created wholly by the worker. Under the capitalist system, the worker is robbed of this dollar because all surplus value goes to the employers (capitalists). So the capitalists get richer and richer.

The capitalists then compete with each other and the big ones swallow up the wealth of the medium and small ones. Thus big fortunes grow still bigger while the former middle-sized and little capitalists are shoved out of the group of "haves" into the group of "have-nots." Now the capitalists insist upon using some of their wealth to buy machines. Marx-Engels say that this is a very curious contradiction because machines do not create wealth. Only labor can create wealth (worth or value). The ordinary observer may suppose that the capitalist invests in new machinery in order to increase his profits, but Marx-Engels insist that the law does not work that way. The money spent for machines does not bring in any profit. The only way that the capitalist can maintain or increase his profits is by exploiting labor more and more viciously. The machines throw men out of work and many of them never find another job. They join the dispossessed little and middle-sized ex-capitalists in a permanent unemployed who are clearly in a miserable situation. Those who do manage to get jobs are not much better off because they are forced to work ever longer hours, at ever lower pay, under ever worse conditions so that the capitalist can make his profit. Eventually this sum total of human misery gets so bad that a violent revolution overthrows the whole capitalist system.

To put it another way, as Marx-Engels did, the capitalist system produces two classes: the bourgeoisie (capitalists) and the proletariat (factory labor). The bourgeoisie includes all private owners, large and small, not excepting the peasants who own land. This class has not only property but also personal freedom. The proletariat, on the other hand, has nothing but its chains—i.e., it has neither personal property nor freedom. The proletariat, moreover, is constantly growing larger and more miserable. Its enmity toward the "haves" is perfectly natural. It is also inevitable and inexorable. When the revolution comes, the proletariat destroys the bourgeoisie and socialism replaces capitalism. But the day of full freedom is not yet because socialism is a transition stage during which power rests in the "revolutionary dictatorship of the proletariat."

This beautifully precise formula fascinated many intellectuals as well as many who wished to be known as intellectuals. It cannot be said, however, to have fascinated the workers to any great extent. Even Marx found this out. The first Communist party, which he and Engels created, consisted of fifteen writers and two typesetters. One of the writers (whom Marx soon kicked out of the party) and the two typesetters were of proletarian origin. The other fourteen were all as bourgeois as Marx and Engels themselves. And when Marx tried his hand at practical politics during the Prussian Revolution of 1848 and with the First International Working Men's Association (1864-74), he soon discovered that he had to keep dictatorial powers in his own hands in order to enforce adherence to his formulas. He talked of the revolution as a mass movement, but in practice he used all the devices of control which are becoming increasingly familiar today. He had his followers pose as genuine liberals and believers in democracy. He had them infiltrate liberal groups. He trained them to dominate these groups (or to try to) by devices both legal and illegal. He used "united front" organizations, hid behind confused liberals, and manipulated fellow travelers. But to no use. The workers stayed away in overwhelming majorities. Some intellectuals continued to be attracted, including a few of the Russian revolutionary intelligentsia.

The first foreign language into which *Capital* was translated was Russian, and a very few Russians began to study and discuss it. Some were repelled by it, some were attracted, but none saw such great possibilities in it as did Vladimir Ilyich Ulyanov. Under the pseudonym of Lenin, this man was able to do what Marx-Engels were not. In the words of a Soviet textbook, "Lenin fully comprehended . . . [and] also further developed these teachings [of Marx-Engels]. . . ." Lenin built, first, a "party"; then, a revolution; and, finally, a state on the basis of his interpretation of the doctrines of Marx-Engels. In the process Lenin made numerous modifications and adaptations of the original. A few of the more important changes ought to be listed here: Marx had regarded the peasants as almost beneath contempt because of their backwardness and because he considered them petty bourgeoisie at heart. Lenin, however, had his chance to apply the formula in a country which was almost wholly peasant in population and outlook. He enlisted the peasants' help in making his revolution and establishing his state. They had already dispossessed the former owners of the land when Lenin appeared on the scene. He acquiesced because he could do nothing else except fight the peasants, in which case he would surely have lost. Later he sought, unsuccessfully, to collectivize the peasants—i.e., to transform them into an agrarian proletariat. Under Stalin, this was done.

Marx paid scant heed to imperialism, which is not surprising because it did not bulk large in his time. But Lenin studied it carefully and came to the conclusion that it represented the dying stage of capitalism. Finance capitalism, he believed, could exist only through imperialism. If imperialism should become impossible or unprofitable, the end of capitalism would be at hand. For these reasons, Lenin sought to use the growing nationalisms of the colonial peoples as weapons against the imperialist, capitalist states. This tactic is still very widely and very vigorously employed. Finally, Lenin, while giving lip service to Marx-Engels' doctrine of a mass movement of proletarians, actually followed their tactics rather than their words. He insisted from the beginning that the revolution must be achieved, guided, and won by a small body of selected, disciplined fanatics who would act in the name of the proletariat. This is what his "party" became and what it remains to this day.

Lenin has been dead a quarter of a century; Marx, for over eighty-five years; Engels, for over fifty. What have these dead men got to do with the present words and deeds of the current rulers of the USSR? There are not lacking those who, though they are outside the Communist party and oppose it, consider themselves the only true followers of Marx-Engels. These persons heatedly deny that the current Soviet regime is in any way carrying out the teachings either of Marx-Engels or of Lenin. What they call "Stalinism" they brand as a perversion of "Leninism." The official Communist parties, on the other hand, just as vehemently maintain that they alone are the true followers of the Marx-Engels-Lenin gospel. As one of the Soviet textbooks puts it: "The teachings of Lenin secured success . . . because they are based on the teachings of Marx, on the most advanced scientific revolutionary doctrine created in the second half of the 19th century by those great revolutionaries, the leaders and teachers of the working class of the world—Karl Marx and Friedrich Engels. . . . After the death of Lenin his closest adherent and pupil, Stalin, continued the cause of Marx-Engels-Lenin." Another schoolbook says: ". . . Lenin continued the teachings of Marx and Engels. . . . Lenin established the Communist Party . . . which led the working class of

Russia to victory in October 1917. . . . Lenin died, but the cause begun by him is continued by his best pupil and follower, Comrade Stalin." And still another official account repeats the same theme in these words: "Just as through the revolutionary period of 1917, Stalin stood shoulder to shoulder with Lenin in the struggle against all deviations from revolutionary Marxism, so in the years following . . . he remained a tower of Leninist strength. . . . The work and heritage of Lenin is intertwined with the leadership [of] . . . Stalin. . . ."

The opponents of "Stalinism" dismiss these claims as mere assertions and as tissues of lies. This is not the place to expound the arguments of either side. Rightfully or not, the Communist party of the Soviet Union (Bolshevik) continually represents itself as the party which follows the Marx-Engels doctrine as refined and interpreted by Lenin and Stalin. How did these norms and values get into the stream of Russian history and combine with those patterns which were described in the preceding chapter?

Russia of the mid-nineteenth century was a land of darkness. The shadows of illiteracy, ignorance, and superstition brooded over all but a few thousands of her people. Autocratic repressions deepened the gloom. Only one pinpoint of light gleamed now and then through the blackness—the tiny group of educated liberals. Their flame, though minute, was brilliant and it cast long rays into strange places. The emancipation of the serfs and the other great reforms of the 1860's seemed to promise a new dawn. But the dark clouds of autocratic conservatism still lingered. Some of the liberals—a minority of a minority—sought to burn the clouds away with their own weak flame. The result was that their flame was quenched by clouds grown heavier. Only a spark remained, smoldering beneath the repression of Alexander III (1881-94). The keepers of this smoldering fire were not many but they were varied. Some were anarchists. Some were socialists of the Utopian school. One of them, George Plekhanov, became a convert to the dogmas of Marx-Engels. Through his efforts the first Marxist study group was formed. Others followed. The groups were insignificant in numbers. Most of the members were intellectuals, but some propaganda work was done among the labor unions which were then clandestinely developing. After several attempts to coördinate the work of these Marxist groups had failed, a few members from a half-dozen groups met in 1898 and organized the Russian Socialist Democratic Labor party.

The long title was perhaps the most impressive thing about this group, which adopted a program based upon the teachings of Marx-Engels. The organizers of the RSDLP were picked up by the czarist police as they left the meetings and their plans perforce were held in abeyance. Few as they were, the adherents of this new party soon fell out among themselves. The rather moderate program of Plekhanov was challenged by a more radical group led by Lenin. When the party held its second convention (congress) in London (1903), the differences crystallized into a split. Lenin's group, which was able to get the support of the majority for most of its points, took the nickname of Bolshevik (from the Russian word for majority, bolshinstvo). The other group, although they won the majority on some issues, were left with the title of menshinstvo, meaning minority. Both groups continued for some time as nominal members of the RSDLP, but as each tenaciously held to its own way the parent party was really split in two. Competition for control continued throughout the 1905 Revolution (in which neither the RSDLP nor either of its "fractions" played much of a part). Finally the two ceased even to meet together. Lenin, meanwhile, with great skill, industry, and patience (but no scruples) was molding the Bolshevik fraction to his will. It is not too much to say that he created the Bolshevik party in his own image.

These were hard years for Lenin and his faithful followers. He was a voluntary exile, as were many of his group. Others were in jail or in Siberia. Their numbers were very small, their treasury almost always empty, their prospects bleak. Russia, under the limited constitutional monarchy set up in 1905, seemed to be stumbling halt-ingly toward a liberal government of the British type. Things were going well in the economic sphere. Industry was booming. Trade was steadily increasing. Agriculture, freed from part of the old restrictions by the Stolypin reforms which broke the monopoly of the mir, was pros-pering. Producer and consumer coöperatives, especially in Siberia, grew in numbers and in membership. All in all, the years from 1907 to 1914 were probably the most pros-perous in Russian history. But Lenin, in exile abroad, continued to dream and to plan. His followers in Russia continued to do what they could, but it was not much. Then came the First World War, and the old Russia did not survive it. That story is sufficiently important to ne-cessitate what may appear to be a lengthy digression. It will lead us back, however, to Lenin and to Marx-Engels-Leninism in Russia.

Three separate events which took place in 1894 had a profound and lasting influence upon subsequent happen-ings in Russia and in the world. Chronologically the first was the completion of a military alliance between France and Russia. This was first directed against Great Britain, but in the early twentieth century a realignment of the powers took place. The French and the British govern-ments in 1904 reached an understanding which was the forerunner of increasingly close coöperation between them. Russia, after her defeat by Japan in 1905, transferred her attention from the Far East to the Balkans and the Near East. Her activities there soon brought her into vigorous competition and conflict with the German and Austrian "drive to the East." The French and the British govern-ments were also more and more at odds with the Germans. Enmity often is a powerful but impermanent cement. The rivalries of the Russians, British, and French against the Germans operated to draw the three powers together against Germany and her two allies, Austria-Hungary and Italy ("the Triple Alliance"). After the British and Rus-

sian governments had settled some of their outstanding
disagreements (1907) there was created an understanding
(known as the Triple Entente) among the three. This
was never technically an alliance, although it certainly
operated like one most of the time. The members of the
rival Alliance and Entente all engaged in building up their
national armies and armaments and in tightening their
two groups against what many regarded as the inevitable
war.

The second event in time sequence in 1894 was the
accession of Nicholas II to the Russian throne. The outstanding characteristics of this little man were a gentleness
and a personal charm which approached the feminine.
Like most weak and gentle people he could sometimes be
mulishly stubborn (usually over the wrong things). One
of the things about which he was stubborn was the maintenance of the autocracy. Another was his devotion to his
wife and his acceptance of her will. That brings us to the
third happening of 1894: the marriage of Czar Nicholas
to the German princess, Alix of Hesse-Darmstadt, and her
coronation as the Czarina Alexandra.

Alexandra had all the strength of character which her
husband lacked, and she dominated him throughout his
reign. Since she was also narrow-minded, stubborn, of
limited intelligence, and, eventually, quite unbalanced
mentally, this was a tragic situation. Alexandra was fanat-
ically devoted to the principle of autocracy and, determined to maintain the autocratic power unimpaired, set
herself against all political reforms. She had perforce to
accept in form the legal limitations upon absolutism which
resulted from the 1905 Revolution, but she also could and
did try with considerable success to undermine and circumvent these restrictions. Her actions along this line
were effective not only because Nicholas was under her
thumb but also because he was so completely lacking in
dependability that none of his ministers could ever count
on having his consistent support and no group could ever
put faith in his promises. Alexandra had, moreover, a

strong streak of superstitious mysticism which made her an easy prey for quacks and charlatans, of whom Rasputin was the most nefarious. Rasputin, Alexandra, and Nicholas must bear a considerable share of the responsibility for the downfall of the monarchy. There were other causes, of course, and these must at least be summarized.

The underlying causes were inherent in the political, social, and economic structure of Russia. Government, despite the changes which grew out of the 1905 Revolution, was still in the hands of a minute minority of privilege. It was also subject to the whims of an autocrat. Nicholas and Alexandra, especially because of their subservience to the will of the notorious Rasputin, who actually ruled Russia from September, 1915, until his overdue murder in December, 1916, had forfeited the respect once enjoyed by the czardom. The cabinet had been ruined by Rasputin, who literally made and broke ministers at will. The Imperial Council, which was the upper house of legislature, represented only the upper classes or a fraction thereof and did not enjoy the confidence of the people. The lower house (Duma) had been elected on a very restricted franchise and did not represent the people either. The bureaucracy, which had never been popular, had lost even more of its limited prestige by its powerlessness, its incompetence, and its corruption. Although its outward appearance in 1914 was healthy enough, the Russian government was actually riddled with decay. The war made its political and moral bankruptcy inescapably apparent.

When the war began in the summer of 1914, Russia had an army which was formidable in size and at least adequate in leadership. It was, however, fatally short in reserve leadership and in materials. The other nations were not so much better off in terms of available supplies, but France, Germany, and Britain had what Russia lacked— the economic and industrial capacity to produce more war materials as the original supplies were expended. Moreover, these powers with their largely literate populations found it possible to train civilians as commissioned and noncommissioned officers. But two out of every three Russian subjects were illiterate, and it is almost impossible to train as leaders men who can neither read a written order nor write one. Russia could fill the ranks of her army, and did so virtually three times over. Her losses in men far exceeded that of any other nation. But she was never able adequately to replace the leaders who so gallantly spent themselves in the first campaigns. Moreover, the Russian armies did not "dig in" as did the forces in the West, where, after the first bloody furies, the battles settled down to trench warfare. The Russians, largely because of the pleas of their allies, flung themselves headlong against the Austro-German forces. This heroic action certainly saved Paris from capture and did much to save the French and British from speedy defeat. Its cost to the Russians in material and leadership was never made up.

Russian morale, gravely undermined by disastrous military losses, by the deprivations due to war and the German blockade, by inflation and its attendant hardships, was further weakened by the czar's stubborn and unwise policies. Nicholas in 1915, against the advice of almost all responsible Russian leaders of all political views—including members of his own family—insisted on taking command in the field. By that action he became directly responsible for what he could not control: the incompetence and corruption of many of his subordinates. What was worse, he left the civil government in the hands of Rasputin and Alexandra, as has been noted. Men of nearly all classes and groups lost all faith in their government and began to seek, rather gropingly, for new leadership. There was none at hand. The power of the old ruling clique had been declining ever since the emancipation of the serfs, and now it had gone. The middle class, which in other European countries had assumed control, was too small, too weak, and too lacking in any common or clearcut program to take over. The peasant masses, untrained, politically mute, and lacking any effective leadership of their own, were likewise incompetent to assume control of the state. Even the tiny city proletariat, contrary to later Bolshevik claims, had neither unity nor effective guidance. That a revolution was inevitable was apparent to at least one foreign observer in 1916, and he so reported to his government. What he could not forecast was the direction in which it would go.

Early in 1917 food riots began in Petrograd (formerly St. Petersburg, later Leningrad). The conditions which produced these riots were partly caused by an actual shortage in food. They were due somewhat more to acute failures in distribution of available stocks, and a very great deal more to the hopeless incompetence of the authorities. Strikes began in the factories and increased almost daily. The strikers joined the crowds and disorders grew worse. Mutinous soldiers from the Petrograd garrisons joined the crowds, which now became armed mobs. It was not planned. There was no plot. Neither the liberal opponents of the czardom nor the Bolsheviks had anything directly to do with it. The movement just grew, like Topsy, and the legal governments—local, regional, and imperial— simply and physically disappeared. The little czar abdicated, and the Duma, after some hesitation, set up a Provisional Government—largely because no one else did so at the moment. Later in the same day, a small group of left-wingers, acting quite on their own hook, proclaimed another potential government, the Petrograd Soviet of Workers' Deputies. Some soldiers came to the first session of the Soviet (which means Council), and so the words "and soldiers'" were inserted in the original title between "Workers'" and "Deputies." This was the March Revolution. The old order was fast falling to ruins. And still there was no sign either of Lenin or of Marx.

Lenin was in Switzerland. The other leaders of the Marxist groups were either in voluntary or police exile or operating secretly on a very restricted scale. The Revolution took them so completely by surprise that when some of them returned under an amnesty given by the Provisional Government they had no plan of action other than obstructionism in coöperation with the Soviet. Lenin tried to guide them by "Letters from Afar" but the results were less than he wished. Then it was suggested to the German High Command and to Lenin that he be allowed to cross German territory in order to get back into Russia. The Germans, correctly judging that he would be a disruptive force, agreed. Lenin, to whom no other route was open since the western Allies controlled the seas, was ready enough to make use of the German offer. He arrived at Petrograd in mid-April, 1917, hailing the world socialist revolution. At once he set to work to gain control.

The goal which Lenin had in mind when he stepped off the train at Petrograd was a world-wide socialist revolution. A series of fortuitous and unexpected circumstances had contrived to make it possible to begin that revolution in Russia. The Communists from Lenin's time forward have never intended that the movement should be permanently confined to that country. During the early months and even years of their power, Lenin and his cohorts thoroughly believed that the day of revolution was close at hand. A later chapter will mention some of their efforts to speed its coming. The optimism was not entirely unjustified in view of what was going on in Europe at the time, but some of it was due to sheer wishful thinking and some to a dead certainty about the reliability of their formulas. It was their great good luck to have as their leader a man who was less a doctrinaire than an opportunist. The Marx-Engels doctrine, after all, would have led one to expect the revolution in a highly industrialized state rather than in a backward and agrarian nation. If Lenin had lived solely by the doctrine, he presumably would not have gone to Russia in 1917 because he would have seen no opportunity there. His flexibility as to times and means served his party very well. It may be that he went to Petrograd with the expectation that it would be only very briefly the headquarters of his movement, but when he found that his stay was longer than anticipated, he shrewdly adapted his tactics to the situation.

The task was not easy. The Bolsheviks were in a minority in the Soviet, and Lenin did not even have control of the Bolsheviks. His proposed program (the April Theses) at first met strenuous opposition even within the ruling clique of the Bolshevik fraction. But he persisted, and by his skill in leadership was able, within a month, to establish firmly his control over the group's executive committee. From then on, things ran his way. He trained and drilled his followers, set up the long-range strategy, planned the day-to-day tactics, and prepared to implement his dreams of revolution. Even so thorough a Marxist as Stalin has admitted that Lenin changed the course of events. The Bolsheviks' Revolution, which was begun by their successful coup d'état against the Provisional Government in Petrograd (November), was Lenin's work. The Provisional Government, which was in almost every way out of touch with the people, went down as suddenly and as completely as the old regime had ten months before.

Lenin, who had first mastered the Bolsheviks and then used them to master the Soviets, had now successfully used the Soviets to master the capital (Petrograd) and such machinery of national government as remained. Moscow fell to the Bolsheviks shortly thereafter, but the Revolution was only begun, not won. The war phases of the movement, in fact, went on until 1921, and it was often touch and go. Lenin, who had complained bitterly about the mild censorship and repressions of the Provisional Government, suppressed, outlawed, and, so far as he could, physically liquidated all opposition as fast as he could. Some fractions of the other left-wing groups were allowed to exist temporarily because the Bolsheviks had a use for them. All others were knocked down at once. When the assembly, which was democratically elected to set up a new permanent government, proved to have an anti-Bolshevik majority Lenin dissolved it by force. That was in January, 1918. Late in the previous month he had created the "All-Russian Emergency Commission for the Combatting of Counter-revolution, Sabotage and Specu-

lation." This title was too much of a mouthful even for a
Russian, and the organization was ordinarily called Cheka.
It was the first of the secret police organizations which
have marked all of Soviet history.

Armed with the Cheka and with the Red Guards (or
Red Militia), which Trotsky brilliantly developed into
the Red Army; making use of all ancient hostilities; deliberately inciting to mobocracy and violence, the Bolsheviks
set out to conquer the enemies which faced them on
almost every side. Some could be won over by the flaming
promises of Marx-Engels-Lenin. Some could be bought
off by concessions and cajolery. But many had to be fought
off and killed off. Lenin skillfully combined all these ways
and, in truth, he needed all his genius. The western Allies
(including the United States) had already begun active
intervention in Russian affairs before the Bolshevik Revolution started. The original purpose was to keep Russia
in the war. The Bolsheviks were attacked because they
were regarded as fighting on the German side. Ideological
opposition developed a little later, primarily because Lenin
and his associates repeatedly proclaimed their belief that
the revolution in Russia was only the first step to revolution throughout the world. The Bolsheviks, or to give
them the name which they formally adopted in 1918, the
Communists, therefore had to fight not only their own
people but also British, French, Americans, Japanese,
Poles, Czechs, and others. It was an exceedingly narrow
squeak, but by 1920 Lenin and Trotsky had managed to
defeat the small forces which the Allies had sent in and
to shatter the disunited Russian opposition. Long before
this victory, the Communist leaders had begun to interject
Marx-Engels-Leninism into the Russian way of life.

The previous chapter pointed out that in certain aspects
of state ownership, state service, and government the new
norms and values were, so to speak, grafted on traditional
norms and values. It was also pointed out that constitutional democracy and peasant proprietorship, both of
which represented norms and values relatively new to

czarist Russia, were destroyed. But it may be reiterated that there were both continuity and change. Some old norms and values were successfully challenged and were replaced by new ones. Other parts of the pattern—the family, for example—were too firmly fixed to be completely rooted out and replaced despite strenuous efforts. Even these elements, however, were more or less changed in the process of attack and resistance. The norms and values of the Soviet Union today represent a compounding and compromising of the ways of old Russia with the ways of Marx-Engels-Lenin-Stalin.

It may also be added that some of the ways of Marx-Engels have been modified or even nullified by the ways of Lenin and Stalin. The changes introduced by Lenin are officially justified and explained by the phrase, "Leninism is Marxism of the epoch of imperialism," which is to say that Lenin brought Marxism up to date. The Stalinist variations are presented as further up-to-dating and enrichment of the Marxist-Leninist treasure. The Communist attitude toward these changes is precisely covered with admirable brevity in the official statement that Marxism is not a dogma but a guide to action. In other words, even the Communists tacitly recognize that Marxist norms and values can no more escape change than can capitalist norms and values. Old norms are challenged by new ones, sometimes successfully. Thus, for example, the Marx-Engels formula on labor was, "From each according to his ability, to each according to his need." Stalin has changed this (in both theory and practice) to, "From each according to his ability, to each according to his productivity." This is a major change and there have been a few others of equal magnitude, but most of the alterations have either been in matters of tactics or of detail or are officially explained as merely "temporary deviations."

Whether one looks at the whole sweep of Russian and Soviet history or merely at the more recent period, he will find an amalgam of continuity and change. And this is true of both domestic and foreign affairs. The two, of course, are not separate and distinct. They are, rather, different aspects of the same thing. The Soviet Union exists in the company of other nations, not in a solitary vacuum, and world affairs have had some part in forming the Soviet way. For the sake of the reader's convenience, however, we shall treat domestic and foreign affairs separately, postponing consideration of the latter to Chapter XIII. The next three chapters will deal with domestic developments since 1917, with emphasis upon the contemporary scene and with special reference to the general theme of this book.

CHAPTER X

The Soviet Way: Early Developments

THE READER will by now be quite well aware of the underlying assumption and general approach of this book, but it may not be amiss to refer to them very briefly. The assumption is that the modern world faces certain problems which are, in some respects, common to all nations. The problem of achieving security is one which confronts all people. The proper relationship of the individual to the various groups of which he is a member is another common problem. Unemployment, poverty, hunger, discrimination, and inequalities are not unique in any single state. These, together with some others, are the great issues of our time. There is a certain family resemblance about them which nobody can deny, and which this book clearly assumes and affirms.

It is, however, the resemblance of distant cousins rather than of identical twins, and the book tries to make this clear by its general approach. National cultural heritages and special circumstances—the norms and values of each society, in other words—have created differences in the problems themselves and in the attempted solutions to the problems. We have attempted to indicate some of the reasons for these differences by sketching the historical backgrounds of each "system" considered. These sketches are intended not only to show why and how the systems differ but also to guard against a common and very misleading oversimplification. Serious confusion has been created by those who have assumed that *similarity* meant identity. Such an assumption can result only in a complete misunderstanding which will lead to erroneous judgments and ill-founded actions. Two specific examples will illustrate the point.

Many people in the United States are properly concerned over problems raised by discrimination against certain minority groups, most notably Negroes and Jews. Some who have been distrustful of our good faith in facing and in attempting to find solutions to these problems, or who have become impatient with the slowness of the process, have been very greatly attracted by a formula which may be briefly paraphrased as follows: (1) The United States has an unsolved minority problem. (2) When the Communists took power in Russia they faced an even graver minority problem. (3) They largely eliminated the problem thanks to their policies. The first statements are accurate without reservation, and there is some truth in the third. But a very serious error is introduced when it is claimed or assumed that the minority problem which faced the Communists is identical with the one which confronts us. Putting aside for the moment the question of whether the Communists have really solved the minority problem, the fact that their problem and ours are not identical disproves the claim that we could solve ours merely by adopting the Communist formula. Actually the common core of the problem begins and ends with the statement that there are minorities in both countries.

It has been justly pointed out, to go on to the second example, that all Western governments have been increasingly concerned for many years with the necessity of assuring to their peoples at least a modicum of economic security. Among the various devices employed to achieve that end, certain ones are commonly lumped together under the label of "planned economy." This phrase has been generally applied without distinction to the systems of Fascist Italy, National Socialist Germany, Soviet Russia, the American New Deal, and British socialism. All these certainly have involved some sort of economic planning, but the implication that the systems are identical is without foundation. New Deal attempts to solve the problem of unemployment were quite unlike the methods employed by the Soviets. The place and power of trade unions under the American and British systems do not at all resemble the situation of unions in Nazi Germany or Soviet Russia. The difference between British socialism and Soviet socialism, to pick up a comparison often heard, is much more than a matter of degree. The problems which the British face and the way in which they face them are not the same as in the Soviet Union except in the very broadest sense. The basic approach and attitudes are sharply different, as the preceding chapters have pointed out.

Not only has planned economy meant different things in these several countries and systems; it has also meant different things within one country or system at various times. Planning Russian economy has been a major business of the Communist party of the Soviet Union (Bolshevik) for over a generation. But, except in terms of the Party's ultimate goal, their "planned economy" has not always had the same meaning. The ultimate goal is today what it was in Lenin's time, namely, the eventual establishment of world communism. Soviet planned economy is a means to that end, and the means have been changed.

The Bolsheviks were committed by their doctrines to an attempt to build a new and untried form of social, economic, and political organization upon a basis radically different from any in existence. They made their first attempts to do this during the years from 1917 to 1921, a period known in Soviet history as "war communism" or "militant communism." There was an overall plan, the Marx-Engels-Lenin doctrine; and there were lesser plans galore. But to stress the plans or to emphasize "planned economy" in describing these years misleads by suggesting an orderliness and system which did not in fact exist. The Bolsheviks were far from omniscient in their planning and actions, nor did they try to cram all of Russian life into their doctrinaire strait jacket. The outstanding characteristics of war communism were its shifts, its compromises, its improvisations and opportunisms, and its harshness. The reasons for these were varied.

The Bolshevik dogmas were broad and general, not detailed and precise. They showed the general direction but no more. Lenin's April Theses, for example, called for such things as the confiscation of landed estates and the nationalization of all land—i.e., the transfer of land from private ownership to national ownership. This followed the catchy slogan of "expropriate the expropriators." It sounded good, but how was it to be done and what did it mean? The doctrine did not prescribe the methods or the machinery for doing these things. Neither did it define its terms with much precision. For one thing, just who were the "expropriators"?

That was fairly easy to answer in the case of those industries (roughly 20 percent of the whole) which continued to operate under the same ownership and management through both 1917 revolutions. But most of the factories had been taken over by workers' committees on a purely local basis. The old owners, if they were not absentee in the first place, soon became so, and most of the managers and technicians withdrew. Self-appointed committees of workers then took over. This was certainly not the same thing as the "nationalization of industry," but what could be done? A government which was seeking power in the name of the proletariat could hardly treat the proletarians as "expropriators." What Lenin did was to give temporary legal sanction to something that he could not stop. He also tried to dissuade the workers' committees from too hasty and violent action, and persuaded about half of them to accept some form of centralized state control. A little later, when he felt strong enough to risk it, he decreed the nationalization of industry. It would be a mistake, however, to assume that the decree was immediately and universally effective.

Somewhat the same sort of thing happened about the land. The dogma clearly demanded nationalization. Engels had written about joint cultivation of the land by the peasants. No one had said how it was to be done, and no one had foreseen the situation which had come into being in Russia. Again, who were the expropriators? Not the old landlords, because, by November, they were no more. Not exclusively or even chiefly the rich peasants (kulaks), because most of them had already been despoiled by that time. During the months of the Provisional Government the peasants had been busy taking the land for themselves. There was considerable variation from section to section, but Maynard has calculated that the peasants, on an average, increased their holdings by about a fifth. Altogether, they took over some 248 million acres of land. Since before the March Revolution the peasants had already owned nearly 80 percent of all the arable land, it follows that they took practically all the rest of it. This peasant ownership was not what the Bolsheviks meant by nationalization, but there was nothing they could do to change it. So they made the best of it by passing a Land Law which said that the land belonged to the nation, and then they put forth the claim that they had given the land to the peasants. That has been good propaganda, but it is historical nonsense. The Bolsheviks couldn't give what the peasants already had. What the Bolsheviks did do, as soon as they were able, was to take the land away from the individual peasants and give the use of it to collectivized groups. That, however, is ahead of our story.

One reason, then, why the economy of the years of war communism was less a result of plan than of circumstance is that there was nothing in the Marx-Engels-Lenin formulas to cover precisely the detailed situations in which Lenin and his cohorts found themselves after their coup. Another reason is that they had to build their new society in a nation which had been the most materially backward of all the major powers, and which, furthermore, had been racked and ruined by a disastrous war that was still going on. Literally and figuratively they had to fight both men and nature. It is worth a momentary digression to point out that all of Soviet history is war history. The Bolsheviks and their followers have had to struggle against Russian and foreign armies; against native and alien "wreckers"; against sloth, indifference, and ignorance; against ancient filth, endemic disease, and recurrent famine; against cold and drought and distance. In trying to figure out the whys and hows of Soviet actions it is important to realize that for over a generation they have not known that peace and security which we habitually take as our due. They have had to fight for every gain, and the sacrifices of the people —given willingly or exacted by force—have been terrific. War communism was the first but not the last period of harshness.

Measurements sufficiently precise and detailed to support a complete description of Russia's economic status from 1917 to 1921 are lacking. There are enough specific, scattered items to show that the situation when the Provisional Government fell was very bad. The late Sir John Maynard gave the following description of it in his valuable study, *The Russian Peasant* (p. 83).

Some of the economic conditions at the November Revolution were these. The cultivated area had been reduced by the war by a sixth, the number of horses available for agriculture by nearly a third, the cereal harvest was down by 14 percent. A very imperfectly industrialized country had been deprived of its access to foreign manufactures except through the north and the far east. The product of industry was little more than three-fourths of what it had been in 1913. The railway system had suffered severely from the strain of war, and from the lack of replacements and repairs. Most of it led toward the most highly industrialized regions: and these had passed out of Russia's hands. Some of the surviving factories catered for luxuries, for which the Revolution stopped the demand. The money in circulation was twelve times as much as in July,

1914. In the country, the paper ruble was worth from a tenth to an eighth of the prewar ruble, though the foreign exchange was rather better than this, doubtless because a virtual blockade had for three years stopped imports, except of war material, as well as exports.[1]

Further figures to bear out the generalization that "life in towns and cities had become an ordeal" could be cited at some length. Thus, the average monthly real wages of employees in all industries, which had stood at eighty-five gold rubles in 1913 and 1914, dropped to thirty-eight gold rubles in 1917. The 1917 production of coal had fallen to 82 percent of the 1913 production. By 1918 it was down to 33 percent of 1913. Iron ore production in 1918 was 9 percent of the production for 1913; steel, 8 percent; salt, 6 percent; matches, 25 percent; granulated sugar, 19 percent; cigarettes, 40 percent; and so on. But most of us are not skilled in translating figures into everyday, human terms. It is likely to have more meaning when we learn that at Odessa fuel was so short that: the electric power station was closed; the water supply was shut off; streetcar service had to be stopped; municipal bathhouses were shut; and one had to stand two days in line to get a little oil. Odessa was not unusual.

Conditions were bad beyond all doubt. But two things ought to be remembered. First, this was not the bottom of the crisis. Russia had not reached, in 1917, the point of economic exhaustion. On the contrary, matters got very much worse before they got any better. The root troubles in 1917 were not so much with supply as with distribution. There was grain in the country. There was coal. There was oil. But the physical and administrative means of getting these goods to the urban areas were totally inadequate. The Moscow bread ration dropped to half a pound a day in the summer of 1917, not because there was no grain in Russia but because there was not enough in Moscow. Second, if the conditions had been literally and univer-

---

[1] Sir John Maynard (S. H. Guest, ed.), *Russia in Flux*, New York, 1948, p. 198.

sally as bad as the cited evidence would lead one to infer, life could scarcely have gone on at all. But life did go on for the majority—the vast majority. Most of the peoples of Russia managed to survive these years of hardships. How did they do it?

A standard answer is that they were tough; and that those who were not hardy enough to stand the gaff died. This is partly true, but it hides a more important fact. Most Russians—probably from 85 to 90 percent of them— did not live in towns and cities. They lived in rural villages. Many of these people suffered in the terrible famines, largely man-made, of 1921-22; and life in the villages was never easy. On the other hand, most of them had clothing and housing which was at least as adequate as what they were used to having. Russia, so to speak, had an economic defense in depth which an industrialized nation would not have had. A very large percentage of the people were not dependent upon industry, nor upon an extensive and complex domestic trade. Their needs could, for the most part, be locally supplied if not self-supplied. Moreover, there was not a great pool of reserves but millions of tiny pools. The sum of these made up a tremendous store without which neither the Bolsheviks nor any other government could have stayed in power. The Bolsheviks coaxed and forced these reserves out of hiding and so managed to squeak by. It was an excruciatingly tight squeeze.

One of the most important cases in point was the matter of food. The theory was that of barter economy with the government acting as the middleman. The peasants, of course, were to raise the food. The surplus, over and above the peasants' personal needs, was to be deposited with the government. The factories were to produce goods and the surplus, over and above the workers' needs, was also deposited with the government. Then the government was to evaluate the foodstuffs and the goods, make some equation of the two, and distribute the goods to the peasants and the food to the workers. The only trouble was that the scheme did not work and could not work. In the first place, the factories could not produce enough to make any reciprocity possible. In the second place, the popular application, which the Bolsheviks sanctioned, of the formula about expropriating the expropriators had destroyed those small merchants and peddlers who were literally Russia's only means of distribution.

But food was an absolute necessity, not only to sustain life but, what interested the Bolsheviks more, to maintain their regime. The Bolshevik strength was almost wholly in the cities, and the cities were hungry. Unless Lenin managed to feed the city workers something more than words, he faced an immediate problem of personal unemployment. The Provisional Government had also faced this shortage of food and had tried to remedy it by levies on grains, but its powers and its ruthlessness were both too little to bring success. Lenin and the Bolsheviks had more power and fewer scruples. They revived the levy in December, 1917, and greatly extended it thereafter. The peasants were arbitrarily classified as "rich," "middle," and "poor," and the latter were encouraged to "expropriate" the others. The class war was deliberately fostered in the villages, partly to increase confusions and troubles (the old divide-and-rule technique) and partly to root out food surpluses. "Committees of the Poor" were organized in the villages, and these coöperated with "Workers' Food Requisitioning Squads" in "food crusades." In less propagandistic language this meant that armed groups from the cities, operating with state sanction, followed up leads supplied by village groups and reinforced the latter in order to seize food. The poor not only were exempt from such seizures but also were given some of the food. The Red Army itself lived off the country, and, in addition, soldiers were sometimes used in these "food crusades."

The peasants fought back with the only weapons they had—evasion and refusal to raise crops. Despite all the orders and all the requisitioning squads and their helpers, large stocks of foodstuffs escaped the net. Demands and regulations were widely evaded, and the enforcement agencies were frequently duped or bribed. More disastrous was the peasant strike, if a completely unorganized and uncentralized movement may be so called. The peasants stopped raising those crops which were subject to requisition. When new items were added to the requisitions, the peasants ceased to plant or harvest them, too. By 1921, only one and a half million of the thirty-eight million acres of arable land in Samara province were cultivated, and the grain yield per acre dropped from 934 pounds to 44 pounds. The peasants also slaughtered and ate much of their livestock to forestall confiscation. The result of all this was a terrible famine in which some three million died directly of hunger and at least twice as many more died of famine-born weakness and disease.

This disaster certainly did not happen because the Communists wanted it or planned it. They were the rulers of Russia, however, and rightly or wrongly the people held them responsible. The economic situation was so desperate by 1921 that the people began to rebel against the Communists. Government food depots and other stock piles were raided and looted. Supplies in transit were highjacked, and there was much banditry. More and more these widespread disorders were directed against the Communist rulers and reached a climax in the Kronstadt Mutiny. There was a certain symbolism involved here because sailors from Kronstadt had played a very prominent part in the November coup. Now sailors from that base revolted against the rule they had helped to create. Their rising was crushed, and the mutineers were annihilated. But the discontent was not banished and other rebels rose against Lenin and his men. The Communist leaders had a choice between sticking to the line they had been following, in which case they were bound to go down, and compromising in the hope of staying in power. They chose the latter course and embarked upon one of those "tactical retreats" for which they have since become justifiably famous. Lenin himself made this decision. At the Tenth

Congress of Soviets in 1921 he announced the "New Economic Policy." The means were changed. The goal remained the same, although the day of its expected achievement was postponed.

The reappearance of private trade and certain other familiar forms of capitalist economy during the period of the NEP (1921-28) led many observers to the conclusion that Lenin had put Russia on the road back to capitalism. It was an erroneous conclusion. The Communist leaders thought and spoke of the NEP as the road to communism. This must also be considered an error unless it is assumed that the leaders meant their own special variety of communism. At any rate, the official explanation was that overenthusiasm had tricked the leaders into making a major mistake. They had overlooked the fact that the dogma said that socialism was a necessary intermediate stage of development, and they had tried to jump directly from capitalism to communism. This was impossible, as the dogma had pointed out, so that it was necessary to acknowledge the blunder, go back to socialism, and begin again. Some of the Communist spokesmen offered a different version. The NEP was not, they said, really a going back even if it looked like it because what they had from 1917 to 1921 was not real communism but merely the sharings and sacrifices demanded by the war.

A more accurate interpretation than any of these is that there were two major aspects to the NEP. One was a restriction in scope and the other was an increase in efforts and controls within the limited area. Lenin, in other words, let go of certain things temporarily in order to get a tighter grip on others. State control was removed or reduced over some activities, and some policies were reversed. The class war in the villages was stopped. The Committees of the Poor were dismissed and the Food Requisitioning Squads were disbanded. The confiscation of foods was ended, and the peasants were allowed to keep or to sell their surpluses. They were, however, obligated to pay a tax which was somewhat higher than it had been before the war. The "middle peasants" (so called) were assisted by gifts or loans of seed and implements, and by new laws on landowning and use. Small-scale domestic trading was allowed under state licenses, and private traders (nepmen) were encouraged to do business. Industries which employed less than twenty workers were also allowed to operate under private ownership. One might say with considerable accuracy and perhaps with some cynicism that one phase of planned economy in the years of the NEP was the use of "expropriators" and "exploiters" as supporters of the Communist regime.

The other aspect of the NEP was the tightening of Communist controls over certain economic and other activities and the experimentation with the methods and machinery of centralized, large-scale planning. Banking, transport, foreign trade, large-scale domestic trade, large-scale industry, and all the machinery of government remained within the Communists' grasp. In fact, these things were more tightly held than they had been before. We may turn aside from the strictly economic matters for a little in order to consider some other parts of the story which bear this out.

The Communist attack on the institution of the family was continued with vigor throughout the NEP despite a strong but largely passive and unorganized popular resistance. Marriage and divorce were merely a matter of registering the fact with the government agency. The new Family Code which was adopted in 1927 made unregistered marriages legally equal to registered ones. Abortions were approved in law and in practice so long as they were performed under officially endorsed auspices. The establishment of communal nurseries and feeding centers also contributed to weakening family ties. It may be noted in passing that these anti-family acts and policies have since been abandoned.

The Communist attack upon churches and upon organized religion was also vigorously carried on throughout the NEP, and the laws against the teaching of religion to minors were strictly enforced for a time. Antircligious campaigns were commonplace, and the "League of the Militant Anti-Godless" flourished. This drive was speeded up after the NEP until the late thirties, when it was gradually slowed down until, during the Second World War, it virtually came to a stop. No Communist, however, can be a member or supporter of any religious group; and it behooves any would-be Communist not to belong to such groups. The insistence upon atheism and irreligion for Party members and aspirants is still in force.

Lenin and his associates very early and very clearly recognized that "education" was or could be made to become an invaluable weapon for the Communist cause and Party.[2] The years of the NEP marked a period of wild experimentation and great quantitative advances in popular education. The experiments included practically all the worst of American "progressive education" of that period as well, of course, as some things of value. The quantitative advance was marked by the spectacular reduction of illiteracy even though the accomplishments in this respect have been considerably exaggerated both in relation to the situation under the czars and in comparison to other countries. By way of restoring the balance somewhat, it may be pointed out that the percentage of illiterates in the Soviet Union in 1940 was only slightly greater than the percentage of illiterates among American Negroes at that time, and the Negroes, of course, were the least favored group of Americans. All "educational" institutions and devices have been and are used by the Communists for the purposes of indoctrination. The autonomy which

---

[2] Presumably it will be clear from the context, but it may also be specifically pointed out here, that "Communist" and "Party" are used with precise and specific connotations throughout the chapters dealing with Russia and the Soviet Union. Communist, written with a capital C, refers only to the followers of Lenin and Stalin or to their theories, policies, words, actions, and organizations. When so written, it is not used to designate a general economic, social, or other philosophy or group or anything else. Party, with a capital P, refers only to what is now called the Communist Party of the Soviet Union (Bolshevik) or to its predecessors.

Russian universities had enjoyed since 1905 was, for example, completely destroyed in 1922. The power of the Communist party took its place, an example of the tightening controls.

The development of the formal theories and machinery of government during these early years is also a case in point, and, further, it illustrates again the merging of old and new.[3] The first Soviet constitution, which applied only to what was the Russian Soviet Republic, was adopted in October, 1918, about a year after Lenin's forces had seized Petrograd. Based upon Marx's *Communist Manifesto* and *Das Kapital*, and upon the experience and legends of the Paris Commune,[4] it sought to introduce new ways and new concepts into Russia. Its descent from the *Manifesto* and the Commune can be briefly demonstrated. The *Manifesto* called for the welding together of the proletariat into a class-conscious group which should then overthrow the bourgeoisie and establish itself in power. The 1918 Constitution said, "Power must belong completely and exclusively to the toiling masses." It then went on to: disfranchise the bourgeoisie, arrange the electoral system in such a way as to give urban labor an unduly large representation at the expense of the peasant majority, and set up a legislative organization which appeared (but only appeared) to vest power in "the toiling masses." The *Manifesto* demanded the abolition of private property and of the rights of inheritance. It also called for the confiscation of all property belonging to those who opposed the new regime or who fled from it. These doctrines had been popularized under the Commune in the slogan, "The

---

[3] The present Soviet government is described in the chapter entitled "The Dictatorship of the Proletariat."

[4] The Paris Commune of 1871 was the uprising of a heterogeneous group of malcontents against the French government. The rebels seized control of Paris and held the city until they were driven out after a bitter siege. There were some followers of Marx-Engels among the rebels, and the Communists, with their customary disregard for historical truth, have always claimed the Commune as their first revolution. It was not theirs.

expropriation of the expropriators." The 1918 Constitution provided for the nationalization of land, resources,
mines, banks, and factories. The preceding chapter noted
that this arrangement was not as foreign to the Russian
experience as it would have been to ours. Here was a
double grafting of old upon new.

The first constitution of the Union of Soviet Socialist
Republics (created in 1922) was adopted in 1924. It also
showed the dominant influence of the Marxist-Leninist
doctrines. Its first section declared that all the world is
divided into two hostile camps: capitalism and "socialism." (That last word is in quotation marks because, as
the Communists use it, it refers only to countries and
systems which they control.) Capitalism, the 1924 Constitution charged, is marked by inequalities, slavery, imperialist brutalities, and war. "Socialism" is blessed with mutual
confidence, the brotherly collaboration of peoples, the
absence of exploitation of man by man, and peace. The
newly created Soviet Union, the document continued,
would serve as a bulwark against capitalism and as a step
toward the inevitable and victorious uniting of all workers
in a World Soviet Socialist Union. This frank statement
of two worlds does not appear in the current constitution,
which is less openly belligerent but no less Marxist.[5]

The key to an understanding of the Soviet government
(as a later chapter will point out with regard to the current scene) does not lie in the constitutions. The methods
by which the Communists retained and were exercising
power during the NEP was once very graphically described
by Miss Anna Louise Strong. Her description is not only

---

[5] It does appear, however, in many other places. For example: "All
the forces of democracy and progress are rallied around the Soviet
Union. The peoples' hopes center in it. Aggressive intentions are
foreign to the Soviet Union which . . . sets the example to all people
who seek the path of progressive, democratic growth. This path is
the antithesis of the path of imperialist robbery and plunder which
the capitalist countries have been following for decades, and which
they are now following under the leadership of the United States of
America." (*Voprosy filosofii*, No. 2, 1948)

historically accurate but also, except for the numbers, currently correct.[6] The italics are mine.

The Communists know all the tricks of politics that are known in any country; the control of press, of election boards, of political machinery. In the elections themselves I could not detect any atmosphere of compulsion. . . . *I have no doubt that, when necessary, the Communist Party uses all the various means known in politics for keeping itself in power.* . . .

It is a marvelous organization, unlike any party known in history. *It is a dictatorship of half a million Communists over one hundred and thirty million people.* Yet it has organized itself to keep in power for a generation, by studying the desires of all the people, over thousands of miles of country, and by supplying those desires, *as far as it finds it necessary,* moulding them always a little further in the direction of its aim.

. . . To be a Party Member is something far more than voting. It is to be organized for life in a compact unit *whose purpose takes precedence over every other interest. You are a Communist first and everything else afterwards.* You are on call always, to go wherever you are sent throughout Russia.

Those half million Communists are scattered throughout the country, at strategic posts of industry and government. Every large factory, every notable village has its Communist nucleus.

Miss Strong later amplified her reference to the "Communist nucleus" by quoting part of a conversation which she had with the chairman of a Workers' Committee in the Kharkov motor factory. The chairman was talking about his own plant, but his statements were equally applicable to any large-scale industry.

"The ultimate responsibility rests," he added after a mo-

---

[6] Miss Strong was for almost a generation one of the most outspoken and effective American champions of the Soviets. Many of her writings had a quasi-official character. All of them demonstrated her unusual knowledge of the USSR and reflected her close association with the Communist movement and its leaders. This gives her writings a definite bias, but it also gives them an especial value. The quotation is from A. L. Strong, *The First Time in History*, New York, Boni & Liveright, 1924, pp. 52, 53.

ment, "neither with the Workers' Committee nor with the Manager, but with the Communist group in the plant. Some of these are in the management, and the rest are scattered as workers through the plant. They have no direct control, but theirs is the moral responsibility of making State Industry succeed."[7]

It will be recalled that banking was one of the economic activities over which the Communists retained control under the NEP. Miss Strong gave a most revealing account of a talk she had with a Mr. Scheinman, who was then president of the State Bank. Scheinman showed her the Bank's gold reserve, and she asked him how it had been acquired. His answer to that question, and her comments upon it, tell something about the methods used and also about the relationships of the various branches of state economic activity.

"We loaned money, for instance, to the Timber Trust. We gave them paper roubles, which they used to pay their bills in Russia. They exported timber to England. They paid us in English pounds. They paid us not only the loan with interest, but part of their profits. Sometimes as much as half of all they made! The fur industry also has been very profitable, making as much as 200 and 300 percent in export trade. On all these profits, the State Bank demanded its share, for making the first loan. . . . It is a question of public policy. . . . We are building up a gold reserve for Russia."

These were the cold, hard tactics of the State Bank. It set out to make all the money it could, and it did not conceal the fact. At the end of the first year it had twenty million dollars in gold; at the end of the second year one hundred and twenty-five million, half in gold and half in negotiable assets as sound as gold.[8]

The State Bank also exacted a high commission (10 percent) for payment to individuals of money sent them from abroad. It speculated in the currency black market and sometimes rigged that market in order to make a

[7] *Ibid.*, p. 81.
[8] *Ibid.*, pp. 85, 86.

profit. As Miss Strong says, "It built itself up into power at the expense of everyone who did business with it. . . ." What she does not say is that the Bank took its profits mostly out of the hides of the Russian people whose rubles were depressed in value by its currency manipulations and who had to pay higher prices because of its actions.

The experimentation under instruments of planning and control revolved around the Supreme Economic Council, which had been created in 1918. This was a very highly regarded body in those days because it was Lenin's belief at that time that all the political organs of the state, except this one, would "wither away." The SEC was expected to be the sole survivor and residuary legatee of the government. Its head was Alexis Rykov, purged as a traitor in 1937, but very close to Lenin in the early years. His associates on the Council were state officials, technical experts, and agents of the trade unions. The officials, who were all Party members, were there for obvious reasons. The technical experts, most of whom were not Communists, were included because the Communists needed their help. The union men were members because unions at that time were virtually masters of industry. Under the original scheme each branch of industry was headed by a committee from the labor unions in that branch. These central committees were supposed to be in full charge of their special industry throughout the nation. The work of all was to be coördinated by the SEC, in which each was represented. The scheme did not work well in practice, partly because the central government was not strong enough to control the local units, which acted pretty much as they pleased.

With the NEP, the SEC was given full authority and responsibility for the management and regulation of large industry. The direct management of each branch of industry was placed in the hands of a trust, which was run by a committee roughly analogous to a board of directors.

Each trust had to submit its plans and reports to the SEC for approval, and half the profits of each trust were assigned to the state. The number of trusts rapidly increased until there were 486 of them. They engaged in cutthroat competition for funds, supplies, labor, and, sometimes, markets so that super-trusts or syndicates had to be set up to regulate the competition, fix prices, allocate raw materials, and regulate the distribution of goods. It was a complex and not very efficient machine but it worked after a fashion. Very gradually the national economy recovered from the effects of wars and revolutions. Since recovery came after the NEP had been in operation for some years, it is generally assumed that recovery was due to the NEP. Perhaps it was, or perhaps it was brought about by the passage of time and the cumulative efforts of many people. At any rate, by 1928 the industrial production had risen to the level of 1913—a very substantial gain over the nadir of 1923. The NEP, furthermore, enabled the Party to hang on to its power and this despite the most serious of intra-Party fights.

Lenin had met opposition in 1917 and he continued to run into it during the rest of his active life. But as long as he retained his health, he also retained control over his party. The break came in 1922-23 when cerebral hemorrhages at first partially and then completely incapacitated him. He died in January, 1924. After the partial breakdown of his health in 1922, the Party created a triumvirate to serve as its chief executive. The trio was composed of three "old Bolsheviks": Kamenev (Trotsky's brother-in-law) and Zinoviev, who had opposed Lenin in 1917 but who subsequently accepted his leadership; and Stalin, who had become the Party's General Secretary in April of 1922. Following Lenin's complete invalidism in 1923, "Stalin became senior triumvir and successor to Lenin in all but name," as Trotsky once put it. Following Lenin's death the struggle for power within the Party came into the open. There were many aspirants for Lenin's place, but the struggle soon narrowed down to two: Trotsky and Stalin. Echoes of this epic battle still reverberate. It is impossible even to sketch it in outline here. Stalin's victory was won bit by bit. Trotsky was fired from his post as People's Commissar for War in 1925, dropped from the Politburo in 1926, expelled from the Party's Central Committee in the summer of 1927. The Fifteenth Congress of the Communist Party of the Soviet Union, held in December, 1927, marks the turning of a page. Trotsky was expelled from the Party and exiled to Central Asia. Two years later he was expelled from the USSR and forced to live the remainder of his life in exile—first in Europe and then in Mexico. He remained a revolutionary conspirator to the bitter end.[9]

The Fifteenth Congress also condemned as heresies any and all deviations from the Party line as laid down by Stalin. His old comrades, who now found themselves in opposition, did not take this meekly. They fought against him by any means at their disposal and Stalin struck back with increasing vigor, ruthlessness, and brutality. The story of this and of the drastic purges and treason trials (1935-38) with which the movement culminated is too complex to be told here. It must suffice to report simply that the evidence shows, on the one hand, that the Stalinist charges of wrecking, sabotage, and treason were exaggerated, and, on the other hand, that there was a basis in fact for the charges. The Fifteenth Congress, to return to 1928, was also remarkable for its decision to end the NEP and to engage in a "renewed socialist offensive" in which the Five-Year Plans were the major schemes of battle. It may be added, in concluding the account of this phase of Soviet development, that long-range national planning did not suddenly spring into being by the action of Stalin's cohorts in the Fifteenth Party Congress. Trotsky (as well as others) had been an early advocate of planning. He was responsible for the drafting of a five-year plan for the

---

[9] Trotsky was murdered in Mexico City in 1940.

metallurgical industries in 1923. The plan was never put into effect. He was also behind an abortive attempt at a general five-year plan which was prepared in 1925-26 by the State Planning Commission. It is clear that some of Trotsky's ideas had greater success than he did. The Trotsky-Stalin feud was more a literal life-or-death battle for power than a conflict of aims.

CHAPTER XI

The Soviet Way: Recent Developments

THE OBSERVANT READER will have noted that the last chapter made no specific, detailed reference to the problems of full employment, labor-management relations, living standards, or civil liberties. These are all parts of the common problems of achieving security and of the relationship of the individual to groups. The four categories just named also represent the selected great issues with which this book is primarily concerned. The virtual omission of them from Chapter X was due neither to oversight nor to that bane of authors—space limitations. While the CPSU(B) did not ignore these problems prior to 1928, it nevertheless met them less by intention than by necessity, and less by planning than by *ad hoc* improvisation. This was partly because first priority had to be given to getting the country back on its feet, and partly it was due to the intra-Party struggles. The planned, concerted, frontal attacks on these problems began with the Five-Year-Plans.[1]

These plans have wrought tremendous changes in most aspects of Soviet life. They are by no means confined to

---

[1] The time spans of the various Five-Year Plans were as follows: First, 1928-32; Second, 1933-37; Third, 1938-42; Fourth, 1946-50. The terminal dates for the First and Second Plans are those officially and arbitrarily announced by the Soviet government. The course of the Third Plan was broken by the war. Special plans covered the years from mid-1941 through 1945.

what we should call an economic sphere. The Very Reverend Hewlett Johnson, Dean of Canterbury—a close friend and stanch supporter of the Communists in the USSR and elsewhere—once explained the scope and importance of the plans in these words: "The dominant word in Russia is PLAN. The Russian world is a planned world. A Moscow babe enters a planned world at birth. Plans secure his birthright. Plans supplement his mother's care. Plan orders his work in adult life. Plan is the most original Soviet contribution to civilized living."[2]

It will not be possible in this chapter either to describe all the ramifications of the Five-Year Plans or to give an account of all aspects of Soviet development since 1928. Since so much has to be omitted the reader is entitled to know the bases of selection. In a general sense, of course, the criteria are set by the pattern of the book. This calls for a comparison of the way in which the several systems have met problems of certain types. An additional criterion is that much of the appeal which the Soviet way undeniably has for many people rests upon the boast that it has solved these various problems. The Soviet leaders and their followers claim that the Soviet system under Communist direction has banished unemployment, strikes, costly work stoppages, and the exploitation of man by man. They boast that the USSR has no economic crises, no second-class citizens, and no fascism. They claim that workers in the Soviet Union are free from the specter of economic insecurity and from the oppression which they say is inherent in capitalism. I shall let them speak for themselves in a moment. If their claims and boasts are supported by the record, then they have indeed found the solution for which the world is waiting. But if the record does not bear out what they say about themselves, the world will have to look elsewhere for its salvation.

The following series of quotations were chosen and are reproduced here without prejudice intended. They are all

---

[2] H. Johnson, *Soviet Russia Since the War*, New York, 1947, p. 129.

taken from Soviet publications of recent date, and even a casual checking of these sources will show that the excerpts are neither atypical nor uncommon. These are the words in which the Soviet rulers report their accomplishments to their own people and to the world. We are not here concerned with whether they should do this. The fact is that they do. The impressions which they wish to create are obvious. Such impressions are bound to be tremendously appealing to the hungry and haunted people of the world. Here are samples of their claims which are made without qualification or limit. (That is, the Soviet rulers do not say that they have solved parts of a problem, or most of a problem. They claim to have found the complete and perfect solution.) The source from which each excerpt has been translated is given at the end of the quotation.

The Soviet Union, as we know, is a country where, in respect to government programs, promise and performance are never at variance. . . . In the Soviet Union, crises and unemployment are unknown because of its political and social system and its socialist planned economy. In our country, postwar reconversion is not hampered by the contradictions and obstacles so characteristic of this process in capitalist countries. . . . There are no antagonistic classes in the Soviet Union so there is naturally a single line both in domestic and foreign policy. (Novoe Vremia, No. 7, Apr. 1, 1946, p. 1)

Soviet democracy provides our people with the fullest possible development of all their capabilities, of all their native talents, and draws upon all the wealth of our native land for the benefit of the working people. (Izvestia, Dec. 3, 1946)

Only the Soviet Socialist State consistently fights for actual freedom, independence and equality for all peoples, great and small. Only the USSR has created a genuine equality of free peoples, a genuine friendship of peoples that have been freed from all forms of exploitation, national oppression, and race discrimination. (Pravda, Nov. 17, 1946)

The Soviet Union met the Second World War and took part in the struggle against fascism already in possession of the most perfect form of social organization. . . . Our most perfect Soviet political system immeasurably facilitates the task of restoring war devastation in our country. (*Izvestia,* Jan. 1, 1947)

That which bourgeois society and bourgeois democracy were incapable of solving, Soviet democracy has solved successfully. (*Izvestia,* Dec. 5, 1946—report of a "learned" paper delivered before the Soviet Academy of Sciences)

For generations the working class has dreamed of the time when unemployment would disappear, and with it the eternal uncertainty of what tomorrow would bring. That is unattainable under the conditions of capitalism, but it has been decisively won forever in our country. Only in the Soviet Union, the country of socialism, where power belongs to the people themselves, and the whole development of the country is directed toward the welfare of the people, has the death blow been dealt to unemployment. . . . To each Soviet citizen we guarantee the worthy employment of his potentialities, abilities and talents. (*Trud,* Apr. 13, 1947)

Unknown to Soviet youth are the exploitations, oppression, spiritual slavery, lack of political rights and the moral humiliation experienced every day by the youth in bourgeois countries. (*Pravda,* Mar. 27, 1949)

The Soviet people make full use of the innumerable advantages of their socialist system which knows neither social nor national oppression, neither crises nor unemployment. (*Pravda,* May 9, 1949)

We are not threatened by the economic crises, so ruinous for industry, from which not a single capitalist country is free. We do not have and will not have unemployment and the impoverishment of the population which accompanies it. (Molotov's speech on Nov. 6, 1947, reported in *Pravda*)

Have the Communist rulers of the USSR found the panacea and created the perfect society which they claim? "Let's look at the record." Some of these things are matters of law in the Soviet Union. The basis of the Soviet system is described and defined in the following articles in their Fundamental Laws (Constitution). The translation is from the official Russian version.

Art. 1. The USSR is a socialist state of workers and peasants.

Art. 4. The economic foundations of the USSR rest upon the socialist system of economy and the socialist ownership of the tools and resources of production, firmly established by the complete liquidation of the capitalist system of economy, by the ending of private ownership of the tools and resources of production, and abolition of the exploitation of man by man.

Art. 11. The economic life of the USSR is directed and ordered by the state national economic plan in the interest of increasing public wealth, of constantly improving the material and cultural condition of the workers, of strengthening the defense of the USSR and of re-enforcing its independence.

What does this mean in more familiar language? Does it mean that a mysterious thing called the state owns everything? No, it does not. Private property legally exists in the Soviet Union. A Soviet citizen may own his house, with its furnishings and appurtenances. He may own an automobile, a bicycle, a radio, books, jewelry—any items of what we call personal property that he is able to acquire. He may own bank accounts, government bonds, life insurance, and any interest or dividends which may accrue on these things. He may own a small business or industry or professional practice provided always that he does not "exploit the labor of others," i.e., become the employer of labor. Several persons may band together in the joint ownership of coöperative or collective enterprises. The individual, however, may not own land, forests, mines, large industries or businesses, or any natural resources. These things are state property.

Many observers, noting that the state is controlled by the Politburo and not by the Soviet peoples, have reached the judgment that this matter of state ownership is a horrible farce. It may be, but there is clear evidence that the masses of the Soviet people do not think so. The individual Soviet citizen is very likely to identify himself with the state and to feel that he rightfully has a share in Russia's vast wealth. He speaks with sincere pride of "our native land," "our factories, mines, and mills," "our collective farms," "our transportation systems," and so on. Perhaps he ought not to do so, but he does. Perhaps he is being fooled, but the observer who fails to grasp the reality of this attitude is fooling himself.

What is a "state national economic plan"? How is it made? What does it include? What is planned for? The planning begins in the first instance not in the government-in-law but in the government-in-fact. The Politburo decides upon the general aims and goals for the plan. The Fourth Five-Year Plan was officially laid before the Supreme Soviet in March, 1946. More than a month earlier, in an election speech, Stalin had announced the broad goals of the plan in these words:

The principal aims of the new Five-Year Plan are to rehabilitate the ravaged areas of the country, to restore the pre-war level in industry and agriculture, and then to surpass this level in more or less substantial manner. . . . The rationing system will shortly be abolished, special attention will be devoted to extending the production of consumer goods, to raising the living standard of the working people by steadily lowering the prices of all goods, and to the widespread construction of all manner of scientific research institutions. . . .

As regards the plans for a longer period ahead, the Party means to organize a new mighty upsurge in the national economy, which would allow us to increase our industrial production, for example, three times over as compared with the pre-war period. . . . That will take three more Five-Year Plans, I should think, if not more.

Mr. Stalin, of course, was speaking not for himself but for

the Politburo and here, then, are the broad objectives of the Fourth, Fifth, Sixth, and Seventh Plans, at least.

It takes a staggering amount of detailed preparation by thousands of people to translate these generalities into action. A tremendous amount of information has to be collected and compiled. Just to give an illustration, here are a few of the questions which had to be answered by the Consumers Cooperative: How many customers were supplied by each unit last year? How many this year? How many are expected for next year? What commodities were (are, will be) supplied and in what amounts? Which of these can be produced locally? regionally? nationally? Which can be produced by the Cooperative? What must be obtained from other Soviet producers? What must be imported? And so on. Industry has to answer questions about past, current, and future production, and about labor. How many workers are available at all levels of skill? How many now in training will become available? How many will be needed? And so forth.

After all this data is collected and compiled for use, the State Planning Commission (Gosplan) must draw up a master plan which will lead to the goals defined by the Politburo. Some idea of the terrific difficulties involved can be had by remembering that the plan must be balanced. It does not do to plan more factories than you can provide steel to build, more blast furnaces than you can mine coking coal to supply, or a greater coal output than you can transport. One region must not be unduly favored at the expense of others. Mistakes in planning on such a scale may not be inevitable, but they certainly have occurred. The First Five-Year Plan, for example, placed such emphasis on quantity that quality suffered. It was soon discovered that it is better to produce one hundred usable units in a given time than to turn out three hundred, of which more than two-thirds were spoiled. The Second Plan therefore stressed efficient production and quality rather than quantity. The Fourth Plan, to cite another instance, attempted too much, and early in 1947 the authorities ordered the abandonment of certain tasks in order to concentrate on others.

When Gosplan's master plan has been approved by the Politburo, it is then submitted to the Supreme Soviet. The Fourth Plan was submitted on the fifteenth of March, 1946, and approved on the eighteenth. In its printed English version, it runs to about 32,000 words. The plan is in four parts: (1) the Principal Aims; (2) the Plan for Increased Production and Development in Industry, Agriculture, and Transport; (3) the Plan for the Material and Cultural Advancement of the People; and (4) the Plan for the Reconstruction and Development of the National Economy of the Union Republics. It will be seen that planned production is only a part, although it is the major one, of a "state national economic plan." The following items will show the scope:

Total volume of Soviet industrial production by 1950 shall be 205 billion rubles, an increase of 48 percent as compared to 1940. The Far East, Siberia, and the Transcaucasus shall create their own sources of supply of iron ore. Peat output is to be increased 39 percent. Tree plantings for the protection of state and collective farms on the steppes shall be restored. Poultry departments shall be organized on all grain-growing collective farms. Automatic brakes shall be fitted to 93 percent of all freight cars, and automatic couplings to 75 percent. The tonnage of ships built in 1950 shall be double that of 1940. The number of children accommodated in kindergartens in 1950 shall be double that of 1940. The manufacture of artificial limbs of high quality for war invalids shall be organized. The paved area of streets and squares shall be extended. By 1950, the production and sale of samovars shall be increased to 200,000. The number of hospital beds in the Byelorussian SSR shall be increased to thirty thousand. It is clear that the Very Reverend Hewlett Johnson did not exaggerate in his statement about plans.

Have the plans solved the problems which were listed at the beginning of this chapter? The matter of employment is laid down in the following articles of the Soviet Fundamental Laws.

Art. 12. Work is the right and duty of every able-bodied citizen in the USSR on the basis that "He who does not work shall not eat." The principle of socialism, "From each according to his ability, to each according to his work," is applied in the USSR.

Art. 118. Citizens of the USSR have the right to work, i.e., they are guaranteed the right of working and of being paid for their work according to its kind and amount.

The right to work is ensured: by the socialist organization of the national economy, by the steady growth of the productive powers of Soviet society, by the elimination of the possibility of economic crises, and by the abolition of unemployment.

Words, even in constitutions, do not always give an accurate description of practices, as witness the political disabilities of certain groups of American citizens despite the Fourteenth and Fifteenth Amendments to our Constitution. Maybe it is the same way in the USSR. It certainly is in some things, but not in the case of employment. Their boast is correct: there is no unemployment in the USSR today. On the contrary, the nation has been plagued by serious labor shortages. Industry, mining, agriculture, and transport have all been hampered by a lack of workers, especially of skilled workers. This is partly due to the tremendous amount of work to be done. But poor planning and difficulties with labor have been much more important causes. It is important to realize the fact that planning alone has not resulted in the abolition of unemployment in the USSR. It should be specifically noted, further, that effective planning on a national scale requires that labor, no less than raw materials and freight cars, be shunted from areas of lesser needs to areas of greater needs. Labor, in other words, cannot be left wholly free to make its own choice of employment under a system like that of the Soviets. In order to get labor where it was wanted, in order to overcome the very serious problem of excessive labor turnover and an equally serious problem of low productivity, the Soviet rulers have used a variety of devices. The combination has been graphically described as "the carrot and the stick." The carrot represents inducements in the form of wage differentials, pension plans, bonuses, better living conditions, and more generous food supplies. The stick represents various means of compulsion. Persistent indoctrination, and "socialist competitions" have also been used.

The 1918 Russian Constitution made all citizens from the ages of sixteen to fifty years subject to compulsory labor. This was replaced after 1922 with a Labor Code which removed the legal compulsion to enter industry except in the case of emergencies. The Labor Code provides that when a worker has once entered into a "work agreement" (i.e., has taken a job) he becomes subject to the code. The law prohibits a worker from leaving his job without the express permission of the head of the enterprise. It has always been difficult and sometimes impossible to enforce this provision. The chief enforcement instrument is the "workbook" or "labor passport" which was introduced in 1938. Under this system, every industrial worker has to have a workbook in which are recorded his name and other identifying data, and his job record. When he takes a job, he surrenders the workbook to his employer, who keeps it and records relevant data. The worker is not supposed to leave the job without getting the passport back from the boss, nor can he legally be hired unless he can deposit the document, properly endorsed, with his new employer. These regulations were largely ignored during the war and immediately thereafter, but vigorous action has been taken since then to guarantee the observance of the regulations by both labor and management.

During the war, workers were "frozen" in certain types of jobs. Railway employees, for example, were placed under martial law. This was in addition to the labor-passport system. Some of these job-freezing regulations

were still in effect in 1950. Railway workers were still
under martial law, and workers who were absent from
their jobs without leave were still being treated as criminals. Workers who are more than twenty minutes late to
work are legally regarded as having been absent on that
day. And one day's unexcused absence is a criminal offense
which may be punished by putting the worker at forced
labor for as much as six months. The postwar price and
currency reforms were also used to compel more young
people, more people over fifty, and more housewives to
take jobs in industry. The first currency reform (December, 1947) bore most heavily on the peasants and forcibly
encouraged them to seek urban, industrial employment.
Because matters of currency, wages, rations, and prices are
part of the general picture of living standards, they will
be discussed in that connection.

There are two other very important instruments of compulsion operated by the Soviet government for the purposes of increasing the supply of labor and controlling its
distribution. These are the State Labor Reserve Schools,
established in 1940 and extended by the Fourth Five-Year
Plan, and the Youth Labor Draft, which was instituted in
1947. The quota for the State Labor Reserve Schools is
filled partly by volunteers and partly by a draft very like
military conscription. Draftees are allowed to indicate
their preferences as to assignments, but—as in an army—
they go where they are sent, and their preferences have
no weight if the high command decrees differently. Grad-
uates of these schools are obligated to work at least four
years in the industry to which they are sent. The Youth
Labor Draft applies to eighteen- and nineteen-year-olds,
who were formerly subject only to military conscription.
The law provides that they may be drafted into coal mining, certain industries, and vocational training.

There is another and integral part of Soviet planned
economy which their propagandists do not publicize. This
is the system of forced or slave labor. Recent studies have

made it clear that slave labor is an organic part of the much-vaunted Soviet way. It is not simply "a corrective measure for the rehabilitation of those who have gone astray"; nor is it primarily a punitive action against a few thousand "wreckers, saboteurs, and traitors." Only the Soviet rulers know how many of their people are held and worked as slaves in forced-labor camps. But it appears that there are more slave laborers in the USSR than there are people in the Dominion of Canada. This fact alone ought to make anyone very hesitant about applying the phrase "economic democracy" to the Soviet system. No system which depends for its continuance upon the enslavement of millions of people has any right to the title of democracy, no matter how that title may be qualified or limited. The fact of slave labor in the Soviet Union makes the promise that there shall be no exploitation of man by man a hollow mockery.

Forced (slave) labor is under the direction of the Chief Administration of Camps, a division of the Ministry of the Interior (MVD). The list of the enterprises which this body carries on by means of slave labor is too long to give here in its entirety. But the list includes: mining; farming; the construction and maintenance of railways, roads, canals, harbor works, and fortifications; fisheries; lumbering; quarrying; and some metallurgical industries. These activities are all essential elements of Soviet economic life. A report presented to the United Nations early in 1950 listed twenty categories of persons in the annexed Baltic states who were consigned to slave-labor camps. The list was compiled from official Soviet documents. The only crime which these people had committed was that of belonging to the designated groups. Among the groups were: those who had occupied important civil service posts, prominent Zionists, small farmers, relatives of persons who had escaped abroad, prominent members of Jewish organizations, and Freemasons. It may be that Soviet socialist economy, "the most perfect form of social organization," as *Izvestia* called it, could operate without this brutal feature. That is anybody's guess. The facts are that it has never so operated.

There are, of course, more Soviet workers outside of the slave-labor camps than there are inside. What are the general conditions of their work? The basic workday is eight hours and the basic work week is six days, so that a forty-eight-hour week is normal. Wherever possible—and in some instances which do not seem possible—labor is on a piecework basis. This means that most Soviet workers are paid only for what they produce. This is not communism. A minimum or basic norm is decreed for each operation. Fulfillment of only the minimum earns only the minimum pay. Overfulfillment is rewarded by a higher rate per unit, by bonuses, by awards, honors, and other perquisites. Those who consistently set up production records are known as Stakhanovites and are especially favored. The basic norms in several industries were substantially raised in 1947 on the ground that better methods and equipment made higher production possible. This was probably true to some degree, but the effect on the worker was to force him to produce more than before in order to get the same pay. There are tremendous differentials in wages. Wages fluctuate so that it is impossible to predict here what the wage scales may be at the time you are reading this. The following examples will give a measure of the differentials as they were in 1947: The average monthly wage of Soviet workers at that time was about 450 rubles. A railway locomotive engineer, however, was paid between 4000 and 4500 rubles per month, and a German scientist reported that the Soviet government had offered him 6000 rubles a month plus food and living quarters to do research on atomic energy. The British Foreign Office reported in early 1950 that the average monthly wages for unskilled Soviet labor began at about 250 rubles. The range for the monthly wages for skilled labor was given as between 500 and 1500 rubles.

The existence of wide differentials in wages, rations,

housing, and other items makes it clear that the usual American stereotype of the Soviet Union as the home of "communist equality" is utterly false. It might also give rise to the question as to whether or not the Communist rulers have abolished classes within the USSR. The answer largely depends on what is meant by "class." To the Communist, "classless" does not mean equality in wealth, rank, or perquisites; it means that no private person can "exploit" others because he happens to own the "means and resources of production." If you accept this definition as adequate, you must logically agree that there are no classes in the Soviet Union. But this is not what "class" usually means to Americans. We are likely to think of classes precisely in terms of wealth, living standards, social status, education, and so on. If the word is used in the American sense, the Communists certainly have not got rid of classes in Russia. The personnel of privilege has been changed, but the fact of privilege has not.

On the basis of normal American usage and understanding one can distinguish four major classes within the USSR: (1) officials, state employees, and intellectuals; (2) workers; (3) peasants; and (4) slave labor. These may be subdivided in a variety of ways. The number one group, for example, is topped by the Party leaders who hold the key jobs. Below them come army officers, scientists, engineers, technicians, authors, and artists. The bottom of this rank, or the top of the worker rank—whichever way you choose to put it—is made up of Stakhanovites, workers who have established production records in different occupations. The distinctions between these classes are apparent in housing, clothing, food, as well as in the quantity and quality of personal possessions, and in priorities on such things as theater tickets, airplane travel, and so on. The Soviets explain this on the grounds that "socialism" does not mean equality and, furthermore, that those who are of the most use and value to the state should have the highest rewards and greatest consideration.

Whether or not this explanation is sound and right is

beside the point. Americans, however, are startled to find that in "a socialist state of workers and peasants" the ordinary worker lives amid squalor and hardships while factory managers and Party luminaries enjoy comfortable apartments, country places, and even yachts.

It is a perfectly normal thing to want to compare Soviet living standards with our own, but attempts to do so are never wholly satisfactory. Wages and prices change in the Soviet Union as they do elsewhere, and since the ruble is not exchangeable on an international market it is difficult to arrive at accurate equivalents. The following table was approximately correct for March, 1950. Prices are given in American dollars at the rate of $1.00 to 4 rubles.

Commodity	Price and Unit
Black bread	25¢ a lb.
Milk	$1.00 a qt.
Ham	$5.60 a lb.
Toilet soap	70¢ a cake
Women's shoes	$63-$134 a pr.
Men's shoes	$50-$117 a pr.

Perhaps the most meaningful comparisons are those which show the hours of labor (computed on the basis of average wages) required to earn the purchase price of various commodities. On this basis, as of January, 1950, the Soviet worker had to work longer to earn food money than did any other European worker, and far longer than American workers. The next table shows the comparison between the United States and the Soviet Union as of January, 1950.

Commodity	Hours of Labor Required to Earn	
	USA	USSR
Toilet soap (bar)	4 mins.	1½ hrs.
Wheat bread (1 lb.)	6 mins.	25 mins.
Butter (1 lb.)	32 mins.	9 hrs., 2 mins.
Tea (1 lb.)	56 mins.	25 hrs., 6 mins.
Woman's woolen dress	12 hrs., 18 mins.	162 hrs.
Man's woolen suit	31 hrs., 35 mins.	425-502 hrs.

This is startling, but it should be kept in mind that even these figures show an improvement in the Soviet living standard since 1945. Between 1945 and 1950 there were wage increases and price cuts. The deepest price cuts, with one or two exceptions, were on luxury goods; the lightest, on foodstuffs. Real wages increased during this period, but wages did not generally increase as fast as the cost of living. The general Soviet living standard had not regained the 1940 level by 1950.

Comparisons may help place the Soviet scene in relation to ours, but they do not contribute much to an understanding of Soviet attitudes. Their relevance is only on the question of the effectiveness of the two systems in establishing and improving the common good. It has little meaning on any other score. The Russian people have never had the same level of living standards as Americans. There would be no reason to point out the current disparities were it not for the Communist insistence that they have not only the best but the only way to a better world. A more meaningful comparison in terms of Soviet attitudes would be to measure their present against their past. Unfortunately there is no satisfactory way of doing this with any precision.

It is the impression of some observers who knew the old Russia very well and who have visited the Soviet Union that the people are materially better off than they used to be. Others do not agree. There is not enough specific evidence, one way or the other, to warrant a dogmatic conclusion. I do not know at first hand either the old Russia or the new. It is my impression, based upon a study of literally hundreds of reports by persons of all shades of political and social views, that the average Soviet citizen under forty believes that he is better off than his parents were, particularly in the matter of opportunity. This is partly because his early memories are of the desperately hard first years. It is partly because he has never had much chance, if any, to make comparisons either with the rest of the world or with the old regime. From the time

that he was a child he has been told by his government
that thanks to the Communist party and the leadership of
Lenin and Stalin he is better off than his parents had been
and better off than workers in other lands.

He was told in the first grade, for example, that "All
children in America do not get hot lunches. All children
in England do not get hot lunches. Only the children in
the Soviet Union get hot lunches in school every day."
Later, in his elementary school career he was told: "The
working people of the USSR are becoming more prosperous all the time, and their life is becoming better and
happier. In the past our country was a backward country;
now it has become the most advanced and mighty country in the world." In his adulthood he reads in his press
that, although certain individuals in America made a great
deal of money in the war, the American worker faces only
disaster and knows only economic insecurity. And he reads
such items as were quoted at the beginning of this chapter.
Perhaps he is being fooled and victimized. Perhaps he is
fooling himself. Perhaps not. That is not the point. The
point is that he appears to believe that the Communist
government has served and is serving the interests of the
Soviet peoples.

There is no evidence to prove, for example, that the
Soviet worker is dissatisfied with the type of labor union
which is provided for him by the Communist party. He
may be dissatisfied with the way some union leaders and
officials are discharging their duties, and, if he is, he will
speak out frankly and publicly about it. He may not criticize the system, but he may and does criticize the operation of the system. What is more, his protests are likely
to have an effect. The union system differs so much from
ours that many an American union man would have
trouble in recognizing a Soviet union.

Soviet unions are set up on an industry and not on a
craft basis. Each factory has its own union. Everyone connected with the factory, from floor sweepers to techni-

cians, managers, and plant directors, is eligible to belong. Most of them do. Membership is not compulsory, but since members get preferential treatment (double sick benefits, for example) most workers and managers do join. Soviet trade unionists claim that from 85 to 90 percent of all Soviet workers are trade-union members. This is a considerably inflated figure because it does not include forced labor, which has no union. Union dues are fixed by law at 1 percent of earnings.

Soviet trade unions are organs and instruments of the government. As the Communist party directive puts it, unions are "to cooperate in every way in the work of industrialization according to the Five-Year Plans." Their job, in other words, is to increase production. They encourage the piecework system and have some voice (but not the final say) in setting the norms. Wages and hours are set by national legislation in accordance with the will of the Politburo. The unions have no effective control over this, and are not supposed to on the ground that in the USSR it is "all for one" and not employer (exploiter) vs. employee (exploited). The unions organize "efficiency courses," vigorously promote "socialist competition and emulation," and take such other actions as they think effective in increasing labor productivity. They administer social insurance and dole out the benefit payments under it. They operate rest homes, summer camps, nurseries, kindergartens, cafeterias, and stores. They promote education and arrange lecture series. They are supposed to provide housing, and they allocate land for workers' gardens. They also take a very active part in political campaigns, nominating candidates and campaigning for them. It is hardly necessary to add that every union is dominated by its Communist party members.

This domination is also true of another very important Soviet institution, the collective farms (kolkhoz, kolkhozi). Most of the arable land in the Soviet Union is leased by the state to collective farms, and most farmers are members of collectives. There is no precise data available except that, as of January 1, 1947, there were some 222,000 large collective farms. Collectivization was one of the objectives of the First Five-Year Plan, but it was not accomplished at that time. Stalin made it the primary objective of the Second Plan, and it was truly the heart of the whole program. It was also a terrific gamble for the highest stakes. Upon the success of the collectivization drive depended the continuance of the Stalinist regime. The peasants were the majority. Stalin saw clearly that not to socialize the majority was to lose all. He could not build a "socialist state" if the largest part of his subjects were not in "socialized organizations." Lenin had tried to accomplish this and had failed because of peasant resistance. The First Plan had also failed. By 1932 (the Second Plan) it was a case of now or never.

Peasant opposition was extremely strong, but it was also wholly disorganized. It is a Communist legend that only the rich peasants opposed collectivization, but it is probably true that they spearheaded the opposition. It is not true that they alone fought against it. It is an anti-Communist legend that the greatest famine of Russian history and one of the greatest in the world resulted directly from this forcible collectivization. Sir John Maynard, whose integrity and technical competence were beyond question, denies this. There was no doubt, however, that collectivization was brutally enforced. The glib phrase that "the kulaks (rich peasants) were liquidated as a class" does not adequately convey the real meaning of the event. There were by Soviet count over five million kulaks. Liquidation meant that most of them were deprived of home, family, possessions, and freedom. Probably the majority were sent into forced labor, which was the equivalent of a sentence to lingering death. By such measures, followed by some compromises, Stalin won his gamble, collectivized agriculture, and secured his regime.

Official actions by the Communist government since

the war prove that many collective farmers tried to escape from some aspects at least of collectivization during the war. The Collective Code of 1935 gave farm members the right to individual use of small allotments of land. Many collective farmers illegally increased their holdings under the confusion and needs of the war. Other postwar decrees show that over half a million persons managed to share in the income of the collectives (which is supposed to be apportioned on the basis of work done) without earning the right to share. Local government and Party officials were also guilty of stealing food, livestock, and money from the collectives. The Fourth Five-Year Plan demanded tremendous increases in agricultural production, and various steps ranging from concessions to drastic compulsions were applied to achieve it. The general technique was to strengthen both the collective-farm system and also the Party's control over it. But reports which continued to appear in the Soviet press five years after the war indicated that the government was still finding it necessary to crack down on the peasants. An example of such a report was an article in the *Moscow Bolshevik* (Jan. 6, 1950) entitled, "Put a Stop to State Farmland Thefts." The article charged that, in spite of all orders and efforts by the Party and the government, collective farm lands were still being taken by the peasants for their own private use. Specific instances of this and other abuses were reported. The newspaper *Ukrainy Pravda* announced early in 1950 that poor labor discipline and frequent violations of the rules governing collective farms had resulted in poor yields on many Ukrainian farms in 1949. The government claimed, however, that the 1949 agricultural production topped that of 1940 and almost reached the goal set for 1950. There is sufficient evidence to suggest that agriculture was still a weak spot in Soviet economy.

Two further comparisons will help to clarify the general picture of Soviet industrial and agricultural production in the postwar period. The first compares the *actual produc-*

tion of certain items in the United States in 1947 with the Soviet production goal for 1965:

Item	U.S. Production, 1947	Soviet Goal, 1965
Coal	Over 613,000,000 tons	500,000,000 tons
Steel	About 77,000,000 tons	60,000,000 tons

The second compares the actual British consumption of certain foodstuffs in 1948 with the amounts of those foodstuffs which the Soviets hoped (in 1949) to produce in 1950. When it is recalled that there are four times as many people in the USSR as there are in the United Kingdom, that 1948 was an "austerity" year for the British, and that the figures for Britain stand for facts while those for the USSR are only imaginative, the figures become more meaningful:

Item	1948 British Consumption	1950 Soviet Production Goals
Foodstuffs	1,900,000 tons	1,300,000 tons
Sugar	2,080,000 tons	2,400,000 tons
Butter	260,000 tons	275,000 tons

The existence of any weaknesses, actual or comparative, in the Soviet system belies their proud boasts. This is in no way to deny that they have made very considerable advances in very many fields. They have remarkable accomplishments to their credit, and it is not intended to take away anything from them which is their proper due. But on the basis of their own records, the Soviets have not achieved what they claim for themselves and their system. Professor Harry Schwartz in his brief but authoritative study of recent Soviet economy summed up his findings in these words:

The history of the Soviet economy, however, casts grave doubt upon the far from modest boasts of Russian publicists. The Soviet Union has had many crises in its three decades of existence, crises born of poor planning, of resistance by great numbers of its people to the regime's overambitious programs, and of the blows inflicted by external and internal forces.

To emerge from its internal crises, the Soviet government has either had to retreat from its original program, as during the time of the New Economic Policy, or suffer tremendous capital and income losses in order to achieve its goals, as was the case with agriculture during the period of collectivization. The USSR does not suffer from mass unemployment, but its people and its economy have suffered grievously from the loss and waste of its inefficient planning system, and the abrupt changes in plans necessitated by internal or external political and economic considerations. One may perhaps even say that the USSR has been in a perpetual crisis since its birth, a crisis whose chief manifestation has been the continued low standard of living of the population despite maximum utilization of all human resources.[3]

The evaluation which one makes upon the matter of civil liberties within the Soviet Union seems to depend more upon one's attitudes and prejudices than upon one's information. The Very Reverend Hewlett Johnson, Dean of Canterbury, who was quoted at the beginning of this chapter, says flatly that Soviet planning is not at all inconsistent with liberty. The Dean is very well informed about conditions in the Soviet Union. He is also a stanch friend of the existing regime. Mr. David Dallin is also a close and careful student of Soviet affairs, and it would be his opinion that civil liberties are nonexistent in the USSR. Mr. Dallin is a distinguished enemy of the existing regime. Let us compare some of the situations in the USSR with situations in the USA.

According to the constitutions of both countries, suffrage is the right of every normal adult. Critics of America are quick to point out that most of our thirteen million Negro citizens are debarred from suffrage. The USSR has virtually no Negroes, but the number of its slave workers (who are adults) is probably greater than our total Negro population, and slave workers do not vote. Those Americans who can vote may vote for candidates chosen by the

---

[3] H. Schwartz: *Russia's Postwar Economy*, Syracuse, 1947, pp. 113-114.

Republican, or the Democratic, or the Socialist, or, in many states, the Communist parties. They can vote a straight ticket or a split ticket. Those who can vote in the USSR may vote only for candidates endorsed by the CPSU(B). There are no split tickets.

An American may not advocate the overthrow of our form of government by revolution or violence, but he may advocate its change by peaceful, legal means. A Soviet citizen cannot advocate any change in his form of government. An American may criticize his President in speech or in print, subject only to such uncertain restraints as may be imposed by fear of libel suits. It is impossible to imagine Mr. David Zaslavsky, a Soviet columnist whose venom is equal to that of Mr. Westbrook Pegler, writing about Stalin as Pegler habitually writes about Truman.

If an American does not like the way in which his local newspaper prints the news, he is at liberty to read another. If he objects to the line of the Chicago *Tribune*, he is free to read the line of the *Daily Worker*. If he dislikes *Harper's*, he may read *Political Affairs*. If the Soviet citizen is not satisfied with the news presentation of *Pravda*, he is at liberty not to read any paper. It will do him little good to shift to *Izvestia* or to any other paper because the news is slanted and interpreted the same way in all of them. Similarly, an American's choice of radio programs is limited only by the capacity of his receiver. All radio broadcasts in the USSR are controlled by the state, which is to say by the CPSU(B). There is no channel of information, communication, or entertainment in the Soviet Union which is not official and is not completely controlled by the Communist party.

An American may send his children to a public school or to a private school. There is no legal bar to his changing jobs and/or residence at will. The Soviet citizen enjoys neither of these freedoms. The list might be extended further, but this should be enough to show that the citizens of the USSR do not have the personal and civil liberties to which we are accustomed. The customary rejoinders of Soviet spokesmen are that such liberties are meaningless without economic security, and "What about discrimination against minorities?" The student is now in a position to judge whether or not Soviet socialist planned economy has given security to the Soviet people. The question of minorities may be examined only briefly within the limits of this chapter.

The minority policy (or what is generally understood to be the minority policy) of the Communist regime has inspired almost universal praise even among those who are highly critical of other aspects of the regime. There can be no doubt of the tremendous publicity value of the story. There may, however, legitimately be questions about some major parts of it. The cold-blooded examination of a topic which by its nature is supercharged with emotionalism is not easy. But it is a necessary part of any search for facts.

The Communist ideal concerning the proper treatment of certain minorities is very high, but it is no finer than the Judeo-Christian ideal of the brotherhood of man—and not as inclusive. The absence of a color line in the USSR contrasts very favorably with Jim Crowism in this country. But there was no Jim Crowism in czarist Russia and its absence in the USSR is not due to the Communists. The various national minorities in the Soviet Union —such as the Armenians, the Kazaks, the Georgians, and others—are not only permitted but encouraged to maintain their own languages, folk songs, native costumes, and literatures. But they are also required to learn the Great Russian language as well as their own, and they are reminded with increasing sharpness and frequency that the Great Russians are "the outstanding people of the Soviet fraternity of nations."

The emphasis which the Communist rulers of the USSR put upon the leadership of the Great Russians may be illustrated by quoting the relevant passages from the speech which Lavrenty Beria delivered on Stalin's birthday in 1949.

The Russian people are the most outstanding in the fraternal family of equal peoples in the USSR. . . . The Russian working class bore the principal burden in the struggle for the triumph of the Great October Socialist Revolution. . . . In the struggle for the triumph of socialist construction, the Russian people were the foreguard of the peoples of the USSR, the detachment which set the standard for all other peoples. . . . During the years of the Great Patriotic War, the Russian people . . . merited their general recognition as the leaders of the Soviet Union among all the other peoples of our country. Comrade Stalin particularly noted that "the confidence of the Russian people in the Soviet government was the deciding force which ensured the historic victory over fascism." . . .[4]

Included in the list of groups to be sent to slave-labor camps were prominent Zionists and important members of Jewish organizations. The inclusion of the Zionists is neither new nor surprising since Zionism has been illegal in the Soviet Union for a generation. But anti-Zionism was expanded in 1949 into an official anti-Semitism, which was new. Some of the reports have been exaggerated and a few have been fabricated. But enough sound evidence has been piled up to prove the existence of an official policy which worked great hardships upon Jewish individuals and groups. It is not clear, however, that this policy was simply and exclusively anti-Jewish. There is good reason to think that the policy was of larger scope and was aimed at the removal of all persons and groups who might be even remotely suspected of having loyalties other than those demanded by the Party. This would be in line with their established actions.

None of the various national groups have been allowed to continue their native cultures, using the word "culture" in the broad sense of a stage and characteristics of a civilization. The Kirghiz people of Asia, for example, had a nomadic culture which was centuries old. The Soviet

---

[4] The speech was reported in *Pravda* for December 21, 1949. Beria, who is a member of the Politburo and head of the secret police apparatus, is a Georgian. So is Stalin.

regime forced them to settle down to industry or to collectivized agriculture. This was not discrimination against them because they were Kirghiz or because they were not Great Russian, however. All people in the USSR, without any exceptions whatever, are compelled to take their appointed place in the political, social, and economic system established and maintained by the dominant Communist minority. The Communists are both more insistent upon this and more effective in implementing their insistence than were the czars about their policy of Russification.

It must be realized that groups set apart by "race," or nationality, or religion are by no means the only minorities in our society. Under our system, though he may suffer certain disabilities for so doing, a man may belong to any one of several nonracial, nonnational, nonreligious minorities. He may be a member of an esoteric political party. He may be part of an economic minority (management, for example—or an Alaskan prospector). He may belong to a social minority such as the pacifists. The list is long and it includes those who are irreconcilably in opposition to the ways and aims of most of us. Such opposition minority groups literally are not allowed to exist in freedom within the borders of the USSR. The difference between discrimination as a price for nonconformity and prohibition against nonconformity is more than a matter of degree. It is a difference in kind. Under our government and system, there are discriminations which should shame us. Under the Soviet government, there are prohibitions.

CHAPTER XII

The Dictatorship of the Proletariat

SOME YEARS AGO a very large number of Americans were unable to say whether the government of the Soviet Union was a dictatorship, or a democracy, or a monarchy, or a republic, or something else. This is attributable partly to sheer ignorance and indifference, partly to calculated confusion created by propaganda and counterpropaganda, partly to the great dissimilarities between the Soviet way and ours, and partly to the fact that it is not easy to describe the Soviet government. Article 16 of the Soviet Constitution, for example, describes the government both as a "federation" and as a "confederacy." Technically the two are quite different and yet the supreme law of the USSR uses them as synonyms. The layman has a right to be confused.

Another difficulty is that the administrative structure and the governmental forms of the USSR have been in a constant state of flux. The present constitution has been in force only since 1936. It had two predecessors, so that there have been three separate constitutions within a single generation. Each of these three, moreover, has been frequently and sometimes extensively amended. Any description therefore runs the risk of becoming outdated and inaccurate.

The Union of Soviet Socialist Republics, as currently constituted, consists of sixteen Union (or Member) Republics. Theoretically these sixteen are all equal, but practically the Russian Socialist Federative Soviet Republic is dominant, mostly for the very simple and obvious reason that it contains two-thirds of all the people and three-fourths of all the land of the USSR. Any Union Republic, at least in theory, is free to secede. Practically, secession is impossible both because of the legal requirement that all Republics must consent to the secession of one and because of the dominance of the USSR.

The federal constitution (known either as "The Stalin Constitution" or as "The 1936 Constitution") grants certain specified rights, powers, and privileges to the Union Republics. Control over all taxes, all revenue, and all economic planning at every level is held, however, by the federal authorities. This obviously makes the USSR a highly centralized state since these things are multifarious and fundamental. On the other hand, as noted in the last chapter, emphasis is placed on the guaranty and development of the cultural autonomy and nationality rights of the Union Republics and their subdivisions. Thus each group may use its own language both privately and officially and is encouraged to develop its own literature, music, and arts. Moreover, each Union Republic, by a constitutional amendment made in 1946, may have its own Ministry of Foreign Affairs and its own distinct military detachments. On the other hand, every Soviet school child must learn Great Russian in addition to his native language, and the recognition of the past and present leadership of the Great Russians, in peace and war, has been increasingly insisted upon during the past few years. Only the federal government, i.e., the USSR, can make and ratify treaties with foreign states, and control of the armed forces still rests with the All-Union (federal) Ministry.

The diagram below is to illustrate the formal, legally established machinery of government at the federal level. This machinery is operated and used, so that it requires some attention, but no amount of study of it will answer the question, Who rules the Soviet Union? It will, however, help to answer the corollary question of how the ruling is done.

The diagram centers on the Supreme Soviet because by constitutional definition this is the highest legislative organ of the USSR and has the unlimited right of control over state administrative bodies. It elects or appoints: the Council of Ministers, the Presidium, the Supreme and Special Courts, and the Attorney General. The actual facts of power and control are somewhat different from the constitutional definition, but before that is discussed let us take a closer look at this Supreme Soviet.

As the diagram shows, there are two chambers. These are coequal. Either may initiate legislation and both must consent to it. The Union Soviet is charged with taking the federal view of all matters, that is, with looking at them in terms of how they affect the whole USSR. This chamber is chosen on the basis of one member to every 300,000 people. The Soviet of Nationalities is given the specific job of looking at matters from the points of view of the national groups within the Union. You will see from the top half of the diagram that each of the sixteen Union Republics elects twenty-five members to this chamber. Each Autonomous Republic, which is a subdivision found in some Union Republics, elects eleven; each Autonomous Region, five; and each small national minority, one. This makes for a very large body. The First Supreme Soviet, elected in 1937, had 569 deputies in the Union Soviet and 574 in the Soviet of Nationalities—a total of 1143. The Second Supreme Soviet, whose election was delayed until 1946 because of the war, had a total of 1339 deputies— 682 in the Union Soviet and 657 in the Soviet of Nationalities. The Third Supreme Soviet was elected in March, 1950. The total membership was 1317, with 679 in the Union Soviet and 638 in the other chamber.

The term of election and, therefore, the life of a Soviet is four years. Two regular sessions are held each year. The length of the session varies slightly, but from four to six

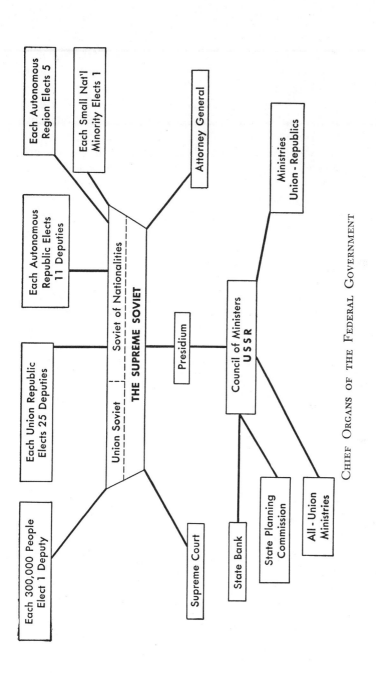

CHIEF ORGANS OF THE FEDERAL GOVERNMENT

days is usual. The first session in 1948, to take a specific example, opened on January 30 and adjourned on February 4. Three days were devoted to a "debate" on the federal budget. During the remaining three days the Soviets approved all interim edicts issued by the Presidium since the preceding session; approved the dismissal of several important ministers and the appointment of their replacements. Considering the magnitude and complexity of these problems, as well as the size of this legislature, it is apparent that its function is more to ratify than to discuss, more to give the prestige of its support to measures already decided upon than to decide those measures.

This generalization is borne out by the following specific details concerning the "debate" on the budget. According to Soviet press reports, forty-seven of the 1339 members spoke on the subject. Only nineteen of these speeches were regarded as sufficiently important to be reported in the papers. Five of the nineteen speeches were made by federal ministers and only fourteen by nonadministrative members. Six of the nineteen speeches offered specific criticisms of certain ministries. Four asked for larger budget allotments to the particular areas which the speakers represented, and nine simply gave full endorsement to the budget as presented. There were no adverse criticisms. At the conclusion of the "debate" the Finance Minister promised to consider all the suggestions which had been made, and the budget as originally presented was then unanimously adopted by both houses. This is the usual procedure.

Something needs to be said about the manner of choice of the members of the Soviets. Candidates for the office are openly nominated by specified kinds of groups, including: Communist party organizations, youth, cultural, and workers' groups. In the words of an official Soviet description of this process, each group seeks to choose a candidate who will be equally acceptable to the Party and to non-Party people. No candidate who was opposed by the Party has ever been chosen, and more than three-quarters of the deputies in the first two Supreme Soviets were Party members. (The figures were 76 percent in the First, 81 percent in the Second.) After the candidates are thus designated, elections are held on the basis of universal adult suffrage. Voting is by secret ballot. The most strenuous efforts are made to see that everyone entitled to vote does so. The results must be highly gratifying to the rulers. In the first election (1937), 96 percent of all those qualified to vote did so. The figures for the 1946 and 1950 elections were, respectively, 99.7 percent and 99.8 percent. Ninety-nine and two-tenths percent of all votes cast in 1946, and 99.73 percent of all votes cast in 1950 went to the official candidates. Of course this may be partially explained by the fact that no other candidates are permitted.

When the Supreme Soviet is not in session—which normally means about fifty weeks out of every year—the Presidium has full authority to issue and interpret laws, to ratify treaties with foreign states, and to appoint and dismiss ministers. It also has the power both to convene and to dissolve the Supreme Soviet, and it controls elections to that body. In other words, the impression originally given by the statement (which is legally correct) that the Supreme Soviet elects the Presidium needs to be somewhat revised. The student can decide for himself which body has the greater power and importance. It should be added for future reference that the Presidium, the Council of Ministers, the Supreme Court, the State Planning Commission, and the Attorney General are all composed exclusively of Communist party members.

It would lead to many technicalities and details to extend this account of the formal machinery to the lower, nonfederal levels. But unless a brief mention is made of one important aspect, the reader's understanding may be marred by an unwarranted impression. This involves the matter of mass participation in elections. There were 101,717,686 electors in 1946; 111,116,373 in March, 1950. These people (or virtually all of them) voted both for a representative to the Union Soviet and for representatives

to the Soviet of Nationalities. (There are two ballots—
one for each chamber.) This was the federal election. In
addition there are six levels of nonfederal soviets ranging
from Union Republic to village. At the time of the local
elections in 1947-48, these totaled over 66,000, to which
were elected about 1,400,000 members. Here is a very real
instance of popular participation in at least the forms of
government. It should be noted that, unlike the Supreme
Soviet, the lower soviets frequently make decisions, subject, of course, to overriding from above. Moreover, the
smaller, local soviets meet frequently. Those in cities and
villages meet once a month; area and district soviets, every
other month; and territorial and regional soviets, every
third month.

What are the functions of the soviets? It has already
been indicated that they range from ratification to some
decision making. To put it more sweepingly, the soviets
serve at least three purposes: First, they give the Soviet
citizen a sense (certainly not entirely unjustified) of being
part of the state system. It is important to know this when
one tries to judge the feeling of most Soviet citizens toward
their government. Second, they serve as a complex series
of ubiquitous gauges of the public mind. Third, and in
some ways most important, the Soviets are the bone, flesh,
and muscle which enclose, protect, obey, and give physical
force to the brain and nerve nets of the body politic. For
make no mistake about it, we have not yet reached the answer to the question of who governs the Soviet Union, although we have begun to answer the question of how it is
done. So far we have described what has been well-called
the government-in-law. Now we must turn to the government-in-fact: the Communist Party of the Soviet Union
(Bolshevik). The matter may be stated boldly at the outset in the words of Stalin himself:

Here in the Soviet Union, in the land of the dictatorship
of the proletariat, the fact that not a single important political
or organizational question is decided by our Soviet and other
mass organizations without directions from the Party must

be regarded as the highest expression of the leading role of the Party.

Our country is the country of the dictatorship of the proletariat, and the dictatorship is headed by a single party, the Communist Party, which does not and cannot share power with other parties. . . .

These frank pronouncements should make it entirely clear that the Communist party is not properly comparable to a parliamentary political party. No leader of the British Labour party or of the American Democratic party, to choose as examples the two which are in office in their respective countries at this time, could honestly or properly say what Stalin said about his party. We must learn a new and alien concept if we would understand the nature of the Communist Party of the Soviet Union (Bolshevik) or of any other Communist party.

One basic characteristic was established by Lenin after an extended and bitter intra-Party fight. Lenin wanted the Party to be a small band of trained, disciplined, professional revolutionaries under highly centralized and rigidly ordered control. His plan to achieve this was originally voted down by the small group of revolutionaries who met in 1903 to organize the Party. Later, however, Lenin got control of a part of the movement and was able to introduce his way. The Party today is, of course, tremendously larger than it was when Lenin first took it over, but it is not yet a mass party. The official figures released in June, 1949, gave the Party membership as 6,100,000. Soviet press releases in April, 1950, seemed to indicate that the membership had increased to about seven million. This is the largest it has ever been, and amounts to 3 percent of the total population, 6 percent of the voting population. The latter figure is the more realistic because it excludes minors.

These percentages, though reasonably accurate, may give a false impression about the relation of the Party to the masses. In addition to the seven million Party members, it was reported at the Eleventh Congress of the

Young Communist League in March, 1949, that the League numbered over nine million members. The Y.C.L. (Komsomol) is officially described as a "non-Party organization," but at the same time it is also officially designated as the Party's assistant and reserve. At any rate, this youth organization (its age range is from fifteen to twenty-six) is completely controlled by the Party. The Y.C.L. in its turn controls the "Children's Communist Organization of Young Pioneers of the Name of Comrade Lenin" and the "Little Octobrists." The Pioneers, of whom there were more than thirteen million in 1949, cover the age groups from ten to sixteen years. The Little Octobrists (age range: eight to eleven years) numbered about sixteen million. These three groups greatly increase the number of contacts between the Party and the people. The Party and these ancillaries have a total membership of over 45,000,000, or better than 20 percent of the total population of the country. This is significant in terms of the relationship of the rulers to the ruled and vice versa. The adult Party, however, remains a self-chosen elite.

Membership in this body, in accord with Lenin's dicta, is not a right open to any adult citizen but a privilege conferred by the Party (and withdrawable by the Party). The rules governing admission and membership have been so frequently revised that they cannot be described adequately in brief compass. In general, the process has worked something like this: Applicants for membership must be sponsored by a certain number of members in good standing. The local group, to whom the application is made, then makes a very careful and detailed investigation of the applicant's record, his character, his daily life and work, his abilities, his qualities of leadership, and his associates. If he passes this screening, and if no contrary orders come from above, the applicant is then admitted as a candidate. This is the probationary stage, which lasts for a considerable time. The candidate (and, remember, he is not yet a member) is tried and tested and watched. If he

ives and works and acts to the satisfaction of the Party he
s then admitted to full membership.

What has he got into? And what are the demands which
iis new position makes upon him? He has joined what the
italin Constitution calls "the leading nucleus of all or-
anizations." In the words of the "Rules of the Commu-
iist Party of the Soviet Union (Bolshevik)," adopted in
939 and still in force when this was written, he has be-
ome a member of ". . . the organized vanguard of the
vorking class of the USSR, the highest form of its class
irganization . . . [which] exercises the leadership . . . of
he entire Soviet people . . . [and] . . . is the guiding
iucleus of all organizations . . . both public and state. . . ."
This is obviously a position of prestige, influence, and
)ower. It is also a place of obligation. As the 1939 rules
)ut it:

The Party is a united, militant organization bound together
)y a conscious discipline which is equally binding on all its
members. It is strong because of its solidarity, unity of will
ind unity of action, which are incompatible with any devia-
:ion from its program and rules, or with any violation of Party
discipline, or with fractional groupings [i.e., the formation of
:liques within the Party] or with double dealing. The Party
)urges its ranks of persons who violate its program, rules or
discipline. The Party demands from its members active and
self-sacrificing work in carrying out its program and rules, in
fulfilling all decisions of the Party and its bodies, and in
ensuring the unity of its ranks and the consolidation of fraternal international relations among the working people of
the nationalities of the USSR as well as with the proletarians
of all countries of the world. A Party member is one who
accepts the program of the Party, works in one of its organizations, submits to its decisions, and pays membership dues.
On all questions he must be guided strictly and unswervingly
by the decisions of the leading Party organs.

The diagram on page 238 shows the schematic relation of the Party organs, as the rules call them, to each

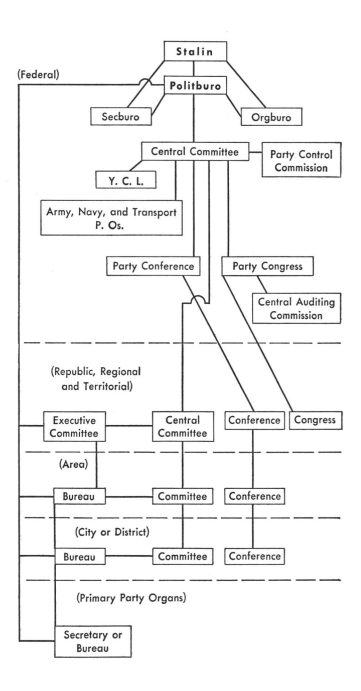

other and to the membership. The upper half of the diagram deals with the organization at the federal level, i.e., for the whole of the USSR. Then, in descending order, come: the Union Republic and other regional levels, the area, the city or district, and, finally, the local party units which used to be called cells but are now known as Primary Party Organs. The comparison is not exact so it must not be taken literally but it may help in understanding to cast this in terms of American political divisions. The federal level would be on a national scale—the United States of America. Next below would come the regional units such as the Middle Atlantic states or New England. (We have nothing which is comparable to the Union Republics.) The area would be a state or a portion thereof if the area were very populous. Thus, there might be a New York State area and a New York City or metropolitan area. The district could be either a portion of a large city or a division like a county which would include several towns.

There were reputed to be 52,000 Primary Party Organs in 1945, a fourfold increase over 1939. Some of these were and are numerically small. (The Party rules make certain special provisions for Primary Party Organs which have less than fifteen members.) Many enterprises, particularly the collective farms, do not have such units. The situation has altered somewhat since 1939 when, out of the 243,000 collectives, only 12,000 had Primary Party Organs, but the Party still remains primarily urban. (In 1941, only 19 percent of the Party members were peasants. The figure is presumably higher now.)

Here at the lowest Party level, as at the highest, there is a contradiction between the formal rules and the facts of power. We may examine both instances briefly, beginning with the Primary Party Organs. According to the Party rules, the top authority at this level is lodged in a general meeting of all the members. This body chooses its bureau or secretary, who is accountable to it. Actually the line of power and control stems from the Politburo, passes

through the Secburo and/or Orgburo, and goes down
through the various levels as shown on the diagram.

At the highest level the theoretically supreme body is
the federal Party Congress, and it used to be so. Since
about 1925, however, the actual importance and power of
the Party Congress has declined until it is little more than
a sounding board for the infrequent announcements of
the leaders. According to the rules, there is to be a Congress at least once every three years. The record, however,
shows that there have been only three during the past
nineteen years. This will explain why the diagram places
the Congress below the Central Committee.

This Committee has undergone a change comparable to
what happened to the Congress. The Party rules still say
that the Committee "during the interval between Congresses, directs the entire work of the Party" and "of the
central Soviet and public organizations." This was once
true, but it is no longer. The Committee has increased
greatly in size, and the frequency of its meetings has de-
creased. Its chief functions now are to confirm and thus
reinforce the decisions made by its technically subordinate
"Buros," to sample the opinion of the Party's more important members, and thus to maintain more effectively the
liaison between the handful of men in actual control and
their lieutenants. The Party Conferences perform a like
function on a lower and broader level. The Conferences
are really meetings of the Party bosses of the conference
level and the one below. That is to say, the federal Party
Conference includes members of the federal Central Committee and of the Republic, regional, and territorial Central Committees. The Conference at the latter level would
be composed of representatives from the Central Committee of that level and of the area level, and so on down the
line. The regularity with which the Conferences are called
indicates that the top leaders find them a very useful way
to measure opinions (all good politicians "keep an ear to
the ground"), rally support for policies, and stiffen Party
morale.

The leading "working organs" of the Party are, to quote the Party rules again, ". . . a Political Bureau [Politburo] for political work, and Organizational Bureau [Orgburo] for the general guidance of the organizational work, a Secretariat [Secburo] for current work of an organizational-executive nature." The Secburo meets daily; the other two, several times a week. Of the three, the Politburo is the most important and we shall concentrate our attention on it. It was first formed in 1917 and permanently set up in 1919. A year later Lenin said that "the Politburo decided all questions of international and internal policy." The Party Congress in 1925 was told that "The Politburo is the highest Party organ in the country" and, in 1934, that it was "the organ of operative direction of all branches of socialist construction." These definitions still hold. The answer to "Who rules the Soviet Union?" is "The Politburo rules the Soviet Union."

As now set up, the Politburo consists of ten members and four "candidates." These are the men who actually run the Communist Party of the Soviet Union (Bolshevik) and, through it, the Soviet Union. In the terms of our earlier figure of speech, which compared the state governmental machinery to the body, the Party is the nerve net and the Politburo is the brain. It constantly receives reports (impulses sensed by the nerve endings and sent along the nerve net), sorts out and interprets the impulses, decides upon the appropriate actions, and sends the necessary orders back over the same apparatus. We shall return to a discussion of this shortly. It is important here to realize that the Politburo is not isolated from the people it rules, and that messages along the nerve net are simultaneously two-directional, reports going to the Politburo and orders coming from it.

It would obviously be important and probably interesting to know a good deal about the Politburo and the men who compose it. But this is where we run into a wall of secrecy and silence. All we know of what goes on in the Politburo is what we can infer from its published orders and directives. Its minutes are not published and the members do not publicly discuss its business except to present its decisions. As to the persons involved, only a very few are known to the world outside of the Soviet Union and some of them are not familiar even to the Soviet people. Even its most famous member, Josef Stalin, has a private life to a degree impossible for any Western politician.

The relationship of Stalin to his Politburo colleagues has been the subject of much speculation and also of differing opinions even in very high places. Is Stalin "the prisoner of the Politburo" or is he its absolute master whose slightest hint must be faithfully and fully obeyed without question? Anyone may guess, but few, if any, outside the Politburo can know.

We know that the members of the Politburo are all tried and tested "Stalin Communists" who operate under the same basic philosophy and within the same framework as Stalin himself. They are, in other words, like-minded men. They are also hard-bitten professionals who have survived a literal life-and-death struggle for power within the Party. Every one of them has demonstrated his ability as a leader in one or in several lines. Beria, for example, efficiently directs the very large, very powerful, and very complex security police. Kaganovich has demonstrated his abilities in various fields including that of running the Soviet transportation system. The point is that each man is a personage in his own right not only in terms of loyalty to Stalin but also in terms of proved administrative or executive ability. They had to be on Stalin's side to get there. Presumably they have to remain stanchly at his side to stay there. But they did not achieve their present status exclusively for that reason. It is a mistake, in short, to think of them as stooges.

It is a guess that Stalin presides over this group just as any skilled leader presides over a group with whom and through whom he must work. This means that on every major issue Stalin patiently elicits opinions, statements, and suggestions from everyone; encourages the thrashing out of the problem in full, free, and frank discussion; and then seeks to formulate and present the general consensus. There are probably some times when Stalin "lays down the law" but in the nature both of the Politburo and of human relationships it seems reasonable to assume that this rarely happens, at least on major issues. It naturally makes it easier to arrive at a consensus when the participants start from the same general place and travel in the same direction. But like-mindedness does not always mean an exact identity or uniformity of opinion. The members of the Politburo all look through the same spectacles—the Marxist-Leninist doctrine—but it does not necessarily follow that they all see things in precisely the same way. So far as we know, the Politburo is the only body in the Soviet Union where such differences may be fully discussed and thrashed out. Once the decision has been made, it is fully and absolutely binding on the members of the Politburo as well as on everybody else. Decisions of the Politburo, like policy decisions of the British cabinet, are presented to the world as unanimous. A situation such as that which developed here some years ago when a cabinet member whose primary responsibility was not foreign affairs publicly attached and belittled the foreign policies of his colleague who did bear the responsibility simply could not happen in the present political framework of the Soviet Union.

This speculation on how the Politburo operates has been presented at some length for the sake of whatever light it may throw on the often heard problem, "What happens when Stalin dies?" The only really accurate answer is that no one knows, but it is, of course, permissible to speculate. Those who assume that Stalin holds all the power in his own hands naturally anticipate a period of great confusion, marked by a struggle of each survivor to pick up all the power himself. This seems unlikely. Others, recognizing that there is an actual sharing of power now, nonetheless expect a knock-down, drag-out fight when Stalin dies or shortly thereafter. This happened after Lenin's death and it may happen again. A third possibility is that the committee procedure—that is, the sharing of power and responsibility by the group—will be firmly enough established to withstand the quarrels which will probably develop. Presumably there are current rivalries within the Politburo, and probably these will be sharpened. Some men may be forced out, but the system will probably continue.

It now remains for us to refer again, briefly, to the diagram for an explanation of the other organs there listed, and then to return to the description of how the Party controls the state and the citizens. The Young Communist League (Y.C.L.) and its relations to the adult Party have already been described and need not be repeated. The "Army, Navy, and Transport Primary Organs" is simply a special division for those whose places of residence are not fixed and who therefore do not fit into a fixed geographic scheme. The Central Auditing Commission supervises the Party's treasury and the accounts of the various Party enterprises. The Party Control Commission is the agent of the Politburo (in fact, rather than according to the letter of the law) in seeing to it that the Politburo's decisions are carried out by the various Party and state bodies. It can demand reports and information from all state officials, institutions, and agencies. It is empowered to suspend the orders and activities of officials and institutions which it is investigating. It can take other disciplinary action, including the dismissal of state officials and the abolition of state organs, agencies, and institutions. This is clearly part of the answer to "How does the Party exercise control?"

Some other parts of the answer have already been given but they may profitably be summarized here. Approximately one out of every ten persons in the Soviet Union is a member either of the Party or of the Young Communist League. The latter is under the direct control of the rulers of the former and in the Party itself seven million men and women have pledged themselves to an iron discipline

which binds them to an absolute and unswerving acceptance of all orders given by the Party leaders. One of the
standing orders is that Party members shall seek to control
every non-Party organization to which they belong. Wherever three or more Party people are gathered, they organize
a Communist group or "fraction" for the purpose of securing at least a place of influence and, preferably, of dominance. They propose their own slate of officers—either
themselves or "front men"—settle what their attitude is
to be on every problem and unanimously support this
position, and vote as a unit according to the decision of
their Party superiors.

Certain of the higher state organs such as the Presidium
of the Supreme Soviet, the federal Supreme Court, and the
Council of Ministers are entirely manned by Communists
so that control is simple. Key ministries like Foreign
Affairs, Foreign Trade, Armed Forces, and State Security
are almost if not entirely Communist in personnel. So is
the State Planning Commission, which touches almost
every aspect of Soviet life. The Supreme Soviet has always
been predominantly Communist in membership, as has
been noted. And of the approximately 1,400,000 members
of the thousands of local soviets. 36 percent (following the
1947-48 elections) were Party members and all had at least
the tacit assent if not the unqualified, explicit approval of
the Party.

To give a specific illustration: If the Politburo decides
on the basis of the information which constantly pours in
upon it that more stringent legislation is needed to control certain recalcitrant collective farmers, it so orders. The
order is conveyed to the Presidium, perhaps by Mr. Malenkov, who is a member of that body as well as of the Politburo, the Orgburo, and the Secburo. Since all his colleagues on the Presidium are Party members who have
sworn to obey such orders there is no difficulty about
getting the desired decrees issued. When the Presidium
reports this action to the Supreme Soviet, the Party people
there ratify it as a matter of course. Communists at every

level are bound to attend to the enforcement of the new law. If any fail to do so—and some do fail since not even Communists are wholly proof against such common political sins as venality and nepotism and sloth—their fellow members will register that fact with the Party's investigating and supervisory bodies and punishment will follow.

If a farmer transgresses against the law and the fact is discovered he will be picked up by the police (Party dominated), brought before a court (also Party dominated), and prosecuted by the state's attorney (who owes his place to the Party if he is not himself a member of it). It ought also to be known that if the law proves unenforceable, as some have, that fact will be reported up the chain of command from thousands of sources. The matter will be reconsidered and a new law or a revision will be started down the chain as before.

Suppose, however, that the transgressor was not just one farmer but a whole collective farm. Suppose, further, that it was one of the many collectives which has no Primary Party Organ of its own. Suppose, also, though this is quite unlikely, that there are no Party members in the collective. How is control exercised in such a case? The collective farm has to lease its heavy machinery (gang plows, reapers, tractors, etc.) from the nearest machine tractor station. The Party has seen to it that these are Communist controlled, and the need of the farm for the machinery is likely to make it amenable to the MTS. The power also might be wielded, of course, by the Communist-run local state machinery.

Now let us look at the other side again for just a minute. Cannot the people say anything critical about the Party? They certainly can, within clearly defined and understood limits; and, what is more, they constantly do. It is important to know this. It is equally important to understand what the limits are. Inefficiency, dishonesty, indifference to the public needs on the part of officials or Party people, and failures to follow established procedures may be freely discussed and criticized. In fact, the Party constantly asks for such criticism. There can, however, be no criticism of the system (which may be the actual cause of the inefficiency) or of the place held by the Party or of the Party's top leaders. Such criticism is officially classified "as a counterrevolutionary crime." Punishment is swift and drastic.

It would be entirely misleading and incorrect to leave the impression that the Politburo rules entirely by fear or by police methods. Both are assuredly very important, but they do not tell the whole story. It is necessary, first, to realize that the majority of the Soviet people probably believe that the Politburo has earned the right to rule them. This belief rests partly upon facts and partly upon the effective work of the Soviet educational system. So it is necessary to take a look at "education" in the Soviet Union. The word is enclosed in quotation marks because "education" as the Soviet rulers use it has a much broader meaning than it does with us.

"Education" under their system includes everything which can be used to mold public opinion. Practically all Soviet institutions, agencies, and groups have a recognized educational function. And this doesn't mean just the formal school system. It also means books, newspapers, magazines, pamphlets, posters, and all other printed material; radio, movies, television, ballet, opera, the theater, and all other types and forms of art; libraries, museums, displays, and even "parks of culture and rest." The Soviet educational system involves trade unions, coöperative societies, the armed forces, collective farm groups, and all Party organizations. In addition to the regular school system for the public there is a special system open only to Party members. According to *Pravda* (Jan. 6, 1950), ". . . a third of the populace is enrolled in the country's educational institutions." The other two-thirds are reached in other ways. The ubiquitousness of the Soviet system of thought control—for that is what "education" means in the USSR—may be illustrated by a series of quotations from Soviet sources. This is not what I think their system to be; it is what they themselves say it is. (The translations are somewhat abridged in order to save space. The source of each one is given in parentheses at its end. The headings and the italics are mine.)

Aims of Education. The teaching of all subjects, beginning with the socio-economic and ending with technical fields, must be aimed at forming the materialist world outlook of our students, and at the unmasking of reactionary, bourgeois theories. (*Pravda*, Feb. 11, 1949)

The Soviet higher schools are called on to train not only qualified experts and technicians, but also highly educated people—idealistic, cultured, conscious builders of communism. The task of the higher school is to arm the student not only with knowledge of special disciplines, but also with the powerful weapon of materialistic philosophy. The young Soviet specialist is a man imbued with the great ideas of the party of Lenin and Stalin, and with a deep understanding of the policy of the Bolshevik Party—which is the indispensable basis of the Soviet state. . . . "In any school, the most important thing is the ideological and political trend of the lectures," emphasized Lenin. (*Pravda*, Oct. 22, 1948)

On History. An essential condition . . . is the correct Marxist-Leninist line. . . . The chief requirement of a correct Marxist-Leninist approach to historical phenomena . . . is to approach them exclusively from the position of historical materialism—to interpret them in terms of socio-economic class conditions. . . . *Only such an approach makes it possible to avoid bourgeois objectivity* in evaluating the phenomena of the past. . . . (*Voprosy filosofii*, No. 2, 1948)

. . . Polish historians can serve their people only . . . [by recognizing] the true meaning of the changes taking place in their country; [by] understand[ing] the . . . inevitability of those changes; and *by actively support[ing] those changes in all their scientific and public activity.* [This can be done] . . . only by renouncing bourgeois ideology, rejecting reactionary methodology in historical science, and by taking the positions of historical materialism. (*Voprosy istorii*, No. 11, Nov., 1948, pp. 157-158)

On Law. The struggle for Soviet patriotism in all branches of cultural progress and in all fields of Soviet legal thought is the most important task of the Soviet science of law. *Bold and militant Soviet patriotism must become the chief criterion* for determining the quality of Soviet legal literature and must be its basic motivating force. (*Sovetskoye gosudarstvo i pravo*, No. 7, Sept., 1949)

In July, 1948, the Central Committee of the Communist party decreed that Marxist materialism proved environment to be the sole determinant of life, and that the Mendelian-Morgan theories of genetics (which are accepted by nearly the entire scientific world) were merely a "bourgeois fraud." It was further decreed that the only possible theory which could be accepted by any Soviet scientist was the Lysenko-Michurin doctrine of acquired characteristics. This doctrine has been rejected as ill founded and unproved by most scientists. Even Soviet scientists had refused to accept the Lysenko-Michurin doctrine before the Party issued this order. Professor Anton Zhebrak, the internationally famous Soviet geneticist, had stanchly opposed the Lysenko-Michurin doctrine as being unsound. But within a month after the Party's order, Professor Zhebrak recanted his fifteen years of opposition on the ground that "I, as a Party member, do not consider it possible for me to continue to hold views which have been declared erroneous by the Central Committee of our Party." (*Pravda*, Aug., 1948)

Soviet Academician Speransky declared in February, 1950, that "bourgeois science is meant to defend the stability of capitalism." Soviet medicine, Speransky said, must rid itself of the influence of antirevolutionary, antimaterialistic, and idealistic positions in the field of pathology. Not even the fantasies of "science fiction" escape the attention of the Party system of thought control. An article in the January, 1950, issue of the *Literaturnaya gazeta* excoriated writers of Soviet science fiction for distorting Soviet realities by yielding to bourgeois influences. Said the article: "The roots of the authors' mistakes lie in the fact that they do not proceed from real life, from Soviet reality, but from outworn western literary cliches. *They strive to be 'entertaining' at all costs."*

Entertainment is not the purpose or the aim of literature or any of the arts under the Soviet regime. Arts, letters, music, science, law, history, and all the rest are merely vehicles for Party propaganda and indoctrination. The amount of influence and power which this complete mobilization of intellectual and artistic efforts gives to the Soviet rulers is tremendous. It is one of their most important instruments of control and government.

CHAPTER XIII

Soviet Foreign Policy from Petrograd to Yalta

THE MANY SINCERE and high-minded persons who regard all "power politics" as an unmitigated evil which ought to be abolished at once would do well to ponder the early history of Bolshevik foreign policy. When the Bolsheviks first seized the government offices in Petrograd, and for a considerable time thereafter, their politics were without power. Russian military strength was smashed. Russian naval power was inconsequential. Russian industrial power, never very great, was ruined. They had neither lands, nor resources, nor strength to offer to the opponents of Germany. They had no power to defend themselves against the Germans. The only thing in their favor was that the other nations were so involved in a life-or-death struggle that only casual and sporadic attention could be paid to Russia. They hoped, and the Western powers feared—both with some reason—that they had an ideological and propaganda weapon which would be effective among the war-weary peoples of Europe. But they had no power. They could bargain neither with their former allies nor with their former enemies. What did they do? They fought with the only weapons they had—words; and they gave up what they could not hold, with as good grace as they could muster.

The first pronouncement of their foreign policy was a strange and curious affair. It was not a treaty, nor a diplomatic note, but a law—legislated presumably for the world by a body whose power hardly extended beyond the city limits of Petrograd. It was "The Decree of the Second All-Russian Congress of Soviets of Workers', Soldiers' and Peasant Deputies" and it began:

The appeal of the workers' and peasants' government to all the belligerent nations and governments to start negotiations concerning a just, democratic peace. Such a peace the government considers to be an immediate peace without annexation (i.e., without the seizure of foreign territory or the forcible annexation of foreign nationalities) and without indemnities.
. . . The government considers that to continue this war simply to decide how to divide the weak nationalities among the powerful and rich nations which have seized them, would be the greatest crime against humanity and it solemnly announces its readiness to sign at once the terms of peace which will end this war on the indicated conditions, equally just for all nationalities without exception.

Even if the other nations had been ready to accept this strictly Marxist interpretation of the causes and issues of the war—which they were not—there was something at least superficially ludicrous in the demand of a powerless government that peace be made on its terms. The Bolsheviks did not really expect that this would happen. What they intended was to put capitalist powers apparently in the wrong and thus be able to claim that the war went on solely because the inhuman capitalists refused a peace offer. It is enlightening to note in this connection that the Bolsheviks in practice renounced only those annexations which they were unable at the moment to make. They first renounced sovereignty over Estonia, to cite only one example; then invaded it (1918); recognized its independence by a peace treaty (1920); and finally annexed that country in 1940. But that is way ahead of our story and reaches a time when Bolshevik politics-without-power had become politics-with-great-power.

The German High Command, which had essentially the same interest as the Bolsheviks in seeking to make the

Western powers appear as warmongers, replied to the appeal just quoted and expressed willingness to start peace negotiations. Their later actions proved that they were acting in perfect bad faith. The Bolsheviks may have suspected this, but it served their purpose to take the German reply at face value and to issue another appeal "to the people of the belligerent nations." This proclamation was also strictly Marxist.

The peace we have proposed must be the peoples' peace. It must be an honest agreement which shall guarantee to every people the freedom of economic and cultural development. Such a peace can be made only as a result of a direct and brave struggle of the revolutionary masses against all imperialistic plans and usurping aspirations.

This was followed within two weeks by a declaration addressed to "all the toiling Moslems of Russia and those of the East" and by an appeal "to the toiling, oppressed and bled-white people of Europe." The former opened with these words, "The reign of capitalist plunder and oppression is crumbling away. The soil is burning under the feet of the imperialistic robbers. . . ." The second contained these paragraphs:

The German, Austro-Hungarian, Bulgarian, and Turkish workers must set against the imperialistic program of their ruling classes their own revolutionary program for the agreement and collaboration between the laboring and exploited classes of all countries. . . .

The liberation of Belgium, Serbia, Rumania, Poland, Ukraine, Greece, Persia, and Armenia, can be achieved not by the victorious imperialists of one of the coalitions but by the revolutionary workers of all the belligerent and neutral countries in the victorious struggle against all the imperialists.

To this struggle we are calling you, the workers of all the lands. There is no other way. . . . The toilers of humanity will be false to themselves and their future if they continue to submit to the yoke of the imperialistic bourgeoisie.

The point of all this is that the first and major aim of Bolshevik foreign policy was the fomenting of world revolution. It is a point which is generally forgotten or deliberately ignored. All the Bolshevik leaders without exception, during the first months and years of their reign, anticipated the almost immediate coming of the world revolution and they worked hard to accelerate it. They regarded their success in Russia as only the first step to a greater triumph and, at first, they valued their Russian victory only because they thought it gave them power to go on. Their actions proved that they were quite ready to sacrifice Russian strengths and interests to promote Bolshevik successes elsewhere. Once this is realized, the policies of the Western powers vis-à-vis Bolshevik Russia seem less mysterious. The so-called Bolshevik peace declarations were actually declarations of revolutionary war against the capitalist states. It was the Marxists who first uncompromisingly defined capitalism as the enemy and not the other way around. With the Bolshevik leaders openly inciting to revolution, one can hardly attack in good faith the powers against whom the revolution was to be aimed because they treated the Bolsheviks as enemies. No capitalist nation could reasonably be expected to give aid and comfort to men who were stridently proclaiming their undying hostility to capitalism and who were giving active expression to that hostility by promoting revolutions.

Another theme frequently repeated in Bolshevik proclamations and declarations was the right of national self-determination. "Free self-determination" was "categorically" proclaimed to be the "inalienable right of the Russian nationalities." "All nations in Russia," a Communist party resolution read, "must have the right of free separation therefrom and the rights of free and independent states." Their fine words were belied by their actions. Lithuania and Finland declared their independence in 1917; Latvia, Estonia, Ukraine, Georgia, and Siberia in 1918. Did the Communist leaders let these people go with their blessing? They did not. They sent armies into all these states and did their utmost to prevent separation and self-determination. But the secession states got support from Germany and/or the Western Allies, and the Communists did not have sufficient power at that time to prevent the secessions. What they could not cure they temporarily endured. The independence of Estonia, Latvia, and Georgia was formally recognized by the Bolsheviks in 1918 and later reaffirmed. The independence of Lithuania and Finland was formally recognized in 1920; that of Ukraine and Byelorussia in 1921. In the face of this, Georgia was overrun and conquered in 1921 and its independence came to an end. Ukraine and Byelorussia were also brought under Russian sway and were incorporated in the new Union of Soviet Socialist Republics when that was established in 1922. Estonia, Latvia, and Lithuania were absorbed by the USSR in 1940; and Finland was brought within the Soviet orbit. But again we have gone from the period of powerless politics to power politics, and must return to the earlier period.

When the Bolsheviks seized control of Petrograd and Moscow, not only were several of the former subject peoples of the czarist empire eager to break away, but also there were many Russians who were far from ready to accept Bolshevik rule. Moreover, the war with Germany was still going on. There were German troops on Russian soil and there were also various agents of the Western Allies who were trying to keep the Germans from complete victory in the east. The first interventions in Russia were not anti-Bolshevik. This is a carefully cultivated myth. The interventions became anti-Bolshevik mostly because of the Bolshevik plans for world revolution, but they began as part of the First World War. The Germans intervened in Russia to further German national interests; the Western Allies, to counter the German moves. Of the two, the German intervention was a much more immediate and dangerous threat to the Bolsheviks and they turned to meet it first.

An armistice was agreed upon between the Bolsheviks and the Central Powers and peace negotiations were begun in early December, 1917. The key fact about these conversations at Brest-Litovsk was that peace at any price was imperative for the Bolsheviks. Their rule was at stake. If they had demanded that Russia try to fight on, they would have been kicked out of power. Because they were powerless to resist German demands, there could be no give-and-take. Their best hope was to use the meetings as a sounding board for their propaganda for world revolution. Peace was their number one aim; propagandizing was their number two. Their agents, especially Trotsky, made skillful use of the opportunity. The meetings were spun out for days by Trotsky's shrewdness, but time was of the essence to the German High Command, who were planning a great spring offensive, and they lost patience. Unwilling to accept the German demands, Trotsky tried to wriggle out by proclaiming to the world, "We withdraw from the war, but we are obliged to refuse to sign the peace treaty. . . . Russia . . . declares the state of war ended . . . the Russian troops are ordered to demobilize entirely along the whole front."

This may have had propaganda value, but it did not impress the Germans, who knew full well that the Bolsheviks had no regular troops to oppose them. The Germans resumed their offensive and advanced almost without hindrance. Lenin and Trotsky wired Berlin that they would sign a peace treaty; and Berlin replied with a treaty which had to be accepted within forty-eight hours, signed within seventy-two hours, and ratified within two weeks. A bitter difference of opinion appeared within the Bolshevik Central Committee. Lenin demanded that the treaty be signed and threatened his complete withdrawal if it was not. The Committee vote was seven to accept the terms; four, to reject; and four did not vote. Lenin won that gamble. He also won the larger gamble. There is abundant evidence to show that he never intended to abide by the treaty. He believed that the Western Allies would win the war and would nullify the Treaty of Brest-Litovsk. A German victory, he knew, would end the Bolshevik rule. The price he paid, at least on paper, was terrific. By the

Treaty of Brest-Litovsk, which the semiofficial German press described as a "peace of understanding and conciliation," Russia lost 34 percent of her population, 32 percent of her agricultual land, 54 percent of her industries, 89 percent of her coal mines, and 98 percent of her oil. Those who think of the Versailles Treaty as the epitome of harshness cannot have heard of Brest-Litovsk. But harsh as it was, the treaty meant salvation for Bolshevik power. Without it, Lenin and his associates must have gone down. With it, they won a respite and, thanks to the German defeat, escaped even the peace terms themselves. Seldom have political leaders so successfully eaten their cake and had it too.

The German war was formally over, but German intervention continued for some months more. It was no longer as grave a threat as were the anti-Bolshevik movements of Russians and their Western supporters. It is customary to refer to the events of November, 1917, as the "Bolshevik Revolution" and to the bitter struggle which lasted from 1918 through 1920 as the "Civil War." This is misleading. It is more accurate to think of the November events as only the beginning of a revolution whose military phases lasted three years. The Bolshevik victory was won slowly and at great cost. It was won piecemeal and not all at once, which is what the customary labeling seems to imply.

Shortly after the conclusion of the Brest-Litovsk Treaty, troops of the Western Allies appeared in Russia. British forces landed at Murmansk in March, 1918, and were later reinforced by other troops, including Americans. British and Japanese marines landed in Vladivostok a month later and were followed within the next six months by British, Japanese, French, Canadian, American, and Italian soldiers. A force of about seventy thousand Czechs became involved and joined the anti-Bolshevik armies. Rumanian troops meanwhile had occupied Bessarabia; and Germans, the Crimea. The Soviets protested these various acts and declared war on the independent Siberian government which had Allied support. More protests were

filed and late in July, 1918, Lenin declared that a state
of war existed between Soviet Russia and the Allies. Later,
British forces occupied the Caucasian oil area and the
French replaced the Germans at Odessa. Poland went to
war against Ukraine, and Rumania annexed Bessarabia
and Bukovina. Soviet peace proposals to the Allies were
ignored, and the Soviets pointedly were not invited to the
Paris Peace Conference which opened in January, 1919.

In that year, the Soviets declared themselves at war
with Rumania, and the Finns declared themselves at war
with Russia. The Polish war continued and the anti-
Bolshevik forces under Denikin won some major successes
in the south. But the Allied troops evacuated north
Russia and the French were driven from Odessa. The Poles
paid no more attention to a Soviet peace proposal than
did the Western Allies. The Allied Supreme Council, however, did remove the blockade of Russia early in 1920 and
sought to encourage trade with the Russians. They were
not willing to open diplomatic relations, however. Some
things went better for the Soviets. The Siberian forces
under Kolchak were routed. American troops left Siberia.
Rumania agreed to an armistice. But some things did not
go so well. The Poles demanded Russian lands which had
not been under Polish control for a century and a half.
Lenin and his associates offered a compromise which the
Poles refused, and the Red Army, largely created by
Trotsky, launched a successful offensive. The Poles yelled
for help and the French and British responded. The Red
Army, in its enthusiasm, overran its strength and was defeated by Polish forces, assisted by British and French
military leaders. Peace negotiations were opened, which
led in 1921 to the Treaty of Riga by which Poland acquired lands which had a majority of non-Polish residents.

This was the last great setback which the Soviets suffered, although they were excluded from the Washington
Conference (1921-22). The barriers, however, had begun
to go down. Nineteen treaties of peace or of friendship
were signed during 1921-22 between the Soviets and their

immediate neighbors. A trade pact was reached with Britain (1921), and the Soviets were invited to the International Economic Conference at Genoa. By this time, also, the Soviets had asked foreign capital to participate in Russian industrial recovery, and had embarked upon the New Economic Policy.

It ought also to be noted in passing that strenuous efforts were made even during these troubled years to promote world revolution. As much aid as possible was given to the German Communists in their revolts of 1918-19 and to the Communist revolt of Béla Kun in Hungary (1919). The Third International was founded under Russian auspices and control in March, 1919. Its openly avowed aim was the furtherance of world revolution by direct action. Communist regimes were installed under Russian sponsorship in Armenia, Azerbaijan, Georgia, and in Central Asia. The Far Eastern Republic, allegedly independent, was annexed in 1922. Two years before that, the Russian Communist leaders had sought to stir up Asiatic nationalisms by means of a revolutionary "Congress of the Peoples of the East." And by 1922, the Russian Communist party had begun active support and direction of the Chinese Communists. The Soviet government, of course, maintained that there was no connection between itself and the activities of international communism. But since the leaders of the Russian Communist party not only dominated the Soviet government but also dominated the Comintern, this was a transparent fiction which fooled only those who wished to believe it.[1]

There was, however, a difference in the bases of formal Soviet foreign policy and the Comintern's policy of world

---

[1] Those who doubt or deny the dominance of the Comintern by the Russian Communists would do well to ponder the following statement by Manuilsky, a member both of the Comintern's Executive Committee and of the Politburo: "Not a document of importance, possessing major international significance, was issued from the Communist International without the most active participation of Stalin in its formulation."

revolution. National policies depend for their success upon the power-in-being of the nation. Power-in-being includes armed forces, economic strength, attitudes of the people, and the bargaining position arising from the relative strengths of the other nations. Comintern policies call for the exploitation of existing conflicts and weaknesses and depend more on the opponents' weaknesses than upon the attacker's own strength. It is a policy of finesse rather than of force and can be carried out by a very small body of trained, disciplined, and unscrupulous professional revolutionaries, operating under leadership of the same type. The Politburo of the Russian Communist party supplied the leadership, and Communists of all nations were obedient to its orders. Soviet power-in-being in the early twenties was, in contrast, very slight. The army dropped from a high in 1921 of almost four and one-half million to a low in 1923 of just over half a million men. The national economy in 1921 had reached so dangerous a crisis that, as has been noted, Lenin found it necessary to retreat toward capitalism on some fronts in order to strengthen the Communist grip on others. This was the New Economic Policy (NEP, 1921-28). It succeeded in its purpose, but success did not come at once. The Soviet peoples, moreover, were war-weary and not war-minded. They wanted to get on with the rebuilding of their country, which had been ruined by years of war and revolution. Foreign adventures had no appeal for them. Finally, the Soviets were still very weak in relation to France, Britain, Japan, and the United States. There was, however, another nation whose power-in-being was small but whose power-in-prospect was good. That was Germany—like the Soviets, also an outcast among nations.

Both Germany and Soviet Russia were invited to the Genoa Conference of 1922. When the conference failed, the Germans and the Soviets reached an agreement of their own: the Treaty of Rapallo. Rapallo was not an alliance treaty. It dealt mainly with economic matters but it did establish a German-Soviet entente which was strengthened by another treaty in 1926. Social, economic, and military ties between the two were quite strong. A lively trade developed and many German engineers and technicians found employment in Russia. One of the most interesting by-products was the mutually profitable coöperation between the Red Army and the Reichswehr.

The Reichswehr was unable to develop and test planes, tanks, and other military equipment at home because of the limitations imposed by the Versailles Treaty. The Red Army lacked such equipment and the technicians to run it. So the Reichswehr sent men and machines and the Soviets provided a testing ground. In the late thirties, Marshal Tukhachevsky and other high-ranking Red Army officers were executed on charges of treasonous conspiracy with Germany. It seems reasonable to assume that whatever connections there were between Tukhachevsky and the Germans began after the Rapallo Treaty.

It should also be noted that even while the Soviet government was developing these ties with the Weimar Republic of Germany, the Comintern actively sought to foment a revolution in Germany in 1923. The effort failed dismally, and that failure, together with similar fiascos in Great Britain (1926) and China (1927), contributed greatly toward a marked change in tactics. The shift was probably due even more to certain changes within the USSR itself. A struggle for power within the Communist party had begun during Lenin's invalidism. After his death it became more open and more bitter. The chief contenders were Trotsky and Stalin, and the issues between them were partly contention for personal power and partly a basic disagreement over tactics. They did not differ as to ultimate goals. This struggle was reflected in the Comintern and in its Central Committee. The Fifth Comintern Congress (1924) recognized that the day of general revolution was not as close at hand as had been expected and set forth a more flexible program which made possible a long-range tactic of slow building toward "the day" rather than an inflammatory incitement to immediate and violent action. Then, for four years no Comintern Congress met. By the end of that period,

Stalin had won his battle with Trotsky, and the Sixth Comintern Congress (1928) minimized world revolution in favor of the Stalin program of protecting and strengthening the USSR. Seven years passed before the calling of the Seventh (and final) Comintern Congress. World revolution was still the ultimate goal, but it had been dropped from first tactical priority to close to the last. It was no longer an immediate hope, nor, temporarily, was it a major tactic.

Once again, the consideration of a topic has led us to outrun the course of events. Now it is necessary to turn back and pick up the thread of formal Soviet foreign policy after Rapallo. For one thing, and this was scarcely surprising in view of their lack of power-in-being, the Soviet diplomats began their sponsorship of disarmament. The Soviet delegation raised the issue at Genoa, and shortly thereafter the Soviet government proposed to Poland and the Baltic states a reduction in armaments. These proposals had no more results than their subsequent suggestions for universal disarmament. However, the newly formed Union of Soviet Socialist Republics did succeed in getting legal recognition from the European states (1924) and some non-European states—but not from the United States.

Soviet diplomatic relations measured quantitatively are almost overwhelming. It has been calculated that between 1920 and 1937 the Soviets entered into 234 bilateral and 57 multilateral international agreements of all sorts. One hundred were on such specific points as consular relations, boundary settlements and postal agreements. Forty-six were concerned with the recognition of the USSR and the establishment of diplomatic relations; thirty-one, with neutrality and nonaggression; and fifty-seven with commercial and economic matters.[2] Most of these were made

---

[2] T. A. Taracouzio, *War and Peace in Soviet Diplomacy*, New York, 1940, pp. 315-342. Quoted by M. T. Florinsky, "The Soviet Union and International Agreements," in *The Political Science Quarterly*, March, 1946, pp. 61-89.

after 1924. The Soviets also entered many international agreements after 1937, but these have not been tabulated. The economic agreements, up to 1937, were well kept. As for the political agreements, he who looks for morality in the record of international relations is bound to be sadly disillusioned. The Soviets observed those agreements when and while it served their interests to do so, and violated them when their interests seemed to require it. Such international amorality is by no means uniquely Soviet.

Soviet proposals for disarmament, as well as its adherence to such well-meant peace efforts as the Kellogg-Briand Pact outlawing war, excited the admiration and won the support of many. It has been noted that the formal Soviet efforts in this line began in 1922. They received their greatest publicity at the time of the Geneva Conference in 1927. Litvinov, the Soviet delegate, startled that conference by proposing complete, general disarmament. No action was taken then or on any of Litvinov's several subsequent reiterations of proposals for disarming. Whether or not the Soviet proposals were made in sincerity has been the subject of repeated and bitter disagreement. There is no conclusive proof on either side. The proposals were made. They were rejected. No nation disarmed because of them. Further discussion of the sincerity of the sponsoring power seems to be singularly fruitless. Much the same may be said of the Kellogg-Briand Pact. The Soviets not only adhered to it; they also put forward an extension of it (the Litvinov Protocol). They later forswore their pledge, but so did all the other signatories, including the USA.

The matter of the USSR and the League of Nations is a like case. Communist Russia was not invited to join the League at its organization, a fact which has evoked much bitter criticism in certain quarters. Since the Communist party program of 1919 (which is still in force) described the League as an "international organization of the capitalists for the systematic exploitation of all the peoples of the earth," it is a little hard to believe that any invitation would have been accepted if proffered. This attitude toward the League was formally repeated by the Soviet Foreign Office in 1923 and officially set forth again in 1926. The 1923 note described the League as a pseudo-international body designed to conceal the aggressive, imperialistic aims of certain great powers. The definition of 1926 repeated the same charges in almost the same words. It was somewhat of a surprise, therefore, when Messrs. Molotov and Litvinov spoke well of the League in December, 1933. Molotov recognized that it had "exerted a certain restraining influence upon those forces which are preparing for war"; and Litvinov conceded that "the tendencies which are interested in the preservation of peace would seem to be gaining the upper hand in the League." Had the Soviets changed? Did they believe that the League had changed? Or were they seeking to use the League for purposes of their own? The answers are much more important to attackers and defenders of the Soviets than to those who are seeking solely to find out and to record what happened. The Soviets, having consistently condemned the League, joined it and for five years their representatives gave vociferous support to projects of peace, disarmament, and "collective security." Then the Soviets attacked Finland and were promptly expelled—something that had not happened either to Japan or to Italy when they had attacked China and Ethiopia. If the Soviets gave reason to doubt their good faith, they certainly had reason to doubt the good faith of others.

Another instrument of Soviet diplomacy which aroused considerable interest and, by and large, enhanced the Soviet reputation as a "peace-loving nation" was the so-called nonaggression pact which she signed with many nations beginning in 1926. There were at least a dozen of these, most of them being renewed at least once. The signatories mutually guaranteed the inviolability of existing frontiers and pledged themselves to refrain from any attack upon the integrity or political independence of the other. The pacts were further strengthened by several formal definitions of "aggression." They proved, however, to be no bar to action when the time for action was judged ripe. The Germans in 1941 violated their nonaggression promise of 1939. The Soviets unilaterally denounced their pledge to Poland on the day the Red Army crossed the Polish frontiers. Both could and did argue with considerable force that the situations had changed since the pacts were signed.

The various mutual-assistance pacts entered into by the USSR were both supplements and complements to the nonaggression pacts. The French-Soviet treaty of 1935 was a defensive alliance of the standard type providing for consultation should either be in danger of attack and for "aid and assistance" should either actually be attacked. The agreement with Czechoslovakia was of the same form. The mutual-assistance agreement made with Outer Mongolia in 1934, on the other hand, was designed to establish Soviet mastery over that land in order to meet the rising threat of Japan. The pacts signed with Estonia, Latvia, and Lithuania after the outbreak of war in 1939 proved to be the prelude to the Soviet annexation of those nations.

Soviet relations in the Far East presented some special difficulties. Japanese troops did not evacuate Soviet soil until 1925 and, although numerous commercial agreements, especially on the fisheries, were made thereafter, serious political and military frictions developed. These will be touched on shortly. Relations with China were complicated by attempts to use the Chinese Communists for Russian ends. This policy seemed very successful in the middle twenties, but in 1927 Chiang Kai-shek expelled the Communists from his party and broke relations with the Soviets. Two years later, the Chinese took over control of the Chinese Eastern Railway in Manchuria. Soviet consuls were withdrawn from China, and Soviet troops entered Manchuria. The affair was peacefully settled, however, and then the Japanese took over Manchuria and erected there the puppet state of Manchukuo. Border clashes between Japanese and Soviet forces in Outer Mongolia became increasingly frequent and furious. Unable at the moment to resist Japanese pressures, the Soviet leaders did what they had frequently done before—namely, cut their losses. The Chinese Eastern was sold to Japan for a song (1935). The border incidents continued despite several formal Soviet protests in 1935 and 1936 until finally they reached the stage of a full-scale though undeclared border war. The Japanese were repulsed. In the process, whatever sovereignty had been left to Outer Mongolia vanished despite Chinese protests. Meanwhile some very important things had been happening in the west.

Hitler and the Nazis had come to power (1933), withdrawn from the League (1933), denounced the Versailles Treaty (1935), and reoccupied the Rhineland (1936). The United States had finally recognized the USSR (1933) and despite almost immediate and continuing disagreement on various points, especially concerning the activities of the Comintern, had entered into formal trade agreements with the Soviets (1935). Civil war began in Spain. The German and Italian Fascists promptly extended material aid, including troops, to the rebels under Franco. The Soviets just as promptly, though perforce to a somewhat lesser degree, sent materials and men to aid the Spanish government. Britain and France set up a nonintervention agreement which was ignored, except for lip service, by Fascists and Communists alike. A German-Italian pact (the Rome-Berlin Axis) was made in October, 1936, and was followed within less than a month by the Anti-Comintern Pact of Germany and Japan. Italy joined it in the following year.

Many observers at the time and later thought that the battle lines between fascism and communism had been clearly and permanently drawn in Spain. It is true that the Soviets continued to support the Spanish government against the Fascist-backed Franco and his rebels. But if the lines of conflict were clear, Stalin and his associates did not appear to think so. Soviet-German and Soviet-Japanese commercial agreements were extended. Stalin, in 1938, demanded that the working classes of all nations be organized to prevent any outside interference with the Soviet Union. Later that year, President Kalinin spoke strongly in favor of a revival of international anticapitalism. The Soviet leaders were increasingly sure that they were going to have to fight. Domestic measures taken in 1938 and thereafter give clear evidence of that, as do various official statements of the time. But it is not at all clear that the Soviets knew who the enemy would be.

A song popular in the Soviet Union at that time bore the title, "If Tomorrow Brings War." Its proudly martial words boasted that the whole land, "from Kronstadt to Vladivostok," would rise, strong and mighty, to rout the invader and that no nation in the world could conquer the USSR. And it summoned the people to be ready to fight. When this song became known in the west—usually in carefully bowdlerized translations—after 1941, the west generally assumed that the song forecast war with Germany. But this could not be deduced from the original Russian version, which did not name any specific enemy or group of enemies.

It ought to be better known, in this connection, that Soviet theoreticians then regarded (and still regard) fascism and capitalism as merely two aspects of the same thing. They describe fascism as "a manifestation of capitalism in its imperialistic phase" and say that fascism is inherent in capitalism and cannot be dissociated from it. During their war (i.e., June, 1941, to August, 1945), they drew a distinction between the capitalist democracies and the fascist aggressors. But no such distinction was made either before they were forced into the war or after the war was over. As the now discredited but then very important Communist, G. Dimitrov, put it at the Seventh Comintern Congress in 1935: "For a successful struggle against the offensive of capital, against the reactionary measures of the bourgeoisie, against fascism . . . it is im-

perative that unity of action be established between all
sections of the working class . . . even before the majority
. . . unites . . . for the overthrow of capitalism and the
victory of the proletarian revolution." This was an announcement of the tactic of the "united front." Somewhat later, "united front" was used to mean a combination
against fascism. But note that in 1935 Dimitrov, then
chairman of the Comintern, called for a workers' union
against capitalism and fascism. And two years later, in
1937, Stalin delivered his famous warning about "capitalist
encirclement"—a warning that has been repeatedly quoted
and referred to in Soviet domestic propaganda since 1945.
Said Stalin:

> Capitalist encirclement means that here is one country, the
> Soviet Union, which has established the Socialist order on its
> own territory and besides this there are many countries,
> bourgeoisie countries, which continue to carry on a capitalist
> mode of life and which surround the Soviet Union, waiting
> for an opportunity to attack it, break it, or at any rate to
> undermine its power and weaken it. . . . Is it not clear that as
> long as capitalist encirclement exists there will be wreckers,
> spies, diversionists and murderers in our country, sent behind
> our lines by the agents of foreign states?

It would be inaccurate and unfair not to point out that
the Soviets could readily find considerable evidence during the thirties to support their theory of an affinity between capitalism and fascism. There were individuals and
groups in Britain, France, the United States, and elsewhere who lauded Mussolini "for making the trains run
on time" and who said, "Hitler has the right idea about
Jews." But this was not all. Except for uttering a few
harsh words which had hurt no one, the Western democracies had done nothing to stop the Japanese rape of
China, or the rearmament of Nazi Germany, or the Italian
aggression against Ethiopia, or the annexation of Austria
to Germany. On the contrary, the democracies, wittingly
or otherwise, had often assisted the aggressors. The surrender of Czechoslovakia to Germany by the Munich

agreement did not create a new pattern. It was rather the continuation of an old design of appeasement which was begun when the Washington Conference permitted Japan to build herself up at the expense of China in the hope that the Japanese would counterbalance the Soviets.

We are still too close to Munich and its aftermath, and there is still too much that is hidden from us both by our prejudices and by actual concealment, to permit a definitive analysis. As Professor Max Beloff wrote in his excellent pioneer study of Soviet foreign policy: "The first point which must be made, and made as forcibly as possible, is that for very much of the history of Soviet foreign policy we still lack the factual information necessary before one can proceed to an analysis of motives."[3] Professor Beloff might well have included the history of the foreign policies of the other powers also because their story has not yet been fully told either although we know more of it. Fortunately, we are here concerned with the effects of the Munich settlement upon Soviet foreign policy in general rather than with a detailed description either of the Munich deal or of Soviet diplomacy. And the essence of that effect was that Munich reinforced the Soviet conviction (which really needed no reinforcement, so firmly was it fixed in their minds) that the USSR was alone in a hostile world.

Soviet isolation was by no means entirely due to Soviet desires and actions or to events which they completely controlled. Faults, mistakes, and guilt were not wholly on one side. But that is not to imply that faults and bad faith were necessarily divided evenly among the contestants. And the purpose of raising the moral issue is not to sit in judgment but only to remind ourselves to guard against the emotional assumption that either side had a monopoly of vice or virtue. This reminder is necessary because we must concentrate on the Soviet record (since that is the subject), and much of it is not pretty. We may lose per-

---

[3] M. Beloff, *The Foreign Policy of Soviet Russia*, vol. i, 1929-1936; vol. ii, 1936-1941, London, 1947 and 1949, vol. ii, p. 385.

spective if we forget that this is also true of the records of the democracies.

To repeat, the Soviets went deeper into isolation after Munich. Their championship of "collective security" (whether made in good faith or not is irrelevant for the moment) had failed. One of the several reasons for its failure was the continuation of the Comintern and of the international Communist movement. This calls for what may appear to be a digression. It is not a digression for, as Dennis Healey once put it: "There is thus no meaning in the problem which often torments non-Communists— whether the primary aim of Russian or Communist policy is the extension of Soviet power or world revolution— since no conceivable conflict between the two aims can ever arise for Communists."[4]

The Comintern, as previously noted, was formed under the auspices of Lenin and his associates in 1919. During the first five years of its existence—probably its most active period—the Comintern was largely dominated but not exclusively controlled by the Russian Communist party. During the next five years (1924-29) the Comintern became involved in the intra-Party struggles and, also, came more and more under the control of the Soviet leaders. There was little free discussion and decision at the 1928 Congress, and none at all thereafter. According to Mr. Healey, since 1929 "the Comintern has been exclusively an instrument of the Russian State" and the 1935 Congress "was called to explain and publicize a change of policy which had already been decided and even, in some cases, put into operation."[5] This Soviet-Comintern policy was by then clearly threefold. First, as Stalin had told the 1925 Congress, it was the Soviet view that "There are being created two principal but opposed poles of attraction; the Anglo-American pole for the bourgeois govern-

---

[4] D. Healey, "The Cominform and World Communism," in. *International Affairs*, July, 1948, pp. 339-359.

[5] *Ibid.*, p. 340.

ments, and the Soviet pole for the workers of the west and the revolutionary east."

The second aspect was linked with the belief that the 1929 depression forecast the final, immediate collapse of capitalism. The Communists' main efforts were centered on the removal of the non-Communist, socialist parties whom they regarded as their most dangerous rivals. It was this policy which resulted, for example, in the frequent coöperation of the German Communists with the Nazis against the German Social Democrats and trade unionists. The third part was once expressed by Dimitrov in the following passage:

"The historical dividing line between the forces of fascism, war, and capitalism, on the one hand; and the forces of peace, democracy, and socialism on the other hand, is coming to be, in fact, the attitude toward the Soviet Union—not the formal attitude toward Soviet socialism and Soviet power in general, but the attitude toward the Soviet Union which has been in existence for twenty years . . . under the leadership of the Party of Lenin and Stalin."

These three points tie into foreign policies in the following way. The 1935 Congress announced, in effect, that the primary job of all Communists everywhere was the defense of the USSR and of the "parent Party." The aim was to strengthen the CPSU(B) against any eventuality. This aim did not change, but contrary tactics were employed to achieve it. One of the tactics was the official Soviet policy of agitating for "collective security." Another was to order the non-Soviet Communists to form a "united front" with any working-class groups or parties who could be inveigled into such an arrangement. A third was to build "popular fronts"—that is, general coalitions which were not limited to "proletarian parties" but which sought to take in all comers. (And many were "taken in" quite thoroughly.)

But offers of collective action and efforts to build coali-

tions at both levels were not allowed to interfere with
pressing forward specific Communist aims wherever possible. While the Communists were trying to get the Social
Democrats, for example, into a "united front," they simultaneously liquidated Social-Democratic leaders. While
they were building "popular fronts," they damaged liberals and liberal movements whenever they could. And
while they were proposing joint actions to achieve "collective security," the non-Soviet Communist parties, which
were under Soviet control, were busily trying to undermine capitalism. Obviously, these tactics were contradictory. The Communists, under Moscow's directions, were
saying one thing and doing another—a situation which is
very baffling to observers. It must also be frustrating to
rank-and-file participants who find their efforts crossed
and blocked by the actions of some of their comrades.
But there was basically no confusion in the matter because the key principle was the advancement of the power
and security of the CPSU(B). All else was secondary—a
matter of expediency only. Is it any wonder that the
governments of capitalist nations were unwilling to place
much confidence in the proposals and promises of the
Soviet leaders? Nor was the bad faith exclusively on the
one side. The Soviets had some reason to believe that
Franco-British policy, in particular, sought to provoke a
quarrel between the USSR and Germany.

The Soviet policy in the months after Munich was essentially a cautious waiting for a break. The Soviets were
ready, to paraphrase Stalin's statement made in 1939, to
keep on doing business with anyone who would do business with them. But they were on guard against being
used as cat's-paws in any conflict, and they continued to
build up their defenses against an attack. A rapprochement
with Germany apparently began in the fall of 1938. Its
growth was interrupted and uneven, but it grew through
German-Soviet trade agreements to a culminating alliance
in August, 1939. Meanwhile, the German advance into
what was left of Czechoslovakia stirred the French and

British into taking some sort of action. The record of their dealings with the USSR in the spring and summer of 1939 is incomplete. There seems to have been bad faith on both sides. But another aspect was probably more important.

The Soviet leaders clearly wanted more time, and probably they entertained the unrealistic hope of avoiding war altogether (just as we did). All that the French and British could offer was an uncertain alliance with uncertain aid but with the certainty of involvement in the coming war. The Germans had a good deal more to give. They could allow the Soviets to annex certain territories, could send them needed materials and equipment, and could offer at least a possibility of keeping out of the war. The Germans, in other words, made a more attractive offer and the Soviets took it. Molotov redefined aggression in such a way as to place the blame for the war on the French and British; and his government took the further positions that this was "an imperialistic conflict," "a phony war" between the "degenerate democracies" and the Fascists. Ivan Maisky, then Soviet ambassador in London, unofficially and privately explained that his government hoped the war would come to a stalemate, in which case the Soviets could become the arbiters of Europe.

Important territorial gains accrued to the Soviets as an immediate result of their alliance with the Nazis. They partitioned Poland, sharing that country with Germany. And in 1940 they incorporated into the USSR parts of Finland; all of Estonia, Latvia, and Lithuania; and Bessarabia. But the German gains and advances were much greater. When France fell in May, 1940, it was apparent that the war was not going to end in a stalemate which would permit Stalin to act as broker. Radio Moscow suddenly changed its domestic propaganda line from an excoriation of the Western Allies to praise and encouragement for the British. But the deal with Germany still went on. On the other hand, evidence—still scanty and incomplete, but growing—indicates that preparations had begun against Germany. It is not at all clear, however, whether these were preparations for defense against a possible German attack or preparations of advance bases for a further step westward, or maneuvers to strengthen the Soviet diplomatic position. All are possibilities, but the last seems the most likely.

There was a good deal of jockeying for position by the two partners, and this increased as months went by. Economic collaboration was apparently mutually satisfactory and profitable during the first year, but friction developed thereafter—the Soviets claiming that German deliveries fell short of what had been promised. There was also some effective naval coöperation, with the Germans supplying naval vessels and equipment in return for port facilities and other aid. This also deteriorated, perhaps because the Soviets asked too much. Relations with Japan complicated matters, especially after the signature of a new Tripartite Pact (Germany, Italy, and Japan) in September, 1940. But the real conflict came over political developments in Europe. To put it very briefly, the Soviets wanted control over Finland and the Balkans, and they demanded more than Germany would give. The breaking point seems to have been reached in November, 1940, when Molotov put forth a series of demands which the Germans found totally unacceptable. At any rate, there were no more significant political conversations after that date although negotiations concerning economic matters were continued. And the master plan for the German attack on the USSR was issued by Hitler's headquarters in December, 1940.

How much the Soviets knew of this plan, and how seriously they took what they knew, is debatable. So far the evidence favors those who hold that the Soviet rulers did not correctly analyze the developing situation, but not all the evidence is in yet. It is thoroughly established that both the British and the United States governments warned the Soviets that Hitler planned a surprise attack. The impression is that the attack, nevertheless, did surprise the Soviets despite the warnings. Maybe the Soviet

rulers expected it. We don't know about that. But we do
know that the news of the German invasion came as a
shock to the Soviet people. They were temporarily embittered and panic-stricken when the German blitzkrieg
pulverized the Soviet defenses and rolled eastward with
apparently inexorable might. But the Soviet people and
their government recovered themselves and, with the help
of those capitalists whom their gospel scorns and despises,
beat back the threat.

Given the desperateness of the Soviet situation during
the first years of their war, one might suppose that their
foreign policy would have been relatively simple, at least
in outline. One might presume that the only aim of the
policy would have been to win the war. The supposition
and the presumption are both incorrect. The primary aim
of Stalin and his associates was to protect and defend the
CPSU(B) both at the moment and for the future. This,
it will be recalled, had also been Lenin's aim. Lenin was
prepared to sacrifice Russia to the Party, if necessary.
Stalin was prepared to sacrifice victory, if necessary. Proof
of this is that Stalin's government began putting out
peace feelers to Germany early in 1943. The Germans were
not then receptive, but they were ready to listen by July.
No agreement was reached, however, and another Soviet
approach was rejected in the early fall. Clandestine negotiations were continued during 1944 on German initiative,
but they got nowhere since no agreement could be reached
about Ukraine. So the Soviet Union remained in the war.
But the very real possibility that the Soviets might make
a separate peace was a continual nightmare to their British
allies and American associates. Much of the so-called appeasement was entered into in order to forestall such an
event.

The Soviet eye to the future is also apparent in their
development of organizations among the German prisoners of war and in their treatment of various non-Soviet
Communist leaders who sat out the war in Moscow.
Probably the creation of the German Officers Corps and
of the Free Germany group served several purposes, in-

cluding that of wartime propaganda. It has clearly contributed to the Soviet power over eastern Germany since
the war. The non-Soviet Communists (Thorez of France,
Bor of Poland, Pauker of Rumania, and others) were
groomed to take over the governments of their native
lands if the chance came.

Soviet relations with Great Britain and the United
States centered on two things, namely, getting as much
material aid as possible from the democracies and getting
their agreement to postwar arrangements which favored
the Communist-Soviet interest or could be made to do so.
They did well in both lines. We cannot trace the story
here even in barest outline but it ought to be emphasized
that if the Soviets were acting primarily in their own
interests (and they were), so were we. The United States
sent over eleven billion dollars' worth of Lend-Lease to
the USSR not out of altruism but because it was to our
advantage to do so. We were no more "helping Russia"
than she was helping us. Our enemies temporarily coincided and it was to our mutual advantage to take some
joint action against them. But relations were never easy
or truly cordial.

We began this story of Soviet foreign policies at a time
when the Communist leaders were forced to play politics-
without-power. We have come, not to the end of the
story, but to the time when they can play power politics
to a degree hitherto unprecedented in Russian or world
history. Their story began with the "peace decree" which
called for peace without annexation and without indemnities. We may close it at a time when the Soviet Union
has completely reversed that principle. "There is," boasted
Lavrenty Beria on December 21, 1949, "no force on earth
which can compel the Soviet people to deviate from their
path as outlined by Lenin and Stalin." The goal toward
which they believe that path will certainly lead was stated
near the beginning of this chapter. It is the triumph of
world revolution under the leadership of the Politburo of
the CPSU(B).

CHAPTER XIV

Development of British Liberalism: Backgrounds

LIBERALISM CONNOTES an attitude of mind. It implies an individual free from narrowness, intolerance, or servitude to authoritarianism or totalitarianism in government, religion, or any human institution. The liberal, therefore, is an intelligent citizen who through study, thought, and debate seeks to arrive at some general understanding as to what is best for all citizens. Moreover, he believes the result of uncensored thought and debate must demonstrate itself in some voluntary agreement by all and that upon the basis of this agreement there should be built a government and society which should aim at keeping the spirit of the agreement, and through further searchings and discussion look toward growth and advancement. For liberalism is not and cannot be a static thing. It must grow not only on the basis of past experience but upon the persistent efforts of enlightened men and women to devise ways that are best suited to the conditions of a rapidly changing world so as to bring about increased satisfactions to all members of the body politic.

Within these limits, the British have evidenced liberalism since the dawn of their history. The inherent virility and toughness of Saxon local government and life (455 ?-1066) was the rich soil out of which many democratic ideas and institutions had their first inception and growth. Then, under the guiding hand of the arbitrary Norman and Angevin kings (1066-1216) a varied assortment of centralizing devices were established. One of these consisted of the creation of a group of central courts, often called the common-law courts, before which judicial actions might be brought from any part of the realm. Granted that the justice dispensed was often brutal and reflected the desires of a privileged ruling class, the bold fact remains that these courts not only bound a far-flung kingdom together but served as a training school for the development of a legal class whose decisions and attitudes the monarchy itself was forced to recognize. Again, these courts, at the request of their kings, carried their law and procedure throughout the kingdom as they journeyed hither and yonder in the interest of law and order. Thus the law which was conceived at the royal palace at Westminster was carried by these itinerant justices into all parts of England until at last it became a law common to all Englishmen.

Through these and other royal officers the early English kings employed a governmental device known as the inquest. Born out of Norman sources, though the possibility of a Saxon influence is not to be dismissed, the inquest was used over and over again as a royal fact-finding body. When William I, for example, wanted to find out the total population and resources of his kingdom (the results of which inquiry appeared in the Domesday Book), he directed certain officers to tour the realm and seek the required information through the inquest. On arriving at any given village these officials summoned before them a group of individuals who under oath were required to answer pertinent questions. So satisfied were the Norman kings with the results of the inquest that gradually they came to use it for judicial purposes. One of the latter's earliest uses was in disputes over ownership of property. The royal judge would select a group of the neighbors of the disputing parties and place them on oath to tell to whom the property rightfully belonged. Out of this procedure, fashioned into more precise form as time moved

on, came the trial jury in civil cases. Meanwhile, the inquest was utilized as a body indicting persons of crime—
the ancestor of our grand jury of today. It was not, however, until many decades after Magna Charta that the
inquest was molded into a trial or petit jury in criminal
matters.

Significant as the use of the jury was in the spread of
English common law and in rendering speedy and on the
whole equitable justice, it is important for us to note that
the jury method necessitated coöperation by the local
community. They, therefore, like the judges, were tutored
and schooled in the art of self-government—a process one
does not find going on in Europe at the time, which goes
far toward explaining England's leadership in freedom and
democracy. It also helps to explain why the English people captured the concept of nationalism during the Middle Ages and how they, first of all Europeans, abandoned
feudalism and slowly felt their way toward a more dynamic
scheme of society.

In the meantime other forces were at work that rocked
the absolutism of the monarchy to its very foundations.
Touched to the quick by repeated violations of existing
law and smarting under the sting of unprincipled punishment, enraged barons rose in revolt against King John and
at Runnymede in 1215 forced him to issue Magna Charta.
Now there is no document in all of English history more
important than Magna Charta. Unfortunately, an opinion
stubbornly still believed by some holds that Magna Charta
was a document of human liberties. It was nothing of the
kind. Rather it was a reactionary document loaded with
restrictions relative to rights and liberties. It in no wise
guaranteed basic rights to the great mass of the people
for the very simple reason Magna Charta was just an agreement which John was forced to issue at the point of the
sword—the sword being in the hands of the barons, who
had little concern for rights of serfs and artisans. Naturally, these feudal lords did not insert clauses in the charter
that would improve the lot of most Englishmen of 1215.

They were selfish in their aims and outlook and insisted only that John promise to protect their lives and interests. Accordingly there is nothing in Magna Charta concerning such matters as jury trial in criminal cases, the right of habeas corpus, or taxation by Parliament. Such principles of democracy were unheard of at the time. On the other hand, the charter did contain one basic principle—one that has become a priceless heritage of all English-speaking peoples—namely, that the king was an Englishman and like all Englishmen *must obey the law*. This enduring feature of Magna Charta carries this implication today: no executive, no official, no court, and no legislative body may or can set itself *up above the law*. In 1215 Magna Charta served as a limiting force upon royal absolutism and operated in this fashion for more than two centuries; today it serves as a limiting force on all governmental authority. For these reasons Magna Charta marked a step toward democracy as we know it today.

John, the most absolute of all absolute English kings, should be remembered also for having been the first monarch to conceive the idea of inviting representatives of the local units to meet him for purposes of offering advice, counsel, and financial aid. These representatives usually met in conjunction with a body known as the King's Council, the combination being styled at a later time as Parliament. During the course of the remainder of the thirteenth century John's son and grandson (Henry III and Edward I) implemented the idea of local representatives from the shires and selected boroughs and gradually evolved during the first quarter of the fourteenth century what became the House of Commons. The genesis out of which this democratic institution had grown was the inquest or jury. Indeed, its earlier meetings were rightly viewed as being nothing more than concentrations of the juries. At these gatherings, which were held with increasing regularity throughout the remainder of the medieval period, Englishmen received what might be described as advanced instruction or schooling in the art of government. Tutored by participation in local affairs, these representatives waxed in political experience and skill the like of which was not to be found on the Continent. And through this valuable experience the members of Commons grew in stature so much that they were able at length to contest with the king for authority and power.

Foremost among the powers won from the king was control over taxation. Although the monarch repeatedly sought to evade Commons in this matter, such avoidances only steeled Commons to greater efforts so that by the fifteenth century that body held the purse strings more than comfortably tight. Closely identified with this struggle for power was the contest involving the responsibility of royal ministers to Parliament, the nature of their duties, the amount of their salaries, the determination and composition of Parliament, and the rights, privileges, and duties of the members of Commons. In these and many other matters Commons gained in power, always at the expense of the king and often at cost to the House of Lords. Finally, it should be noted that in 1327 and again in 1399 it deposed Edward II and Richard II respectively and determined succession to the throne by legislation.

Despite the gains of the medieval period, Parliament, and especially Commons, was by no means so firmly established as to prevent strong monarchs from finding ways of circumventing it. Particularly did this become true during the reign of the Tudor rulers (1485-1603) when the impact of foreign and domestic wars, the rise of private capitalism, the discovery of the New World, and the implications of the Renaissance and Reformation favored the growth of royal power. So well did Parliament reflect the desires of the English people that it was possible for a writer in 1589 to declare: "The most high and absolute power of the realm of England consisteth in the parliament." And Peter Wentworth, a commoner, in addressing the House upon good Queen Bess's sharp command for the Commons to keep its hands off her business, said: "Free speech and conscience in this place are granted by special law. . . . It is a dangerous thing in a prince [sic] to oppose or bend against her nobility and people." Imagine anyone saying that before the king of France, the pope, or the emperor of the Holy Roman Empire!

Thus when the day came in the seventeenth century that Englishmen were called upon to defend their hard-won rights and privileges against the arbitrary government of the early Stuart kings (1603-49) they were prepared mentally and spiritually for the contest and the victory. The word "spiritually" is used advisedly; for had not the long contest over the moot question of church and state culminated in the triumph of religious freedom from Rome during the stormy days of the Reformation?

Democracy and liberalism, however, are not static things; if they were they would have disappeared long ago. Impressive evidence for this statement may be found in the events centering in the reign of the unfortunate Charles I (1625-49), who inherited a host of political, religious, and economic problems left unsolved by Elizabeth and James I. One of these concerned the ever widening gap between royal income and expense incident to the conduct of government. Parliament was as aware of this as Charles but, detesting the latter's foreign and domestic program, willfully withheld much-needed revenue in the hope that an impoverished king would reign but not rule England. Charles attempted to circumvent Commons by demanding loans from wealthy subjects, imprisoning those who refused, and keeping them in jail despite their resort to habeas corpus. But when all was said and done Charles failed; he still was short of funds. And so he came to Parliament, and in a manner highly irritating to Commons bluntly asked for help. Commons refused to yield, and Charles was compelled to accept in 1628 the Petition of Right, which asserted that no man should be "compelled to make or yield any gift, loan, benevolence, tax or such like charge without common consent by Act of Parliament" and that no freeman should be imprisoned without due process of law. Two other contemporary abuses—the quartering of troops upon civilians without their consent and resort to martial law in time of peace—were also forbidden. Actually the passage of the Petition of Right was only a lull before the storm because in a short time Charles took matters into his own hands and ruled eleven years without Parliament. But the day of reckoning came when, after a year or two of parliamentary struggle for compromise, the entire issue was thrown into the uncertainties of a civil war. Out of this conflict came the trial and execution of Charles, the establishment of the Commonwealth and Protectorate, and the appearance of England's first and only written constitution—the Instrument of Government. It was from this document that Americans were to profit when they drafted the Federal Constitution of 1789.

The Commonwealth and Protectorate, however, was not successful, and in 1660 conservative opinion in England restored the monarchy in the person of Charles II, who until his death in 1685 skillfully managed to check the liberal tendencies favoring a more democratic form of government and life. His successor, James II, seemingly did everything he could to hurt the cause of monarchy and constantly played into the hands of the more progressive elements, who, in the Glorious Revolution of 1688, forced James off the throne and into exile and arranged for the succession of William and Mary to the throne. To implement its triumph and to secure the fruits of the Civil War and Glorious Revolution, Parliament passed in 1689 the Bill of Rights. The salient features of this time-honored document provided that the king could not suspend or dispense with law and the execution of law without parliamentary authority, that all monies for the use of the king (i.e., the state) must be voted by Parliament, that all commitments and prosecutions incident to the Right of Petition were illegal, and that the raising or keeping of a standing army in time of peace was the sole privilege of Parliament. It was also stipulated in the Bill of Rights that there should be free and frequent elections to Parliament, that there should be complete freedom of speech and debate in that body, and that excessive bail ought not to be required or excessive fines imposed, or cruel and unusual punishments inflicted.

There then followed a century of continued growth and development during which the English people renewed their faith in the wisdom of their forebears and augmented their heritage by various innovations in government, such as the cabinet system, which have stood the test of time and which today invoke confidence at home and respect abroad. Toward the close of this century, however, George III sought to halt the development of democracy and restore the authority of the crown. Too wise to walk in the footsteps of his ancestors, he disdained using the sword. He availed himself, however, of existing forces such as the party system, the press, a loyal body of nobles, and an obedient church. Success at first attended his efforts, but success strengthened the opposition. Alarmed by the political-boss tactics of the crown and convinced that George's power must be curtailed at once, the Whig party took up cudgels in defense of the rights and liberties of Englishmen. Against that defense the king beat in vain.

In this respect reference should be made to the American Revolution. The factors that led to that conflict have been treated earlier, but there is one aspect that relates to our problem and that was George's own attitude toward the colonial issue. In the formulation of that attitude the king was profoundly influenced by the liberal opposition within and without Parliament—an opposition which wanted a conciliatory policy toward the colonies. In order to beat down an opposition *in England* which was seeking restriction of royal power within that realm, George elected to throw his political influence in favor of coercing the rebellious colonies. Other considerations, it should be remembered, aided George in making up his mind, but the conflict between absolutism and liberalism in England deserves special emphasis. And as it is well known, absolutism suffered the defeat.

Close upon the heels of the American Revolution came
a far greater upheaval that shook the political, economic,
and social foundations of Britain in much the same manner as communism does today. That a meeting of the
States-General in France (1789) should give rise to a
French Revolution no serious-minded person in England
would have believed for one minute. Indeed, British opinion was at first largely sympathetic toward liberal reform
in France, but as the movement drifted into violent channels and sought to carry a new philosophy of life throughout western Europe, British friendship became British
enmity. There then followed what are known as the
French Revolutionary and Napoleonic Wars. Now one of
the most unfortunate aspects of these conflicts was the
effect they had upon British democracy. Stated briefly,
these wars halted for a time the onward march of liberalism. All the careful and constructive work of reforming
groups in governmental and economic affairs was swept to
one side in an endeavor not only to defeat Bonaparte but
to make England a safe place for conservatism. Burke,
Pitt, and others whose voices had been raised in defense
of the American colonials now thundered against those
who read Paine's *Rights of Man* and who by deeds attempted to save British democracy from the hands of its
enemies. Parliament echoed the sentiments of the reactionaries by enacting legislation calculated to curb and
crush all signs of liberalism. Every local gathering was considered seditious, postal authorities read private correspondence, spies were planted in factory, shop, and reading circle, the Habeas Corpus Act was suspended, and
scores upon scores of persons were thrown into jail.
Others, more fortunate, were pronounced criminals and
transported to New South Wales to become, in the view
of later decades, the First Families of Australia. Hysteria
of this type was matched by the defeat of measures in
Parliament designed to improve the lot of agricultural
workers and chimney sweeps, to afford religious toleration

to Roman Catholics, to revise the penal laws, and to modify the acts affecting lunacy.

Meanwhile, and with irresistible strength, England's entire structure was being transformed by what has been called the industrial revolution. Antecedents of this far-reaching upheaval had occurred as early as the fourteenth century with the breakup of the static manorial system; later came the impact of the discovery of the New World and the influence of the Renaissance and Reformation; nor should one forget the tremendous change in England's economy that took place during the Tudor and early Stuart age (1485-1649). As a consequence of these and other factors there emerged, during the late eighteenth century, the industrial revolution, which for present purposes may be defined as the application of machinery and motive power to production and distribution. New techniques and machines were introduced that upset long-established methods of production and distribution. Savery, Newcomen, and Watt produced steam engines which simplified coal and iron mining, permitted the tapping of new seams, and increased the annual output of English mines. To illustrate, during the years 1681-90 the yearly average of the British coal mines equaled nearly three million tons; from 1781 to 1790 it amounted to over ten million tons. Kay's flying shuttle, Hargreaves' spinning jenny, Arkwright's water frame, Compton's mule, and Cartwright's power loom completely revolutionized the textile industries. The value of cotton goods at the opening of the eighteenth century, for example, was £23,000; in 1764 it was £200,000.

The results of the industrial revolution, however, were not limited to greater productivity in manufacture or new facilities for transportation. A marked increase in population followed, especially within the industrial urban centers. With this increase came problems which even today remain partially unsolved. Inadequate housing, a deficient sanitary system, fire hazards, distorted family life, and gangsterism are but a few samples. The factory town, in short, had come into being. Wide-scale employment of women and children followed, who, together with men, labored as much as ten and twelve hours a day amid conditions that would turn the stomach of even the most rugged individualist of today. Nor were conditions any better in the mines or on the railroads, canal boats, and steamers. And in defense of this vast exploitation of human and physical resources there arose many speakers and orators. From the pulpits of the Anglican churches, from the floor of the House of Commons, and from the drawing rooms of the captains of industry and counting houses of bankers, the voice of conservatism was heard. In support of their thesis they could cite the phenomenal expansion of England, the growth of trade and industry, and the multiplication of the necessities and luxuries of life. Moreover, the absence of restrictive legislation gave sanction to the new England. Then there were economists, like Adam Smith, Thomas Malthus, and David Ricardo, who in their writings tended to exalt free competition, laissez faire, and individual rights. In justice to these men, it may be noted that they also indicated the shortcomings of the new industrial age, but these were lost and forgotten by conservative readers, who remembered and quoted only those portions that reflected their own views and desires.

Depressed conditions among the laboring classes led to labor disturbances. With mill workers at Glasgow earning five dollars a week, women operators no more than three dollars a week, and undernourished children receiving much less, it is not surprising that labor demonstrated its feelings by smashing machines and burning factories and mills. The Luddite riots of 1810-11, though quelled by force, putting some to death and exiling others to the Australian penal settlements, did not stifle the opposition. Eight years later another demonstration—this time in favor of parliamentary reform—led to the Peterloo Massacre at Manchester. Local officers, in an attempt to enforce the law against assembly, lost their heads and ordered the military to fire upon a mixed crowd. Fortunately, only a few were killed or injured, but this did not deter a conservative government from enacting even more repressive legislation.

Nor were conditions any better in the agricultural sections. Although machinery and motive power were not to appear upon the farms for many a decade, an agrarian revolution did take place. The inception of this movement may be traced to a number of different sources, not the least of which was the draining of the rural population away from the farms to the industrial towns and cities. The increase in urban population that naturally followed stimulated the demand for more food, and this in turn led to the enclosure movement. The fencing-in of land for agrarian purposes had begun in the seventeenth century, but it was not until the middle of the next century that enclosures became quite common. The evident advantages of large-scale farming, the rising demand for more food supplies, and the high prices offered for grain in the urban markets excited action among landlords, investors, farmers, and lawyers. The effect of these enclosures, plus certain scientific discoveries, upon production was enormous. The yield per acre, for example, of wheat rose from twelve bushels in 1714 to fifteen in 1750, and by 1815 it had climbed to twenty; additional increases were to follow. But what is more astonishing, these increases in production did not yield lower prices. Meanwhile the small tenant farmer was squeezed off his holdings (the enclosure process permitted his eviction, often without any compensation), while the free cottage tenant was jostled into the status of a rural proletarian.

Contemporary sources of this age bristle with protests by the agricultural laborers. "Man's memory of misfortune, however, is exceedingly short; and historians in general have overlooked the destruction wrought upon England by enclosure." Time-honored rights enjoyed by independent rural workers and tenant operators were tossed to one side, and a trek, marked by excessive suffering, began from the farm to the factory. Goldsmith glimpsed the meaning when he wrote, "A bold peasantry, their country's pride, When once destroyed, can never be supplied." Equally penetrating was the mind of Gray, whose pen depicted, "Some village Hampden that with dauntless breast, the little tyrant of his fields withstood." Those who remained, and they probably accounted for more than half of the island's population in 1830, eked out an uncertain existence. Their protests, however, grew in volume, and in the hope of strengthening their position they frequently banded themselves into organizations comparable in structure and purpose to the unions in the cities. Unfortunately, some of them, like the Friendly Society of Agricultural Laborers in Dorset, in the hope of keeping their membership pure exacted strict oaths of allegiance, surrounded by an elaborate and secret ritual. Straightway the government under Lord Melbourne became convinced that these societies plotted the overthrow of the government and monarchy and the establishment of a workers' republic. Witch hunting, strongly suggestive of present tendencies, disguised by legal proceedings overwhelmed the Dorset group. Arrests, trials, convictions, and deportation followed.

In the meantime, the same classes that worshiped at the feet of a Ricardo, whose iron law of wages was like a Daniel come to judgment, put through Parliament newer, bigger, and better corn laws. These acts, aiming at protection for landlords and wheat producers, maintained a high and almost prohibitive tariff upon the import of foreign grain. Not only were the English consumers denied an adequate food supply but that which they did obtain was purchased at high prices. A casual examination of any economic history of this period will provide ample illustrations of the operations of the corn laws and their social consequences. The trilogy by J. L. and B. Hammond on the lot of the town, skilled, and village laborers is of special significance. The picture one will gain is a somber one and not any happier than that which has been roughly sketched in the preceding pages. But a knowledge and, one trusts, an appreciation of the terrible conditions in which British labor lived are essential if one would understand the soil out of which modern British liberalism had its immediate inception. For even in the midst of this dismal age forces were at work that gave promise of a better world in the future.

Those who were interested in this future were partially recruited from the intelligentsia of England; others were of the governing classes. Then there was the "Clapham Sect," so called because the members held their meetings at Clapham, southwest of London. Although most of these were communicants of the Church of England, they were more interested in the humanitarian and evangelical program of Christ than in the doctrines of the church. And for daring to advocate a return to the gospel of the Good Samaritan they were dubbed by their critics as the "Saints of the Clapham Sect." Another group, believed by some to be atheistic, was known as the "Utilitarians" or "Benthamites" because they walked behind their leader, Jeremy Bentham, who had declared himself in favor of "the greatest happiness of the greatest number." Nor should one forget 16 Charing Cross, London, the home of Francis Place, a retired tailor of comparative wealth. He was a radical reformer for those days, and his home was well stocked with tracts and literature which his disciples scattered throughout the country.

Closely allied in purpose and objective were the avowed humanitarian societies such as the Society for the Suppression of Vice and the Society for the Abolition of the Slave Trade. Organizations of this type freely indulged in petitioning Parliament for remedial legislation. Among those within the halls of Parliament who favored these movements was Sir Samuel Romilly, a brilliant lawyer and intimate friend of Jeremy Bentham. In 1808 he had the fortune of sponsoring and fathering through Parliament a bill reducing the penalty for pocket picking from death to transportation to New South Wales. Later he tried to lessen the number of cases entailing the use of the death penalty, but the House of Lords, whose members represented church and property, and not people, was hostile and defeated Romilly's endeavors by heavy majorities. Some relief, however, was gained through the passage of measures prohibiting disemboweling and quartering of convicted criminals. Meanwhile the Quakers, though laughed at and ridiculed by the "respectable" elements, sought to improve conditions within the prisons, but in only a few instances were they able to clear the religious and property hurdles in the Lords.

Another venture that proved more successful was the reform which centered about slavery. Captained by William Wilberforce, a Claphamite, this reform slowly influenced public opinion, permeated Parliament, and in 1807 succeeded in passing a measure providing for the abolition of the British slave trade. A quarter of a century later, slavery was abolished throughout the British Empire. Then there was the effort to abolish war. Condemnation of war had been heard during the fourteenth century from the great humanitarian John Wycliffe; pacifism had also been advanced by George Fox, the founder of the Society of Friends in 1660. William Penn's *Plan for the Permanent Peace of Europe* (1693) received a wide audience, as did the many other tracts and pamphlets that were issued extolling peace and condemning war. Later Dr. David Bogue and William Allen founded the "Society for the Promotion of Permanent and Universal Peace." And as the Napoleonic Wars came to an end the crusade for peace attracted increased attention and effort.

Britain's position as a world power was immeasurably strengthened by its victory over France in 1815. A rival of no mean stature had been humbled; strategically located islands and naval bases had been won; and the domestic theater had been cleared for a vast development in industry, agriculture, and trade. The revolutions in agriculture and industry, previously noted, had made Britain the outstanding nation of the world. Small wonder was it that Englishmen viewed with pride their nation's mastery on

land and sea, in the field of science and invention, and in
the productivity of her expanding industry and trade. And
with that material sense of satisfaction and accomplishment came the confidence of England's superiority in
government. Of course those who felt so well pleased were
also those who managed and controlled the social, economic, and political structure of the realm and empire.
Particularly significant was their direction of government.
Elections were dictated, bribery and intimidation cowed
a limited electorate, and local and national offices were
staffed with those who knew their master's voice. All of
which was accepted as being ethically and morally sound.
For decades privilege had enjoyed such power, and it was
recognized by existing constitutional law and applauded
by the wise and learned of England. Those of mean birth
or those who traff ked in business were debarred from a
role in government.

It should not be assumed that, because wealth and
property were enthroned in government, the latter was
necessarily always corrupt, inefficient, and self-centered.
Any résumé of British political history between the Glorious Revolution of 1688 and the opening of the nineteenth
century will reveal accomplishments and contributions of
priceless value for the growth and promotion of liberalism
and democracy. In W. S. Holdsworth's *History of English
Law* and H. J. Laski's *Political Thought in England from
Locke to Bentham* there is suggestive and pertinent material on this subject. At the same time it should be remembered that British democracy and liberalism did not materially, politically, or spiritually shower many favors upon
the masses during this era. Evicted from ancestral homes
and rights in rural areas, by reason of the enclosures,
crowded and packed into expanding industrial towns, and
denied any adequate opportunity of gaining redress of
grievances, these depressed individuals joined hands with
the already exploited urban proletariat and flatly rejected
the ideals and assumptions of the property classes. What is
more, they wanted a change, and, since there was scant

prospect that any material change would be initiated by those in power, English labor determined to force the change, cost what it might to established privilege and order. England, in short, faced a revolution the magnitude of which seemed likely to eclipse that which France had experienced but a half-century earlier.

Although it is dangerous to generalize, one may be forgiven for observing that a revolution has at least two marked phases. One constitutes the intellectual preparation for revolt and is led by what one may call a party of the idea. The other denotes action—violence if necessary—intended to implement the new ideology, and this aspect is led by a party of action. The former predates the latter and in many ways is far more significant in that it provides the party of action with a platform, a body of ideals, symbols, and objectives. Demonstrations, parades, mass meetings, petitions, political activity, and even brute force are generally void of meaning and will necessarily flounder and probably fail if the party of the idea has not cultivated the mind in favor of revolt.

Some of this spadework since the opening of the last century and continuing thence to date has been undertaken by men and women who were born in the ranks of labor. Reference has already been made to the humble tailor of Charing Cross, Francis Place, who sitting cross-legged on his workbench stimulated and impelled many a young Englishman to thought and action. Then there was the journalist William Cobbett, whose sojourn in America led to a lasting friendship with Thomas Paine. Cobbett's writings, such as the *Parliamentary History* and the *Register*, the latter being issued in cheap editions so labor might see and read for itself, became bywords among the factory and mining hands of his age. Other cheap and so-called radical publications appeared: Carlile's *Republican*, Wade's *Gorgon*, and, more latterly, *Justice* by Henry M. Hyndman, *The Miner* by Keir Hardie, *The Labour Elector* by H. H. Champion, and *The Clarion* by Robert Blatchford.

Meanwhile the condition of unrest among labor had
attracted individuals of larger means and better education,
such as Jeremy Bentham, of whom mention has been
made. Convinced of the justice of labor's cause and anxious to promote a fuller life for all Englishmen, they used
their pens and exercised considerable influence in many
ways. William Morris, for example, an English poet and
craftsman of some wealth, advocated socialism through
the *Commonweal*, the official organ of the Socialist
League. Then there was *The Link* by Annie Besant and
the *Fabian Essays* written for upper- and middle-class
readers by members of the Fabian Society, which was
founded in 1883. Basically rationalist in their thinking,
the Fabians all but turned a deaf ear to the trade unions
and coöperative societies. Some of them frankly admitted
at a later date that they had not known of the existence
of these laboring groups who, egged on by the writings of
a Hyndman or Hardie, were doing so much for the future
British Labour party. They were aroused, however, from
their ivory towers by the quickening of unrest among the
English workers by the strike of the London dockers in
1889, and from the ready pens of their members, such as
Mr. and Mrs. Sidney Webb, George Bernard Shaw, and
G. D. H. Cole, there appeared what was known as the
Fabian Tracts, in which a definite interest in the lot of
labor was evidenced. With this came the recognition
of the role organized labor should play in the growth of
socialism in England. At the same time, as G. D. H. Cole
stated, "its endeavors . . . were directed rather toward
drawing the trade unions into socialist politics than toward
working out an industrial socialist policy."

The Fabians were socialists who, unlike their rival, the
Social Democratic Federation, which adhered to the Marxian philosophy, stressed the evolutionary transition of
society from capitalism to socialism. Fundamentally Marx
was and is important in the history of socialism for his
emphasis upon class conflict through which, as he reiterated over and over again, and only through which man

might achieve equality and freedom in all things. This doctrine the Fabians repudiated or ignored. Class warfare had no place in Fabian thought. Equality and freedom, therefore, were to be gained by convincing men through sound and logical arguments that the rewards and blessings of socialism do not depend on revolution.

Fabian interest in politics led the society to move closer to the British Labour party. Especially did this become apparent after the close of World War I, when the Labour party adopted a new constitution that reflected to a marked degree the Fabian concept of orderly evolution. So complete was the union that G. D. H. Cole is of the opinion ". . . that the recent comparative inactivity of the society is largely due to the fact that the Labour Party is a larger reincarnation of Fabianism."

During the years the Fabian Society was waxing in stature and thought there were others who did their bit in promoting the cause of labor. In this respect mention should be made of John Stuart Mill, whose essays *On Liberty* and *Treatise on Representative Government* rank as classics in the field of political science. Equally significant were R. H. Murray's *Studies in the English Social and Political Thinkers of the Nineteenth Century* and W. E. Lecky's *Democracy and Liberty*. Historians, sociologists, economists, and theologians joined in the movement, which also enlisted the support of many scientists and philosophers. Finally, a word more should be said of Karl Marx, who, exiled from Germany, made his home in London. Here he propounded his thesis about the death of private capitalism and the establishment of a proletarian world. British labor listened with considerable interest and read and reread his monumental tome, *Das Kapital*, and some went so far as to aid in founding the "First International Working Men's Association" in 1864. Second and sober thought exposed basic defects in Marx's thesis and British labor parted company with the great communist, who even today has relatively few followers in Great Britain.

CHAPTER XV

From Liberalism to the Labour Party

THE FRUIT of the literary activity and propaganda, already noted, becomes apparent as one reviews the nature and scope of parliamentary legislation during the last and present centuries. Steps in this direction were taken prior to the French Revolution, but it was not until after the close of the Napoleonic Wars (1815) that agitation for reform of Parliament attracted serious attention. But thereafter many different groups appeared in support of the movement. In one instance it was the Hampden Clubs of London; in another, it was an association of manufacturers; and in still another it was a union or organization of labor. Each of these had some particular interest to forward. They did, however, have one thing in common, and that was an extension of the franchise in respect to parliamentary elections. As things stood—say, at the opening of the 1830's—the right to vote was restricted by laws and ordinances that dated back to the Middle Ages. Property qualifications of the Middle Ages were still operative. Moreover, considerable corruption, fraud, and intimidation characterized every election, and since there was no secret balloting individual voters frequently were at the mercy of evil forces and evil men.

To alter this situation, British workers undertook direct action, their hope being that once they had won the right to vote they would be able to elect men to Commons who would sponsor and carry measures calculated to give relief from the baneful influences and results of the industrial revolution. Mob violence frequently occurred, and many were the boroughs and cities that witnessed street demonstrations and burned buildings. Similar scenes were enacted in the rural areas, until finally the privileged classes, fearful of a violent revolution, reluctantly consented to reform Commons. The determination to yield was hastened by the Whig victory in the election of 1830. Led by men like Earl Gray, the Whig party, which gloried in the achieve· ments of the Bloodless Revolution of 1688-89, introduced into Parliament and finally carried, in the face of stiff opposition, the Reform Act of 1832. According to the terms of this measure, the suffrage was lowered so as to give the vote to the middle class, most of whom lived within the urban centers. Companion acts provided for a redistribution of seats in the Commons and an extension of the franchise in Ireland and Scotland. Three years later, and by a Commons elected on the basis of the acts of 1832, various municipal governments and elections were reformed. Other measures, such as a Factory Act, a new Poor Law, and the abolition of slavery within the Empire were passed.

But the acts of 1832 had not granted the vote to labor, and so the fight for franchise continued. In 1867, and this time by a Tory party, the suffrage requirements were lowered so as to grant the vote to the laboring classes in the boroughs and cities. Later, in 1884, the agricultural laborers were enfranchised; in both years similar measures were passed for Ireland and Scotland, and in 1885 there was another general redistribution of seats. The United Kingdom now had universal manhood suffrage, but it was not until 1918 and 1928 that the vote was given to women.

In the achievement of these ends considerable credit should be given to the movement of British labor known as Chartism. The members of this group gained their name from a charter which, in imitation of Magna Charta, set forth their rights and objectives. A perusal of this

document reveals that its friends desired universal manhood suffrage, the secret ballot, the abolition of property
qualifications for membership in the House of Commons,
the payment of a salary to members of that house, equal
electoral districts, and annual elections to Commons. Universal manhood suffrage and equal electoral districts were
won by 1885. The secret ballot was gained in 1872, and
the removal of property qualifications for membership in
Commons in 1858. Annual elections have never been won
and in view of parliamentary procedure that calls for annual sessions there is little likelihood that this demand
will ever be granted. The campaign for payment of salaries
was fought well into the present century, and in 1911 this
principle of the Chartists, who as a body had long since
ceased to exist, became law. Also during the twentieth
century the power of the House of Lords, an unrepresen-
tative chamber, was seriously curtailed. Its power of veto
over money bills was abolished, and its legislative power
over all other bills that passed Commons was drastically
restricted.

Numerous other laws were enacted that altered the
political structure of Britain. One of these, the Supreme
Judicature Act of 1873, reorganized and consolidated the
courts of the realm, thus affording better justice to British
labor. Of equal importance to labor were those laws and
court decisions that established complete freedom of the
press. Definite progress in that direction had been made
during the first thirty years of the reign of George III
(1760-1820), but this was abruptly halted by the wave of
reaction which swept over the island following the advent
of the French Revolution. And it was not until after 1832
that the fight for a free press got under way. Between that
year and 1861, for example, various duties on advertisements and paper, as well as a stamp tax on all newspapers,
were abolished. Meanwhile, by Lord Campbell's Libel Act
of 1843, a defendant was permitted, as had not been the
case before, to plead the truth of a statement he had
previously made, which statement had been denounced as

inflammatory and was therefore indictable. At the same time the criminal liability of a publisher for the unauthorized acts of his agents was abolished. Today, nothing is heard of state prosecution for libel. On the other hand, it is true that during periods of national emergency, such as war and economic depression, the government has interfered with the freedom of the press. It should be noted, however, that this interference takes the form of restricting the amount of newsprint and of taxing advertisements because of economic exigencies of the moment. Thus the government claims its conduct is not predicated upon any policy of censorship.

Closely related to the question of free press is that of religious freedom. At the opening of the nineteenth century the right of religious worship and assembly were generally restricted to members of the Anglican Catholic Church (the Church of England) and certain approved Protestant communions such as the Methodists. All non-Anglicans, however, were denied basic political rights, such as voting, membership in local and national government, and in some instances employment in the civil and military services of the country, unless they had taken certain required oaths of loyalty and allegiance. If by religious freedom is meant freedom of conscience, then England in 1800 had religious freedom. But if religious freedom means the right of public worship, the right to speak, write, and legislate in behalf of that freedom, and to enjoy immunity for the free exercise and practice of one's faith, then England did not have religious freedom. And to gain such ends, which must exist if men are to be free men, steps were taken by those concerned. In 1828, after a stout battle, Protestants with but few exceptions were accorded full political and religious rights, and in the following year Roman Catholics, except for several minor instances, were given the same privileges. Subsequent decades witnessed the removal of most of these restrictions, and today in democratic Britain complete religious freedom, as defined above, is in force.

Among the powers exercised by the Anglican Church, at the turn of the eighteenth century, was control over education. Today, although that faith still enjoys prestige and caste, it has no priority. The stripping of this power from the church was by no means an easy fight. But thanks to the infiltration of Protestants into Commons and the advance of liberalism throughout the island the battle was won and the way was paved for a broader and more democratic system of education. Elementary training for every child was provided by 1880; by the same time attendance either in state or church schools, both of which received grants-in-aid, was required for all between the ages of five and fourteen. Within thirty years, the number of elementary school pupils jumped from less than a million to over six million. Strides were also made in secondary schools, which, by the Fisher Act of 1918, received considerable financial assistance. Unfortunately this measure, which contained other benefits, never fully operated because of the expenses incident to World War I and the depression that followed. And it was not until 1944, under the war government of Churchill, and in 1946 and 1947, under a Labour government, that a more satisfactory educational program was initiated. The school age has been raised, a variety of social services have been introduced, and the door has been opened for nation-wide entrance into institutions of higher learning, a privilege heretofore largely enjoyed by those of greater means.

Finally, there were a number of acts that removed the dead hand of the past in matters of trade, commerce, and industrial behavior. In all of these activities, vested interests, proud in prestige and the power that came to them from swollen profits, battled most determinedly against those who thought in terms of production for use. Aiding the latter in their struggle for free trade were men like Adam Smith, England's greatest economist and foremost advocate of laissez faire. According to Smith, excessive governmental control and regulation inevitably tended to stifle production and distribution. Government, he insisted, should leave the direction of industry to business, which if unbridled could double and triple the national output of domestic manufacturers. These finished goods, because of their inherent superior quality and through the ingenuity and skill of British merchants, would find extensive markets at home and abroad. State interference, he continued, always led to national confusion and loss. Follow natural laws and allow business to function under free initiative and competition, and the results would benefit capital and labor alike. Special consideration was given by Smith to the corn laws and the navigation system, classic examples, he said, of governmental blundering and error. Smith's opinions, expressed in *The Wealth of Nations*, appeared in 1776 and may well be considered as a declaration of freedom in economic affairs. The validity of his views, however, was slow in gaining acceptance, and it was not until after the American Revolution, and more particularly not until the advent of William Huskisson, that positive steps were taken in the direction of free trade.

During the years Huskisson was at the Board of Trade definite inroads were made upon the navigation acts, which through their operation restricted England's foreign trade in a manner that pleased the captains of industry and finance but bore down most unfairly upon those who toiled in factory, mine, or shipyard. Finally, during the 1840's, Sir Robert Peel, who, like Huskisson, was a member of the Tory party, led a successful attack against these laws. In 1845 came the consolidation of the navigation acts and the complete abolition of export duties. In 1849 Parliament declared England's foreign trade open to all nations, and in 1853 permitted foreigners to engage in the coastwise trade. All of which spelled liberalism in trade, and for the next sixty years England's economic stature in respect to other nations might be likened to a giant among pygmies.

At about the same time, Peel challenged the right of the landed class, the large farmers, grain brokers, merchants, and exporters to dominate the domestic produc-

tion of grain, the foreign trade thereof, and the price of
corn in local markets. These and many other privileges
had accrued to these vested interests through the operation
of the corn laws. In theory, these acts aimed at protecting
both producer and consumer, but judging from the high
price of grain during the first four decades of the last
century, and the mounting fortunes of those who dwelt in
marble halls, it was the consumer who paid and paid.
North German and American wheat, every bit as good as
England could raise, was generally denied access to British
markets by reason of high tariff rates most carefully and
delicately stated in the corn laws. Continued opposition to
these measures led to the formation of the Anti-Corn-Law
League, which, joining ranks with Peel, ultimately gained
the victory. Drastic reductions in rates took place in 1846;
three years later, the corn laws died, the mourners being
very few in number.

Meanwhile other reforming groups were pushing manufacturers and mine owners for concessions as to conditions
of work, shorter hours, elimination of child and woman
labor, higher wages, and a score of other matters of vital
concern to those who labored amid circumstances that pass
all understanding. A parliamentary committee, for example, found in 1842 that children of four years of age
were employed in the mines. Others, slightly older and of
both sexes, wearing only loincloths, crawled on hands and
knees through narrow and low passageways, frequently a
foot deep with water, pulling heavy carts of coal or ore.
Moral conditions were appalling. "No brothel can beat
it," one member of Parliament declared. And when informed of an accidental death, the average mine owner or
operator replied, "Oh, it is only another collier." Equally
alarming, from the point of view of national health, were
the factories.

Conservative opinion admitted the existence of such
abuses but flatly denied labor's right to generalize on the
basis of what it insisted were isolated and uncommon
cases. The Mine and Collieries Bill of 1842, for example,

was roundly condemned because it interfered with the market of labor and because it attempted to "enforce morality by an act of parliament." But those who argued so were championing a lost cause, and the bill, prohibiting employment of women and children in the mines, was passed. Two years later, liberalism won again with the enactment of a Factory Act, which restricted working hours for women and children and provided for the installation of safety devices on dangerous machinery. Subsequently, additional measures were passed improving the lot of the worker in factory, mine, shipyard, and wherever labor was employed—in the city, on the farm, in the fisheries, or in merchant shipping.

Probably none of these reforms would have become law as soon as they did had it not been for the rise of labor organizations and the entrance of labor into politics. All during the medieval period and well down into modern times, the right of labor to organize for self-protection and promotion was generally unlawful. Attempts to correct this inequality were made in the late eighteenth century, but it was not until 1825 that William Huskisson, stimulated by the brilliant Francis Place, brought the matter before Parliament and secured the passage of an act allowing labor the right of organization. Trade unions immediately sprang up in all parts of the realm, and before long strikes in favor of higher wages, shorter working hours, and the like became the order of the day. At first these unions were local in origin and activity, but as time went on they became regional and national. John Doherty's National Association for the Protection of Labor, founded in 1830, the Grand National Consolidated Trades Union of 1834, the Miners' Association of 1841, and many others made their appearance in rapid order. In their wake came others, most of which today are organized in the powerful Trades Union Congress.

Among those who played an active role in these nineteenth-century activities was Robert Owen, the son of a poor Welsh ironmonger. By dint of hard work and application, Owen rose from the rank of a factory hand to the managership of one of Manchester's largest manufacturing plants. Later he became the owner of a factory at New Lanark. Owen assumed that the well-being of his workers was as vital to him as to them. Accordingly, he reduced hours of work, increased wages, afforded educational advantages to the children, and provided improved housing for his help. In spite of these increased costs, he was able to amass a respectable fortune. Owen, it might be said, was a practicing socialist, and from his example and writings, British labor received early instruction in Utopian socialism. He deplored militant methods and saw little value in strikes and sabotage. Labor, he insisted over and over again, would conquer only through education and coöperation. By the latter he meant the establishment of coöperative societies. His idea of coöperative stores and exchanges gradually spread, and in 1844 there appeared a society known as the Rochdale Pioneers. This organization sought to create retail stores for groceries, clothes, and other necessities, and to build homes and recreation centers. The society controlled its own supplies, eliminated the middleman's profit, and returned profits to the members in proportion to their purchases. Success attended these efforts, and similar groups made their appearance elsewhere. Most of these then consolidated in the Coöperative Wholesale Society of the 1860's. By this time the effort had expanded itself and the society began manufacturing goods for its members. Plants and factories were located throughout the realm and empire, and even in foreign countries. Later the society enlarged its services by engaging in the banking and insurance business. Today, the coöperative movement is most significant in the British economy, and like trade unionism has entered into all phases of industrial, agricultural, and commercial production and distribution.

The impact of these various organizations and efforts resulted, as has been shown, in the passage of numerous social, political, and economic reforms by Parliament.

Labor's influence within and without Parliament had become well established. Labor captured its first seat in Commons in 1830; other seats were won in the years that followed, but it was not until 1852 that the first trade unionist, William Newton, entered Parliament. Later the London Working Man's Association and the Labour Representation League were formed. Little, however, was accomplished until 1874, when fifteen labor candidates ran for office, two of whom were elected. During the course of the next two decades avowed laborites were returned to Commons from time to time. Although these men may be called labor members they were counted and voted as Liberals in Commons. This Liberal-labor alliance served a useful purpose, but it fell far short of doing for labor what labor wanted. Thus, the demand arose for direct political action.

The genesis of an independent labor party may be traced to the socialistic teachings of Robert Owen and Karl Marx. Additional stimulus came through the foundation of the workingmen's clubs of the 1870's. One of the leaders of this group was Henry M. Hyndman, who succeeded, in 1881, in uniting the clubs into the Democratic Federation. At first Hyndman avoided socialism as such and endeavored, through party action, to secure the passage of measures that were reminiscent of Chartism. Trade unionists and the radical elements within the clubs were unwilling to follow so moderate a program, and Hyndman was forced to mold the Federation into a militant socialist group known as the Social Democratic Association. It advocated land nationalization, state aid in housing and education, and the establishment of workshops to care for the unemployed. The Federation attracted a wide variety of reformers, one of whom was William Morris. Morris joined with Hyndman in condemning trade unionism, which still refused to adopt socialistic party action. The absence of the powerful trade unions, plus internal dissension, led finally to Morris' withdrawal and the founding of the Socialist League. As the latter opened its doors to anarchists and Communists its influence waned and shortly after Morris' retirement (1889) the Socialist League disappeared. A similar story could be told of the Federation, which, by 1890, had given ground to a new movement initiated by Keir Hardie.

In 1889, Hardie founded the Scottish Labour party. Three years later the London Trades Council founded the London Labour Representative Committee, which strongly advocated the creation of an independent labor party. At this juncture there appeared Robert Blatchford's *Clarion* and the more famous *Fabian Essays*, composed by members of the Fabian Society. These activities plus the election of fifteen laborites, including leaders like Keir Hardie, John Burns, Havelock Wilson, and Joseph Ash, to Commons encouraged the socialists to form, in 1893, the Independent Labour party. According to its platform, the party stood for an eight-hour day, the collective ownership of production and distribution, and other socialistic measures. The program, however, was too radical for the trade unions, and several years passed before an alliance was established between the unions and the party. In 1900, thanks to able direction by men like Keir Hardie, Ramsay MacDonald, and George Bernard Shaw, a Labour Representative Committee was founded. The key to the latter's success lay in the compromise that a trade unionist might vote for a candidate of the Independent Labour party without necessarily indicating acceptance of socialism.

In 1906 the Committee changed its name to the Labour party and in the election of that year won twenty-nine seats in Commons; in the same year, the Independent Labour party returned seven members. During the years that followed, candidates of both parties have been elected to Parliament, and for a brief period the two parties consolidated. Meanwhile the voting strength of labor increased. In the January, 1910, election it gained some 500,000 popular votes and forty seats in Commons, though in the December contest of the same year there was a marked decline due to the strong appeal the Liberal party made in the campaign. In the famous "khaki election" (so called because all men in service were granted the vote regardless of other qualifications) of 1918, the two labor parties won over 2,700,000 votes (chiefly in the boroughs) and fifty-nine seats in Commons. Four years later with a popular vote of about four and a half million labor had 142 seats. In December, 1923, with the Tory party advocating a sharp departure from free trade in favor of a protective tariff, labor gained in popular votes and registered an astonishingly high level in Commons with 191 seats. Owing to the inability of the Tory party to control a majority vote in that chamber and because of an alliance between the Labour and Liberal parties, Ramsay MacDonald, leader of the Labour party, became Prime Minister. For the first time in English history His Majesty's government was in the hands of a socialist party.

It was, however, a hollow and premature victory. The electorate had not really returned a Labour majority to Commons, and when the working agreement with the Liberals encountered rough sledding the MacDonald government fell and a general election followed in the early fall of 1924. This time the Tory party conducted a most vigorous campaign and was able to gain 412 out of the 615 seats in Commons, labor having to be content with 151 and the Liberals with but 40 seats. Five years later a sharp swing to the left was registered. Labor won over eight million popular votes and captured 288 seats in Commons, sufficient to give it control of government for the second time. In 1931, owing to a split within the Labour party over the question of economy, including reduction of social services and the maintenance of the gold standard, the Tories were returned to Parliament, capturing all but sixty-one seats in Commons. In November, 1935, with a rejuvenated party, labor cut into the Tory control, increasing its popular vote by nearly two million and winning 154 seats in Commons.

One therefore may conclude that the British Labour party, through its socialistic liberalism, had offered the

British people a democratic way of life that captured the imagination and support of a considerable number of voters. It had, moreover, by its constant advocacy of socialism forced and educated Tory and Liberal alike to promote liberal and socialistic measures in Parliament. In 1906 the Liberal party enacted a Trade Disputes Act which freed unions from any liability resulting from damages committed during a strike. Five years later, after the House of Lords had ruled it was illegal for union funds to be used as compensation for time served in Commons, the Liberal party provided salaries for all members of Commons. In the same year the Liberal party pushed through the famous Parliament Act of 1911. According to this measure: (1) all money bills (and the determination of what was a money bill was left to the Speaker of the Commons) were to be presented to the king for signature within one month after passage in Commons, regardless of the action of the Lords; (2) all other measures were to be referred to the king, irrespective of the wishes of the Lords, provided they had passed Commons in three consecutive sessions and provided they had been presented to the Lords one month prior to the close of a session, and provided that two years had intervened since the measure was first introduced; (3) the life of Parliament should be five years. Also, under a Liberal government, Britain embarked upon a far-reaching program of social reform including such matters as old age, accident, health, and unemployment insurance. Nor have the Tories been at all backward in advancing liberal legislation, particularly after their advent to power in 1922. Indeed, a very good case may be made for the statement that more progressive social legislation has been passed by the Tory party since 1922 than by any other party prior to the great Labour victory of 1945.

Socialism, as the British Labour party sees it, is democratic in structure, procedure, and objective. For several decades the party has reiterated over and over again that England is a country of rich natural resources and that its sturdy inhabitants are highly skilled in administrative and productive capacity. The Labour party also believes that the English people possess a bountiful historical heritage of experience in handling social and economic as well as political problems. Not for one moment has it ever viewed the mother country as a Garden of Eden, but it always has insisted that the British Isles could and should be made a better place—a place in which no man, woman, or child need go without or be short of the good things of life. To the British Laborite, this is but a twentieth-century restatement of the Sermon on the Mount or, if you prefer, the gospel of the Good Samaritan.

The British Labour party does believe in public or social ownership of the essential resources and utilities of the nation. But it does not stand for the concept that state ownership involves ownership of everything. As a matter of fact, it believes there is too little private property in the world. Man, the party declares, ought to have more private possession. Private ownership, however, of property which involves the welfare, health, and safety of all the people is thoroughly condemned. The party believes that private ownership of this type produces not only an inequitable but a socially bad distribution of wealth and income; that it often results in the production of things not conducive to the needs of human welfare. Again, the party is convinced that much too little is produced to obtain those standards of living which the growth and spread of human knowledge have made possible for man.

The British Labour party leaders are not simply idealists. They are basically level-headed, sensible men and women who frankly admit their goal cannot be reached overnight. The complete fruition of their program, therefore, entails the temporary postponement of many desirable changes; or, putting it differently, the Labour party has both a short- and a long-term set of objectives. These attitudes and concepts were well brought to the front during the months preceding World War II in a series of notable pamphlets such, for example, as *For Socialism* and *Peace* and *Labour's Immediate Program*. Other publications have appeared from time to time since the close of that conflict, and although none of these individually or collectively may be viewed as a blueprint or, as a Russian is used to saying, a five- or a ten-year program, they nevertheless give the lie to those who assert that the British Labour party does not have a well-thought-out plan and program.

Bolstered by these publications and numerous articles and addresses by its leaders, the Labour party went into the election of 1945 with a rather clear idea of what it was after and what it wanted. Among other things it promised a wide assortment and variety of social services. It believed that if elected its attention should be turned to the troublesome problems of childhood and youth; that the worker and the unemployed should be cared for; that sickness, accident, and sudden death should be cared for; that men and women should not want because of the infirmities of age; and that up and down the islands there should be adequate housing and extensive slum clearance. Secondly, they proposed that there be a thorough overhauling of the kingdom's educational program; that the youth be kept in school longer; that the curriculum be broadened and extended, not merely along cultural but along vocational lines; and that governmental assistance make it possible for an increasing number of young men and women, regardless of economic or social background, to obtain desired higher education and training. Thirdly, it announced, particularly in view of the difficulties caused by the war, that the islands' agricultural economy should be reviewed with the aim of trying to provide a maximum amount of food from native resources. Again, it declared that the government should take over, own, and control the sick coal industry and that gas and electricity should likewise be nationalized. Fifth, in a long list of pronouncements, the party called for state ownership of all means of transportation and with that went a large share of the English hotels throughout the islands, since the railroads

at the time had built and operated an extensive chain of
hotels. Nor was industry overlooked, and a promise was
made not only to nationalize steel and control the armament industry but to modernize the textile industry and
possibly place it under government control. The platform
also promised extensive and far-reaching changes in the
existing financial and banking structure, and a reappraisal
of taxation with a view to producing a more equitable distribution of national wealth and income. It also hoped to
establish an overall program of national planning whereby
these and other matters might be carefully studied and
evolved not only to prevent error but to correct such error
as might creep in or develop. Finally, and in entire agreement with its concept of democracy, the British Labour
party of 1945 definitely announced that if elected it would
reorganize the government so as to make it a democratic
institution and not one that continued to reflect the de·
sires and ideas of the people of a century ago.

Any fair appraisal of the party's conduct of the campaign of 1945 must reach the conclusion that the party
went into the election with a program and a promise of
what it would do if elected. And this, incidentally, is not
what the Tory party did in so precise a manner. The result
was that, in spite of Mr. Churchill's plea for his own re-
election on the ground that he and he alone could save
England, the country went socialistic by a rather comfortable majority. Over twelve million voters out of a total
of almost twenty-five million supported the British Labour
party, which thereby gained 392 seats in Commons, and
control of His Majesty's government for the third time.

How well did Labour carry out its pledges? The answer
to this question must remain a matter of opinion. Tory
and Liberal have found fault with Labour's legislation and
have made considerable noise within and without Parliament in expressing their views. But the surprising thing
is not that these defects were mentioned—and Labour
frankly admitted the existence of some and has sought to
correct them—but that generally speaking both of these

opposing parties accepted in principle the program Labour has carried out. In respect to the latter, reference should be made to the nationalization of the Bank of England, the coal industry, the transport (bus, rail, canal, and hotel) industry, electricity, aviation, and the steel industry. In addition vast changes were effected in the nation's health, housing, and educational activities. In government the most significant achievement was the Representation of the People Act, by which plural voting and the university seats were abolished and a new distribution of seats in Commons was established. In overseas affairs, the party accorded Commonwealth status to Ceylon, India, and Pakistan; enabled Eire and Burma to achieve independence outside of the Commonwealth; legislated in a manner so that Newfoundland might become a province of the Dominion of Canada; extended local self-government throughout the British Empire; and through the Colonial Development and Welfare acts appropriated large sums of money for the economic and social development of the Empire. Time and time alone will tell whether these various undertakings abroad and at home were wise and expedient. But for the present, few would deny that Labour tried to fulfill its promises made to the electorate during the summer preceding the election of 1945.

Ill-advised individuals in Britain as in the United States have confused British socialism with Russian communism. Surely it is not difficult to discern the bias and prejudice behind most of this confusion. Ignorance, one readily admits, is blissful but nothing but condemnation should be showered upon those who constantly repeat as truth what clearly has been established as error. It is demonstrable that British socialists and Russian Communists have agreed on some ultimate aims but so have Democrats and Republicans in America. Mohammedanism and Christianity also have much in common but that does not prove that both have the same notions about salvation and life hereafter. No, the British socialist is not a communist. He is not overly concerned about theory and he has been cold to the long-winded discourses that have come from Moscow.

The British socialist most certainly does have a philosophy, and the constitution of the Labour party refers to the "common ownership of the means of production, distribution, and exchange." But when it comes to implementing these generalizations the party does so in keeping with the democratic process and with the rule of reason. The limits and ways of British socialism have always been tempered by what the Labour government considers expedient. Speaking in 1922, the late Arthur Henderson, a prominent Laborite of his age, stated: "The difference between British Labour and Russian Communists was the difference between democracy and dictatorship, between a political method which trusted and derived its strength from the people, and a political method which made use of dictatorship in the name of the people without their consent." Comparable statements have been made since by leaders such as Attlee, Bevin, and Cripps. British socialism is utterly opposed to the use of revolutionary methods. It does not preach the idea of the "International." And it does not maintain a fifth column. It rejects completely the concept of the inevitability of class conflict and war. And when it fulfills its pledges through nationalization it follows the procedure of compensation, not confiscation.

These basic differences have been ever present in the British theater since 1922. And British Labour in its annual conferences and in Commons, or its members in their own units such as the Trades Union Congress, have ever reaffirmed their undying loyalty to British political democracy. There have been exceptions. But in meeting these exceptions evidence of party faith has been revealed. The record of British Labour shows it means what it says.

And what has that record been? Founded in 1900, the Labour party quickly sensed the dangers of affiliation with communism, which openly scoffed at socialism in Britain. "It was no secret," so Dr. Carl Brand writes in an article in the July, 1949, issue of the *South Atlantic Quarterly*, "that communist policy was to capture the socialist parties or to destroy them in order to erect new structures on their ruins. Lenin himself ordered a fight without mercy against the 'social patriots' as he styled their leaders. 'I want to support Henderson with my vote in the same way as a rope supports one who is hanged.' " But Labour leaders of the 1920's were not blind to realities and while struggling at home to avert intervention in Russia they nonetheless turned a deaf ear to Communist infiltrators within the party. Evidence of their strength came in 1921 when in response to a request for affiliation by the British Communist party Labour at its annual meeting rebuffed communism by a vote of 4,115,000 to 224,000. "Since that day the issue has been repeatedly raised, but the decision has always been reaffirmed." It is also of interest to note that in the election of 1945 and also in 1950 wherever a Communist candidate ran for a seat in Commons he was opposed by a Laborite. Finally, it might be added that in foreign affairs, Labour since 1945 has been on tiptoe in respect to Soviet penetrations at home and abroad. Its record in western Germany, its role in the airlift to Berlin, its handling of communism at home, and above all the outspoken utterances of an Attlee, a Bevin, or a Cripps should leave no doubt in the mind of anyone. Critical as Churchill, Eden, and others have been of Labour's domestic policy, their approval in the main of Labour's attitude toward Russia cannot be dismissed as faint praise.

Foreign and Commonwealth problems, while present in the pronouncements of all parties in the general election of February, 1950, figured much less prominently than did domestic issues. The political campaign, though short in time—three weeks—enlisted tremendous interest but on the whole was quiet and orderly. Prime Minister Attlee expressed the view that the contest was quieter than usual, and Mr. Churchill said it was "the best conducted and most demure" in all his long experience. In the election, 28,769,477 voters went to the polls, a figure that equaled about 84 percent of the total electorate. Of the votes cast, Labour (including 4112 Independent Labour party votes) received 46.4 percent; Conservatives and their associates, 41.7 percent; Liberals, 9.1 percent; National Liberals and Labour Conservatives, 1.8 percent. The remainder gained 1 percent, of which the Communists had .3 of 1 percent, which incidentally recorded a drop from the vote in 1945 and should do much to allay the fears of Britain's going communist. Although the Tory vote exceeded the vote won by that party in 1945, it still fell short of the figure for 1935. On the other hand, Labour increased its vote to a total of 13,295,736, the largest number ever cast in any British election. The Liberal party also increased its popular vote, but owing to the peculiarities of a British election actually lost rather than gained seats in Commons. Had there been any scheme of proportional representation, the Liberals might have won approximately fifty seats; as it was, they secured but nine. The second largest block of votes in Commons is Tory—298—with Labour ranking first with 315. The Irish Nationalists gained two, which with the Speaker made a House of 625 seats.

From these statistics it may readily be seen that Labour enjoys the unenviable distinction of having a small and precarious majority in Commons. This kind of a situation will call for unusual skill and patience on the part of Prime Minister Attlee and his colleagues. Not only must the Labour government deal cautiously with the thrust and attack of the opposition, but it must be alert as to how to keep its own ranks unbroken. Similar situations have arisen in the past, and it may be that the Labour government will be able to stave off defeat for some time. An election day probably would not alter conditions to any degree, and the best Tory advocates might expect would be to trade places with Labour on much the same basis as now exists. Possibly Churchill with his zeal and ambition might welcome such an opportunity, though others in his party would prefer Labour to suffer and sweat under existing adverse conditions.

It is, however, too early to make any positive generalizations. This much may be said, namely, that neither a Tory nor a Liberal government would materially alter what Labour has enacted. Nationalization and the welfare state are not Labour creations. The friends of these concepts are to be found in varying degree in all three major parties. The British world, under the aegis of a social philosophy common to all but the Communist, has sought and seeks to advocate the well-being of the United Kingdom and its democratic-loving peoples.

CHAPTER XVI

British Democracy Goes Overseas

THE AMERICAN REVOLUTION marked the beginning of the end for the British Empire of the eighteenth century. Based upon a philosophy which has been termed the old colonial system, the English colonial world was generally conceived as only a means to an end. The end was the economic and political power and greatness of Britain, the mother country; the means was the founding and promotion of colonies so as to achieve that power and greatness. Thus, the colonies were to furnish Britain the raw supplies necessary to sustain an expanding industrial order at home and in turn to provide a safe and protected market for the sale of Britain's manufactured goods. To gain these ends numerous laws and directives were issued, such as the navigation, hat, coin, and molasses acts. Trade and manufacture in the colonies was thereby harnessed to the cart tail of British economy.

It would be wrong, however, to imply that the colonies were but chattels and that their waking hours were devoted to enhancing England's treasure. An impartial analysis of colonial economy will reveal that the colonists prospered in their own right. England, for example, did not so seriously restrict domestic manufacturing that the colonies had none of their own. Shoes, paper, glass, bricks, paints, iron goods, rum, and scores of other products were made in America. Shipbuilding engaged the labor of many persons, and so far as domestic coastwise trade was concerned the colonials enjoyed a complete monopoly; almost the same may be said of the trade between the colonies and the British West Indies. It is also clearly established that the British were not always able to enforce the prohibitive measures mentioned. Hats were made, paper currency flourished, violations of trade laws became commonplace, and the molasses act was poorly enforced. Meanwhile, a country that was predominantly agricultural and commercial made great strides along these lines.

It is also contrary to fact to state that England gained her North American empire by force of arms alone. Exceptions may be noted in the West Indies and in old Canada, but no British men-of-war, supported by regiments of the line, ever conquered the area occupied by the thirteen colonies. Moreover, it was a private trading company and not the crown or Parliament that actually promoted and developed the colonies during the first half of the colonial age. Finally, it should be observed that in governmental activities the trend was distinctly toward local autonomy. In every colony political power, in a realistic manner, came to be lodged in the people of that colony through a local legislature—a legislature, moreover, which had eclipsed the governor. Precisely where this growth would have led the colonies one does not know. It might have been directed into separatism and independence; it might have developed into Dominion status. Although the American Revolution brought independence, there was nothing within the colonial system prior to 1763 that would of itself have necessitated independence. But the Revolution did take place largely because the British government elected to embark upon an imperial defense program that entailed taxation of the colonies by Parliament.

These facts are of primary importance not only for an adequate understanding of the American Revolution but for a clear knowledge of the progress of British liberalism and democracy in the colonial world. The development of this movement, moreover, was demonstrated even before 1776, as may be seen, for example, in the establishment of a free-port system within the framework of the navigation acts. By the free-port system, the British opened ports, at first within the West Indies, to the free trade of all nations. This trend continued after 1783 and was gradually extended elsewhere. The impact of this free port idea did much to stimulate those who followed the laissez-faire views of Adam Smith. As has been shown, Britain by the middle of the nineteenth century threw overboard the navigation system and established free trade throughout the British world.

The promotion of free trade and the development of local self-government within the Empire after 1783 were paralleled by the withdrawal of the British garrisons from most of the colonies. The reasons prompting this movement were varied; probably the most significant was the widespread feeling in England that the expense of a military establishment, except in respect to bases like Gibraltar, Hong Kong, and the like, should be borne by the colonies and not by Britain. Actual withdrawal, however, was both difficult and gradual; it was often dependent upon internal as well as external considerations. A native uprising in New Zealand, or the Canadian fear, during the American Civil War, of the military might of the United States, not only checked withdrawal but for the time being led to the arrival of reinforcements. By the late 1870's, however, these disturbances and others had died down, and the withdrawal of British troops, save for military bases and where the colonies requested their retention (though at colonial expense), was complete. Only in India were garrisons kept and here there were special reasons no one questioned at the time.

The withdrawal of the garrisons, the abolition of the navigation acts, and the development of local self-government in the colonies were in part predicated upon British notions of democracy and the lessons learned from the American Revolution. Other forces also operated, not the

least of which was the rise of a new colonial philosophy—
a philosophy that ultimately led to what some have called
Britain's Second Empire. At first, this new concept
stressed the shortcomings and failures of the old, though
after the latter showed signs of disappearance the emphasis
was upon increased local autonomy and independence
under the crown. As illustration, an examination of the
writings of Adam Smith is instructive. Smith insisted that
the old colonial system was an anchor around the economic
neck of Britain and the colonies. Open Empire trade, and
both the colonies and the mother country would prosper.
Even from a military angle, Smith believed their cost out-
weighed any benefit. He was not, however, for giving them
up; rather he argued for colonial representation in Parliament. Such a device, he concluded, would lead to a reform in empire government. In sharp contrast stood
Josiah Tucker, eminent economist and Dean of Glouces-
ter Cathedral. Like Smith, Tucker saw little but evil in the
old colonial system, though he parted company with him
on the question of what to do with the colonies. If he had
his way, he was wont to say, he would release them from
all ties and grant them complete freedom and independence. On hearing of Cornwallis' surrender at Yorktown he
congratulated his countrymen upon their defeat. More
constructive were the comments of Major John Cartwright, who in 1775 suggested the establishment of a
Grand British League and Confederacy. Within this structure would exist a state extending from the St. Lawrence
to the Mississippi possessed of a free and independent
legislature, popularly elected, and in no wise bound to
Britain except through its allegiance to the crown. What
is of interest in this thesis is that Cartwright clearly anticipated the Dominion system of today.

These men, and there were others like them, had little
influence at the time, but their ideas were not forgotten.
Once the hysteria of defeat in 1783 had vanished in
Britain, and the French and Napoleonic Wars had passed,
Englishmen took stock of their colonial policy, recognized

existing faults, and advocated significant changes, such as the abolition of the trade laws already mentioned. Year after year witnessed the development of a new attitude toward colonials. Missionaries, historians, philosophers like Edward G. Wakefield, Charles Butler, John Stuart Mill, George Grote, and Jeremy Bentham wrote in behalf of this movement, and a number of private societies were formed to promote colonial expansion and development, all of which bore distinct fruit as Britishers began to fill in the open spaces of Canada, Australia, New Zealand, and South Africa. Bit by bit the control by Parliament slackened. Finally, in 1867, Britain created the Dominion of Canada. Later, in 1901, Australia was raised to the same rank, a distinction that was accorded to New Zealand in 1907 and South Africa in 1909. Elsewhere in the Empire local self-government was promoted as conditions warranted.

Meanwhile, the British government, conscious of its responsibilities and sensitive to the problems inherent in the new order, studiously cultivated the friendship of its children. The existence of a common historical heritage was never forgotten, members of the royal family visited the far-flung Empire. Britannia's navy cruised in colonial waters, and the advantages of improved communications were utilized to cement an alliance that became stronger as the years went by. Loyalty to the mother country grew. Conscious of the value of these connections, the Dominions aided Britain in the hour of need. Australians and Canadians joined in Britain's Sudan wars of 1885; a decade later, more blood was shed by these colonials in the Boer War; and during the First World War all of the Dominions furnished large supplies of life and treasure. More significant were the coöperative efforts which promoted greater economic intercourse; and trade connections stimulated imperial defense. In support and praise, the pens of James A. Froude, Sir Charles Dilke, Sir John Seeley, Cecil Rhodes, and Sir George Grey were used with telling effect. In their wake came the Royal Colonial Institute and the

Imperial Federation League. It was the latter organization that sponsored the idea of a colonial conference to be held in conjunction with the Empire's celebration of Victoria's Jubilee of 1887.

During the spring of that year representatives from the colonies gathered in England and discussed matters of defense and trade. Another meeting was held a decade later —the topic of discussion being imperial unity. A third conference was held in 1902, when it was agreed that similar gatherings should convene every four years. In preparation for these assemblies much time and effort were spent, and at one gathering a draft of a constitution for future Imperial Conferences was drawn. As the war clouds loomed in Europe, the conferences devoted much attention to the impending conflict and in order to implement their activities the Dominions gained the right of receiving confidential information as to the conduct of British foreign affairs. The exigencies of World War I argued for increased coöperation; the premiers of the Dominions were accorded seats in the British cabinet, which generally became known as the Imperial War Cabinet. The conference of 1919 was of special significance for here it was decided that the Dominions, for the first time in history, would be represented at the Peace Conference as free and sovereign states. From a constitutional angle, the 1918 conference was more important. According to the resolutions of that year, direct communication on all matters between the Dominions and Britain was agreed upon; moreover, during the interval between conferences each Dominion was to be represented at London by its Prime Minister or by a Dominion minister. Again, in accordance with the Treaty of Versailles, the Dominions were recognized as free nations, and in the years that followed many states, such as France, United States, Russia, and Germany, received Dominion ambassadors and consuls.

The effect of this growth was likewise shown within the structure of Empire government. At the Imperial Conference of 1926, Britain formally admitted Dominion na-

tionalism and announced that each Dominion possessed
equality of status in domestic and foreign affairs. Additional discussion followed in 1930. As a result of these
conferences and in keeping with the express wish of the
Dominions the British Parliament in 1931 enacted the
famous Statute of Westminster. According to this act, the
Dominions were recognized anew as independent states
within a British Commonwealth of Nations, of which
Great Britain was a member on equal terms with the Dominions. Each was to be master of its own domestic and
foreign affairs and thus could not be embroiled in war
except by its own consent. The British Parliament was to
have no authority over the Dominions, nor could it dis-
allow any act of a Dominion Parliament. Appeals to the
Privy Council were to be allowed in all matters concerning
disputes between the provinces of a Dominion or those
that arose over Dominion legislation. But the right of this
appeal could be abolished by the Dominion. Each Dominion recognized the British king as sovereign, an agent
of whom was to preside over Dominion Parliaments but
to possess only nominal power. The British Parliament,
moreover, was not to alter the line of succession or royal
titles without the consent of the Dominions.

The Statute of Westminster, in brief, legally recognized
that a large part of the British Empire had been molded
into a British Commonwealth of Nations. As instituted in
1931, the Commonwealth consisted of the Dominions of
Canada, Australia, and New Zealand, the Union of South
Africa, Eire, and the United Kingdom of Great Britain and
Northern Ireland. At the time of its birth, a few misin-
formed critics asserted that recognition of Dominion independence foreshadowed a dismemberment of the Empire and a collapse of British imperial solidarity. But
loyalty to the mother country was patent before 1931, and
it has grown in quality and significance since. B. S. B.
Stevens, one-time Prime Minister of New Zealand, remarked shortly before World War II:

The problem of the Dominions, insofar as foreign policy is concerned, is not such a difficult one; and in practice there have been no great divergences of opinion. I am convinced that, even if we thought that Great Britain had made a mistake, the citizens of the overseas Empire would never consent to wash their hands of the consequences. The tie of sentiment has a very real value under these conditions. . . . It is an empire of the spirit, its bonds are above self-interest or legal exactitudes, its ties defy rational or juridical explanations, it is a unity accepted without question in a fashion so inevitable as to be almost mystical.

It is true that no political connection of any value exists between Britain and the Dominions, or for that matter between the Dominions themselves. Their detachment at times reminds one of the blood frankness existing among relatives. Eire, for example, saw fit not to respond to its king's invitation to attend the wedding of Elizabeth, heir presumptive to the throne, in November, 1947. And South Africa has said some sharp things about the conduct of India. The solidarity of the Commonwealth, however, is beyond all question. The death of George V in 1936 was mourned in Melbourne as in London; nor did Edward VIII's abdication a few months later dent the structure of the Commonwealth. More striking testimony was evidenced at the outbreak of World War II, when all the Dominions of their own free will and accord, with the exception of Eire, joined England in the war against Hitler and his evil followers. Finally, one has to recall the tremendous gifts in treasure the Dominions have poured at the feet of the mother country during the latter's years of discontent that have followed since 1945.

Of course the pact is not all one sided, as the United Kingdom repeatedly has evidenced its responsibilities in a score of different ways. Eire's neutrality and security, for example, were respected even though it meant loss of life and treasure. Britain's concessions in matters of imperial trade should be remembered, and it should not be forgotten that the bulk of Britain's fleet has provided and still provides protection on the high seas. The story of Britain's new colonial policy, however, does not stop there; it has extended itself throughout the British Empire, which, it should be remembered, is not synonymous with the British Commonwealth of Nations. The latter includes all of the Dominions and the United Kingdom, whereas the British Empire consists only of those areas under the king and British Parliament such as Bermuda, Hong Kong, and Aden; it does not include the Dominions.

Foremost in proof of Britain's liberalism in colonial matters is the grant of Dominion status to Pakistan and India in August, 1947. Regardless of what immediate antecedents were behind this grant, the bold fact that the Indian people were led to democracy and Dominion status as the result of Britain's occupancy of India is beyond question. Gandhi, Nehru, Patel, Jinnah, and other Indian leaders have admitted this time after time; they only differed with British leaders over the timing of the grant of independence. They wanted it before 1947 and it seems likely, in view of Tory opposition to the India Independence Bill, introduced in Parliament on July 4, 1947, that Dominion status would not have been granted had that party rather than the Labour party been in power. Meanwhile the socialist government has forged forward and has elevated Ceylon to Dominion status. A similar story was all but finished in respect to Burma, which, after ninety years as a part of the British Empire, was offered Dominion status in the summer of 1947. The Burmese people, however, graciously declined the honor, preferring independence outside of the Commonwealth, and in January, 1948, the Burmese state came into being. The friendship between Burma and Britain may be illustrated in part by the commercial treaties entered into by these states, the reception of a British military mission to the exclusion of others, and the permission granted Britain to use Burmese airfields. In commenting on these happenings, Prime Minister Attlee stated:

It was the hope and desire of the Government that the people of Burma would recognize the great advantages which accrue from membership of the Commonwealth—a membership which as one of the Dominion Prime Ministers said is not a derogation from independence but an addition to it. But they have decided otherwise. In our view, nations have the right to decide on the nature of their own government. The British Commonwealth of Nations is a free association of peoples, not a collection of subject nations. When, therefore, after due consideration the elected representatives of the people of Burma chose independence, it was, I believe, the duty of His Majesty's Government to take the necessary steps to implement that decision.

Equally significant in the annals of the Commonwealth and illustrating again the peculiar relationships existing within the same was the passage in the spring of 1949 of the Ireland Bill by the Parliament of the United Kingdom. The occasion for this measure was the decision of the government of Eire to leave the Commonwealth. It was a decision deeply regretted throughout the Commonwealth but exercised a right accorded Eire under the provisions of the Statute of Westminster. In other words, the right of secession is constitutional under the framework of government within the Commonwealth. Indeed, if that right were not admitted the Commonwealth as it now stands would not exist. "I do not pretend," so spoke Prime Minister Attlee in Commons, "that the solution . . . is completely logical—very few things in the relationship between these islands have been completely logical—but I believe they are practical and I believe that they are to our mutual benefit." The Prime Minister went on to point out that Eire's action had been entirely unilateral and that announcement of her decision was made by the Prime Minister of Eire during the course of a visit to Canada. "It came," he continued, "without any peculiar notice to us."

Eire's action forced a decision relative to No. 'ern Ireland, which since 1922 had been an integral part of the United Kingdom though having a Parliament of its own.

The island of Ireland, in short, was divided politically into two sovereign states: the Irish Republic (Eire) and Northern Ireland (Ulster). This division was accepted by the Irish Republic at that time—a decision that was not forced upon it by the United Kingdom. In recognizing the right of Eire to leave the Commonwealth the United Kingdom was also compelled to recognize the right of Northern Ireland to remain within the Commonwealth. "The view of His Majesty's Government in the United Kingdom has always been that no change should be made in the constitutional status of Northern Ireland without Northern Ireland's free agreement." (*Hansard*, Oct. 28, 1928; May 11, 1949)

The consequences, therefore, of the Ireland Bill for the time being are twofold: (1) It admits Eire's right to withdraw from the Commonwealth; (2) it admits the right of Northern Ireland to remain in or leave the Commonwealth. And Northern Ireland voted to remain where she has been for the past two decades, namely, within the Commonwealth. Ill-advised comments have been made as to "partition," about English bayonets forcing the ways upon free peoples, etc., etc. But the clear, indisputable facts tell a different story. Faithful to its past treaty obligations, in keeping with its ideas of democracy, and in accord with the Statute of Westminster, the United Kingdom followed a correct and precise course of action. She admitted the rights of the governments of both Eire and Northern Ireland to do what they wanted. Democracy knows no better way.

The year 1949 is also important in Commonwealth life for the happy solution that arose out of India's desire to adopt a Republican form of constitution and yet to remain within the Commonwealth. The issue raised was subject of much debate at a meeting of Commonwealth ministers held at London in April last. After full and frank discussions it was agreed that India would retain full membership within the Commonwealth and would accept the "King as the symbol of the free association" of the independent members of that association and "as such the head of the Commonwealth." The other member nations accept a "common allegiance to the Crown" as the symbol of "their free association." From a practical point of view the declaration makes very little difference to the previously existing situation. It is designed to meet India's political ambition to demonstrate her independence in a special way but also to meet her clear desire to remain in intimate association and full membership with the Commonwealth. Logically, it may be added, this formula might well be the bridge by means of which Burma may return to the Commonwealth; it might also lead to Eire's return.

The British government, therefore, expresses a liberal policy in colonial affairs. Comparable statements may be found in Britain's attitude toward the Sudan; here the British stand ready to withdraw when and if the Sudanese express a wish to that effect. Elsewhere throughout the British Empire colonials are being led as rapidly as conditions warrant toward local self-government either within or without the Commonwealth. Those who accuse the British of being slow and reluctant to make these concessions are grossly ignorant of facts or else they refuse to recognize the inherent difficulties involved in educating backward peoples to the democratic process. Out of the millions of black British citizens scattered throughout the Empire there are relatively few capable of handling government in accordance with democratic notions. Few know what the vote means, few have ever heard of a parliament, congress, or assembly, and few have any notion of what common law is. They can understand that they have a king, though many of them last year in South Africa were bitterly disappointed and shocked to see that their King George was not twelve feet tall; others wagged their heads in bewilderment when they discovered he had but one wife. It is an old adage that runs: One cannot make bricks out of straw; it is equally true one cannot make a democratic state out of a primitive and backward people by merely granting them independence.

Much idle talk has been heard in respect to the British
West Indies, though in 1947 a gathering of representatives
of these colonies at Jamaica was offered Britain's services
in promoting a West Indian Federation. The Federation
of Kenya, Uganda, and Tanganyika is underway, and similar efforts are being made in West and Central Africa.
Meanwhile, increased governmental powers have been
given to the residents of Cyprus, Gibraltar, and Malta—in
fact, there is hardly a colony that has not benefited from
concessions of this type. British colonial policy of today,
born out of the loss of the American thirteen colonies, has
thus moved decidedly to the left—a way, we believe, objective minds must conclude is wise. "We realize," so a
commoner recently stated in Parliament, "that the only
right attitude for an Imperial power over territories which
may still be subordinate to it is the relationship of guardian
to ward. We are responsible for their territories just as
long as it is necessary for us to supervise them. All the
time we should be aiming at preparing them for independence. That is now the accepted and enlightened
view." And to this leaders of the Liberal and Tory parties
have given their complete endorsement.

The role of a guardian does not stop at educating a ward
to self-government. It also involves the promotion of
physical fitness in the colony, the founding of hospitals,
maintenance of schools, construction of improved roads,
development of natural resources, and a score of other
allied activities. Tremendous strides in these directions
have been made in every quarter of the Empire and
usually at the expense of the English taxpayer. In 1940,
to illustrate, and after a feeble start in 1929, the British
Tory government, though involved in a war with Germany,
renounced its former policy that colonies should be finan-
cially self-sufficient unless they were in a state of solvency.
In lieu, a sum of five million pounds a year for ten
years was voted to meet pertinent improvement plus a
grant of half a million pounds a year for colonial research.
In spite of the war, the effort received favorable applause

and in February, 1945, a bill passed Parliament authorizing the expenditure of 120 million pounds for colonial development and research between then and 1956. In the wake of this measure several agencies such as a Committee on Colonial Research, were set up to carry out the purposes of these acts.

Significant as this was, the Labour Government took another step when in February, 1948, it enacted an Overseas Resources Development Bill. In sponsoring this measure the government paid a compliment to the splendid work already done by private entrepreneurs in developing colonial resources. It promised—and the promise was repeated in the summer of 1949—that private interests would be encouraged to play an important role in the entire undertaking. "We are the greatest of Colonial powers," a speaker stated, "and we can not afford a deserted Empire, " not only because of a deranged world but because the colonial peoples need new development of their means of production and of their natural resources. Indeed, if something is not done and that right soon "it is not too much to say that ruin and starvation" may overtake some of the colonials. To prevent the latter the Overseas Resources Bill provided for the setting up of a Colonial Development Corporation financed by loans and advances from the Treasury up to 100 million pounds. The corporation was not confined to the production or promotion of any one type of commodity or project and it could operate generally throughout the Empire including the mandated areas. The act also provided for an Overseas Food Corporation with loans and advances from the Treasury up to fifty million pounds. Unlike the Development Corporation, the Overseas Food Corporation operated not only within the Empire but in the Dominions and even within foreign states. Its objective is a permanent increase in the food supply of the Commonwealth and Empire.

The first project of the Colonial Development Corporation was the Gambian egg production scheme. At a cost of over a half-million prounds ten thousand acres of forest are being cleared for the production of coarse grain to feed poultry, and a poultry farm to produce table poultry and about twenty million eggs a year is being set up. Cold-storage facilities are being employed. The project is located about fifteen miles south of Bathurst and will reach full production by 1951 or 1952. The Overseas Food Corporation's first project was the East African groundnuts (peanuts) scheme, which illustrates quite well the spirit with which Britain is meeting the twin problem of native backwardness and the world shortage of foodstuffs; it also demonstrates the tremendous hurdles such pioneering efforts have to face. The area chosen for this unprecedented undertaking was in the mandated territory of Tanganyika and Northern Rhodesia, whose total size is somewhat larger than Texas, California, Nevada, and Utah combined. As originally conceived there were to be ninety-seven units set aside for the development of groundnuts, each unit consisting of thirty thousand acres or about seven square miles. Most of these were to be in Tanganyika, especially in the vicinity of Kongwa in the Central Province some 240 miles to the west of the port of Dar-es-Salaam on the Indian Ocean. Here as elsewhere the country was relatively flat, interspersed with hills rising in some places to five thousand feet. It was densely covered with a thorny, tough, and almost impenetrable bush which pushes its way through a red soil which is usually dry and porous. Roads in the modern sense did not exist. And what of the natives? They were almost as primitive and naked as the country from which they eked out an existence.

To harness this wild area was an undertaking of no mean proportion. And it is not to be wondered at that unforeseen difficulties arose which retarded progress and revealed how careless in some respects the original surveys and plans had been. The absence of adequate transport facilities, the shortcomings of the port of Dar-es-Salaam, the constant turnover of native labor, the resignation of certain key British officials, and above all the impact of drought caused no end of trouble. Nor should one ever forget the far greater battle being fought by man against his greatest enemy the tsetse fly. The recent discovery of antrycide has pushed the fly back in some quarters but it is far too early to make any safe predictions. The well-known capacity of life, in any form, to develop immunity, and the reluctance on the part of natives to pay for the cost of antrycide are factors that have to be remembered. The combination of these and other problems has distinctly limited the output of the groundnuts units; indeed, it has fallen far below expectation, but this in no wise should be interpreted as failure. It is the opinion of those who have visited and studied the area that there is more than a reasonable chance for success. All of which will bring relief to the British housewife whose cupboard and icebox are not loaded with necessary fats and oils.

Other examples, the product of Britain's new colonial policy, include the rehabilitation of the Malayan railroads, the construction of new railroads in Tanganyika, the opening of new ports and the improvement of old, the development of copper production in Northern Rhodesia, the exploration of the lead mines in Tanganyika, the Fiji hydroelectric scheme, and the Owen Falls project in Uganda. Nor should one forget the improvements that have been made in sugar production in the Queensland Province of Australia. And though a fair portion of the fruits of these undertakings will accrue to the advantage of the English taxpayer—and there are few who would argue that the latter is not heavily taxed and not in need of increased food supplies and raw materials—the greater and more important results will be seen in the colonies themselves. Steady and profitable work is being provided for natives who heretofore had to depend upon the caprice of nature for food, shelter, and clothing. Roads have been constructed, wild life has been fenced in, so to speak, schools, hospitals, stores have appeared, and a hundred and one other things have happened that promise much for the future.

Moreover, the contributions of many of the above-mentioned schemes will in all probability affect every country in the world. In its international aspect this is a major British effort toward world reconstruction and development. "Here," said John Strachey, British Food Minister, in talking about the East African undertakings late in 1947, "is the redemption of the pledge we gave at the Hot Springs Conference and reiterated to the Food and Agriculture Organization of the United Nations that we British mean to play our part in increasing the world's foodstuffs and primary products." Although the international features of these various British schemes are not the burden of this chapter, it should be evident to all who read and think that continued growth in the colonial world raises new and very significant problems. Surely the British taxpayer will in the long run be unable to meet his own needs at home in the way of schools, hospitals, roads, and the like while meeting those of native populations whose fecundity passeth all understanding. Experts have concluded that birth control measures will have to be encouraged, but here as in respect to housing, health, education, and a score of other essentials of good living the problem will have to be handled on an international rather than on a national basis. Thus the cycle of British democracy, political, economic, and social, will have rendered another service to the world.

CHAPTER XVII

Patterns of Western Europe: Germany

THERE ARE STILL seventy million Germans living in the strategic heart of Europe. Thousands of these are highly trained soldiers and sailors. In Germany are Europe's richest coal mines, greatest steel mills, finest chemical plants, and most skillful engineers and business organizers.

The prize is rich, and the world's rival philosophies of government are contesting for it. Russia naturally hopes and works for the victory of communism in Germany; a communist Germany, closely allied with the Soviet Union, would greatly diminish the danger of capitalist attack from the west. But security for Russia would mean insecurity for England and the United States. A powerful communist Germany allied with the Soviet Union would make so formidable a combination that Englishmen and Americans shudder at the thought. The American ideal would be a new Germany, democratic in government and peace-loving in disposition, strong and prosperous enough to serve as a bulwark against the westward expansion of communism but not strong enough to be a threat in itself. The British share this ambition to democratize Germany, but they differ with us over the control of German industry. They feel that the chances of a peaceful, democratic Germany would be improved if moderate German Socialists were to gain control and put through a nationalization of the key industries of the country. Most American policy makers oppose this; they would put more trust in a country where private enterprise was at a maximum.

German Political Traditions: Monarchy

Study of the origins of American, English, and Russian institutions should make us skeptical of the possibility that the Germans can be completely made over into any foreign pattern. Certainly, if we would understand the factors at work in the German situation, we must know something of the past political experience of the German people themselves.

When we turn to German history, the first thing that impresses us is the absence of a great constitutional tradition like that of England, or of an obstinate insistence on the right of self-government like that of America. No great national legislature like Parliament developed in medieval Germany. The heroes of modern Germany have not been spokesmen for human liberties, but strong men like the Great Elector, Frederick the Great, and Bismarck, who accomplished things through the ruthless use of force. There were Germans with other ideals, who sought to pattern German institutions upon those of Great Britain and the United States. But, although the liberals won limited victories in securing constitutions and parliaments in some of the German states, they failed in their larger objects. Again and again they were defeated, and many of them—in despair of achieving real democracy in Germany —emigrated to the United States.

This does not mean that the institutions of imperial Germany were totalitarian. Although an extreme conservative, Bismarck was shrewd enough to see the advantage of making certain concessions to nineteenth-century liberalism. The German Empire, created in 1871 as a result of Bismarck's policy of "blood and iron," was organized along federal principles with distinct areas of authority reserved for the governments of the various German states. For the Empire as a whole, there was a representative body called the Reichstag, elected by universal manhood suffrage. Here German political parties ranging all the way from conservative to socialist enjoyed freedom of debate.

But the Reichstag exercised no such real power as the English House of Commons. The chancellor was responsible only to the emperor, and the Reichstag was kept from exercising any effective check on the policies of the government. Especially was this so in foreign affairs and army matters, where the emperor exercised almost unlimited authority.

Closely allied with the emperor in the exercise of political power was the Prussian aristocracy. These so-called Junkers—one of the most highly privileged groups in Europe—lived in eastern Germany on vast estates worked by hundreds of agricultural laborers. In politics the Junkers were extreme reactionaries who exercised great influence. Bismarck and other chancellors were drawn from this class, and the same group secured the best posts in the German diplomatic corps and in the civil service.

But the area where the Junkers were most firmly entrenched was in the imperial army. The generals and high-ranking officers were almost exclusively drawn from this Prussian aristocracy. They studied the art of war with such avidity that they became the world's greatest specialists in military science. The army was a powerful factor in determining government policy. Instead of being the servant of the state, it was one of the masters of the state.

The extraordinary expansion of German industry between 1871 and 1914 created another extremely wealthy class—the big businessmen. In some particulars this group's interests conflicted with those of the Junkers, but the two were allies in supporting the monarchy, the bureaucracy, and the army against the German factions who were demanding a more democratic regime.

The Weimar Republic

The old order suffered a great, though temporary, loss of prestige through Germany's defeat in World War I. During the weeks just before the armistice in 1918, there were demands for reform in the Reichstag, mutinies in the navy, and great strikes in the factories. On November 9, 1918, responsibility for government was turned over to the German Socialists. The humiliation of the old regime seemed complete. Almost without resistance, it had surrendered to the spokesmen for democracy and permitted the establishment of a republic.

But although power had been attained with surprising ease, the republic found the exercise of power much more difficult. The Socialists were divided as to their next step. A minority, influenced by events in Russia, became Communists. They wanted to retain all power in the hands of councils of workers and proceed to the speedy socialization of the entire German economy. But the Majority Socialists opposed the dictatorship of the proletariat. They were content with gradual steps toward socialism and were determined to entrust the task of drafting a constitution to a freely elected assembly. When the Communists resorted to violence in an attempt to secure control, the Socialists used the army to oppose them.

The Socialists were of course right in opposing the Communist attempt to deprive the German people of an opportunity to choose for themselves their future form of government. But in their fear of the Communists, the Socialists became too conservative. Germany had never had a real revolution, and it needed one. Democracy would never be safe in the nation so long as the Junkers continued to hold their great estates and to control the army and so long as German big business continued to be dominated by the same interests as before the war. Fearing disorder, the Socialists never took the steps that were necessary to purge the German bureaucracy and army of antidemocratic elements, to break up the large Junker estates, and to neutralize the excessive power of the great industrialists. The new republic was not a clean break with the old regime but a compromise with it—a compromise in which the old regime continued to control the real centers of power while the democrats were permitted to occupy the most prominent government posts and to struggle with the thankless tasks of a difficult reconstruction period.

The most democratic election that Germany had ever seen took place in January, 1920. The constituent assembly, thus freely chosen, met at the little town of Weimar and drafted a republican constitution for the country. It was based on federal principles like that of the United States and provided for a central government with carefully defined functions.

In some respects the institutions established by the Weimar Constitution were more democratic than those of the United States or of Great Britain. But it takes more than a democratic constitution to make a democracy. It takes a strong democratic tradition, whereas the German tradition was weak. It also requires substantially unanimous acceptance of the system by the people, and this acceptance the Weimar Republic never secured. The Communists did not accept the finality of the constitution and continued to agitate for a worker-dominated state. More dangerous still were the enemies of the right—the monarchists, militarists, ultranationalists, landed aristocrats, and great industrialists. These reactionaries were responsible for numerous political assassinations during the early twenties; they had many powerful allies in the regular army, and they organized private armies of their own.

The precarious majority supporting republican institutions was made up of the moderate political parties—the Social Democrats, the Democrats, and the Catholic Center party. These groups derived their strength from the industrial workers and the middle classes. If these elements in German society attained reasonable security, the republic had a chance for survival. But stable economic conditions did not materialize. From 1919 to 1923 there was a colossal currency inflation, which ruined thousands of the lower middle class. This important section of society became embittered with the republic and provided the new Nazi party with most of its converts. The alienation of the middle class was a fatal blow, but a blow that was for six years suspended. In 1924 Germany's reparations burden was reduced by the Dawes Plan, and the government was able to balance its budget and stabilize the currency. This encouraged large-scale investment in Germany by foreign bankers—particularly American. German industry enjoyed a remarkable revival, and with the restoration of prosperity the Weimar system became more popular.

But in 1930 the republic's borrowed time began to run out. The great depression set in; American investment in Germany ceased; German trade was paralyzed; factories closed down and unemployment spread. More and more German voters lost patience with the moderate democratic parties. The vote for the Social Democrats, the Catholic Center party, and other supporters of the republic shrank at an alarming rate, while that of the extremist parties—the Communists on the left and the National Socialists and Nationalists on the right—grew rapidly. On January 30, 1933, the Weimar Republic received its mortal wound when President Hindenburg designated Adolf Hitler Chancellor.

Nazi Totalitarianism

The National Socialist, or Nazi, party had been born during the chaotic period following the armistice. Hitler was not its first member, but he joined in 1919, while the party was still very small, and soon won the leadership. From the beginning the Nazis had an extreme program. They aimed at the overthrow of the Treaty of Versailles and the revival of Germany as a great military power. They despised the republic and advocated authoritarian rule. They blamed Germany's postwar political and economic difficulties on the Jews, whom they promised to drive out of German life. They hated both Socialists and Communists and carried on incessant street fighting with these rivals. In order to win support from the lower middle class and from the workers, the National Socialists promised certain drastic economic measures. But many German big businessmen, receiving confidential assurances that their interests would be safeguarded in a Nazi state, provided funds for Hitler's propaganda against the republic. The Nazi cause had also many powerful friends within the German army.

For some time during the last months of the Weimar Republic the Nazis, although they had become the largest party in the Reichstag, were kept out of power through the hostility of the Nationalist party. This faction was dominated by the friends of the old regime—the monarchy, the army, the aristocracy, and the great industrialists—and they had an important ally in President Hindenburg—a Junker general. They hoped to take advantage of the collapse of the republic to establish government by gentlemen like themselves instead of by roughnecks like the Nazis. But the Nationalists found themselves too weak to rule without the help of the Nazi masses. They struck a bargain with Hitler, and the first Hitler cabinet was a coalition of National Socialists and Nationalists. Thus in the end the Junkers, the generals, and the great industrialists became accomplices in the destruction of the republic and the delivery of Germany into the hands of fanatics.

The old schism between the Socialists and the Communists also contributed to the tragedy. In a common front the German workers might have defeated the Hitler movement, but during the months of crisis the Communists failed to rally to the defense of the republic. Instead they played their own game, hastening the downfall of the Weimar system in the hope that the chaos would work out to their advantage. Nothing could have been more short-sighted and foolish. Not only did these tactics divide the natural enemies of the Nazis, but anti-Red hysteria stampeded thousands of timid Germans into voting for Hitler.

Within a few months the Nazis had established a completely totalitarian state. They abolished Germany's federal institutions and centralized all power in Berlin. They induced the Reichstag to vest in the Nazi cabinet full authority to levy taxes and make laws. All political parties except the National Socialist were outlawed. The Gestapo, or political police, was organized to ferret out any opposition to the regime, and soon the concentration camps were jammed with prisoners. Nazi storm troopers now had full opportunity to spite themselves against the Jews. Thousands were assaulted, forced out of business, imprisoned, or hounded out of the country in poverty.

The Nazis deliberately plotted to seize the territory of their neighbors even though they knew that this meant eventual war. Step by step the German army was built up again in defiance of the Treaty of Versailles. Although the democratic powers protested, they took no action even when Hitler seized Austria and Czechoslovakia.

But in 1939 the war finally came. In two years the great German war machine overran Poland, Denmark, Norway, Holland, Belgium, France, Yugoslavia, Greece, much of North Africa, and all of western Russia. It was in their hour of victory that the Nazis threw off all restraint and showed their true character. Consider the deposition of one Rudolf Hoess, presented at the Nuremberg war crimes trial of 1945:

I commanded Auschwitz until 1 December, 1943, and estimate that at least 2,500,000 victims were executed there by gassing and burning, and at least another 500,000 succumbed to starvation and disease, making a total of 3,000,000. This represents about 70-80 per cent of all persons sent to Auschwitz, the remainder having been selected and used for slave labor in the camp industries.

Included among the executed and burned were approximately 20,000 Russian prisoners of war. . . . The remainder of victims included about 100,000 German Jews, and great numbers of citizens, mostly Jewish, from Holland, France, Belgium, Poland, Hungary, Czechoslovakia, Greece and other countries. We executed about 400,000 Hungarian Jews alone in the summer of 1944. . . .

I visited Treblinka to find out how they carried out their exterminations. The Camp Commandant at Treblinka told me that he had liquidated 80,000 in six months. He was principally concerned with liquidating all the Jews from the Warsaw Ghetto.

He used monoxide gas and I did not think his methods were very efficient. So when I set up the extermination building at Auschwitz, I used Cyclon B, which was a crystallized prussic acid which we dropped into the death chamber from a small opening. It took from 3 to 15 minutes to kill the people in the death chamber, depending upon climatic conditions. We knew when the people were dead because their screaming stopped.

After the bodies were removed, our Special Commandos took off the rings and extracted the gold from the teeth of the corpses. . . .

Children of tender years were invariably exterminated since by reason of their youth they were unable to work. . . .

Auschwitz was only one chapter in the terrible book of crime. According to the Nazis' own estimate, they killed about four million Jews in extermination camps and about two million in other ways. The International Military Tribunal, which tried Goering and his associates, found that the Germans had been guilty of murdering and torturing prisoners of war, of performing terrible medical experiments on human guinea pigs, of compelling millions of their conquered populations to work in Germany as slaves, and of wholesale looting of conquered territories. In the judgment of the International Tribunal: "War crimes had been committed on a vast scale never before seen in the history of war. The majority of them arose from the Nazi conception of total war and they were, for the most part, the result of cold and criminal calculation."

ALLIED OCCUPATION OF GERMANY

Obviously, it would not be an easy task to erect a democracy in a country whose population had been indoctrinated and brutalized by twelve years of Nazi rule. Yet this was one of the principal objectives which Allied occupation of Germany was intended to serve. When the

Big Three—Stalin of Russia, Attlee of Great Britain, and Truman of the United States—met in Berlin soon after V-E Day, they drew the first partial blueprint for Germany's future in the so-called Potsdam Declaration of August 2, 1945. They stated the purposes of military occupation to be:

1. The complete disarmament and demilitarization of Germany and the elimination or control of all German industry that could be used for military purposes. . . .
2. To convince the German people that they have suffered a total military defeat and that they cannot escape responsibility for what they have brought upon themselves, since their own ruthless warfare and the fanatical Nazi resistance have destroyed German economy and made chaos and suffering inevitable.
3. To destroy the National Socialist Party and its affiliated and supervised organizations, to dissolve all Nazi institutions, to insure that they are not revived in any form and to prevent all Nazi and militarist activity or propaganda.
4. To prepare for the eventual reconstruction of German political life on a democratic basis and for the eventual peaceful cooperation in international life by Germany.

Since Germany's evasions of the Treaty of Versailles were made easier by the fact that Allied occupation after World War I was confined to the Rhineland, this time occupation was extended over the whole country. All eastern Germany was occupied by Russian troops, while western Germany was divided into a northern zone occupied by the British, a southern zone occupied by the Americans, and a small zone along the Rhine occupied by the French. At Berlin—divided into separate Allied sectors—an Allied Control Commission, composed of the commanding generals of the four armies of occupation, had its headquarters. Matters affecting Germany as a whole were dealt with by the Control Commission; all local or regional matters were handled exclusively by the commander of that particular occupation zone. Although no provision was made for a central German government, the Potsdam

Declaration did stipulate that there should be certain administrative departments, staffed by Germans, to handle economic problems affecting the country as a whole.

BREAKDOWN OF THE POTSDAM AGREEMENT

The Potsdam Agreement proved to be extraordinarily difficult to administer. The central administrative departments which it stipulated were never established. In the earlier months of the occupation France offered the most serious obstacle, since she feared that an economic unification of Germany would be the prelude to a speedy German revival. As French objections were gradually quieted, Russia prevented the establishment of central administrative departments by making her consent conditional on terms which the western powers were unwilling to grant. As a result, the four occupation zones in effect divided Germany into four separate countries, governed in conformity with different philosophies and carrying on trade with each other under difficult conditions. This resulted in near-starvation economic conditions for the German population and dangerous suspicions among the Allied governments.

In the American zone primary importance was placed upon rebuilding German political life as speedily as possible. Advisory councils were elected, first at the local level and thereafter in the larger subdivisions corresponding to our counties and states. Each of the states adopted a new constitution drafted by a constituent assembly. The principle of federalism—sacred to Americans and familiar to the Germans from the days of the Empire and the Weimar Republic—was followed in the establishment of a federal council for the whole zone. Although both elected and appointed German officials performed their duties under the close scrutiny of American military government officials, the American policy was to interfere as little as possible and to throw responsibility upon the Germans. The newly built political structure was based on the essential democratic foundations of a free press, free functioning of political parties, and free elections.

The removal of Nazis from all positions of political and economic influence, although stipulated by the Potsdam Declaration, was not easy to carry out. During their twelve years of power the Nazis had established themselves in every part of German life. In the early days of occupation, American military government officials were severely criticized for allowing Nazis and near-Nazis to hold important positions, either through ignorance or because they placed more importance on the maintenance of efficiency than on the promotion of democracy. But General Patton and others who were overly tolerant of Nazis were removed from their posts in October, 1945, and thereafter denazification was more energetically carried out. Action was required at many different levels. Major offenders, who had taken a prominent part in plotting for World War II or had been responsible for war crimes, were tried by special military tribunals. Nazis and near-Nazis who held key posts in the bureaucracy or in industry were dismissed. Finally, the new German governments in the American zone passed their own denazification law and set up hundreds of tribunals to classify all adult Germans as to their relationship with the Nazi movement and punish those found guilty of active collaboration.

As we have seen, the Nazis were helped to power by many of the great German landowners and industrialists. It was not always easy for American administrators to recognize the need for drastic measures to curb the power of these classes. But timidity in this field not only threatened the future of German democratic institutions but played into the hands of the Communists, who contrasted American lenience with the stern measures taken in the Soviet zone to break the power of the Junkers and big businessmen. After some delay, the United States laid down a policy of dividing all estates of 250 acres or more into small holdings and breaking up the industrial cartels.

German Socialists considered this program inadequate and called for the nationalization of key industries, but American officials resisted any immediate steps in this direction. They believed industrial recovery would be retarded by nationalization and most of them disliked socialism in any case.

On various issues, British and French occupation policy in the early months differed somewhat from American. The British, for example, were much more sympathetic toward the nationalization program of the German Social Democrats. They believed that such a policy was particularly adapted for the great Ruhr industries, which lay within the British occupation zone. But this sympathy was not translated into action. The British were deterred from drastic steps by their own economic crisis and that of Germany. Feeding its occupation zone was an intolerable burden upon the weakened British nation, and it seemed imperative to build up German exports to pay for at least part of the imports. The British therefore decided to leave control of the great industries temporarily in the hands of experienced German businessmen. A further reason for avoiding hasty action was British fear of American disapproval. American influence over British policy was much increased by the economic union of the British and American zones, established in principle January 1, 1947, and implemented during the following summer.

The major conflicts of policy, however, were not between the United States and England but between the western powers and the Soviet Union. Although the Russian officials claimed to permit freedom of political activity in their zone, their policies strongly favored the German Communists. In the summer of 1946 the Social Democrats were induced under pressure to ally themselves with the Communists in a new Socialist Unity party. The Soviet occupation authorities then favored this group in various ways—by allotting more paper to the Socialist Unity newspapers, by timing Russian concessions to the occupation zone to coincide with elections, and by hampering opposition parties through police and information controls. Soviet tactics succeeded to the extent that the Socialist Unity party received a clear majority over its rivals in elections held in the eastern occupation zone.

Russian policy seemed clearly directed toward strengthening the Communist position throughout the country so that the Soviet-oriented party would be able to dominate Germany after the end of military occupation. But Russian methods often defeated their ends. The Social Democrats of the western zones resented Communist tactics and spurned invitations to join the Socialist Unity party. In the first western elections the Communists polled less than 10 percent of the vote. The Communist cause was further injured by Soviet reparations policy. In desperate need of immediate help, Russians dismantled and sent to the Soviet Union plants and machinery representing perhaps one-half the industrial capacity of their zone. These wholesale removals deepened for millions of Germans the anti-Communist sentiments inculcated by years of Nazi propaganda.

The reparations problem provided material for bitter recriminations between the occupying powers. The western nations rebuked Russia for indiscriminate seizure of German factories without adequate accounting. The Soviet Union condemned the other powers for not carrying out the Potsdam Agreement on reparations, which provided for extensive allotments of plant and equipment to Russia from the western zones, where most of German industry was concentrated. The western powers justified their policy with the argument that the Potsdam Declaration had contemplated the economic unity of the country and that reparations from the west could not be made to the Russians so long as Soviet policy blocked the flow of foodstuffs and raw materials from eastern to western Germany.

Obviously, what was imperatively needed was four-power agreement as to both occupation policy and the future status of Germany. But conferences of the foreign ministers at Moscow in March, 1947, and at London in

December of the same year ended in failure. Not only were the diplomats unable to write a peace treaty for Germany, but they could not even provide for the economic unification of the country. The Soviet government placed great emphasis on two points. They asked for ten billion dollars of reparations, to be paid from the current production of all Germany; they asked also for the creation of a strongly centralized German government. United States Secretary of State George Marshall rejected these demands, because he considered them part of a Russian scheme to extend Communist control over the whole country by establishing "a centralized government, adapted to the seizure of absolute control of a country which would be doomed economically through inadequate area and excessive population, and would be mortgaged to turn over a large part of its production as reparations, principally to the Soviet Union."

THE BERLIN CRISIS

After the failure of the London Conference, the western powers abandoned efforts to secure a four-power agreement and concentrated on the problem of building a state of Western Germany from the three western occupation zones. A first step toward this end had already been taken in the economic union of the British and American zones during 1947. Further steps required the coöperation of France—not easy to secure since the French had a legitimate fear of steps that might permit Germany to again menace her neighbors. The French were particularly reluctant to see the great industries of the Ruhr under German control. From February to June, 1948, a new London Conference—to which the Soviet Union was not invited but Great Britain, the United States, France, Belgium, the Netherlands, and Luxemburg were—wrestled with the problem of restoring Western Germany without jeopardizing the security of Germany's neighbors. The plan eventually accepted provided for the creation of a federal state of Western Germany and the establishment of an International Authority of fifteen members to control the Ruhr industries.

The new policy represented an attempt not only to cut through the four-power impasse on Germany but to contribute to the economic recovery of Europe. The United States was contributing large sums for this purpose under the Marshall Plan and it seemed imperative to revive the economy of Western Germany and integrate it with that of its neighbors. As a necessary preliminary to all this, the western powers instituted a currency reform in the three western occupation zones. This plan involved the substitution of new Deutsche marks or "West marks" for the almost worthless reichsmarks then flooding the country. The new sound currency helped to kill the black market and make available food stores hoarded by the farmers.

These decisions by the western powers were highly displeasing to the Russians, who denounced them as contrary to the Potsdam Agreement. Soviet disapproval was given tangible form by the Berlin "blockade." All railroad, highway, and canal traffic from the western occupation zones across the hundred-mile Soviet occupation zone corridor to Berlin was halted. The Russians based their action on the pretext that introduction of the West marks into the British, French, and American sectors of Berlin made drastic controls necessary. They issued a new currency of their own—the East mark—through whose manipulation they sought to dominate Berlin economic life. But this complicated currency war was only one phase of a more fundamental struggle. Russia's real objective was to bring about the unification of all Germany under conditions that would permit a Communist seizure of power. By the Berlin blockade she hoped to force an abandonment of the project for a Western German state. Failing this, she hoped at least to force the western powers to withdraw from Berlin. Since the historic capital was a symbol of enormous importance, such a withdrawal would be a humiliating defeat for the democracies. It would, moreover, permit the establishment of a Soviet-dominated regime at Berlin, which would claim to be the true government of Germany, thus undermining the prestige of any Western German government.

But the western powers were determined both to stay in Berlin and to proceed with their plans for a Western German state. On June 26, 1948, two days after the Russian blockade was instituted, the Berlin air lift began its remarkable operations. To transport supplies by airplane to sustain an urban population of two million persons seemed fantastic. Even with the imposition of strict rationing of food, fuel, and electricity, some four thousand tons of imports a day were required. By a miracle of organization, this daily average was not only achieved but sufficiently surpassed to provide a modest stock pile against bad flying days and other emergencies. The skeptical conceded that the air lift might succeed in the summer, but they were convinced that it would fail in the winter, when fuel requirements increased and flying weather was often bad. Yet despite hardships the great German city was kept supplied in January as it had been in August.

The air lift not only saved the western powers from a humiliating diplomatic defeat but gave all Europe a striking demonstration of the determination of the democracies to hold their ground at all cost. The Russians lost correspondingly. Anti-Communist feeling in Berlin and the western occupation zones was intensified by the Soviet blockade. Moreover, the counterblockade of the western powers deprived the Soviet zone of much needed goods. These developments resulted in a Russian decision to lift the blockade in May, 1949. For their part, the western powers agreed to a new four-power conference at Paris to discuss the whole German problem. But the foreign ministers, although agreeing to minor provisions for increasing east-west trade, remained deadlocked on major issues.

The West German State

Meanwhile, the West German State was in the process of creation. From September, 1948, to May, 1949, delegates from the three western occupation zones, meeting at Bonn, debated the provisions of a new German constitution. Agreement was difficult, since the two principal parties, the Christian Democrats and the Social Democrats, had equal representation in the Bonn assembly and were fundamentally opposed on certain major issues. The Social Democrats advocated such a distribution of powers between central and state governments as would permit the nationalization of key industries and strong regulation of industry by the central government. The conservative Christian Democrats advocated relatively weak central institutions and the retention of large powers by the states. The occupying powers, seeing in states' rights an obstacle both to the revival of aggressive nationalism and the capture of power by the Communists, gave their support to the Christian Democrats.

Finally, the necessary compromises were made and the constitution secured the assent of the Bonn assembly, the various German states, and the occupying powers. It provided for a federal republic, composed of eleven *Laender* or states. Provision was made for the admission of new states in the hope that the five *Laender* of the Soviet zone would eventually join what the Germans at once nicknamed the *Kernstaat* (kernel state). For the time being, the capital was to be Bonn—once again German aspirations were clear: the eventual capital ought to be Berlin. In other details the Bonn Constitution showed points of similarity with the Weimar Constitution of pre-Hitler days and the constitutions of Great Britain, France, and the United States. A two-house legislature was provided: the lower house (the Bundestag) was to be elected by universal secret ballot under a system of proportional representation; the upper house (the Bundesrat) was to be elected by the state governments. The President, an official of narrowly limited powers like the President of France, was to be elected by the Bundestag and an equal number of state representatives. The Chancellor, whose powers resembled the French Premier or

English Prime Minister, was to be chosen directly by the lower house and might be overthrown by a no-confidence vote. If the Bundestag were unable to agree upon his successor, the Chancellor might order dissolution of Parliament and new elections.

The powers of the new government were limited not only by its constitution but by the Occupation Statute, an agreement of Great Britain, France, and the United States defining their relations with the new German state. Occupation troops were to remain in their respective three zones under military commanders, but Allied military government as such was to be ended and a new Allied High Commission, composed of civilians, established. The German state was to have "full legislative, executive and judicial powers"—subject to important limitations. Through the Allied High Commission, the occupying powers would continue to exercise authority in matters relating to disarmament, reparations, civil aviation, foreign affairs, and foreign trade. Control of the Ruhr industries, including the distribution of Ruhr coal, coke, and steel production, was to be vested in the International Authority provided for earlier. Symbolic of the occupation's new phase was the resignation of General Lucius D. Clay as United States Military Governor and the appointment of John J. McCloy, a civilian, to succeed him. McCloy, destined to be the American member of the new Allied High Commission, enjoyed a reputation for administrative ability gained as head of the International Bank for Reconstruction and Development.

First elections under the Bonn Constitution were held on August 14, 1949, after spirited campaigning by the several parties. The results provided an index of the political situation as the new republic began its history. The Communists, who condemned the Bonn Constitution and the whole idea of a West German State, did poorly, receiving 1,360,443 votes (15 seats in the Bundestag). This was only 6 percent of the total vote in contrast with the 10 percent that they had received in the elections of

1946. The Social Democrats put up a strong fight and received 6,932,272 votes (131 seats), but were beaten by their principal rivals, the Christian Democrats, who had 7,357,579 votes (139 seats). The conservative trend was further emphasized by 2,827,948 ballots (52 seats) cast for the Free Democrats, 986,606 votes (17 seats) for the Bavarian party, and 940,088 votes (17 seats) for the German party.

In September the newly elected delegates assembled at Bonn to set the governmental machinery in operation. Dr. Theodor Heuss, a member of the Free Democratic party, was elected President and Dr. Konrad Adenauer, the head of the Christian Democrats, became Chancellor. Adenauer's cabinet was a coalition of Christian Democrats, Free Democrats, and German party members. The government parties were all conservative in philosophy. The Christian Democrats, drawing most of their strength from the Catholics, who composed about one-half the population of the West German State, advocated cautious reforms but opposed any step toward socialism. The Free Democrats were also middle-of-the-roaders, placing their principal emphasis on a minimum of regulation for business. The German party was supported by nationalists and authoritarians, whose distaste for Western democracy was scarcely concealed. That the Adenauer government would be hostile to communism was obvious; that it would rule in the spirit of liberal democracy was much less certain.

The Struggle for Germany

The Soviet Union countered the establishment of the West German State by prompting the German Communists to form a rival government in the eastern zone. The procedure by which this was done is illustrative of the difference between Communist and democratic methods. The steps just described, by which representatives from the various political factions of Western Germany met to frame a constitution and submit their proposal to the various states for ratification, had no parallel in the Soviet occupation zone; nor did the elections by which a government for the new Western state was chosen. In the eastern zone the procedure was to summon to Berlin members of the so-called People's Council—an appointed body composed of members of various political parties, trade unions, youth, and agricultural groups. Addressing this body on October 7, 1949, Wilhelm Pieck, German Communist leader, asked its members whether they wanted to become the lower house of an all-German Parliament. All in favor stood up and cheered while Pieck announced: "The People's Council has proclaimed itself the People's Chamber of Parliament." This rubber-stamp body designated Pieck as President and Otto Grotewohl as Prime Minister of the "German Democratic Republic." Elections were postponed for a year.

The effect of four years of military occupation was thus to divide Germany, for the time being at least, into two nations—each desirous of absorbing the other on its own terms. By many standards, the West German State was stronger than its East German counterpart. West Germany's forty-seven million population was more than twice that of the East; West Germany before the war accounted for 86 percent of German steel production, 80 percent of its coal, and 61 percent of its industrial products. Its most serious deficiency was food, since only 45 percent of the prewar German food production was from this area.

Yet the Communist-dominated East German State was not without powerful assets. A government calling itself "the German Democratic Republic" with its capital at historic Berlin was likely to provide a more powerful rallying point for German nationalism than a "German Federal Republic" with a capital at a provincial city like Bonn. The Soviet Union, pushing relentlessly toward control of the entire country, encouraged the formation of a National Front of patriotic Germans to bring about reunification of all Germany. So strong was the nationalist sentiment that there was danger that the unification movement might mount to dangerous dimensions despite its obviously Communist character. Part of the propaganda drive was to encourage the hope that the Soviet Union would soon negotiate a peace treaty with the German Democratic Republic and withdraw its occupation troops. Such a Russian move would place the western occupying powers in a difficult position. If they continued to insist on occupation, they would expose themselves to angry condemnation from all German nationalists. If they withdrew their troops along with the Russians, the West German State might collapse and Germany might be united under circumstances that would permit the Communists to seize control over the whole country. Particularly disquieting was the growth of an efficient, well-armed, and thoroughly loyal Communist police force in the East German State.

The Adenauer government, no match for the Communists in the game of propaganda, tried to demonstrate its nationalism by demanding concessions from the western Allies. Arguing plausibly that the dismantling of German factories was inconsistent with the Marshall Plan, the West German government was able to secure a curtailment of the dismantling program. The German republic also contended that strengthening western Europe against communism required lifting the limitations on German steel production and returning the Ruhr industries to unfettered German control. Although these demands found a sympathetic response in many American quarters, they were regarded with natural suspicion by France and other neighbors, who remembered the aggressive use to which German steel production had been put in the past. Even more controversial were proposals that the West German State should be permitted to rearm as an ally against Soviet imperialism.

Western policy makers were obviously facing a dilemma. To keep the West German State weak was to paralyze an area which could add much-needed strength to the defense of western Europe. To allow the West German State to grow strong was to revive the danger of German aggression. Indeed, on the basis of history, there was nothing to prevent a restored Germany from deserting the western Allies and joining Russia in a war against the democracies.

To many observers the most hopeful escape from this dilemma was to merge the industrial and military potential of western Germany in some larger whole. Projects for a western European federation were seriously discussed, but practical steps toward this goal were taken with what seemed to most Americans exasperating slowness. One of the most helpful suggestions for lessening national economic rivalries was offered by Foreign Minister Robert Schuman of France, who suggested in May, 1950, that the entire coal and steel production of France and Germany should be pooled under the direction of a joint commission.

The future for democracy in Germany was still uncertain. By Western standards the Adenauer government had disturbing tendencies toward overriding opposition and limiting freedom of speech and press. But its sins against democratic ideals were far less serious than those of the Communist-dominated East German State, where life became steadily more regimented and the penalties for nonconformity more drastic. Indeed this object lesson in Communist methods was one of the strongest supports for opposition to communism in the western occupation zones. Anticommunism, however, is never an adequate guarantee of democracy: it leads, indeed, all too often to authoritarian conservatism. Not yet have the foundations been laid in Germany for a broadly democratic movement, dedicated to maintaining the liberties of the people, promoting the general welfare, and living in peaceful coöperation with neighboring peoples.

CHAPTER XVIII

Patterns of Western Europe: France

ONE OF THE MOST SERIOUS RESULTS of World War II has been the eclipse—temporarily, at least—of France as a great power. Badly defeated by Germany in 1940, occupied and exploited by the Germans for four years, the French people went through a psychological experience of the most damaging kind. Since the liberation the nation has had to deal with a succession of difficult problems—runaway inflation, low industrial production, poor harvests, and a succession of political crises related to the economic problems both as cause and effect. The French Communist movement, believing the nation ripe for a capture of power, has maintained a ceaseless agitation. At the other extreme, factions with thinly disguised fascist aims have whipped up anti-Red hysteria in the hope that they may establish an authoritarian regime. Amid this confusion French moderates have tried to reëstablish democratic institutions and restore order and prosperity. The task has been almost impossibly difficult—the more so since French democrats disagree among themselves upon the extent to which the French economy should be reorganized along socialist lines.

A great question mark hangs over France's future. Not only France but the whole world is vitally concerned in the outcome. A genuine French recovery would be a most important contribution to the establishment of international stability.

POLITICAL TRADITIONS: MONARCHY AND REPUBLIC

France has a great tradition of political liberty, but it is a tradition neither so old nor so universally accepted by the French people as the traditions of representative government in England and the United States. The French States-General was similar in its origins to the British Parliament, but it failed to establish control of the purse or legislative powers. From 1614 to 1789 the French kings carried on their government without convening the ancient body. They imposed such taxes and made such laws as suited their royal pleasure. Nor did Frenchmen secure the same protection through their courts as did the English. Arbitrary arrest and imprisonment were frequent. There was not the same evolution toward freedom of speech, press, and assembly as across the Channel, while the French nobility and the Roman Catholic clergy retained privileges far more extensive than the parallel groups in England.

But not all Frenchmen acquiesced in these conditions. During the eighteenth century, French philosophers and men of letters repeatedly criticized the inequalities and injustices of the political and social system. They laid the yardstick of right reason against French institutions and demonstrated that the latter were deficient. Montesquieu and Voltaire made damaging criticisms of the old regime, but it remained for Rousseau to inflame the literate classes with a zeal for reform. Borrowing most of his ideas from Locke and Montesquieu, Rousseau stated them so strikingly that he reached a much wider audience. In the *Social Contract* (1761) Rousseau said that "all the rulers of the earth are mere delegates of the people, who, when they are displeased with the government, have the right to alter or abolish it."

The old regime in France eventually dug its own grave.

The expenses of many wars and an extravagant court brought the nation to the verge of bankruptcy in 1789. In desperation Louis XVI revived the institution of the States-General to secure the support of the nation in meeting the crisis. But when the historic body began to sit again, the representatives of the middle class immediately objected to the medieval organization under which the so-called third estate might always be outvoted by the first two estates, composed of the clergy and the nobility. In defiance of the king's orders the middle-class representatives organized themselves as a National Assembly and invited the representatives of the first two estates to join them.

This was the first episode in the great Revolution which was to transform the French nation. The National Assembly proceeded to enact fundamental reforms. The special privileges of the clergy and nobility—their exemptions from taxation, their monopoly of many civil and military offices, their servile dues and tithes, their feudal monopolies and hunting rights—were swept away. As a first step toward drafting a constitution for the kingdom, a Declaration of the Rights of Man was adopted. Drawing both from British and American precedents and from the philosophy of Rousseau, the Declaration was a magnificent document. Such striking statements as these were included:

The aim of all political association is the preservation of the natural and imprescriptible rights of man. These rights are liberty, property, security and resistance to oppression. . . . Law is the expression of the general will. Every citizen has a right to participate personally, or through his representative, in its formation. It must be the same for all, whether it protects or punishes. All citizens, being equal in the eyes of the law, are equally eligible to all dignities and to all public positions and occupations, according to their abilities, and without distinction except that of their virtues and talents. . . . No person shall be accused, arrested or imprisoned, except in cases and according to the forms prescribed by law. . . . No one shall be disquieted on account of his opinions, including his religious views, provided their manifestation does not disturb the public order established by law.

Although the king and the more conservative factions among the privileged classes offered some resistance to these initial reforms, they had to submit because of the overwhelming demand of the nation. But the destruction of the old regime soon went so far as to arouse bitter hostility. When the National Assembly confiscated the vast properties of the church to apply upon the national debt, and when it attempted to extend the authority of the state over the church, it made powerful enemies. The Roman Catholic clergy denounced these steps vehemently, and their influence was great—particularly with the peasantry of western France. Meanwhile many of the nobles had gone into exile and were intriguing abroad to secure the intervention of foreign kings to restore the old regime. In 1792 France became involved in war with Prussia and Austria. The effect of this was to force the revolution into more radical channels. The attempt to establish a constitutional monarchy was abandoned; the king was deposed and imprisoned; a republic was proclaimed.

The First Republic had a stormy history. Confronted with enemies on every hand—both outside France and within—a Committee of Public Safety was set up with dictatorial powers. The war against foreign enemies was successfully organized and insurrections by the conservative peasantry were put down. Louis XVI and Marie Antoinette, accused of treasonable correspondence with foreign courts, were brought to trial and executed, and hundreds of other domestic enemies of the Republic—real or imagined—were sent to the guillotine. The Reign of Terror was brief, and in 1794 the radicals lost control. A conservative constitution was drafted, granting the franchise only to property owners and vesting the executive power in a Directory of five members.

The Man on Horseback

The Directory was hated by most of the French population because of its corruption and inefficiency. There was, therefore, little opposition when in 1799 Napoleon Bonaparte, the most brilliant of French generals, suddenly used the army to overthrow the republican government and establish a dictatorship. By a plebiscite in 1804 the French people approved Napoleon's assumption of the title "Emperor."

In many ways Napoleon showed himself more intelligent than his imitators of the twentieth century. He realized that despite the disorder and bloodshed of the Revolution there had been a great deal of constructive reform which should be perpetuated. He accordingly protected the peasantry in their new rights of ownership; he opposed the restoration of feudal privileges; he preserved the principle of equality before the law. Furthermore, he instituted certain great reforms of his own. He codified the law, reorganized the national administrative system, promoted the cause of education, and brought an end to the feud with the church. Above all, he provided order and stable government—conditions sorely needed for the restoration of French economic prosperity.

Thus, a third French tradition was founded. The first tradition had been that of the monarchy and the old regime with its deference for the privileges of the church and the nobility. The second had been that of the French Revolution and the republic, with its great motto, "Liberty, Equality, Fraternity." The third was the tradition of "the man on horseback"—the strong leader who quieted all internal dissension and brought order and stable government.

Of course, the man on horseback brought other things as well. He brought the extinction of liberty and popular participation in the government. Freedom of debate, speech, press, and assembly was terminated. The arbitrary arrest and imprisonment of political offenders were restored. Elections were manipulated, the legislative body became a rubber stamp, and the emperor himself became the real source of all new law. But the heaviest price that the French paid for acquiescing in the rule of the man on horseback was perpetual involvement in war. Napoleon's restless ambition resulted in a tragic waste of France's wealth and manhood and eventually united all Europe against him. In 1815 the emperor met his final defeat and spent the rest of his life as the prisoner of the English.

THE TWO FRANCES

Throughout the nineteenth century France's political life was subject to revolutions, coups d'état, and crises. Following the downfall of Napoleon, the Bourbon dynasty was restored. At first, the kings recognized the need to follow constitutional principles, but the clergy and the nobility intrigued for a more complete restoration of the old regime. The steps taken in this direction so alarmed the liberals that in 1830 the Bourbons were overthrown and Louis Philippe, an Orleanist prince, was made king. This "July Revolution," as it was called, resulted in vesting the real power of government in the hands of the wealthier elements of the middle class. In 1848 another revolution occurred. The Second French Republic was set up, but its life was short. The French people elected—of all persons—Louis Napoleon Bonaparte, the nephew of the great Napoleon, as their President. The inevitable happened. By coups d'état and plebiscites Louis Napoleon first illegally extended his term as President, then bestowed the title of "emperor" upon himself. The Second Empire, like the First, brought strong government and material prosperity but also deprivation of liberty and, eventually, war. In 1870 Napoleon III was captured by the Prussian army, when the French suffered a disastrous defeat at Sedan. For several years after the Franco-Prussian War France's political future was uncertain, but eventually the Third Republic evolved and attained sufficient stability to survive until 1940.

But on several occasions the Third Republic seemed in grave danger. By no means did it have that substantially unanimous acceptance which is necessary for successful democratic government. As the situation was frequently described, there were two Frances. One was republican France, loyally defended by those who cherished the ideals of the French Revolution. This France had the allegiance of most of the French middle class, a part of the peasantry —particularly those of the Southeast—and most of the urban proletariat. But republican France was never loved by authoritarian France, which yearned either for the restoration of the monarchy, the aristocracy, and the state church or for the man on horseback who would rule with an iron hand. Authoritarian France had the allegiance of the nobility, most of the professional military class, many of the Roman Catholic clergy, and many big businessmen. The antirepublican right also had a certain following among the peasantry and among members of the middle class who feared radicalism.

France's tendency toward civil strife is illustrated by events during the 1930's. Just as in Germany, the effect of the great depression was to confront the democratic parties governing the country with almost impossible problems. Authoritarian France began to bestir itself. Numerous fascist leagues were formed, and there were serious demonstrations. The gravest of these occurred in February, 1934, when so much disorder was stirred up that the liberal government of the day had to resign in favor of a more conservative one. The republic appeared to be in great danger, but it survived the crisis owing to several circumstances. Fortunately, there were several would-be men on horseback, and the fascist movement was never consolidated. Moreover, the French Communists learned something from the experience of their German brothers. Although they too had been guilty of

GREAT ISSUES

agitating against the republic, they were sufficiently warned
by the rising strength of the French fascists to change
their tactics. They rallied to the support of the republic
and coöperated in the creation of a great Popular Front,
composed of themselves, the Socialists, and the so-called
Radical Socialists—who were neither radical nor socialist,
but a strongly republican middle-class party. The Popular
Front enjoyed a sweeping victory in the French elections
of 1936. Léon Blum, the leader of the Socialist party,
became Premier, and a broad program of social reform
was enacted. The measures of this French New Deal were
by no means radical, but they aroused great resentment on
the part of French industrialists. France had been temporarily saved from fascism, but the cleavage between the
two Frances was sharper than ever.

France in World War II

This lack of unity was fatal to France's war effort in
1939 and 1940. Many Frenchmen—some of them in high
positions in the army and in industry—feared a French
victory almost more than they did a French defeat. They
reasoned that the defeat of the Nazis would be a great
victory for the French left, who would gain a secure control of the government. "Better Hitler than Blum," was
their slogan—certainly a disastrous one for a nation at war.
But the French left was itself divided. Because of the
Soviet-German nonaggression treaty of 1939, the French
Communists argued that the war was not in the interests
of the workers. Strikes in the factories and desertions
from the army resulted from this Communist position.
Probably France would have been defeated in any case
because of Germany's greater population and industrial
potential, but the defeat was rendered more humiliating
by the evidence that many Frenchmen had not been
whole-hearted in their patriotism.

Authoritarian France returned to power from 1940 to
1944. The so-called Vichy government of Marshal Pétain
and Pierre Laval substituted the slogan of "Work, Family,

Fatherland" for the old "Liberty, Equality, Fraternity." It ruled by decree without the participation of the French parliament. It sought to reorganize French social and educational life in order to promote the interests of the army and the church. It collaborated with Nazi Germany, Fascist Italy, and authoritarian Japan.

But only a minority of Frenchmen were ready to follow the Vichy regime in its repudiation of democracy and its coöperation with the Axis. During the great disaster of June, 1940, General Charles de Gaulle, then Undersecretary of State for War, escaped to London and addressed the French people over the British radio. "France has lost a battle," De Gaulle asserted; "she has not lost the war." His words proved a rallying cry for thousands of his fellow countrymen. Denying the authority of the Pétain government, De Gaulle organized what was known at first as the Free French movement and later by other names. The Free French organized an army on British soil and, with British support, ousted the Vichy faction from control of some of the outlying parts of the French Empire.

Of course, the number of Frenchmen who could escape from France and serve directly under De Gaulle was relatively small. But within France itself much could be done to sabotage French munition plants working for the Germans and to resist Vichy's efforts at collaboration. Above all, patriotic Frenchmen could spy on the Germans, secrete arms, effect a military organization, and generally prepare to take the field against the Germans when the Allies finally attempted the invasion of France. Under the noses of the Germans the French Forces of the Interior (FFI) took form as a great secret army. The resistance movement played an important role in the eventual liberation of France; it was of decisive importance also in laying the basis for future political developments.

In the heroic days of the resistance movement when Frenchmen risked their lives to associate with it, there was a minimum of partisanship. Many individuals who had been associated with the right refused to follow

Pétain and Laval into the Axis camp. In the FFI such conservatives worked side by side with moderates and leftists. The German attack on Russia in June, 1941, gave the French Communists a lesson—that should not have been necessary—in the need for all-out resistance to the Germans. They now provided much of the boldest and most active participation in the resistance movement. The resistance also won the vigorous support of many Catholics who spurned the clericalism of Pétain and threw in their lot with the fighters for democracy.

The moratorium on partisanship resulted in general acceptance of De Gaulle's leadership. Before the war the general had been an outstanding advocate of tank warfare and a critic of the backwardness of French military thought, but in other ways he had been a typical professional soldier, sharing the conservative political views characteristic of his class. Despite this, De Gaulle became the great hero of a movement predominantly leftist in its following. The paradox, of course, is easily explained. The general's political philosophy was of little interest so long as the German boot was still on France's neck. In the great hour of decision De Gaulle had defied the Nazis and their Vichy puppets, and for the moment this was all that mattered. De Gaulle was the symbol of the unvanquished French spirit, and patriotic Frenchmen of every political hue rallied around him.

PROBLEMS OF THE FOURTH REPUBLIC

De Gaulle's prestige continued to grow until after V-E Day. The United States was for many months unwilling to give official recognition to his leadership. This was due at first to our wish to continue diplomatic relations with the Vichy regime in order to exert counterinfluence against the Germans and to prepare the way for the invasion of North Africa. After that, we dealt with leaders like Admiral Darlan and General Giraud, since their orders to cease firing would be obeyed by many French officers who would not have obeyed De Gaulle. But during 1943 the

Free French leader secured effective control over the administration of North Africa and the next year, when the Germans were driven out of France, he set up a Provisional Government in Paris.

By this time the parties which were to participate in postwar French politics had emerged. Despite the patriotism of many individual members of the right, this section of French politics as a whole was in disgrace because of the activities of the collaborationists. Even the Radical Socialists, the moderate party which had provided most of the premiers of the thirties, were in disrepute because of their bad record in Munich days. The three parties whose zeal in the resistance movement had given them great prestige all belonged nominally at least to the left. Two of these were the Communists and Socialists, whose leadership and program were familiar to the nation from prewar days. The third party, the Popular Republicans or MRP (*Mouvement républicain populaire*), was new. Its membership was originally drawn largely from Catholic trade unions and Catholic young people; its program was anticapitalist, calling for the nationalization of much of the French economy, national planning, and a broad program of social reform, but it was also clerical, proposing that private Catholic schools should receive subsidies from the state.

In October, 1945, the French voters went to the polls in the first postwar national election to choose representatives for a Constituent Assembly to draft a new constitution. The results were significant. In contrast with prewar French politics, when a large number of factions divided the ballots, about 80 percent of the vote was cast for the three great parties. For the first time in French history, the Communists secured more votes than any other party. Second in strength were the Popular Republicans while the Socialists were a close third.

De Gaulle's prestige was still tremendous and the Constituent Assembly unanimously elected him President of the new Provisional Government. But partisan politics soon revived. On the basis of their success in the election, the Communists demanded the right to name such key officials as the Foreign Minister, the Minister of War, and the Minister of the Interior. When De Gaulle refused to entrust any of these vital offices to them, a political crisis developed. Eventually, a compromise was arranged: De Gaulle remained as president; the Communists secured several important posts but none of those in dispute; other posts were divided among the Socialists, the Popular Republicans, and certain independent groups.

But the truce between De Gaulle and the Communists was soon broken. In January, 1946, a crisis arose over the provisions of the new constitution. The general was convinced that the history of the Third Republic had demonstrated the need for a stronger executive. Instead of the figurehead president of prewar days, De Gaulle advocated constitutional provisions which would give the French President approximately the same powers as those of the President of the United States. But the Communists, fearing that such an executive might obstruct radical economic change, called for a weak presidency and an all-powerful assembly which would designate the cabinet and fix its policy. The Popular Republicans supported the general on this issue, but the Socialists sided with the Communists—remembering probably how the delegation of strong executive powers had delivered the First French Republic into the hands of Napoleon I and the Second Republic into the hands of Napoleon III. Unable to have his way, De Gaulle resigned the presidency of the Provisional Government. A Socialist, Félix Gouin, succeeded him.

De Gaulle out of office was perhaps a more potent political influence than De Gaulle in office. Now he could not be blamed for any of the failures of the Provisional Government, but could throw his enormous influence into the balance on crucial issues. This was illustrated in May, 1946, when a constitution representing principally the ideas of the Communists was submitted to the French voters and was rejected. A new Constituent Assembly had to be elected. In this election of June 2, 1946, the Popular Republicans went ahead of its two rivals and became the largest party in the Assembly; the Communists were second in strength and the Socialists remained third.

A compromise constitution was now drafted. Instead of the unicameral legislature advocated by the Communists, it provided an upper house or Council of the Republic with power to delay actions of the Assembly if it disapproved measures passed by the latter body. The President was to be elected by the parliament for a seven-year term. He was given the right to ask the Assembly to reconsider any law with which he disagreed. If two governments fell within eighteen months, the Assembly might be dissolved and new elections held. In such particulars as these, the new constitution was more conservative than the proposal rejected in May. De Gaulle was not satisfied, since the strong presidency which he advocated was not included, but in October, 1946, the new constitution was adopted.

THE COMMUNIST PROBLEM

One of the most troublesome problems for the Socialist and Popular Republican leaders was that of whether or not to include the Communists in the government. The practice of giving cabinet posts to the extreme left had begun under De Gaulle in recognition of the great efforts that the Communists had made in the resistance movement. In 1946, however, De Gaulle began to attack the Communists as being subservient to Moscow and likely to compromise France's independence if they gained too much power. He advocated excluding them from the government. But for many months the responsible Socialist and Popular Republican leaders continued to include them. Georges Bidault, the Popular Republican President of the Provisional Government during the latter half of 1946, gave cabinet posts to the Communists as had the Socialist Gouin during the first half of the year.

The reasons for including the Communists were several. Their creditable record during the period of German occupation was one; their large popular vote in the postwar elections and their heavy representation in the Constituent Assembly were others. But above all, it was believed necessary to include the Communists because of their dominant position in the French labor unions. Although the rank and file of labor were divided between the Socialists and the Communists, the Communists had gained control of the most important unions of the country and were particularly strong in the great Confédération Générale du Travail (CGT). France's economic situation was desperate. Above all things, she needed maximum production from her industry and agriculture. The inclusion of Communists in the government seemed to contribute to this end. They used their influence to keep strikes at a minimum, and they gave valuable support to the so-called Monnet Plan for modernizing and expanding the French economy.

The Communist position seemed strong and was made stronger by the results of the first elections under the new constitution in November, 1946. The Communists increased their vote and became the largest party in the new Assembly, while both the Popular Republicans and the Socialists showed a loss of strength since the June elections. Despite the fact that the Socialists had done particularly poorly they held the balance of power between the Communists and Popular Republicans and had to undertake the responsibilities of leadership during a difficult period. Socialist Vincent Auriol was elected President, Socialist Paul Ramadier became Premier. The cabinet was composed of representatives of the three great parties.

But as time went on, the advantages of including the Communists in the government became less obvious than the disadvantages. Although Communist ministers were often intelligent and efficient, they took their orders in important matters from their own party leadership rather than from the head of the government. Seeking to increase their popularity with the workers, the Communists supported the wage demands of French labor despite the nation's desperate need to break the cycle of inflation.

The showdown came in May, 1947. When Premier Ramadier opposed the demands of strikers in some of the country's leading industries, the Communists in the Assembly voted against the policy of the government. Thereupon Ramadier expelled the Communist ministers from his cabinet, and the attempt at a three-party coalition was abandoned. Although the crisis seemed to arise out of a purely domestic problem, undoubtedly the trends of world politics in 1947 were involved. Only from the United States might France hope to get the economic assistance necessary for its recovery, and the French Socialists and the Popular Republicans obviously believed that their chances of American aid would be improved if they purged the cabinet of Communists. The government was now in the hands of moderates who were thoroughly devoted to the Fourth Republic. But their problems were tremendous. Out of the government, the Communists of course had no need for restraint. They fomented labor disturbances of an increasingly serious character in an effort to demonstrate that it was impossible to govern France without their support. They carried on a campaign of propaganda against the Marshall Plan, which they labeled a clever piece of capitalist imperialism.

To add to the government's burdens, General de Gaulle emerged from retirement and launched a new political movement called the Reunion of the French People (RPF). To combat communism, he called upon patriotic Frenchmen of all parties to join in a great common front. Municipal elections on October 9 and 26, 1947, demonstrated the strength of the new movement. The De Gaullists secured 40 percent of the vote and became the largest party in the country. At the other extreme, the Communists retained most of their strength with about 29 percent of the vote. The Socialists were third, and the Popular Republicans were the principal losers, falling from second to fourth place. Obviously, the more conservative members of this moderate party had deserted Bidault for De Gaulle.

The political situation created by this election was extraordinary, since the new De Gaullist movement, although now the largest party in the country, was unrepresented in the National Assembly. The general called upon Ramadier to resign and clear the way for new elections to the Assembly. More than ever, he insisted upon the need for amending the 1946 Constitution by granting large powers to the executive. Attempting to resist this pressure from the right, the Ramadier government found itself also subjected to new and much more serious attacks from the left. A new wave of strikes began to sweep over France. The Communists, obviously seeing the impossibility of further increases in their popular vote, were engaged in a desperate effort to demonstrate the contention that the French economy could not function without their consent.

The Ramadier government was drowned by this sea of troubles, and Robert Schuman, a member of the right wing of the MRP, became Premier with a cabinet composed of right-wing Socialists, Popular Republicans, and Radical Socialists. The initial result of Communist demonstrations had been to bring about a shift toward conservatism. Schuman, the first Premier of the Fourth Republic to favor free enterprise over socialism, advocated drastic measures to curb the wave of strikes.

THE THIRD FORCE

Politics in France continued to revolve around the efforts of the Communists and the Gaullists to capture power and the efforts of the moderates to prevent this. A working alliance of Socialists, Popular Republicans, and Radical Socialists attempted to build up the so-called

"Third Force" as a counterweight to the extremist parties. The alliance was not easy to maintain, because, although the three parties agreed in their devotion to democracy, they disagreed on other fundamental issues. To conquer inflation, the Socialists advocated strict government controls, the Popular Republicans more moderate controls, the Radicals a return to free economy. The issue of state aid to Catholic schools also divided the parties: the Popular Republicans supported such proposals; the Socialists and Radicals were both opposed. As a result of recurrent cabinet crises, the Third Force governments were several times reshuffled to bring new figures to the fore. The Schuman government lasted only from November, 1947, to July, 1948; the Marie government, which succeeded it, fell a month later and was replaced by a cabinet headed by Henri Queuille, a Radical Socialist. Queuille managed to hold his cabinet together until October, 1949, when after a serious political crisis the Popular Republican leader, Georges Bidault, became Premier of a new Third Force coalition government. In February, 1950, the Socialists in the cabinet resigned, but Bidault continued as Premier and the Socialists refrained from using their votes to overturn the government.

The Third Force, walking its precarious tightrope, was confronted by frequent strikes. Behind most of these were Communist labor-union leaders, using their power in an attempt both to force the Communists back into the government and to reduce French production as a blow to the European Recovery Program. But the strikes generally had the support of non-Communist workers as well. Since wages were controlled more effectively than prices, the workers suffered much through inflation. The most serious strike was that of October, 1948, in the coal mines. Operations were halted for a month—a heavy blow to the French economy. The Queuille government sent soldiers and police into the mines; the Communists retaliated with acts of violence and serious sabotage. In the end, the government granted a partial wage increase and the miners went back to work. The episode increased the prestige of the Queuille cabinet and injured that of the Communists. The Communists threatened serious trouble again in March, 1950, when their protests against American arms shipments to France took the form of strikes, sabotage, and rioting in the Assembly. Through firm measures the Bidault government succeeded in restoring order.

What the Communists sought by politically inspired strikes the Gaullists attempted to gain by mass meetings and demonstrations of strength. De Gaulle's expectations were obvious. He believed that the republic's problems were impossible of solution under its present constitution and waited for the moment when the nation, weary of party strife, would restore him to power. The Gaullists continued to clamor for a dissolution of the French Chamber of Deputies and a general election.

The political trends of 1949 were reflected in elections held in March for members of the department councils— roughly equivalent to American state legislatures. The Communists received about 23.5 percent of the vote—a substantial reduction from the 29.3 percent they received in 1946. Gaullist strength also fell off and this group received 25.3 percent of the vote as compared with 38.6 in 1947, but it still retained the prestige of being the largest single party in the country. The principal Third Force parties received 36 percent of the vote, distributed thus: Socialists, 16.8; Radical Socialists, 11.1; Popular Republicans, 8.1.

The Fourth Republic seemed to be slowly gaining strength. Although budget deficits and high taxes continued to worry the nation, industrial production increased to better than prewar levels, and good harvests eased the food situation. But democracy in France was not yet secure. A reverse on the economic front would obviously bring serious political repercussions. Moreover, the Third Force stood in some danger of falling to pieces through internal frictions. Conservative elements among both Popular Republicans and Radicals admired General

De Gaulle and there was always the possibility of a rightist coalition, which would bring him to power. To prevent such a development, Socialists and middle-class antifascists might form another Popular Front with the Communists. Any such split right and left in French politics would carry with it a very serious possibility of civil war.

CHAPTER XIX

Patterns of Western Europe: Italy

THE PROBLEMS OF POSTWAR ITALY we might expect to be very similar to those of postwar Germany. Both countries suffered the overthrow of parliamentary institutions; both were subjected to a long period of totalitarian rule and fascist indoctrination; both embarked upon a course of military aggression against their neighbors; both were completely defeated in World War II; both were placed under Allied military occupation.

But at this point the similarities cease and significant differences must be noted. Unlike Germany, Italy was not divided into separate zones; the country was under the joint occupation of British and American troops without the complicating factor of Soviet participation. The political and economic unity of the country was thus preserved. A central government, staffed by Italians, functioned throughout the occupation period. A final important difference was the relatively early negotiation of a definitive peace treaty so that by the early months of 1947 Italy was no longer in suspense as to her future boundaries and reparations obligations. This has permitted a gradual evacuation by the British and American armies and placed Italy in control of her own destiny.

With the termination of Allied occupation the problems of Italy began to bear a closer resemblance to those of France than to those of Germany. The Italians, like the French, are struggling to regain their morale after a national humiliation, to rebuild their war-ravaged economy, and to establish stable government. They too have a strong Communist party eager to perpetuate disorder in order to serve its own ends and, at the other extreme, Fascist factions intriguing for a return to power.

ITALY BEFORE MUSSOLINI

During the first half of the nineteenth century Italy was only a geographical expression. Within this bootlike peninsula there were, as there had been since the collapse of the great Roman Empire, numerous separate states. Some of these were ruled by the Pope; some by kings; some by nobles with various titles. All of them were characterized by the absolutism of their political institutions. There were no constitutions, parliaments, or guarantees of individual liberty.

As important for the future of Italy as the great Revolution for France was the Risorgimento (Resurrection). This was the awakening among the Italians of a passion for nationalism, an overwhelming aspiration to submerge the petty provincialisms of the princes in a larger patriotism. The political result of the Risorgimento was the establishment of the Kingdom of Italy in 1861.

The tradition of the Risorgimento was in the spirit of liberal democracy. Three men were heroes of the movement. The first was Mazzini, the prophet of the new nationalism. He lived most of his life in exile, and his influence was largely in the intellectual realm. He believed passionately in the sovereignty of the people and hoped that unification would be achieved in the form of a democratic republic. Garibaldi became famous as a man of action. The most colorful episode of the Risorgimento was the fabulous campaign of Garibaldi and his thousand "Red Shirts"—a campaign that brought to an end the despotic rule of the Bourbons over Sicily and Naples. The Red Shirts should not deceive us. Garibaldi was no totalitarian seeking to establish a personal dictatorship. In his

3

78 GREAT ISSUES

hour of glory he turned over his conquests to the new
king of Italy and retired from public life—despite his
strong preference for republican rather than monarchic
institutions. The third of the great trio, Cavour, resembled
Bismarck in several particulars. He too was a member of
the nobility, who became Prime Minister of his country—
in Cavour's case, the country of Piedmont in northwestern
Italy—and through adroit diplomacy and the provocation
of war created a new European nation. The unification of
Italy was consummated under Cavour's leadership, and
Victor Emmanuel II of Piedmont became king of the
new nation. But, unlike Bismarck, Cavour was a liberal
with a great faith in constitutional government. He admired English institutions and tried to give the new
Italian parliament powers similar to those of its English
prototype.

But Italy was not England. After the age of giants came
an age of dwarfs in Italian history. Large, well-disciplined
parties did not emerge; governments were based on coalitions and blocs. There was inefficiency and corruption.
Much of the trouble might be laid to political immaturity.
The transition from absolutism to reasonably democratic
institutions had been rapid.

Other disrupting factors were more fundamental. They
arose in large part from the nation's poverty. Italy had a
large and rapidly increasing population; the amount of
good land for agriculture was limited, and much of it was
in the hands of great landlords. Italy's industrial life was
backward, and operated under a serious handicap, since
the country lacked the coal and iron on which modern
industrial strength is based. Such industry as she did possess was largely concentrated in the north. The poorly paid
workers were bitterly class conscious.

CHURCH AND STATE

Problems arising out of the relations of church and
state were common in most Continental European countries, but nowhere did they take so acute a form as in Italy.

This was because Rome was the historic center of the Roman Catholic faith. Except for brief intervals the popes had resided there for almost two thousand years. For centuries, moreover, the popes had been chosen from the Italian clergy, and the College of Cardinals had been largely Italian in composition. Beginning in the early Middle Ages and continuing to 1870, the Pope had been a temporal sovereign as well as the head of his church. It was necessary for the Pope to rule over the territory on which he resided, so the Catholic argument ran, because only in this way could he be assured of uninterrupted communications with the rest of the Catholic world. If he surrendered his independence and lived under some national sovereign, the church would lose its international prestige and be suspected of being under the influence of a particular nation.

The jealously guarded temporal sovereignty of the popes ran into direct conflict with the aroused Italian national-ism of the Risorgimento. Mazzini, Garibaldi, and Cavour sought to bring the Papal States, along with the rest of Italy, into the new nation, and the Pope of the day, Pius IX, bitterly opposed this. When the Kingdom of Italy was first proclaimed in 1861, the Pope lost to it all of his terri-tory except the city of Rome. This capital he held onto ten years longer, thanks to a garrison of French troops provided by Napoleon III, who was courting the French Catholics. But Italian nationalists were unhappy until the most famous of Italian cities became the Italian capital. The Franco-Prussian War provided the patiently awaited opportunity. When Napoleon III had to withdraw his troops for other duties, Italian forces soon moved in despite the Pope's efforts to resist them.

Having gained its objective, the Italian government promptly sought reconciliation with the church. It passed a law of papal guarantees, setting aside the Vatican and other places to be under the exclusive authority of the Pope and providing annual annuities to compensate for the loss of income suffered in the disappearance of the

Papal States. But Pius IX refused to accept this settlement
on the theory that his status could not be dependent on
the legislation of any national state. He shut himself up
in the Vatican, where he proclaimed himself a "prisoner."
He denied the authority of the Italian government and
stubbornly insisted on referring to Victor Emmanuel as
king of Piedmont rather than of Italy.

As a corollary to the papal refusal to recognize the
existence of the Kingdom of Italy, Catholics were forbidden by their church to vote or to accept public office
under the new government. This extreme measure of dis-
pleasure was gradually relaxed—in large part because the
Vatican perceived that the abstention of good Catholics
from politics would inevitably surrender Italy to the control of Socialists and anticlericals. Many Catholics supported the Popular party founded in 1919 and pledged to
moderate social reform, the coöperation of capital and
labor in economic life, and full liberty for the church to
teach.

The emergence of this Italian center party repeated a
pattern that had originated in German politics many years
before and somewhat later in France. A closely related
development was the organization of separate Catholic
trade unions. The strategy of the church was obvious. It
hated and feared Marxian socialism. Yet to associate with
the extreme right, as many of the clergy had done since
the days of the French Revolution, was to alienate the
church from the workers and peasants and from believers
in democracy. So the Catholic parties based their appeal
on demands for social reform based on Catholic principles, while emphasizing the continued need for the state
to defer to the church on issues relating to education and
morals. Much of their inspiration was drawn from the
papal encyclical, *Rerum Novarum*, issued by Leo XIII in
1891. The Pope warned that hostility between capital and
labor was growing because of the tyranny and the greed
of employers, and that the condition of the lower classes
must be improved. The remedy was not socialism, since

the principles of this movement violated the natural right to property and incited to class hatred, which was un-Christian. Harmonious relations between capital and labor were the solution. Workingmen were enjoined to be peaceful and loyal to their employers; employers were enjoined to treat their laborers as Christian freemen and not to exploit them as slaves.

Rerum Novarum is still a living document, giving inspiration to millions of good Catholics. Like other great documents, different and sometimes contradictory conclusions have been drawn from it. Catholic liberals have been inspired to profess republican and democratic loyalties and to crusade for social justice. This may be illustrated by the career of Monsignor John A. Ryan of Catholic University, Washington, D.C., or by that of the influential French philosopher, Jacques Maritain. But while Catholic liberals have placed greatest emphasis on Rerum Novarum's plea for social justice, Catholic conservatives have based their program on the famous encyclical's condemnation of class warfare. In extreme cases, this has resulted in clerical fascism—support for dictators like Dollfuss and Schuschnigg in Austria, Franco in Spain, or Peron in Argentina, or antidemocratic demagogues like Father Coughlin of Detroit. It is this great divergence in the forms which Catholic political action may take that makes it so difficult to predict what the ultimate influence may be of such contemporary movements as the German and Italian Christian Democrats or the French Popular Republicans.

Fascist Italy

Before World War I the path of liberal government had been thorny enough in Italy; in the immediate post-war years it became almost impassable. Italian nationalists, oblivious to the large annexations of Austrian territory permitted to Italy at the Paris Peace Conference, condemned their government for not securing more. Economic life had been greatly disrupted by the war, and the

---

postwar recovery was slow. As in other countries during 1919 and 1920 there were serious labor disputes. Many of the factory workers went on strike; many agricultural laborers rebelled against the landlords. Conservatives, alarmed at all this, were particularly disturbed by an incident of 1920 known as the occupation of the factories, when thousands of Socialist workers attempted to take over the factories of the north in disregard of the rights of the owners.

All this gave rise to a somewhat hysterical fear that Italy was following the example of Russia and falling into the hands of the Reds. The danger of this happening, however, was never very great. The occupation of the factories failed without the government's taking any drastic measure, and moderate Socialist leaders succeeded in imposing restraint upon their followers. By 1921 all observers agreed that whatever danger there had been of a Communist seizure of power was over.

But, even so, the possibilities for exploiting the Red scare were still great. Benito Mussolini bluffed his way to power and secured great credit, both in and out of Italy, for saving his country from a nonexistent peril.

Before World War I Mussolini had been a Socialist newspaperman. During the first months of the war he had demanded vociferously that Italy remain neutral. Then he had abruptly and mysteriously changed his position and advocated that the country enter the war on the side of the Allies. Since this reversal was contrary to the principles of the Socialist party, he was expelled. The new Fascist party had its origin in 1919 in a group which organized in Milan under the leadership of this renegade radical. Hating the Socialists with whom he had quarreled, Mussolini's first effort was to steal their thunder by advocating a program more radical than theirs. He approved the occupation of the factories and counseled the workers not to evacuate until they had won concessions.

But this phase was soon over. Entirely without principles of his own, Mussolini found it more profitable to oppose the Reds than to outbid them. He secured from Italian industrialists and landlords the cash he needed to finance his movement; he drew enthusiastic recruits for his party from the ranks of the lower middle class, who feared and hated the labor unions. Strong-arm squads were organized to wreck union headquarters, to beat up Socialists and Communists, and to assault peasants who lacked the proper deference for their landlords. Such activities were of course pure gangsterism, and they attracted to the Fascist movement many underworld characters as well as rakehells from the upper classes. Mussolini's roughnecks benefited enormously from the feeling among influential members of the Italian government that the Socialists had become too powerful and that it would not be a bad thing for them to be pushed around a little. The police were usually tolerant of Fascist violence, whereas they were prompt to punish disorders on the part of their antagonists.

Italian politicians, who were confident that the Fascists could be permitted to break up the Socialist movement and afterwards easily restrained, had a bitter disillusionment. By 1922 the Fascists felt strong enough to demand official power. Although they were still only a small minority party in the Chamber of Deputies, their reputation for violence was enough to intimidate the nation. At a great Fascist Congress in Naples in October, 1922, the party demanded that Mussolini be appointed Premier. As a demonstration of their strength, Fascists from all over Italy began to converge on the capital—the so-called "March on Rome." A resolute government would have resisted this attempt to gain power through the threat of force, but the king and his advisers were timid men. The cabinet, after much vacillation, decided on a proclamation of martial law, but the king refused his consent. He accepted the resignation of the Premier and appointed Mussolini to succeed him. In this way Victor Emmanuel III betrayed the principle of constitutionalism and became the accomplice of the Fascists.

Italy's transformation into a totalitarian state during the twenties was not as rapid as that of Germany in the thirties. Mussolini had less support in the parliament and had to base his government for some time on a coalition with the conservative parties. Nor was he strong enough at first to outlaw the opposition. But the Fascists used their dominant position in the cabinet to extend their rule. Terrorism continued and proved an effective weapon for imposing Fascist control over local units of government. In 1924 Italy and the outside world were shocked by the brutal murder of Giacomo Matteotti, a young Socialist who had been courageous enough to condemn Fascist terrorism and corruption in speeches before the Chamber of Deputies.

Although Mussolini at first disavowed the Matteotti crime and promised to punish its perpetrators, the eventual result of the affair was to demonstrate the degree to which democratic elements in Italy had become divided and weakened after two years of Fascist rule. Mussolini now found it possible to push boldly ahead. He banned all parties other than his own; he centralized all legislative power in himself; he extended Fascist control over all newspapers and sources of information. The Ovra, a secret police force directly responsible to Mussolini, arrested persons suspected of anti-Fascist sympathies. Thousands of these were imprisoned on the Lipari Islands.

Despite the brutality of the Fascists, many Englishmen and Americans defended them. In part, these observers were overly impressed by certain superficial achievements of the regime. The trains ran on time; the cities were cleaner and more orderly; marshlands were drained and brought under cultivation. Many foreigners were interested in the new Fascist legislation concerning capital and labor. Strikes and lockouts were prohibited. Wages and working conditions were stipulated by agreements between syndicates of employers and syndicates of workers which replaced the old labor unions. All Italian economic life was organized in so-called corporations in which the employer and employee syndicates were represented along with the Fascist party and the government. Eventually the old Chamber of Deputies was abolished and a Chamber of Fasces and Corporations was substituted. Gullible foreigners believed that this was a distinct contribution to the science of government, since it based representation on economic groups instead of old-fashioned geographical districts.

Mussolini's corporate state was one of the greatest strokes of modern propaganda. Even with Mussolini dead and the Fascist party dispersed, the idea persists in many quarters that the principle of the corporate state has much to commend it. General de Gaulle has indicated interest in a "reform" of the French labor unions which is disturbingly reminiscent of the Italian experiment. It is to be feared that many other Frenchmen, naturally disturbed by too many politically inspired strikes, may be attracted to the idea of a radical reorganization of the relations of capital and labor. A closer examination of the Fascist experiment, however, should make them cautious. Peace between capital and labor in Italy was purchased at an intolerable price. Italian workers completely lost their independence with the loss of their old unions. The new syndicates were simply instruments for regimenting labor in the interests of the Fascist party. The employer syndicates served a similar purpose for that class. The whole idea that the corporations represented a mechanism for industrial self-government was a deception. In actual operation, the system proved to be ingeniously contrived to bring all Italian economic life under the domination of the state and the Fascist party.

Relations with the Roman Catholic Church

Another development in Italy that for a long time helped to mislead foreigners into thinking that fascism was less sinister than communism was Mussolini's shrewd manipulation of Italy's religious problem.

In 1929 the Fascist government and the papacy signed

the so-called Lateran Accord, composed of three important documents. One was a treaty, recognizing the 107-acre Vatican City as a completely sovereign state; the second was a financial agreement under which the Italian government paid the Holy See about ninety-five million dollars as compensation for its losses during the unification period; the third was a concordat, proclaiming the Roman Catholic faith to be "the sole religion of the state." Religious instruction under the direction and control of the clergy was made compulsory in the public elementary and secondary schools, marriage was recognized as a sacrament, and divorce was not to be permitted. The church for its part promised to consult with the government in appointing its archbishops and bishops. The latter, moreover, were required to swear loyalty to the Italian government before assuming office.

The Lateran Accord was advertised to the world as a first-class Fascist achievement. Had not Mussolini settled on a reasonable basis a problem that pre-Fascist governments had struggled with unsuccessfully for half a century? Good Catholics in foreign countries were much impressed. Certainly this Mussolini who had liberated the "prisoner in the Vatican" could not be such a bad fellow.

But such an interpretation of the Lateran agreements was decidedly misleading. It revealed a misunderstanding both of the position of the church in Italy in the days of the constitutional regime and of the purposes of Mussolini in entering upon the Accord.

Even though the church and state had never come to an explicit agreement in the days before Mussolini, they had long since buried their quarrel. The Pope enjoyed perfect liberty within the Vatican City; his de facto sovereignty was respected even if it had never been formally recognized in a treaty. The church suffered no persecution, and only a small minority of Italian politicians were aggressively anticlerical. Not only had the church's prohibition on Catholics' participating in Italian political life been lifted, but one of the largest Italian parties had been the Catholic Popular party. Democratic Italy and the papacy had learned to live together long before the Fascists ever came to power.

Mussolini was not a better Catholic than the average Italian politician before his time, but a poorer one. His early writings were replete with insults to the church. But after he came to power, he was shrewd enough to see the advantage of making a magnificent gesture toward the church in a country where the great majority of the population were Catholics and where the papacy and the clergy had great influence on public opinion.

The Pope, for his part, might well have hesitated before giving his consent to an agreement which would provide a cloak of respectability to a government based upon violence and the suppression of popular liberties. But the very brutality of the regime seemed an argument for defining the relations of church and state in a written document. Moreover, the concordat offered the church privileges that it was particularly eager to secure.

In actual practice, the Lateran agreements by no means ended all problems of state and church. The Pope discovered to his sorrow that Mussolini's object was more to utilize the church for the benefit of his party than to dedicate his party to the ideals of the church. On several occasions before his death in 1939 Pius XI expressed public condemnation of the un-Christian policies of the Fascist government. A leading Catholic historian has concluded that many more of the Catholic clergy suffered imprisonment during the ten years following Mussolini's famous settlement with the church than during the half-century that preceded it.

But the truth about the character of fascism drifted only slowly to the outside world. The belief that the Roman Catholic Church had been persecuted in democratic Italy and was emancipated by Mussolini became one of the most persistent and dangerous of modern myths.

BIRTH OF THE ITALIAN REPUBLIC

Like all dictators, Mussolini was fatally attracted to adventures in foreign affairs. In defiance of the League of Nations, he attacked and conquered Ethiopia in 1935. In 1939 he seized Albania. In reckless disregard of Italy's best interests, he allied himself with Hitler and plunged his country into World War II in 1940. The result was a startling revelation of the hollowness of the Fascist regime. The government, instead of being the efficient machine which Fascist propagandists had advertised, proved to be corrupt and inefficient. Even tiny Greece was able to halt the vaunted Italian army, and Italy's campaigns against the British and Americans in Africa were featured by defeats of the most humiliating character.

After Italy's loss of Sicily in 1943, Mussolini's prestige was entirely gone. Even the Fascist Grand Council turned against him, and on July 25, 1944, Victor Emmanuel, with the support of the army, deposed him and ordered his arrest. The government was then entrusted to an elderly general, Marshal Pietro Badoglio. For a few weeks the new government attempted to continue the war against the Allies, but, understanding at last that Italy's defeat was certain, Badoglio arranged an armistice. This, however, did not bring peace. The Germans turned Italy into a battleground, contesting the Allied invasion with great bitterness and giving up territory only a bit at a time. Not until the spring of 1945 were the Germans finally pounded into surrender in northern Italy.

For two years, therefore, the political situation in Italy was highly confused. The legal government of Victor Emmanuel and Badoglio sought to restore Italy to international respectability by declaring war on Germany and collaborating with the Allies. But in northern Italy a rival government was organized around Mussolini, whom the Germans, by a bold stroke, released from imprisonment and used as a convenient puppet. Northern Italy became a battleground between the Fascist government in its last incarnation and numerous Italian partisans, who carried on guerrilla activities against Mussolini and the Germans. Italian workers—most of them Communists—were prominent in this movement. In the final days of the war, the partisans captured and executed Mussolini and his mistress.

The Badoglio government was very conservative. For a time the Allies endeavored to keep it in power in order to lighten the tasks of military government. But the Italian people were in no mood to get rid of the Fascists only to fall under the rule of near-Fascists. Badoglio was compelled to resign, and a government representing the more aggressively anti-Fascist elements in the country was substituted.

Until the summer of 1946, the great question was what Italy's future form of government would be. Many British and American military government officials, fearful lest Italy's revolution go too far, hoped to perpetuate the monarchy. But Victor Emmanuel was too thoroughly tainted with collaboration with the Fascists to save the dynasty. Not only had he weakly allowed Mussolini to become Premier in 1922, but he had accepted with apparent willingness the empty honors that Mussolini subsequently offered him. Realizing that he could no longer hold the crown himself, Victor Emmanuel abdicated and went into exile on May 9, 1946, in the hope that this might preserve the monarchy for the dynasty. His son, Crown Prince Humbert, succeeded him.

But Humbert's reign was exceedingly brief. On June 2 and 3, 1946, the Italian voters went to the polls for a dual purpose. They elected delegates to a Constituent Assembly to draft a new constitution and by a special referendum they indicated their choice as between republican and monarchical institutions. For the republic 12,717,923 votes were cast; for the monarchy 10,719,284. Humbert went immediately into exile, and the new Italian republic began its troubled existence.

The elections for the Constituent Assembly revealed that the largest party was that of the Christian Democrats, who secured 207 seats; the Socialists were second with 115; the Communists third with 104. Five other parties—mostly of the right—were represented with an aggregate of 127 seats.

The situation obviously had many similarities to that in France. In each country there were now three major parties with a number of smaller groups. In the case of the Communists and the Socialists the parties bore the same name in the two countries; the third party in each case was made up of Catholic moderates. In Italy as in France the Communists were included along with the other two parties, and some of the minor groups, in the cabinet.

But Italy's different political traditions have resulted in somewhat different political trends. The Vatican is both a bigger influence and a bigger issue in Italy than anywhere else. Obviously, this influence is one of the great assets of the Christian Democrats, helping Premier Alcide de Gasperi, the leader of that party, to remain in office through several cabinet crises and reorganizations. The church won an important victory when the Lateran Accord of 1929 was made a part of the new republican constitution. To the surprise of many observers, the Communists gave their support to this solution, explaining that they did not want to precipitate religious warfare. Perhaps a more truthful reason was the desire of the Communists to court support from the Italian peasantry, sympathetic to radicalism in politics but conservative in religion.

But the perpetuation of the 1929 religious settlement does not mean that the church is no longer an issue in Italian politics. On the contrary, fear of clerical reaction is still very strong among Italians of the left. This probably explains why most Italian Socialists have followed a different policy from that of the French Socialists. In Italy a People's Bloc, composed of Communists and left-wing Socialists, has been formed. This group had its first test in the election of the Rome City Council in November, 1946. On this occasion the People's Bloc gained 189,000 votes—the most that any party received. Aggressive anti-communism also appeared in this campaign, and the so-called Common Man party, whose tendencies were fascist, won the second largest number of votes—106,000. The Christian Democrats received only 104,000. Obviously Italian politics seemed to be tending toward the two extremes.

Despite growing friction between Premier de Gasperi and the Communists, the latter continued to be repre-sented in the Italian cabinet until May, 1947. A cabinet crisis of that month eventuated in a new de Gasperi government which excluded both the Communists and their Socialist allies. It was made up entirely of Christian Democrats and independents. The crisis followed soon after the similar one in France, and the desire for Ameri-can aid was presumably an element in the Italian situation as it had been in the French. But the Italian reorganiza-tion marked a more drastic shift to the right than had the French. De Gasperi's cabinet looked dangerously narrow in composition, but he clung successfully to power.

The Struggle for Italy

Early in 1948 the Communist threat in Italy seemed particularly grave. With 2,300,000 members the Italian Communist party was probably the largest European Communist group outside Russia. Most of the labor unions were dominated by the party and the country was repeatedly racked by strikes and slowdowns in protest against the Marshall Plan and in demonstration of the slogan: "You can't govern without the Communists, nor against the Communists." The party also gained ground among the impoverished tenant farmers, to whom it promised a redistribution of the land. The Communists would probably have been even stronger except for Italian resentment over the Soviet Union's reparations demands and its backing of Yugoslavia in the latter's territorial disputes with Italy.

On April 18, 1948, elections were held for the Italian Chamber of Deputies in an atmosphere of great tension. It seemed that the People's Bloc might win an absolute majority of the seats and come legally to power. Moreover, a large Communist vote, even if less than a majority, might pave the way for the party to seize power by threat of force as they had in Czechoslovakia only a few weeks before. The bitter campaign was fought over international issues quite as much as domestic. The Christian Democrats warned that a vote for Togliatti, the Communist leader, was a vote for Stalin. The Communist posters read: "Vote for the peace front! A vote for de Gasperi is a vote for Truman!" Intervention from the United States took both unofficial and official forms. Italian-Americans wrote thousands of letters to relatives and friends in the old country urging them to vote against the Communists, and Secretary of State Marshall warned that a Communist Italy would receive no help from the European Recovery Program. The American, British, and French governments took this occasion to recommend the restoration of Trieste to Italy. The Roman Catholic Church made no pretense of neutrality. The Vatican announced that Catholics might vote only for candidates who would "respect and defend the rights of the Church." Despite Communist disclaimers of any intention to interfere with religious freedom, priests all over Italy interpreted the Vatican decree as authority to exhort their parishioners to vote against the Communists.

The election returns showed the effectiveness of these tactics. The People's Bloc received only 30.7 percent of the vote (182 seats) as compared with 48.7 percent (307 seats) won by the Christian Democrats. Probably the belief that Italy's salvation lay in continued American aid under the European Recovery Plan was the most important factor in the Christian Democrat victory. The anti-Communist trend continued after the election. Over the next twelve months Communist party membership was estimated to have suffered a 15 percent decline. The de Gasperi government dealt with Communist-inspired strikes and disorders with increasing boldness, while improved economic conditions helped to stabilize the political situation.

But the rightist trend was not without dangers of its own. Although the need for energetic reform to combat bad social conditions was great, many landlords and industrialists appeared to believe that the conservative victory made concessions to the peasants and workers unnecessary. Within the Christian Democratic ranks there were diverse factions—some eager to use the party to further the ends of social justice, others to use it in defense of the *status quo*. Premier de Gasperi reflected this party situation by advocating reform in general terms but moving very cautiously toward achieving it. In April, 1949, the government at last formulated a program for breaking up some of the larger estates and selling the land to the peasants. Even after this there were exasperating delays in carrying the policy into effect. In the fall of 1949 impatient peasants in some areas of southern Italy seized land without waiting for government authorization. De Gasperi responded to these demonstrations—partly spontaneous, partly Communist inspired—by making local concessions. But drastic redistribution was still avoided, perhaps out of fear that such a policy would seriously reduce Italian food production.

In any event, the future of Italy was not bright. Italy's overpopulation problem was growing more acute each year. Even with the most equitable division of land there was not enough to go around. Nor could the country's millions of workers be adequately absorbed by industry, since Italy's lack of resources and capital was a continuing handicap. Emigration had been a palliative before 1914, but by 1950 most countries were as little disposed as the

United States to admit large numbers of aliens. Peace, economic security, and democracy for Italy appeared in the long run to depend on heroic remedies—perhaps in a surrender of Italian sovereignty to some future United States of Europe.

CHAPTER XX

China: The Evolution of Self-Government

THE INDEFINITELY OUTLINED geographic area called China not only is one of the world's largest territorial units but contains nearly one-fifth of the world's population. China's political divisions, also ill defined, are usually given as: (1) China proper with its eighteen provinces; (2) Manchuria, and the one-time dependencies; (3) Tibet; (4) Sinkiang; and (5) Mongolia.

The area of this once-great empire exceeded four million square miles, but with the vast appendant territories cut away the real China is left with slightly more area than Mongolia, or approximately half the size of the United States (1,530,000 square miles). Manchuria now has a population of thirty million and the vaguely estimated population of the other three outlying areas is about two million each—possibly nearer three million for Sinkiang. No one knows the population of China proper within millions; however, it is most often stated in very round figures to be more than 450 million. One out of every five men in the world is Chinese.

A more natural division of China proper than north, central, south, and west might appear to be the grouping of the provinces around the three great river basins: the Yellow (Hwang) River (Ho) in the North, the Yangtze reaching throughout all central China, and the West (Si) River (Kiang) which flows into the ocean at Canton in the south. The rivers of China have had an intense influence in molding the characteristics of the people and have played important roles in their history. Still the chief means of transportation, connected by many canals, China's three waterways (particularly the three-thousand-mile Yangtze, which is navigable by steamers for a distance of two thousand miles) have served to bind the country together and to produce some degree of homogeneity among the people.

Nevertheless, a number of authorities declare that a threefold division of China, following the main river valleys, leaves out Manchuria as well as other areas and does not recognize the essential unity of the central and southern provinces. They maintain that the most realistic division of China is into north and south, for, as Professor Cressey points out: "There are two Chinas, each with distinct characteristics in sharp contrast to those of the other."[1]

According to Dr. Cressey, North China is a land of limited rainfall, disastrous floods and droughts, cold winters and hot summers, semi-arid climate, precarious agriculture with a short growing season, grassless, treeless, and dust-blown in winter, mud-walled houses, and a smooth coastline with poor harbors. Here fishing is unimportant. The people of North China emigrate to Manchuria, have their contacts with foreigners by land, are an essentially uniform race with Mongolian mixture, speak the Mandarin dialect throughout, and are in general classical in their culture and conservative in their attitudes.

South China, almost in direct opposite, is a land of abundant rainfall, canals and irrigation, long growing season with two or three crops, intensive cultivation, profuse vegetation, woven bamboo walls and thatch-roofed houses, irregular coastline with many good harbors, and excellent fishing. The foreign relations of the people of South China have been by water, and they emigrate to

---

[1] G. B. Cressey, *China's Geographic Foundations*, New York, 1934, pp. 13, 14-16.

the "South Seas." There are many racial variations and a great diversity of dialects, but most significantly, the Southern Chinese tend to be more radical and restless.

HISTORY

Chinese history is the story of the rhythmic rise and fall of dynasties. Some lasted only a few years, others for centuries. Out of a period of unrest or disunity a strong leader would appear to reëstablish a sound government. China would expand and prosper. Then weak rulers would sit on the dragon throne and corruption would bring a decline. Inevitably the result was the same—a popular revolution, civil war, and an able leader became emperor and founded a new dynasty.

China now suffers from a period of civil strife and war, but the Chinese philosophically feel certain it will come about in due time and again they will become the "Great Middle Kingdom." What is a mere forty years of chaos? During their 3500 years as a nation they have experienced periods of disunity lasting over a hundred years, but they always came back stronger than before!

The accompanying historical chart brings out the parallel, or sometimes earlier cultural developments in the Chinese world, and, in marked contrast to the rise and fall of many nations and empires in the Western world, the ages-long continuity of Chinese national history. This may be partly explained by China's isolation from the rest of the world, and by the great barriers that existed between the "Middle Kingdom" and other powerful nations. However, China was eventually invaded both overland and by sea. Therefore, the stronger reasons for the steadfast integrity of the Chinese nation must be found in its firmly established traditional bonds, social, economic, and political.

Chinese cultural unity was accomplished under the nine-centuries' rule of the Chou Dynasty which, though a feudal system, held together the many states that then made up China. In the latter half of the Chou suzerainty

COMPARATIVE HISTORICAL CHART

B.C.	Western World	Dynasties	Chinese World	B.C.
1800	Hammurabi. BRONZE AGE.	HSIA	NEOLITHIC AGE. Agricultural communities in Yellow River Valley cultivated loess soil with stone tools. Grew millet. Used potter's wheel. Domesticated dog and pig. Hunting and fishing tribes in Yangtze Valley. Ox, goat, sheep, horse domesticated. BRONZE AGE.	1800
1700				1700
1600				1600
1500	Egyptian New Empire.	SHANG	Yellow River city-states. Probable irrigation. Beautiful bronze castings. Oracle bones. Writing. Silk culture and weaving. Wheeled vehicles. Stone carving. Writing brush and ink.	1500
1400				1400
1300	Moses.			1300
1200				1200
1100				1100

Year (B.C.)	China		West
1000	Books of bamboo slips. FEUDALISM. Expansion from Yellow River to Yangtze Valley. "City and country" cells. Increased irrigation.		IRON AGE. Solomon.
900			Lycurgus.
800			Carthage founded. Hebrew prophets.
700	Astronomy.		Greek lyric poets.
600	IRON AGE.	CHOU	THE GOLDEN AGE OF GREECE.
500	CLASSICAL PERIOD. Confucius, Lao-tse. Water clocks and sundials. Bronze mirrors.		Persian Wars. Socrates.
400	Lacquer. Round coins. Mencius. Loadstone. Chopsticks.		Plato. Dramatic Poets. Aristotle. Alexander.
300	BEGINNING OF EMPIRE. Great Wall		ROMAN POWER AT HEIGHT. Punic Wars.

COMPARATIVE HISTORICAL CHART—Continued

	Western World	Dynasties	Chinese World	
200		CHIN	begun. Palace architecture. Trade through Central Asia with Roman Empire. Football.	200
100	Carthage and Corinth destroyed. Julius Caesar.			100
A.D.	Birth of Christ. Jerusalem destroyed.	HAN		A.D.
100	Marcus Aurelius.		Paper. First Buddhist influences.	100
200			Tea.	200
300	Constantine. Roman Empire divided.	3 KINGDOMS	POLITICAL DISUNITY but cultural progress. Buddhism flourishing. Coal.	300
400	Odoacer takes Rome.	PERIOD OF 6 DYNASTIES	Kite. Firecracker.	400
500	Justinian.	SUI	UNIFICATION. Grand Canal.	500
600			ZENITH OF CULTURE. Geographical	600

Year	Chinese developments	Dynasty	Western events	Year
700	expansion. State examination system. Chinese culture reaches Japan. Mohammedanism. Revival of Confucianism weakens power of Buddhist monasteries.	TANG	Mohammed's Hegira.	700
800	Gunpowder. First printed book; porcelain.	TANG	Moslems stopped at Tours. Charlemagne. Alfred.	800
900	Poetry; painting; sculpture. Rise of Khitan.	5 DYNASTIES	Holy Roman Empire.	900
1000	Classical renaissance. Paper money. Compass. Navigation. Movable type. Gardens.	LIAO / SUNG		1000
1100	Mathematics. Cotton textiles.	SUNG / CHIN	Crusades.	1100
1200	MONGOL AGE. Jenghis Kahn. Marco Polo. Operatic theater. Novels.	YUAN	Magna Charta.	1200
1300	RESTORATION and stagnation.	MING	Hundred Years' War.	1300
1400	Portuguese traders.	MING	RENAISSANCE. Printing. Turks take Constantinople.	1400

COMPARATIVE HISTORICAL CHART—Concluded

	Western World	Dynasties	Chinese World	
1500	AGE OF DISCOVERY.		Jesuits. Medical encyclopedia.	1500
1600	Religious Wars.		Nurhachi.	1600
1700	(American, (French revolutions. (Industrial revolution.	CHING	Canton open to Western trade.	1700
1800			Opium War. Unequal treaties. Western culture. Factories and railroads.	1800
1900	First World War. Russian Revolution. Second World War.	REPUBLIC	Boxer rebellion. 1911 Revolution. Sun Yat-sen Nationalist Revolution. Chiang Kai-shek. Japanese invasion and World War II.	1900

the classical period of China (contemporary to the golden age of Greece) produced the great teachers, Confucius, Lao-tse, and Mencius. Although their teachings are not well known to Americans, it is probably true that their philosophical way of life has had a greater influence on more people than the works of their contemporaries Socrates, Plato, and Aristotle.

The internal warfare which marked the last generations of the Chou was ended by the victory of the Chin over its rival states. The achievements of this short-lived dynasty (less than fifty years) are of noteworthy significance. The Chin abolished feudalism—fifteen hundred years or more before Europe began the elimination of this great obstacle to the creation of a nation-state—and set up the first emperor of China in 221 B.C. Outstanding as was the start of the Great Wall, the Chin are to be remembered for the transfusion of a common administrative system and political philosophy throughout the truly established Chinese Empire.

The Han Dynasty, like their contemporaries of the Roman Empire, was a period of great conquerors. Under the Han the geographic outlines of the continuing Chinese Empire were largely fixed. They strengthened the central authority taken over from the Chin, along with the bureaucratic system, and made Confucianism the national philosophy.

After two thousand years, the imperial structure created by the Chin and the Han persisted, especially the appointive bureaucracy. The cultural unity that they fostered survives, and although Confucianism is no longer enforced by the state it continues as the dominant attitude of mind in China today.

There is no need to give here a further account of the historical events after the fall of the Han Dynasty. China was repeatedly invaded and twice conquered and ruled by outsiders—the Mongols (Yuan Dynasty) and the Manchus (Ching Dynasty). There were some foreign cultural contributions to Chinese life. The most influential was

Buddhism, which introduced new concepts of spiritual philosophy and gave added expression to various forms of art. Fundamentally, however, China entered the nineteenth century with slight modifications in culture and politico-economic institutions from those existing in the third century. Although the results of the coming of the Westerners during the nineteenth century were very far reaching, the truly revolutionary changes in the Chinese way of life have come only in the recent few decades of the twentieth century.

CHINA'S NATIONAL ECONOMY

China is well endowed with practically all the natural resources and, within the limits fixed by an archaic transportation and distribution system, is relatively self-sufficient. With large-scale industrialization of recent origin, the wealth of China is still largely taken from the land. Possibly the most important vegetable products are rice (food), tea (drink), mulberry (silk), and bamboo (construction and implements). The rich soil and wide range of climatic conditions provide a well-diversified agricultural production. Staple crops, in addition to rice and tea, include sugar, soybeans, wheat, barley, millet and other cereals. Meat, especially pork and chicken, besides fish, gives a wide variety of food in contrast to the ordinary Japanese diet. Practically every kind of fruit in the world is produced in China. For textiles, in addition to one-fourth of the world's silk, China is well supplied with cotton and wool.

Like all other countries, including the United States, the mineral resources of China vary considerably. Probably ranking third among the nations in known reserves, China has more than enough coal for a highly industrialized economy. Like coal, iron ore is widely distributed throughout the provinces, but unfortunately the deposits are inadequate for the demands of modern industry. The same is true for copper. China is poorly supplied with gold and silver, but has modest reserves of lead, zinc, manganese, mercury, and nitrates, and a fair amount of tin. Only in antimony and tungsten (important steel alloys) is China outstanding as the world's principal source of these minerals.

The great historical differences and the tremendous lag in material progress between China and the West make any attempt to describe Chinese economy, using English words, extremely difficult if not quite meaningless. The thin veneer of modern economic practices, seldom instituted by Chinese, but superimposed by Western imperialism and Japanese controls, has been worn through by the past two decades of civil and international wars. The basic features of Chinese economy are still one or two thousand years old. Here and there may be observed some fragmented economies trying desperately to emulate Western methods and to work their way out of backwardness in technology and general helplessness. But these isolated examples, to be found mostly in the larger seaport cities, are exceptions and not the rule in China.

Confucianism was not only a strait jacket on social change, but along with woefully inadequate communication and transportation it stifled progress in the development of a modern national economy. The antique social system, in dreadful alliance with weak central political authority, made each community in China cell-like, autonomous, and autarchic. The increase in wealth was kept within each community, to the chief benefit of the rich landed families and their commercial allies of that community. It was not spread out to wider mutual benefits or to provide an economic advance throughout the larger framework of the province and nation.

From a nation whose best estimates of its population may vary by twenty-five million, one can hardly expect even reasonably accurate statistics. The most common assumption is that at least three-fourths of the people of China find their chief occupation in agriculture. That would mean that over 300 million people in one country are in farmers' families. Then, to picture the landscape, note that Chinese farmers do not live on their scattered farms, as in America, but always in compact villages.

Chinese farmers have shown considerable skill in the cultivation of a wide variety of plants for food, clothing, and shelter. They have proved adept in conserving the fertility of the soil, in the rotation of crops, and in the use made of compost. But there are many serious defects in the utilization of land, with responsibility resting upon the government probably more than on the farmers. Soil erosion has followed denuding the hills of their forests, especially in North China. Much good land still goes untilled for lack of proper reclamation methods. The Chinese are backward in their seed selection and in the protection of plants from diseases. And over all, the enormous expenditure of human labor in cultivating the soil without any agricultural machinery makes for extreme poverty as the lot in life for the average Chinese farmer.

No one seems to know the percentage of Chinese farmers who own the land they till. It is probably somewhere between 30 and 50 percent, but it really makes little difference. The small farm owner was actually no better off than the tenant farmer. The tenant gave up 50 to 80 percent of his cash crop to his landlord, but anyone could tax the small freeholder and usually did. The petty pilferings of local officials took what little might be left after paying the exorbitant government exactions. In many sections of China taxes practically amounted to confiscation of the year's harvest. And the army added its demands as soldiers felt free to take any food they could lay their hands on while passing through the district.

Chinese, like any other farmers, need credit, but despite government efforts to break up the system, loans were available only from the village broker at interest rates which ran from 30 to 60 percent a year. Once caught in the usurer's grip there was small chance of breaking free.

The ancient trinity of landlord, loan shark, and merchant (in most villages often one and the same family) represents a system that has shackled China's rural development for centuries. Appeal by the farmer to his government for some relief from his unbearable conditions was useless. The same landed families and merchants, in practically all of the hundreds of thousands of villages throughout China, were the local government. The above is put in the past tense only because no one knows what changes may be taking place now that China has come under control of the Communists.

No other great nation has as large a proportion of its population bound to the land. The Chinese farmer is the framework, the body, of the Chinese nation. What hope for democracy when several hundred million people in one country are subjected to extreme poverty and ignorance? The large majority of the Chinese people live under inconceivable conditions of squalor, disease, and malnutrition. They had no one to turn to, for no one could or would help them.

Although the average Chinese family does not provide much of a market for manufactured goods, in such a vast population there are many families living in comfortable circumstances, which in the aggregate constitute sizable numbers. Large-scale industries and mass production factories, usually controlled by foreign interests, have been only recently established in China. Chinese manufacturing is still overwhelmingly in the handicrafts stage. This means that except in a few of the largest cities there is no industrial class, and no sharp division between employers and workers.

Chinese industry and commerce was, and still is, organized into crafts and guilds. The great bulk of consumer articles are produced in small establishments which often serve as both home and shop for the master craftsmen and their apprentices. The latter receive maintenance but no pay during the many years of apprenticeship. Larger undertakings are based on partnerships, for there are relatively few corporate or joint-stock company organizations in China.

The various crafts are separately organized into guilds

which the master craftsmen belong to and support. The more important guilds form independent hierarchies extending up through provinces to even national offices. Historically the guilds controlled prices, fixed quality, and determined minimum wages. Often owning their large meeting halls, most guilds served as a social as well as an economic agency in the community. Chinese guilds are still so powerful that in most cases the local government officials find it expedient, to put it nicely, to consult with a guild before imposing new taxes or regulations, and in general to keep on good terms with the guild officers.

Chinese traders and merchants were organized in much the same way as the artisans except on a broader territorial basis. Their guilds were often more informal organizations —clubs in the metropolitan centers to which foreigners might belong.

The interchangeable use of past and present tenses above must be confusing to the reader. What are the conditions in China today? One answer might be that it is impossible to give any reasonably accurate description which would apply generally throughout China. A better reply would be that, although there have been many innovations and some economic changes during the past fifty to one hundred years, the national economy of China is still very largely organized as it has been for over a thousand years.

The points to be remembered are: first, that the entire economic life of China is largely self-controlled by guild organizations which are relatively free from interference by the national and even provincial governments; second, that transportation is so crude, roads so few, that each community or district operates almost as an isolated entity.

This problem of inadequate transportation and communication has been repeatedly referred to. It cannot be overemphasized for an understanding of China. It is the lack of transportation and communication which accounts for the nonestablishment of national markets which would tend to fix relatively uniform prices. Furthermore, without adequate railways no effective means is available to equalize surplus and deficit areas. Instead of further elaboration, this point may be driven home by the startling fact that there is more railroad track mileage underground in the subways of metropolitan New York than in all of China proper.

China's Political Foundations

Before beginning the discussion of Chinese politics, which from the point of view of a "Westerner" is sure to be critical, let it be remembered that "No other society comparable in size, duration and extent has ever existed; the Chinese Empire, from the beginning of the Chin (221 B.C.) to the end of the Manchus (A.D. 1911), remains the greatest social edifice mankind has yet brought forth."[2]

The principal historical reason for this stability was previously stated as the Chinese cultural unity based upon the Confucian doctrines of obedience, filial piety, and right conduct toward one's neighbors. This repeated reference to Confucianism calls for some further comment, especially because the average American commonly associates it with ancestor worship as the religion of China. But in the Orient ancestor worship is not a religion in the same sense that Occidentals think of religion. To the Chinese it is "filial piety" due preceding generations, as taught by Confucius, for the inherited blessings of life.

Confucianism is not a true religion, but rather a philosophical way of life. The elements of worship are perfunctory and the emphasis is placed upon right living. The Great Teacher did not make pronouncements as to God or an afterlife. He made no attempt to create a system, but only to systematize the moral experience of the past; to get back to the ideal life rather than go forward to it. This overemphasis on the past inevitably stunted development, and made for a static society with many unfortunate consequences to China.

---

[2] Paul M. A. Linebarger, *The China of Chiang Kai-shek*, New York, 1941, p. 2.

There was also a political unity in China, definite enough to be considered apart from the cultural whole. It, too, was based upon the dogmas of Confucianism. The first was the position of the emperor and of the bureaucracy (the latter recruited through competitive examinations and steeped in Confucian traditions). The second was the place of the Chinese family, not only as the basic unit of society but as the foundation of government.

Three out of the five Confucian ethical relationships— prince and minister, father and son, husband and wife, elder brother and younger brother, friend and friend—had to do with the family. The individual in China had no status alone and apart from the family or clan association of both the past and his own generations. His primary loyalty, almost exclusive, was to his family and clan. Thus, the outstanding difference from the political concepts of Western nations was that in China the family, not the individual, was the constituent unit of society and therefore of legal responsibility.

The family assumed many functions ordinarily ascribed to government: primary education, care of unemployed, support of its aged, and punishment of those who violated established law or custom. Actually, an individual in China was subject to few governmental controls. The state held the family accountable for the actions of its members. Inasmuch as Chinese families do not live apart, but congregate their several generations of immediate and in-law relations in village or town, the next step was obvious. Centuries ago the villages and small towns became practically autonomous, not only in their economic self-sufficiency as previously noted, but in their local self-government.

Parenthetically, it may be said that this situation has been the salvation of China throughout the many periods of disunity and chaos in her long history, especially during the last two generations. When the central government was weak, or as in the case of the recent conquests of Japan when large areas were under foreign rule, the craft guilds, village and family governance carried on as it had for centuries. With no aid or direction from above the activities of the people were controlled within each community.

As a generalization it was true for the vast majority of the Chinese people, in marked contrast to Western nations, that the individual seldom had any relations with government officials. The real control over the lives of the people resided in the selected leaders of the village. The independent Council of Elders, the patriarchal heads of the principal families in the community, was the seat of authority and the policy-determining body. The village headman, or mayor, was selected by the Council and responsible to it. To show the degree of noninterference by the Chinese government: even the taxes were (and usually still are) collected by the village headman and then turned over to the district magistrate.

This freedom from officials appointed from above, along with reliance upon authorities of their own selection, gives credence to the proposition that Chinese politics rests on a democratic base. In terms of the wide latitude in local self-government this may be true. However, if democracy consists, in part at least, of the popular election of government officials and their responsibility to the people, even in the Chinese village this concept is not adhered to. The elders and the headman more or less assume their positions year after year. They are invariably the semi-autocratic heads of the few wealthy families. Their chief concern is in their own families' land holdings and vested interests—certainly not, as a general rule, in the conditions of the people and the community as a whole. It is on this traditional "democratic" base that China attempts to establish a constitutional republic with national and provincial officials, as well as local officers, elected by the people.

The Chinese political system was frequently described as an "autocracy superimposed on a democracy." Some doubts were raised above in regard to Chinese democracy, but there is no question about the absolute autocracy of the imperial government. Supreme theocrat and patriarch, the occupant of the Dragon Throne was the source of all appointments and laws, the highest court of appeal, the religious and intellectual head of the state, head of the imperial clan, and father of the nation. In theory a divine ruler, the emperor alone faced heaven. However, this great power at the same time made him personally accountable if famine or flood befell the people. In other words, although he was an extreme autocrat, actually in fact and in practice the powers of the emperor were circumscribed by old customs and established precedents kept alive by the scholar officials.

At the height of Chinese power, the emperor ruled over the four dependencies, Manchuria, Mongolia, Tibet, and Sinkiang, in addition to China proper, and received tribute from such neighboring vassal states as Korea and Indo-China. The structure of the imperial hierarchy was relatively simple. At the top was the emperor, who, presumably, was advised daily by one or more ministers from his Council of State, made up of the heads of the administrative departments. These departments had not changed in name or number for over two thousand years, being the same six boards established under the Chou Dynasty: Civil Appointments, War, Public Works, Finance, Rites (religious and other ceremonies), and Punishments (courts). A seventh, Board of Foreign Affairs, was added in 1861.

One special agency should be mentioned because it persists under the republic and is provided for in the new constitution. Under the Empire the Censorate was called the eyes and ears of the emperor. The scores of Censors scattered throughout the central and provisional governments were to criticize freely all they observed and report directly to the emperor.

The metropolitan or central government at Peking (imperial capital) was highly organized and rigidly controlled. In the provinces, however, the viceroys or governors enjoyed a large measure of autonomy. This was true of other more subordinate authorities for, as long as appropriate revenues were received by the imperial treasury and no serious disturbances arose, they were not checked in the exercise of wide discretionary powers.

The provinces were in turn subdivided into administrative circuits or prefectures. Below them, forming the broad base of the governmental hierarchy, were the almost countless districts under magistrates. These administrative officers for larger towns and clusters of villages were by far the most important officials in the whole imperial system. Their duties included the complete range of governmental responsibilities, and the magistrate was the only official within the cognizance of the vast majority of the Chinese people. The district magistrate, as the symbol of imperial authority, provided the strongest, if not the only, link between Peking and the country.

All imperial officials were appointed in the name of the emperor. The viceroys and governors were responsible directly to the emperor; the subordinates in turn were responsible to their immediate superiors. An official was never appointed to his native province or district, and usually reassignment came after three or six years in one place. Another practice, still being followed, was the attempt to balance off one rival political faction against another through the distribution of appointments. However, the distinguishing feature of China's bureaucracy was the requirement that applicants for civil service appointments must first pass a series of extremely difficult competitive examinations. This would seem to be highly desirable and of course would have been if the material on which they were examined had included anything calculated to prepare the prospective official for public administration. However, the examinations neither included any problems of government nor tested administrative ability, but stressed only the writing of essays on the Confucian classics.

The subversion of education through the centuries to

these civil service examinations added to the tremendously heavy price China paid for the resulting cultural and political unity. Until the establishment of missionary schools and colleges, practically all formal Chinese education was to prepare for the government examinations. Tutored by the local sage and spurred on by the promise of wealth and distinction in store for the successful scholars, thousands of students took the first of a series of examinations given annually by the district magistrate. The 2 percent that passed could wear a metal button and take the prefecture exam. Every three years an examination was held in each of the provincial capitals.

The less than 1 percent who passed this second series were given degrees and the right to take the final series in Peking. By this time the students were mature men, and of the few thousand that were left from the several hundred thousand that started about two hundred every three years achieved the highest honor of being titled a "scholar." The highest-ranking scholars entered the Royal Academy, the others finally gaining appointment as top officials in the provincial administrations or imperial departments.

When a nation's education consists of pumping up the minds of a few scholars with the philosophy of the ancients, and the only textbooks used were written one or two thousand years before, one can hardly expect much material progress or development. Naturally the Chinese scholars who stood to lose their high positions blocked all efforts at change, and it took a modern revolutionary overthrow of the entire imperial system to make even a start in educational and civil service reforms. It can be said without much fear of contradiction that one of the chief reasons for the backwardness of China and her inability to stand up to the impact of the West was the deadening curse of the examination system. The obvious result was a governmental bureaucracy totally unprepared to meet the problems of contemporary public administration. China had great scholars for officials but in 1900 was the most illiterate nation in the world.

In summation of China's political foundations there are several further considerations. The brevity of discussion does not imply less significance. First, Chinese officials have always been grossly underpaid. Even when their meager pay was supplemented by a much larger allowance it generally would not meet their ordinary living expenses. From time immemorial the "squeeze" (to Americans a "rake-off" or a "cut") has been the established practice by which governmental employees recompensed themselves. Corruption today goes back many centuries before the republic, for the administrative system in China has always been permeated with graft.

Second, although the old Chinese government was rigid and strongly centralized at the top, it became progressively decentralized into very loose controls as it approached contact with the people. This undoubtedly encouraged local initiative, but it resulted in more or less complete popular indifference to national affairs. With primary loyalties so strongly localized, the creation of a national consciousness, so essential to the establishment of democracy, is made doubly difficult.

Finally, that the Chinese are a passive, easily subjugated people is entirely fallacious. Their whole history is replete with rebellions, local and national. The Chinese people have a thoroughly inculcated respect for authority, but from district magistrate to the emperor himself their "mandate" to rule gave them in turn the responsibility for the maintenance of peace, order, and comparative prosperity. When times were bad the people complained. If improvements were not forthcoming there was a boycott, followed by armed force when necessary. A successful rebellion, as taught by Confucius, was sure proof that the "mandate of heaven" had been withdrawn. In other words, public opinion was a dominant force even under the Empire. Both in theory and in practice the "right" of revolution is fundamental in the political thinking of the Chinese people.

THE GROWTH OF CONSTITUTIONAL GOVERNMENT IN CHINA

The development of the Chinese republic falls into five periods: (1) the establishment of the republic, 1911-16; (2) the period of provincial rule by war lords, 1917-26; (3) the inauguration of the National government, 1927-36; (4) the war period, 1937-45; (5) constitutionalism, 1946-49.

The turning points were: the overthrow of the Manchu Empire by Sun Yat-sen's revolutionaries (1911); the death of the dictator-President Yuan Shi-kai (1916); the Great Revolution by the combined Kuomintang-Communist forces (1927); the Sian kidnaping of Chiang Kai-shek (December, 1936), followed by Japanese invasion (July, 1937); and the adoption by the Chinese National Assembly on December 25, 1946, of a "permanent" constitution.

According to Professor Linebarger, the government of China was the successor "of a wide variety of decaying imperial administration, experimental modernism and outright confusion."[3]

Describing the recent Japanese war as a part of a revolution, he goes on to say:

It is a continuation of the Nationalist revolution, begun against the Manchus, continued against the imperialist powers, and [then] directed against the Japanese. . . . At the same time, this revolution struggles to incorporate in its dynamics the drive of an endemic peasant rebellion, Communist in its extreme phase. Nationalist in supreme emphasis, the revolution finds its highest expression in the articulation of an effective state—something not known in China for twenty-two centuries.[4]

From the beginning of the republic, the Chinese have been drafting, amending, replacing, or suppressing constitutions. These organic laws did not interfere with practical

[3] Ibid., p. 5.
[4] Ibid., p. 6.

politics, for it was not until the National government was established at Nanking that there was even any similarity between the constitutional structure and the actual government. Constitutionalism has played a much more subordinate role in China than in most Western states. The early constitutions copied too much from the West and disregarded the peculiar political needs of China. They were not put into effect.

The Provisional Constitution of 1931, based on the theories of Sun Yat-sen, was elaborated in the Draft Constitution of 1936. It was under this last document that the National government ostensibly operated during the war. Actually, of course, China has never been governed under a constitutional system. Therefore, the avowed relinquishment of dictatorial authority by Chiang Kai-shek and the proposed establishment of a constitutional government was, even if only in principle, of great significance.

The first article of the Constitution, which was promulgated on January 1, 1947, declares: "The Republic of China, founded on the San Min Chu I (Three People's Principles), is a democratic republic of the people, for the people, and governed by the people." Under Article 2, "The sovereignty of the Republic of China resides in the whole body of citizens."

Following the American pattern of a Bill of Rights, there is an impressive list which specifies duties as well as rights. This includes such political rights as freedom of speech, religion, petition, voting, holding office, habeas corpus, and the right to work and own property. The duties of paying taxes and of performing military service are imposed, and education is defined as both a duty and a right. The infringement of an individual's civil liberties by a public official is punishable under the Constitution, as well as under civil and criminal law.

The government which was organized under the 1947 Constitution consisted of three elected bodies, the National Assembly, the Legislative Yuan, and the Control Yuan; and three appointive organs, the Executive, Judicial, and Examination Yuans. In addition there was the President and Vice-President of the republic.

This was China's government before it fell to the Communists and it evidenced very real progress in native Chinese political theory during recent decades. Although it had adopted, with modifications, some principles of organization from the West, the Chinese built upon ancient forms and constructed a constitutional system designed to meet the future demands of a democratic China. For a complete understanding one should study carefully the very extensive system of checks and balances exercised among the several bodies, but that is far too complex for description here.

One feature of the Constitution is worthy of further note. Chapter XIII was devoted to an expression of the fundamental national policies for China. It enunciated the guiding principles for national defense, foreign policy, and the economic system. It contained statements that no one may use the armed forces "as an instrument in the political struggle for power," and that no military man in active service may "concurrently hold a civil office." Article 141 required adherence to the United Nations Charter, the only such reference in any national constitution. It proposed that public utilities and enterprises of a monopolistic character were to be socialized, but the private ownership of land was guaranteed. Other principles were in the form of instructions to the government to secure an equitable distribution of landownership, to extend social security, and to stress the importance of free public education.

Taken as a whole, this last national Chinese Constitution was liberal, democratic, and an admirable instrument for popular responsive government. However, too many historic examples prove that a constitution alone is no guarantee of democracy or of a representative form of government. Latin-American countries (under dictators) have long had constitutions modeled after that of the

United States, and the Soviet Union has (in writing) a splendid "democratic" constitution!

Unless many far-reaching reforms were made this Constitution for China was ordained to remain merely an outline of good intentions. In addition to the general encouragement of democratic processes, especially in local government, the two main objectives that had to be accomplished before there could be any true constitutional government in China were: (1) the end of one-party rule and (2) the elimination of Kuomintang control over the military and financial power of the nation. No honest effort of any real significance was made under Chiang Kai-shek along either line. The complete failure of the Kuomintang leadership in China, particularly after World War II, to follow the policy enunciated in the Constitution, to motivate essential reforms, and to put the organic law of the nation into being, is the basic reason for the collapse of the Nationalists and the victory of the Chinese Communists.

The Future Government of China?

It is too early to ascertain what kind of constitution will be framed and what form of government will eventually evolve under the Chinese Communists. At the moment, the new rulers of China are struggling with many strange and complex problems in both practical administration and ideological principles. The theoretical base of the new regime has passed through many phases as it first fought for survival and now seeks to enlist various classes from China's population in active support. It is a period of transition that defies sharp analysis or definite conclusions.

In searching for some clues to the future Chinese Communist government one starting point might be the Communists' First All-China Congress of Soviets which convened in Kiangsi on November 7, 1931. The 610 delegates proclaimed a "Constitution of the Chinese Soviet

Republic," and a government was established with Mao
Tse-tung as chief executive. The Constitution provided
that: "All power shall be vested in the Soviet of Workers,
Peasants and Red Army men and in the entire toiling
population." "Only capitalists, landlords, the gentry, militarists, reactionary officials and monks—all exploiting and
counter-revolutionary elements—shall be deprived of the
right to elect deputies to participate in government and
to enjoy political freedom." "In the Chinese Soviet Republic Supreme Power shall be vested in the All-China
Congress of Soviets. . . ." "In the interval between Congresses the Supreme organ of power shall be the provisional All-China Central Executive Committee of the
Soviets."

This first attempt by the Chinese Communists to
establish a centralized system of government was crushed
when they were forced out of Kiangsi in 1934-35 and with
the Long March settled in northern Shensi province.
During the intervening years of guerrilla fighting and war
with Japan no attempt was made to rewrite a constitution
or revitalize a central government over Communist territory. A Border Area Government was established within
the united front against Japan, and as Communist influence expanded, temporary local governments were created
in the "liberated areas." In other words, for the past fifteen
years Communist governments in China have been on a
local basis with central authority concentrated in the party.

With no precedent except the short-lived Soviet government in Kiangsi the Chinese Communists are preparing now to establish a new national government in
China. During the past decade the Communists have
called for a "democratic coalition" for China. This slogan
has had great appeal and many intellectuals have joined
the Communist movement. In 1945 Mao Tse-tung wrote
a book On Coalition Government in which he stated "in
the present stage" China "should not attempt to realize
a Socialist system of state"; on the contrary ". . . we
should establish a united front, democratic coalition sys-

tem of state with the absolute majority of the people of the whole country as its basis."

The slogans used most frequently by the Communists characterize the proposed government as follows: "republican," "coalition" (on a class basis under Communist leadership), "federal" (referring mainly to relations between minorities and the majority Han Chinese), and organized on the principle of "democratic centralization."

However, the present trend in Communist thinking on governmental questions, as revealed in the book *On People's Democratic Dictatorship*, seems to revert to the pre-1935 period in many respects. There is no indication that the Communists are returning to "extreme Sovietism," and the concept of a "New Democratic" transitional period is still accepted, but the latest definition of policy emphasizes "class dictatorship" and the restriction of political rights on a class basis more than any policy declarations during the past decade.

Early in 1949 Mao Tse-tung pronounced the abolition of the constitution, laws, and political organizations inaugurated under the "Kuomintang reactionary government." On October 1, 1949, the Central People's Government of the People's Republic of China was proclaimed in Peking.

The structure of the new Chinese government follows the familiar Soviet pattern. Within the "people's democratic dictatorship" there is to be an elaborate system of "people's congresses," responsible to the people, which in turn elect government councils responsible to their corresponding congresses. But all local governments throughout the country, no matter how "responsible" they may be to the congresses which elect them, must obey the central government, which, in turn, is to be elected by the All-China People's Congress.

Various provisions of the new organic laws and Common Program insure the central government full control over the policies and personnel of all lower levels of government. And until an All-China People's Congress is elected, the Chinese People's Political Consultative Conference, completely controlled by the Chinese Communist party, is to exercise its powers and functions as the supreme legislative body.

The effective legal power in China today is exercised by the Central People's Government Council of fifty-six members, "elected" by the Chinese People's Political Consultative Conference. The latter meets triennially. The CPGC can "enact and interpret the laws of the State, promulgate decrees and supervise their execution." It determines all administrative policies, concludes treaties, can declare war, and appoints or dismisses all important officials on both central and local governmental levels.

Under the supervision of the Central People's Government Councils are: (1) the State Administration Council, which directs the ministries and other agencies of the national administration; (2) the People's Revolutionary Military Council, which controls the People's Liberation Army and other armed forces; (3) the Supreme People's Court, with administrative control over inferior courts; and (4) the People's Procurator-General's Office, which inspects the observance of the laws and functions along parallel lines to the traditional Control Yuan.

To appreciate the effective control enjoyed by the Communists over the government of China it should be sufficient to note the positions held by members, usually high officials of the Communist party. As would be expected, Mao Tse-tung is chairman of the Chinese People's Political Consultative Conference, the Presidium and its Standing Committee, and the National Committee. The Communists have an absolute majority of the all-powerful Central People's Government Council with four party officials including Mao from the small Communist Politburo. Mao is also chairman of the People's Revolutionary Military Council, and other Communist party members dominate all of the other subordinate administrative agencies.

In theory the Communists consider themselves free

from the restraints of precedent. But the old social traditions, economic forms, and political institutions cannot be cursorily passed over. Regardless of the Chinese Communists' allegiance to Marxism and alliance with Russian communism, the pressures from the past—the 2000-year-old Empire structure, the permeating influence of Confucianism, the first republic and the principles of Sun Yat-sen, and the national Constitution of 1947—cannot be safely underestimated.

These and other forces, past and present, must be realistically evaluated by the contemporary Chinese leadership if they hope to establish a stable government and retain their power. And the whole should be adroitly weighed by the United States government in formulating policies for its relations with the "New China."

CHAPTER XXI

Meeting of East and West

THE PEOPLES OF EASTERN ASIA, including India, developed a distinctive type of civilization over a period of several thousand years without much cultural or political intercourse with the other great contemporary nations of the world. Both India and China had land barriers which cut them off from easy contact with peoples further west, and any considerable trade relations by sea awaited comparatively recent times. However, it would be a serious mistake to assume that China and India had been completely isolated, without knowledge of, or trade with, western Eurasia, particularly the Mediterranean civilizations.

Before the beginning of the Christian Era there was extensive commerce between India and the Mediterranean traders. During the first two centuries A.D. the Chinese had established protected trade routes westward until they reached the eastern edge of the Roman Empire. Chinese silk was so prized it was literally worth its weight in gold, and many other Chinese products found their way to ancient Greece and Rome. In return, glass, precious stones, enamels, and fine horses moved eastward into China.

Although the modern history of eastern Asia begins with the forcible opening of China and Japan (by British and Americans), the preceding contacts with Europeans should not be entirely overlooked. Nestorian Christian missionaries reached China sometime during the seventh century A.D. and exerted some influence during the Tang Dynasty (618-907) before being persecuted. The Polo

424

brothers, Venetian merchants, lived at the court of the great Kublai Khan during the last quarter of the thirteenth century and, on their return to Europe the *Book of Marco Polo* became the chief source of information on eastern Asia for many years.

Under the vast and powerful Mongol Empire the overland route to China was kept open. Over it went several Roman Catholic missions; the first, led by a Franciscan, Friar John of Montecorvino, reached China in 1292. During the first half of the fourteenth century, prior to the decline of the protective Mongol rule, the Catholic missions claimed to have converted "more than 30,000 infidels."

Then the growing power of Mohammedan rulers in central Asia formed a wall between East and West. (Constantinople fell to the Turks in 1453.) To reach eastern Asia required the navigation of the oceans and rounding the Cape of Good Hope. Portuguese traders, already established in India, and with their base at Malacca on the Malay Peninsula, sent a convoy of trading ships in 1517 which entered several Chinese ports. Some years later they were the first Europeans to discover Japan. Macao (on a small peninsula seaward from Canton) was in the nature of a leasehold, the first of its kind. The Portuguese settled there during the latter half of the sixteenth century, and it gave them a considerable advantage in the trade with Canton for over a hundred years.

The Spaniards, after conquering the Philippines, traded with China indirectly from Manila, founded in 1571. The Dutch came next in 1604 but were denied permission to trade in Canton. They established themselves on Formosa (driving out the Spaniards who were there) and carried on intermittent trade along the southern coast of China. Incidentally, the Dutch were the only foreigners allowed to trade with Japan (under very humiliating limitations) after the Exclusion Act of 1638. Although British ships arrived at Canton about three decades earlier, the British

East India Company did not actively enter the Chinese trade until 1664.

It may be of interest that long before the coming of the Portuguese the Arabs had for several centuries been traders by sea with China. This fact led to a historic chain of recriminations. The Arabs, who were in good standing with the Chinese, warned them about the Portuguese, who in turn told horrible tales about the Spaniards and Dutch, and so on. This must have caused considerable wonderment to the philosophical Chinese. When in fact the worst descriptions were actually lived up to by the actions of many Europeans, it can be appreciated why the Chinese considered all foreigners barbarians and treated them accordingly.

Another interesting fact of still greater significance is that Russia was the first European nation to establish formal relations with China. After repeated conflicts in the Amur River Valley (the Chinese army victorious in every battle), officials representing the two empires signed the Treaty of Nerchinsk in 1689. This was the first treaty China had made with a Western power. It fixed the boundary line (one of the most permanent in modern history) between Manchuria and Siberia along the Amur River. Here, even today—at least officially—the Russians are separated from Chinese territory. Following the treaty the Russians developed considerable overland trade with China, established an embassy, and built a Russian church in Peking. The Chinese government maintained at St. Petersburg their only ambassador to a foreign court, over a hundred years before the British finally forced diplomatic recognition. Furthermore, the Chinese long considered their relations with Russia far more important than those with the maritime nations.

It was probably historically inevitable that the expansive forces of European imperialism in the nineteenth century would break into the extensive, but restricted, trade of eastern Asia. Unfortunately there is not space here to describe the series of events, sometimes romantic but more often oppressive, which accomplished the opening of China. Many nations took part in the increasingly profitable Chinese trade, and although all involved smarted under the restraints and exactions of Canton's officials, few could hope effectively to coerce the vast Oriental empire. Even with the more modern ships and armaments it was no small task to prepare for an attack upon so large an organized population on the other side of the world.

Only the British, in the period following the Napoleonic Wars, were prepared to open the gates by having the following essential qualifications: first, undisputed naval supremacy (in European waters for security of the homeland) as well as command of the seaway to the Far East; second, a great power base, India, and the advance base of operations, Singapore(secured through the foresight of Sir Stamford Raffles); finally, the means, and the stubborn will to achieve what they considered justice—the establishment of trade and diplomatic relations on the basis of accepted international practices.

By the first quarter of the nineteenth century foreigners trading with China faced three options: (1) to abandon trade; (2) to continue being limited to one port, Canton, and existing while there in the cooped-up "factories" under abominable conditions; also, submitting to the arbitrary regulations of the "Hoppo"; or (3) to resort to force to compel the Chinese government to institute official relations including the commonly adopted commercial policies.

The British tried a peaceful approach for over three decades, but their various missions (two of them reached Peking as "tribute bearers") accomplished nothing. The attitude of the imperial government seems to have been that China was self-sufficient and did not want to be annoyed by the "barbarians" or their trade. The special Chinese officials in Canton, authorized to deal with the foreigners, became convinced that the traders would always yield in their demands (they always had for over a hundred years) at the threat of stopping trade.

Opium imports, even though considered a direct cause, were incidental to the so-called Anglo-Chinese "Opium" War of 1839-42. The underlying causes—beyond just commercial restrictions—were: (1) the refusal of the Chinese government to trade with other nations on any basis of equality; (2) questions of jurisdiction over nationals; and (3) the vast difference in the concepts regarding the administration of justice, especially enforcement of criminal law. In an attempt to stop the traffic in opium a special Chinese commissioner seized and destroyed all stocks in Canton. They were valued at several millions of dollars. Then he virtually imprisoned all the foreign traders. This led to armed clashes, and Canton was blockaded by the British fleet. The British tried repeatedly to establish contacts with Peking, but all efforts failed until Canton was occupied and Chinkiang, on the Yangtze River, captured. The latter move divided China, and the imperial government finally entered into negotiations.

The Treaty of Nanking (1842) provided that: (1) five "treaty" ports—Amoy, Canton, Foochow, Ningpo, and Shanghai—should be open to trade, with the right of residence by British subjects, along with the right to appoint consuls who were empowered to treat with Chinese officials; (2) relations between British and Chinese officials were to be on a basis of equality; (3) a uniform and "fair" schedule of tariff duties (imports and exports) was to be drawn; (4) China would pay indemnities to cover opium destroyed, debts owed British merchants, and British war costs; and (5) the island of Hong Kong was ceded to Great Britain without any limitation.

Other treaties followed which opened the five ports to nationals of the other trading states on equal terms. The United States treaty (1844), negotiated by one of America's outstanding diplomats, Caleb Cushing, elaborated the principle of extraterritoriality (the curse on China for the next hundred years). It clearly stated that "citizens of the United States who may commit any crime in China

shall be subject to trial and punishment only by the Con-
sul or other public functionary of the United States." The
French treaty assured toleration to Roman Catholic missionaries, and a later decree extended the privileges to
Protestants.

Following the opening of the five "treaty ports" trade
with China increased rapidly, accompanied by intensifi-
cation of Western interests. Through the operation of the
"most favored nation" clause in the various treaties, every
treaty nation obtained the same most favored position that
any one Western power exacted from China. Thus the
Americans and practically all European nationals enjoyed
extraterritoriality—the right to live and do business in
China under their own laws exempt from Chinese law
and taxation. However, the Chinese continued to consider
themselves superior, and many of their officials were extremely arrogant. A series of incidents led to increasing
friction and a second Anglo-Chinese War (1856-60), in
which French forces joined the attack.

The United States and Russia entered with France and
Great Britain into the negotiations of the treaties of
Tientsin. The principal terms of this series of treaties
finally concluded in 1860 were: (1) opening eleven additional ports for foreign trade and residence; (2) opening
of Yangtze River to foreign merchantmen; (3) foreign
embassies to establish residence in Peking; (4) permission
for foreigners to travel in the interior of China; and
(5) additional protection for the propagation of Christianity. Russia obtained full title to the territory east of
the Ussuri River where construction was begun on the
port of Vladivostok.

These treaties, combined with the conventional tariffs
(which surrendered China's right to fix her own customs
duties), definitely limited Chinese sovereignty. The fact
that none of the rights or privileges granted to Westerners
in China were reciprocal to Chinese nationals in Europe
or the United States seems to warrant Chinese resentment
toward the "unequal treaties." Furthermore, the various

foreign powers soon built exclusive residential and business "settlements" and "concession zones" in the treaty ports, and even operated their own postal systems. Western troops were stationed in these foreign areas of Chinese cities, and warships were anchored in the ports or patrolled the rivers of China.

During all this period China was being ruled by the Manchus—foreigners who had conquered China two hundred years before. But they had been absorbed and had adopted Chinese culture as their own according to the age-long pattern of Chinese history. On the other hand, the Westerners, barbarians though they were to the Chinese, did not have the "inferior" culture of preceding foreign conquerors. In fact, their material advancement gave them not only superior military power but techniques of control which proved more effective, at far less cost, than overall conquest. Before China could readjust conditions to meet this new type of approach it was too late.

China was not overrun by one nation; rather its metropolitan centers became virtual colonies to all nations whose merchant ships called at Chinese ports accompanied by warships. To this last statement should be quickly added that with all the encroachments China remained a nominally sovereign state and, in the vast hinterland away from the seaports, an independent nation. In part, the foreign treaty rights were based upon the principle of competition, which checked the rule by one power such as had taken place in India.

Yet it does not seem possible that several states on the other side of the globe, using only a handful of soldiers and a few ships, could dictate to the government of such a great nation. The chief explanation is that the European impact came at the most inopportune period in the historical Chinese cycle—the decline of the ruling dynasty. The Manchus came to power in 1644 and by 1800 had passed their zenith. Western power hit a corrupt imperial government under weak rulers who knew little and cared less about matters in the distant, decentralized provinces.

Plagued by foreign intervention, the Manchus also faced their most serious internal threat, the Taiping rebellion, which occupied most of the imperial forces during the crucial period. Beginning in the 1840's with a strange mixture of Western ideas, some Christianity, and just good old-fashioned peasant uprisings, the Taiping or "Great Peace" armies held the Yangtze Valley in turmoil for over a decade. The "revolution" was not suppressed until 1865, and then with some foreign aid.

Probably the main reason why the Manchu Dynasty did not fall in the middle of the nineteenth century was the dominating personality of the empress dowager, Tzu Hsi. In all world history few women have had such a spectacular career. Rising from concubine to coregent Tzu Hsi, who combined many of the characteristics of Lucrezia Borgia and Catherine the Great, practically controlled the Chinese government from 1861 until her death in 1908. However, upon Tzu Hsi must rest a heavy responsibility for delaying by four or five decades the various reforms so absolutely essential to Chinese recovery and maintenance of power. China's small neighbor, Japan, utilized the same years to learn and copy from the West. With this knowledge and modern arms the island empire was equipped to take away forcibly from China the leadership of eastern Asia.

War and Diplomacy in Eastern Asia

Within fifty years there have been six major international wars (all of them involving China or Chinese territory), numerous border conflicts, repeated armed intervention, several serious revolutions, and almost continuous civil warfare. In fact, it is practically impossible to designate a single year since 1894 when peace reigned throughout eastern Asia. Furthermore, there are no signs of a cessation of hostilities in the immediate future. This situation of almost constant reliance upon military force for over half a century should temper our often too hasty

opinions about the slowness of reform and progress in
China and other countries.

In the first two wars Japan demonstrated her strength
and became a world power. Two weeks after she signed
an "equal" treaty with Great Britain, which signaled her
victory for treaty revision, Japan precipitated a war with
China, in July, 1894. The war was fought over the control
of Korea. However, the Japanese objective was more than
the removal of Chinese suzerainty. It was to prevent the
establishment of Russian domination over "the dagger
pointed at the heart of Japan." The superior Chinese
forces (on paper) were no match for the smaller but
better led and equipped Japanese navy and army. Korea
was easily cleared of Chinese troops and the Japanese
overran southern Manchuria. By the Peace Treaty of
Shimonoseki (1895) the full independence of Korea was
recognized, and China ceded to Japan the great island of
Formosa; also, Japan laid claim to the Liaotung Peninsula
at the southern tip of Manchuria.

During this first interim period between wars several
important events must be briefly chronicled to give understanding to later policies. Japan's impressive victory served
to combine the Western powers against the new competitor in "cutting up the Chinese melon." Russia, backed
by Germany and France, forced Japan to return the
Liaotung Peninsula to China in return for an increased
indemnity. The Japanese never forgot, and the three European nations were checked off for future revenge. The
humiliation of giving back their "just spoils of war" turned
to bitterness when Russia "influenced" China to lease
the tip of the disputed peninsula. Here the Russians
fortified Port Arthur and joined the seaport Dairen to the
Russian-built South Manchurian railway.

The next series of events evolved out of the Boxer
uprising in China, a violent antiforeign movement probably encouraged by the "Old Buddha," Tzu Hsi. An international force, including American and Japanese with
European troops, fought their way from the coast to re-

lieve the besieged Western legations in Peking. The capital was shamefully looted and the government forced to pay a huge indemnity. China was on the verge of complete collapse. It was at this point that American diplomacy irrevocably entered Far Eastern politics.

The United States had just acquired the Philippines by dubious but internationally acceptable means. The American decision to retain the Philippines was made with a view to their use as a base for trade with eastern Asia. But by that time all except Japan was staked out into colonies, leaseholds, or exclusive spheres of interest by Europeans. Thus the famous "open door" notes of the American Secretary of State are easily associated with ulterior motives. Too late to secure zones of influence on the Asiatic mainland, American commercial interests, it was said, promoted for their benefit this policy of equality of trade opportunities for nationals of all countries. Regardless of the degree of truth in such assertions, Secretary Hay was sincere in his attempt to prevent the breakup of China. The "open door" for China became a traditional American policy, and it stood out in world politics as the only forthright declaration of the territorial integrity of China.

Hay's overtures for an international policy in China received only calloused lip service from the other powers. Russia was too busy taking advantage of the situation to even bother to reply. Her troops were increasingly concentrated to dominate Manchuria and North China. Although the British lost some influence around Peking they were preëminent in the rich Yangtze Valley, and Hong Kong gave them prestige in Canton. France added Hainan Island to her previously gained control of Indo-China and her sphere of interest in the southern provinces. Germany, though last, established her interests in the peninsula of Shantung, the richest province in China.

It should always be kept in mind that international politics in eastern Asia were seldom disconnected from European diplomacy. In this period there was a close correlation between the moves of power politics in the Far East and the developing Triple Alliance and Triple Entente in Europe. It is in this light that the Anglo-Japanese Alliance of 1902 must be pictured. Incidentally, this full military alliance with the British was long a high-water mark of Japanese diplomacy and the great achievement toward her objective of recognition as an equal. With the world's greatest naval power as an ally Japan was diplomatically ready, being assured a free hand to fight Russia alone.

The natural antagonism between Russia and Japan over their competing interests in Manchuria was increased by Russian penetration in northern Korea and intrigues with the Korean government in Seoul. Japan repeatedly offered proposals for a settlement of differences and actually made real concessions, but the proud Russian czar remained adamant until it was too late. The Japanese chose the most propitious time to strike and in February, 1904, set a new pattern for modern warfare all too familiar to us now. With a sneak surprise attack upon Port Arthur the Japanese crippled the Russian naval forces in Far Eastern waters. The declaration of war followed.

Again Japan's enemy was much stronger on paper, but there were many compensating factors including a strong revolutionary movement in Russia. The shorter lines of communication and supply by way of Korea were a real advantage to the Japanese compared to Russian reliance upon the single-track Trans-Siberian Railroad. Russian armies were pushed north to Mukden. Russia's European fleet sailed around the world only to be annihilated in the Straits of Tsushima by the waiting Japanese. Russia, although beaten, still had great reserves of manpower to call upon; Japan, although victorious, was exhausted. Both welcomed the proffered mediation of the ubiquitous American President, Theodore Roosevelt.

The Treaty of Portsmouth (New Hampshire) has significance beyond the settlements reached, for it marks the turning point in American-Japanese diplomacy. Prior to

1905 the relations between the two were extremely amicable and characterized by sincere mutual respect. But the Japanese negotiators, to save face for not bringing home an indemnity (which the Russians absolutely refused to pay) blamed it upon President Roosevelt. This attitude was difficult to understand, particularly when Japan came out so well. In the treaty settlements Russia acknowledged Japan's paramount interests in Korea, transferred her twenty-five-year lease of the Liaotung Peninsula and gave up the South Manchurian Railroad; also she ceded the southern half of the island of Sakhalin to Japan. With a strong foothold on the Asiatic mainland, Japan had become a real empire.

Not resting on her laurels Japan continued to move skillfully. The rest of the world was intent upon happenings close to home such as the death of Tzu Hsi and the convocation of a National Assembly for China's first republic; and in Europe, each succeeding diplomatic crisis brought ever closer the threat of war. In 1910 Japan incorporated Korea into her Empire, and both America and Great Britain acquiesced; no other power was in a position to oppose the *fait accompli*. And in 1911 the third renewal of the Anglo-Japanese Alliance gave Japan a diplomatic cause for declaring war on Germany in August, 1914.

World War I gave Japan a great opportunity to expand both her political and her economic empires with slight risk and small costs. With the Western Powers locked in a death struggle on European battlefields Japan enjoyed a relatively free hand in eastern Asia. Crossing off the check mark against Germany, the Japanese captured the German leasehold of Tsingtao, chief port for Shantung. They attacked from the land side in as wanton a violation of Chinese neutrality as the German march through Belgium. Then Japan proceeded to pick up the German Pacific islands (to be later awarded to her at Versailles in the form of mandates).

Taking full advantage of the situation, Japan secretly submitted to the Peking government the so-called

"Twenty-one Demands." Soon disclosed, it was obvious that, had they been complied with, China would have become a protectorate of Japan without a struggle. This was in 1915 and before the United States entered the war. The American government opposed this peaceful conquest of China. However, the credit should go to the Chinese nationalists and their unaccustomed strong resistance to Japanese pressure. Japan gave way, but her nationals, backed by their government, acquired many valuable economic concessions.

The Treaty of Versailles was very largely a European settlement which left several troublesome problems in the Far East unsolved. Japan had gained support for her claims by secret treaties with the Allies before American entrance into the war. The United States had not committed herself and stood alone in opposition. The Japanese, however, retained the former German rights in Shantung, plus an extension of her own rights in South Manchuria. Nevertheless, Japan was defeated in her chief objective, the inclusion of a clause on racial equality in the treaty.

After the Paris Conference the United States continued to oppose both Japan's position in Shantung and the continued Japanese army intervention in Siberia after the other Allied troops had been withdrawn. The United States had a "big stick" then, a navy which was fast becoming the most powerful in the world. Japan could not hope to compete in a naval building race and prepared to negotiate.

The Washington Conference, called in 1921, was ostensibly for limitation of naval armaments. As the first time proud sovereign states even deigned to discuss such a subject, let alone reach an agreement, this diplomatic gathering is a milestone on the road to world peace. Of at least equal significance toward international coöperation was the settlement of Far Eastern questions. The leaders in Tokyo were under pressure from several sides. A short-lived liberal party government was attacking the Japanese militarists at home. The Japanese Foreign Office was reticent about an open discussion at Washington. As a result, although other factors such as an effective Chinese boycott were involved, the Japanese government restored Shantung to Chinese control and withdrew her last troops from Soviet Siberia (as it had now become).

The prerequisite for any naval treaty was the renunciation of the Anglo-Japanese Alliance. As a face-saving device for Japan, the twenty-year-old alliance was replaced by the rather meaningless "Four-Power" Treaty of consultation among Britain, France, Japan, and the United States. But by far the greatest achievement of the Washington Conference was the Nine-Power Treaty—an international "Magna Charta" for China. The other eight powers, Japan, the United States, and the six European nations with interests in China, signed with China the following pledge: "To respect the sovereignty, the independence, and the territorial and administrative integrity of China; to provide the fullest and most unembarrassed opportunity to China to develop and maintain for herself an effective and stable government."

The American unilateral declaration of policy contained in the Hay notes had finally become a multilateral policy— a strong free China as the basis for peace in eastern Asia. It was true, as the cynics verified by pointing to later Japanese aggression, that the Nine-Power Treaty had no teeth, no means of enforcement. This may or may not have been a weakness. Force alone has failed to prove a lasting guarantee for security or peace. But regardless of varying points of view on this open question, it would seem clear that there can be no hope for peaceful stability in the Far East (and that may well mean for the whole world) until the principles quoted above are firmly reëstablished. One might add that this applies to other nations in eastern Asia besides China; in fact, "to respect the territorial and administrative integrity" of all other nations throughout the world must be universally adhered to by all nations. This is the prime essential to international peace.

The wars and diplomatic events from 1922 to 1945 will be most briefly highlighted here. To describe with any meaning at all the extremely complicated and far-reaching effects of the world depression on national and international politics would take a chapter in itself. The depression, starting with the American stock market crash in 1929 and soon felt in every country on earth, is one of those great turning points in world history. From it came the basic general causes of World War II. And in the Far East it was because of the serious repercussions of the depression upon the Japanese economy, coupled with another opportunity to take advantage of the world situation, that Japan struck again. The date, September 18, 1931, marks the beginning of most violent international conflict, which continues throughout the world today.

The conquest of Manchuria, an integral part of China, by the Japanese army was not just another war of expansion on the old pattern of imperialism. Conditions had changed, or at least the large majority of the peoples of the world believed that a new standard of international morality had been inaugurated. Symbolic of the comparative peace which had followed World War I was the Covenant of the League of Nations. In its Article X the member states undertook "to respect and preserve as against aggression the territorial integrity and existing political independence of all Members of the League." Although not a member of the League, the United States had promoted the Paris Peace Pact of 1928, in which the sixty signatories, including Japan, renounced their right to use war "as an instrument of national policy." Japan had arbitrarily violated her pledges under both the Covenant and the Peace Pact, as well as the Nine-Power Treaty.

With only verbal censure by the great democracies and with no effective restraints imposed by the League of Nations, Japan set a course which lends credibility to the incredible Tanaka Memorial. The puppet state of Manchukuo was her answer to the profoundly fair Lytton

Report. When criticized Japan withdrew from the League. This signaled the failure of collective action, and the world's first attempt at international organization was doomed. The revolt against established world law and order, begun in eastern Asia by Japanese militarists, was extended to Europe by Mussolini and Hitler. An international civil war eventually developed into World War II. Force took over from reason and armed conquests under the modern title of aggression followed in rapid succession. To name only the main examples there was Ethiopia, 1935; Spain, 1936; China again, 1937; Austria, 1938; and then "Munich."

Japan made the most out of each European crisis, pushing down into North China and finally provoking war for the subjugation of all China. She did not forget France, the third member of the triumvirate that had blocked her way in 1895. Riding on the successes of Hitler in 1940, Japan invested Hainan Island and French Indo-China. Here she paused before making her most momentous decision.

China had not collapsed as anticipated. Four years of war on the continent plus the tightening American blockade were seriously straining Japanese economy and military effectiveness. Japan had been permitted to put herself into a position where a compromise was no longer possible. She could not wait, and her course of action must be either to withdraw ignominiously from her uncompleted conquests or risk all in war upon the Western democracies. If Japan won, she would rule perhaps the greatest empire in all history. Hitler's assurance of victory and the supposed degeneracy and pacifism of the United States gave real promise for success. The die was cast at Pearl Harbor.

By way of review it should be remembered that the United States from 1910 to 1922 forcefully blocked Japanese expansion. At the Washington Conference the United States, relying on Japan's pledges in the Nine-Power Treaty, agreed to a *status quo* on fortifications in the

Pacific. Even with the inferior ratio of naval strength, this granted Japan undisputed naval supremacy in the waters off eastern Asia.

After 1931 American public opinion restrained the government from using even the threat of force. But the "Stimson Doctrine" of nonrecognition of Manchukuo set our policy. The United States refused to compromise with aggression and gradually increased its opposition to Japan by economic measures. "Pearl Harbor" united the Americans with such strong resolution that Japan was beaten by the summer of 1945. The atomic bomb merely gave the Japanese leaders a face-saving excuse for surrender.

As a final postscript, Russia entered the war after the first atomic bomb was dropped and a few days before the obvious Japanese capitulation. As was promised her at Yalta as part of the price for Soviet participation, Russia, after forty years, is now reëstablished at Port Arthur and Dairen on the Liaotung Peninsula, and in control of the Manchurian railways. Again the Russians govern all of Sakhalin, and have taken the former Japanese Kurile Islands that run north to Kamchatka. History may not repeat exactly, but the close parallels in wars and diplomacy, especially in regard to strategic areas, may well be noted in looking into the future.

United States Relations with China, 1942-49

The American "white paper"[1] on China is remarkable in several ways. It is "based on the files of the Department of State," which are not ordinarily opened for publication until twenty-five years have passed. Never before has such a volume of classified documentary material been made available to the American public—and to the world—so close upon the events covered. It is a post-mortem before the corpse is actually buried. Although seemingly a bit forced it is in keeping with the principles of American

---

[1] *United States Relations with China: With Special Reference to the Period 1944-1949.* Department of State Publication 3573, released August, 1949, Washington, D.C.

democracy, for it frankly admits the complete failure of American diplomacy in one of its most decisive spheres of action.

The 1054 pages (400 pages of textual analysis, the balance in documents) are a treasure house for the research student. Of course it does not tell the whole story. Later historians, with access to other files, are necessary to round out the picture; but the main frame of reference from the American official point of view is substantially drawn. In brief, the debacle in China was the responsibility of Chiang Kai-shek and the Kuomintang. True and correct in general as this conclusion undoubtedly is, it does seem unsportsmanlike, to say the least, that nowhere can be found any blame placed on the policies and actions of the United States government or its officials.

Few issues in the history of American foreign relations have generated such heated controversy as our recent policies toward China. Seldom have such extreme positions been so stubbornly held by various segments of American private and official opinion. It might be desirable to await the future interpretations of history, but the dynamics of contemporary world politics demand action.

The pressures of the cold war and the rapid advances of communism in eastern Asia make a sound American policy imperative. Assuming that forward-looking statecraft builds upon the past, the following pages will chronicle the highlights of American policies and actions in China since Pearl Harbor.

Upon United States entrance into the war China became an Ally and, with American promotion, one of the "Big Four" in the United Nations. The program of military and economic aid, started earlier in 1941 under the Lend-Lease Act, was expanded. An initial loan to China of 500 million dollars was made early in 1942. American military and civilian advisers were sent to assist China in her war effort.

Constructive steps were taken by the United States government to demonstrate its intention of treating China as an equal and generally to strengthen Chinese national-ism. These included the relinquishment by the United States of extraterritorial and related rights in China; the repeal, also in 1943, of the Chinese exclusion laws, replac-ing them by an annual Chinese immigration quota; and an act of Congress making legally admitted Chinese eli-gible to naturalization as American citizens.

The reports on conditions in China from American diplomats and other observers were unanimously discour-aging. China's plight after four years of single-handed fight against Japan was beyond comprehension. The vi-cious struggle and the conquest of the materially advanced sections of the country had critically weakened the Chi-nese government militarily, economically, and politically —also, of equal significance, in general morale. The Kuo-mintang leadership seemingly floundered in corruption and self-seeking power. They were fast losing the loyalty and confidence of the mass of the Chinese people.

In a superb effort American air transport "over the hump" from India brought in essential supplies. In return, by superhuman labor, the Chinese people fashioned great airfields for the American planes. However, when the costly procured weapons were given to those Chinese Nationalist troops which faced, in attempted containment, the highly successful Chinese Communist troops, the Americans were dismayed.

Obviously, the renewed Kuomintang-Chinese Commu-nist feud seriously weakened the united front against the common enemy, Japan. The unity of action by China's two prime military forces, so effective in the early years of the war, was considered a first priority for victory. This demand for unity inside China, as well as by the American military advisers, became the crux to the immediate and future situation.

General Joseph W. Stilwell, the American Chief of Staff to Generalissimo Chiang Kai-shek, reached the con-clusion that the United States should give military aid to the Chinese Communists as well as to the Nationalist armies and that he should be empowered to integrate their tactical employment. President Roosevelt sent a message to the Generalissimo on July 7, 1944, in which he strongly recommended that Chiang place General Stilwell "in command of all Chinese and American forces, and that you charge him with the full responsibility and authority for the coordination and direction of the operations required. . . ." Chiang Kai-shek first agreed in principle, then stalled, and finally refused to comply.

Without comment the summary and prophetic report by General Stilwell to the American Chief of Staff on September 26, 1944, is quoted as follows:

Chiang Kai-shek has no intention of making further efforts to prosecute the war. Anyone who crowds him toward such action will be blocked or eliminated. . . . Chiang Kai-shek believes he can go on milking the United States for money and munitions by using the old gag about quitting if he is not supported. He believes the war in the Pacific is nearly over, and that by delaying tactics, he can throw the entire burden on us. He has no intentions of instituting any real democratic regime or of forming a united front with the communists. He himself is the main obstacle to the unification of China. . . . I am now convinced that, for the reasons stated, the United States will not get any real cooperation from China while Chiang Kai-shek is in power. I believe he will only continue his policy and delay, while grabbing for loans and post war aid, for the purpose of maintaining his present position, based on one-party government, a reactionary policy, or the suppression of democratic ideas with the active aid of his gestapo.

Regardless of rationalizations, the facts are that when faced with a possible showdown the framers of American policy retreated. Chiang Kai-shek's adamant position, including the demand to retain control over the allocation of American supplies brought into China, was acceded to. President Roosevelt ordered the recall of General Stilwell. This exciting opportunity to weld the rival Chinese parties into a unified nation during the war, for the later problems of peace, was lost by default.

Half-hearted efforts to create unity were continued by the special presidential envoy Patrick J. Hurley, aided by Stilwell's successor, General Albert C. Wedemeyer. The American Ambassador Clarence E. Gauss resigned and handsome Pat Hurley became nominal head of the American mission to China. It soon became apparent in Chungking that the American representatives stood for outright support of the Nationalists regardless of the degree of actual coöperation on the part of Chiang Kai-shek. The War Department wrote off the China theater as a base for the final decisive attack upon Japan. And most conditions drifted from bad to worse in China until the surrender of Japan.

The defeat of Japan ended the gravest threat to China's independence in a century of foreign aggression. But it did not bring peace. Civil war broke out simultaneously, as the Nationalists and the Communists raced to take over the Japanese-occupied areas. In this contest the United States gave material aid by air transport of Kuomintang troops to key cities in northeastern China, where they accepted the Japanese surrender before the Communists could enter. United States marines landed to help protect the railroads for use by the Kuomintang.

Against this background Ambassador Hurley brought together Chiang Kai-shek and Mao Tse-tung, the Communist leader, and they announced an accord on general principles. But the civil war continued with no quarter asked or given. Mr. Hurley, his policy having failed on all counts, resigned, and President Truman named Chief of Staff George C. Marshall as special envoy. General Marshall was initially successful in the cessation of hostilities while a Political Consultative Conference was held by representatives of all major Chinese parties. A substantial and hopeful agreement was reached. China was to have a transitional coalition regime, followed by a constitutional government.

Probably the two extremes—Kuomintang rightists and Communist leftists—recognized that they and their objectives were bound to lose out. At least, the civil war was renewed in even greater intensity. General Marshall returned home and his report might be summarized as a "plague on both your houses." American policy makers were in a quandary and public opinion was hopelessly confused.

The United States postwar policy for China was logical *if* reasonably normal conditions had prevailed in China and in world politics. China, with American backing, was to be the strong stabilizing force in eastern Asia. Unfortunately, if not unforeseeably, America's Far Eastern bulwark deteriorated fast under the continued single Nationalist party leadership. The failure of promised Kuomintang reforms bothered American liberals, but few paid much attention to them. The snail's pace of transportation and distribution rehabilitation, and of fundamental agricultural recovery, gave fair warning of national economic disintegration. The increasing support of or acquiescence in the Chinese Communists' program seemed to cause no undue alarm in Washington.

There was no reassessment of China's strategic position in the increasingly overshadowing East-West split. American diplomacy did not seem to recognize that Chiang Kai-shek might be relying upon China's old policy of playing one great power off against the other. No one seemed to realize that the sought-for peace and unity between two bitterly rival groups would be difficult to obtain while the mediator continued materially to aid only one side. Finally, China was seemingly viewed in a vacuum, and little concern was manifested for the rest of Pacific Asia or the potent existing interrelationships. So the collapse of Nationalist China in the fall of 1948 found American diplomacy in the Orient completely bankrupt.

A few Congressmen and certain former military and diplomatic leaders, aided and abetted by one of America's most influential publishers, launched a campaign for all-out aid to Chiang Kai-shek. But except for a small appropriation, as a preëlection political move, the general response of American public opinion was negative. Probably owing to a realistic estimate of the situation by both the State Department and the armed services, it seems to have been recognized in Washington that it was too late to bring about the needed changes in the Kuomintang or to stop the Chinese Communists with the means available.

There was never any question about the sympathies of the American people. The traditional bonds of friendship assured the Chinese people our best wishes. But wishful thinking was no more effective in 1948 than it had been in stopping Japan in 1938. The more than two billion dollars' worth of material aid given to Chiang Kai-shek's regime since V-J Day had been used on both the propaganda and actual battle fronts more effectively by the Communists than by the Nationalists. More dollars and arms to the Kuomintang were evidently not the solution.

Even more basic was the fact that Chiang Kai-shek had repeatedly refused to follow sound American military and political counsel. This was particularly true in regard to leaving Manchuria alone until he had first consolidated his position south of the Great Wall, and in urging the demobilization of at least half of his mass armies of crudely conscripted and poorly equipped soldiers. The latter measure would have augmented the much-needed labor supply for rehabilitation while actually increasing the efficiency of his combat troops. In view of these experiences there was no reason to expect that in 1949 Chiang would follow new suggestions any better than he had those of General Stilwell and the other Americans who had succeeded him.

It all seemed to boil down to the proposition that the only effective means of keeping the Chinese Communists from overrunning North China and probably the whole country was to send a number of American combat divisions to China supported by naval and air units. With the difficulty of maintaining even five divisions in the United States at near strength, the drafting of thousands of young men to fight in China's civil war was politically unthinkable at home. And it was questioned whether such intervention in a purely Chinese affair would win many friends abroad.

Furthermore, the probability of Russia's taking counter-steps in active support of the Chinese Communists, if America should embark upon such a course, opened the vista of a beginning of World War III. Thoughtful Americans were of the opinion that if the United States must fight Russia, our moral position is of utmost importance. Certainly, if the break should come over American military support to the corrupt and dictatorial Kuomintang, our position before the world, and especially in the eyes of Asia's millions, would be exceedingly weak.

In the summer of 1949 Nanking fell to the Chinese Communists. Their armies overran Shanghai, crossed the Yangtze River, and marched into South China practically unopposed. All United States forces were withdrawn and further aid to the Nationalist government was stopped.

Chiang Kai-shek, his forces completely shattered on the mainland, withdrew to the island of Formosa with some army divisions, Kuomintang naval units, and the remnants of the Chinese national air force. He had been preceded by several hundred thousand wealthy Chinese and Kuomintang leaders. On the large island stronghold they prepared to make their last stand.

Throughout the winter and early spring of 1950 those Americans who had continued their pressure for aid to Chiang now demanded that the United States use whatever means was necessary to prevent the Communists from seizing Formosa. Cooler heads won out and President Truman decided in favor of the State Department's advice of nonintervention in Formosa.

This was not a continuation of the negative policy of waiting until the dust settled in China, as implied in the "white paper." By January, 1950, the Department of State had formulated a policy of confining communism to China by attempting to halt its spread across China's southern borders. The Truman administration sought to strengthen the nationalist and anticommunist elements in

Indo-China, Thailand, the new United States of Indonesia, Burma, India, and Pakistan. Congress gave support by appropriations for the Point 4 program and for specific aid to individual countries.

The question of United States recognition of the Chinese Communist government, anticipated as a big issue to come before the 81st Congress, never materialized. The actions of the Chinese Communists in restraining United States consular personnel for months, and the fact that the British government, which quickly recognized the Communist government, had never been permitted to send their ambassador to China, were not encouraging. Finally, the Sino-Soviet Treaty made clear that, regardless of American attitudes, the Chinese Communists had no desire to reëstablish diplomatic relations with the United States.

The "Treaty of friendship, alliance and mutual assistance between the Union of Soviet Socialist Republics and the Chinese People's Republic" was signed in Moscow on February 14, 1950. Along with the two published agreements and regardless of suspected secret codicils, this treaty creates the framework of a strong and practical Chinese-Russian political, economic, and military alliance.

Although it cleverly avoids reference to the United States, there is no question of the country toward which the alliance is aimed. "Both Contracting Parties undertaking jointly" to carry out "the necessary measure of preventing aggression" by Japan "or any other State" directly or indirectly associated with it (i.e., the United States). "In the event of one of the Contracting Parties being attacked by Japan or States allied with it . . . the other Contracting Party will immediately render military and other assistance with all the means at its disposal."

There can be only one conclusion: If war should break out between the Soviet Union and the United States, Russia will draw upon the uncounted millions of Chinese manpower.

CHAPTER XXII

National Self-Determination in China

SELF-DETERMINATION is the "right" of a nation to choose its own form of government and to select its own authorities without any external direction. This cry for sovereignty appears to be almost instinctive throughout world history. Toynbee says that "the criterion of growth is progress towards self-determination." The rise of the European and later world states system is the story of struggle for national self-determination. But the nations of eastern Asia had governed their own destinies for many centuries—long before the modern nations of Europe became states.

The contemporary urge for self-government in the Orient is comparatively recent and should not be compared to the historic drive toward statehood. It is more like a revolution to regain their independence lost to the white man's imperialism. This basic fact, coupled with the strangely different cultural foundations of Oriental peoples, greatly complicates many issues and leads to much confusion in thought. Nationalism, democracy, and communism, as known to the Westerners, will not be found to be the same in eastern Asia.

NATIONALISM

Nationalism is commonly rated as the greatest single force in international relations. Almost everyone refers to it, accepts it, but few attempt to define it clearly. The

449

writer is no exception, for nationalism is such a complex psychological behavior pattern, with so many forms and changing manifestations, that it defies any brief specification. As a generalization it may be said that nationalism is the political foundation of the modern world community. It made the great powers; also, it helped create mass armies and total wars. Nationalism almost made Napoleon master of all Europe; in its most extreme form it almost made Hitler dictator over half the world. Yet, more than anything else, nationalism saved China from complete Japanese subjugation.

In eastern Asia nationalism has similar basic characteristics as elsewhere. Large nationality masses think of themselves as an identity held together by strong bonds of common race, language, religion, or, more important, their own long-standing history and culture. A national entity is distinguishable, at least in its own consciousness, from other national groups. Yet in Asia, in addition to its newness, the chief feature of nationalism and its most powerful motivation is resistance to the disliked foreigner. So the cycle is completed—imperialism, born of economic nationalism, creates its own nemesis in native nationalism. However, to give balance it should be added that all imperialism today is not "Western," nor are all foreigners white men. Not counting the short-lived Japanese imperialism, the developing antagonism to (Asiatic) aliens throughout eastern Asia is an outstanding nationalistic manifestation.

Siam may be the best example, but only because it has enjoyed independence longer than others. The several million Chinese nationals, many years resident in Siam (and parallel conditions exist in the Malay States, Indonesia, Indo-China, Burma, and the Philippines), are added to each year by scores of thousands of immigrants. The Chinese (foreigners) dominate much of the economic life of the country and make "the Chinese problem" increasingly critical. The rising nationalism of both Siamese and Chinese encourages friction and develops conflict. Indian nationals, although not as strong competitors as the Chinese, occupy a similar position in southeast Asia. The potentials of a new imperialism and future wars should be quite obvious, if and when China and India become the two great powers of eastern Asia—that is, if they follow the policies of great powers in the past and insist upon "protecting the rights" of their nationals doing business in weaker states.

To discuss some implications of nationalism in the future before describing its origins may be inconsistent, but to ascribe a date for the beginnings of nationalism in any country is practically impossible. Nationalism is a mass movement, and it takes long periods of preparation and education throughout all the people. In eastern Asia the great mass of the people were illiterate; furthermore, it was difficult to arouse them to resistance, for they had long been acquiescent to foreign rule. There had been numerous minor outbursts, but they were incidental because the doctrine of white supremacy was generally accepted by the masses for one reason or another. By the end of the nineteenth century a number of leaders and Western-trained students were sowing the seeds of nationalistic sentiments, but with the exception of some development in small sections of China, India, and the Philippines modern nationalism did not blossom in eastern Asia until the period of World War I.

Although some nationalistic tendencies can be discovered earlier, and certain characteristics of nationalism may be noted in the Taiping and Boxer rebellions, the first large-scale expression of nationalism in East Asia was the Chinese Revolution of 1910-11. The chief difference between it and the countless previous revolutions in China's long history was Sun Yat-sen, the father of the Chinese republic, and his three great principles: (1) nationalism—freedom from imperialism and complete self-determination; (2) democracy—a constitutional republic and a democratic form of government; (3) livelihood—a higher standard of living for the Chinese people. This first Chinese republic was overwhelmed—betrayed by Yuan Shi-kai, one of the worst traitors of all history, and by Japanese aggression—during the confusion of World War I.

Near the end of the war, President Wilson announced the famous "Fourteen Points" as a guide to peace settlements. They included the right of national self-determination. At Versailles were established an independent Poland, Czechoslovakia, Yugoslavia, and Hungary. Why not independence for India, Korea, the Annamites, and the Indonesians? India was promised Commonwealth status; Burma was given more local autonomy; the Philippines were assured again of eventual independence; but for the others only minor concessions, such as advisory councils to the governor, were reluctantly granted by British, Dutch, and French. Denied any real voice in their own governance and driven underground, the persecuted native movements of nationalism continued and grew stronger. More far reaching, their radical elements turned responsively to the persuasive doctrines of a new international force born of World War I, communism, which spread throughout the Far East.

The Growth of Chinese Nationalism

Limited space will permit discussion of the growth of nationalism after World War I in only one country. China is selected not only because it is the greatest nation in Asia but as the best illustration of the interplay of the forces of imperialism, nationalism, and communism.

After World War I, Sun Yat-sen set up his headquarters in Canton (South China) and formed the Kuomintang (National People's party). He appealed in vain to the great democracies, the United States and Great Britain, for aid or at least encouragement in his program of democracy for China. As a last resort he invited the Chinese Communists to join and turned to Russia. Moscow was happy to send Comrade Borodin and others. These trained Communist organizers and agitators were of great help in the early days of the Kuomintang.

In 1925 Dr. Sun died, but Chiang Kai-shek, one of his chief disciples and the most capable military leader, took over and carried on the plans for the second revolution. The Kuomintang army began its march north from Canton to unify the country. It was preceded by well-organized propagandists who roused the common people against the war lords and in support of nationalist ideals. The advance was rapid, and in 1927 captured Nanking was named the new capital of the Chinese republic. Then a most important event took place, an appreciation of which is essential to understanding contemporary China.

The Communist leaders in the Kuomintang who were operating in the industrial cities of Hankow and Shanghai took matters in their own hands. They refused to obey Chiang and called for strikes. Then they followed with such extreme measures as the looting and murder of Europeans. It was not a question of unruly mobs, because it was definitely planned and executed. By the Communist leaders' own admissions they wished to create general chaos out of which they hoped to set up a communist soviet state. It should be noted that Chiang's prior advances involved the Nationalist party forces' overthrowing one war lord after another. It had not been very violent; in fact, "silver bullets" accounted for more victories than lead bullets. The actions by the Communists brought imperialist intervention by the great powers for the protection of their nationals and property.

Chiang Kai-shek had to make a decision. He still faced the strong war lords in Peking and the North. He had little money, few supplies. The wealthy Chinese who could help, would not while he associated with Communists. British and American warships were on the Yangtze, and armed intervention would surely mean the collapse of the Kuomintang movement. And to carry out Sun Yat-sen's principles the first essential was to unify China. Chiang Kai-shek broke with the Communists and repudiated them, driving them from the Kuomintang. The Russian advisers fled, and many thousands of Chinese

Communists were cruelly put to death. Twenty years ago
the breach was sprung which has ever since widened and
hardened the gulf between right and left party politics in
China.

By the summer of 1928 the Generalissimo, Chiang Kai-
shek, had taken Peking and defeated the last northern
war lord, Chang Tso-lin, ruler of Manchuria. China had
been unified and was ready for the next step proposed by
Sun Yat-sen, political tutelage under a single-party national government. Chinese nationalism surged forward
with enthusiasm. The government of the republic, recognized by all the powers, was able to recover control over
foreign concessions in the interior cities and finally won
the right to fix her own tariff on imports. Extensive surveys were made, but real economic progress was obstructed
by the entrenched position of the foreigners. The imperialist interests held tightly to their remaining privileges, and
foreign governments or individuals were reluctant to give
positive assistance to the Chinese.

Chinese nationalists lost out in their first test of strength
when they unsuccessfully tried to oust the Russians in
1929 from the Chinese Eastern Railway (across northern
Manchuria). However, a great victory was theirs in winning over Manchuria to the Kuomintang. The Japanese
had the old Marshal Chang Tso-lin murdered in hopes of
better controlling his son, Chang Hsueh-liang. But the
young Marshal (who was to engineer the later Sian coup)
rebuffed the Japanese, declared allegiance to the Generalissimo, and opened Manchuria to nationalist organizers.
This situation, combined with other signs of increasing
Chinese strength, caused the Japanese Kwantung army to
act before more progress was made. Manchuria was overrun in 1931 and, though a great loss, it taught the Chinese
a lesson. Reliance on the League of Nations or the United
States was of small avail; the security of China rested on
its own efforts and power.

The vitality of China is amazingly shown in the very
real progress, social, political, and economic, during the

five years 1932 to 1937—this in spite of the constant military actions by Chiang against the Chinese Communists. His costly success in driving them from their base in Kiangsi province, south of the Yangtze, is best known by the famous Communist march of ten thousand miles (one of the great exploits of military history), which finally settled the Communists in their strategic strongholds of the northwest province of Shensi. The kidnaping of Chiang Kai-shek at Sian, in December, 1936, and the resulting truce between the Kuomintang and the Chinese Communists, was a most significant historic event. A situation which Japan had counted on as impossible—the unification of the two strongest factions in China—had been realized. Facing a common front instead of a divided nation, Japan struck again while she still had superior power.

The general outline of the war beginning in 1937, which was merged four years later into World War II by Pearl Harbor, is familiar to most readers. Here was the real test of the enduring vitality of Chinese nationalism. The heroic efforts and consuming sacrifices of the numberless masses of Chinese people, faced with staggering losses and inconceivable handicaps, is one of the most glorious chapters in all world history. One-fourth of their country was occupied by a rapacious invader. This included their two capitals, most of their seaports and industrial centers, and two-thirds of their railways. Yet the Chinese seemingly had only begun to fight. Chinese nationalism had proved itself; China was a nation.

Factory machinery was dismantled and actually transported on the backs of coolies to be reassembled over a thousand miles into the interior. Essential production was maintained under tremendous difficulties. A remarkable development of coöperatives in all types of activity educated millions of refugees in a true political economy while making constructive use of their energies. The Communist forces organized the most effective guerrilla tactics of modern warfare, while leaving the positional fighting to the troops of the central government. For the first year or two of the war close coöperation existed between the two forces under the overall command of the Generalissimo. China had become more truly unified than at any period of her three-thousand-year history.

The great tragedy of China, in fact for the whole world, is that somewhere, somehow, during the last year of the war and soon after the Japanese surrender, China lost its inspiration. Faced with the enormous task of reconstruction, the harmonious spirit of patriotism, which had supported the government of Chungking when China alone in the world fought aggression, was gone. China was again torn asunder by sanguinary internal strife. So today Chinese nationalism and true patriotism are confronted with an even more severe test than during the darkest days of the war—a supreme test of its inherent qualities.

The Force of Imperialism

Imperialism means domination and control over peoples and areas by a foreign power—usually, but not necessarily, an overseas state. Imperialism comes in all shapes, sizes, and colored packages. Controls range from military or total political governance to indirect, but no less effective, economic controls and extraterritorial rights or special privileges. The rights of dependent or native peoples run the gamut from practical slavery to a considerable degree of local autonomy, but all have in common the restrictions on political or economic independence, plus the denial of self-determination.

There is no point in enumerating the many abuses practiced under imperial controls. They are well known to all, and much better appreciated than the other side of modern imperialism. That there is another side to imperialism comes as a surprise to many who have always supposed that all imperialism was all bad. Under an imperial flag, with a few exceptions, colonial administrations in the last generation have shown definite improvements in the social, political, and economic conditions of the dependency peoples. Beyond the more intangible results of the missionaries and their religious teachings are the hospitals, modern medicine and sanitation, schools and colleges, plus improved agricultural methods and better distribution through developed transportation and communication. Increasingly important today is the mixed blessing of the industrial "know-how" imparted to natives by Westerners.

But any general consideration of imperialism should appreciate that it has never been exclusive to Europeans. For ages immemorial, long before the coming of the Westerners, the peoples of Asia had been repeatedly conquered and subjected to successive alien empires. Maybe the fact that this ancient imperialism was more brutally autocratic than that of the nineteenth century partly explains the almost ready acquiescence to the white man's rule. There is no question that the recent Japanese imperialism, Asiatic over Asiatic, was far more cruel and abusive than any experienced under former European and American regimes.

It should be further acknowledged that Western imperialism would have been relatively powerless without the enthusiastic collaboration of native subordinates. The most ruthless exploitation of native labor throughout eastern Asia is by native bosses, with or without the direction of Westerners. Political independence to the countries particularly of the western Pacific and southeast Asia holds no assurance of relief to the ignorant, laboring masses. There are many evidences that the worst forms of exploitation usually associated with irresponsible imperialism will continue in eastern Asia long after all Western controls have been removed.

Eastern Asia's acceptance, for over three centuries, of the superiority of Western materialism (if not civilization!), and the imprint on three generations of Asiatics under imperial controls, cannot be quickly erased. It may be true that the yellow and brown men no longer bow subserviently in awe of white men's supremacy. The prestige of Western states and their nationals was irredeemably lost in their overthrow and humiliation by an Asiatic conqueror, Japan, in World War II. The later crushing defeat of Japan may reëstablish the recognized military power of certain nations, but the natives' respect for Westerners is gone. It probably can never be fully restored, certainly not by force.

However, imperialism is normally much more than political domination. Even though native nationalism may achieve governmental self-determination, Western enterprise and management are so deep rooted and essential to the national economies of eastern Asia that any immediate or drastic changes would bring economic calamity. The determining factor in the economic development of eastern Asia was, and in the foreseeable future will continue to be, a decisive insufficiency of capital. The West not only possessed the necessary finances but provided the essential skills for the profitable exploitation of Asia's resources. Except to a limited degree in India, China, and Japan, it will be extremely difficult for individuals or groups to amass the means (both capital and technology) to take over and successfully operate the modern large-scale enterprises owned by Westerners.

Another consequence of Western economic administration was the concentration on production of raw materials and foodstuffs for industrialized Europe and the United States. In eastern Asia (and the western Pacific) this has seriously increased the one-sidedness of the national economics. Furthermore, the deliberate prevention of industrialization adds to economic instability. The prosperity of the nations of eastern Asia is largely dependent upon the fluctuating world market in a relatively few products such as tin, rubber, tungsten, sugar, and tropical foodstuffs.

Local manufacturing was discouraged so that the imperial interests might retain a native market to help pay for the exports of raw materials. All in all, to win political independence—as the experience of the Philippines clearly shows—may well accentuate the economic dilemma of new nation-states. It is essential for them to achieve some semblance of a balanced economy or relative self-sufficiency —at least in the manufacture of ordinary consumers' goods. But they cannot switch over their basic production of raw materials and plantation products, for that is their principal source of national income; furthermore, it is in the hands of Westerners and protected by law.

To industrialize, the new proud yet poor states must seek foreign capital and skills. Where will they turn for help? About the only available source is the already entrenched imperial interests. The strings attached to investment by such groups in all probability will mean the broadening and strengthening of their grip on the nation's economy. Obviously political independence without economic independence is a mockery.

Political imperialism is definitely on the way out of eastern Asia, and some forms of economic imperialism may have changed on the surface, but imperialistic exploitation for alien profit will remain a very real force to be reckoned with for many years to come, unless farsighted and enlightened policies are readily adopted by the United Nations led by the United States.

What a wonderful opportunity is presented in the true interests of international economic stability and peace! What an exciting challenge is proffered by President Truman in his "fourth point" (of inaugural address of January 20, 1949) quoted here:

. . . We must embark on a bold new program for making the benefits of our scientific advances and industrial progress available for the improvement and growth of underdeveloped areas.

More than half the people of the world are living in conditions approaching misery. Their food is inadequate. They are victims of disease. Their economic life is primitive and stagnant. Their poverty is a handicap and a threat both to them and to more prosperous areas.

For the first time in history, humanity possesses the knowledge and the skill to relieve the suffering of these people.

The United States is preeminent among nations in the development of industrial and scientific techniques. The material resources which we can afford to use for the assistance of other peoples are limited. But our imponderable resources in technical knowledge are constantly growing and are inexhaustible.

I believe that we should make available to peace-loving peoples the benefits of our store of technical knowledge in order to help them realize their aspirations for a better life. And, in cooperation with other nations, we should foster capital investment in areas needing development.

Our aim should be to help the free peoples of the world, through their own efforts, to produce more food, more clothing, more materials for housing, and more mechanical power to lighten their burdens.

We invite other countries to pool their technological resources in this undertaking. Their contributions will be warmly welcomed. This should be a cooperative enterprise in which all nations work together through the United Nations and its specialized agencies wherever practicable. It must be a worldwide effort for the achievement of peace, plenty, and freedom.

With the cooperation of business, private capital, agriculture, and labor in this country, this program can greatly increase the industrial activity in other nations and can raise substantially their standards of living.

Such new economic developments must be devised and controlled to benefit the peoples of the areas in which they are established. Guaranties to the investor must be balanced by guaranties in the interest of the people whose resources and whose labor go into these developments.

The old imperialism—exploitation for foreign profit—has no place in our plans. What we envisage is a program of development based on the concepts of democratic fair dealing.

All countries, including our own, will greatly benefit from a constructive program for the better use of the world's human and natural resources. Experience shows that our commerce with other countries expands as they progress industrially and economically.

Greater production is the key to prosperity and peace. And the key to greater production is a wider and more vigorous application of modern scientific and technical knowledge.

Only by helping the least fortunate of its members to help

themselves can the human family achieve the decent, satisfying life that is the right of all people.

Democracy alone can supply the vitalizing force to stir the peoples of the world into triumphant action, not only against their human oppressors, but also against their ancient enemies —hunger, misery, and despair.

DEMOCRACY AND COMMUNISM

Democracy in terms of the American concept and communism in terms of the Russian precept are completely foreign, in every sense of the word, to the cultures and political traditions of East Asian peoples. Thus it is extremely difficult for a Westerner even to attempt to assess their forms or influence in the Far East. Except in the Philippines under somewhat earlier American inspiration, democratic and communist ideologies are very recent. The seeds of both were first sown in China and at about the same time. In fact, democracy and communism were largely introduced or encouraged after World War I by Sun Yat-sen.

It would be silly to try to invent any conceivable basis in Asiatic culture for the principles of Marxism. However, the centuries-old form of village government in China, as described in a preceding chapter, had some elements of democracy, but hardly a basis for a modern democratic state. And in no other Asiatic country outside of China was there any usable foundation for the building of native democracy. Even in the Philippines today the pilings for democracy are not too deep or sturdy. Throughout the Far East there is a lack of any experience in local self-government or representative institutions. The force of the old traditions of a hereditary status and of arbitrary rule—of authority and obedience—still predominate.

Democracy and communism, like nationalism (but unlike imperialism), are imports from the West, and no Western idea can enter the Orient and remain unchanged. Sun Yat-sen studied and was influenced by what we would consider somewhat contradictory ideas—nationalism, democracy, and socialism. He saw no inconsistency in welcoming Russian Communists as trusted allies in the revolution for national liberation. And it cannot be overemphasized that Sun Yat-sen's second principle—democracy—was not, and undoubtedly never will be, American democracy. As expressed so neatly by Professor Linebarger: "Western ideas served largely as a mold; when the mold was removed, the form was Western but the content was still Chinese."

While discussing the "isms," some mention should be made of fascism. The totalitarianism and regimentation associated with fascism were never confined to Europe; nor did the miserable deaths of Mussolini and Hitler signal their obliteration. The chief attributes of modern dictatorship—the all-powerful "leader" supported by an "elite"—could be found throughout the Far East long before it was more definitely symbolized in "*der Führer.*" The potentials were appreciated, for similar controls had often been part of national experiences, if not traditions. Japan made the most of some of the new techniques, but they were widely copied in other Asiatic countries. The military capitulation before the Allied Anglo-American and Russian "democracies" drove fascism under cover. But it would be calamitous wishful thinking to assume that fascism is dead. In Asia, as elsewhere throughout the world, fascism is a latent power against which all freedom-loving people everywhere must be on their guard.

The fear and condemnation of fascism adds to the confusion, especially in China. It is easy for those in critical opposition to assert that Chiang Kai-shek was a dictator. There is no denying that the Red Circle and other secret societies, one-party Kuomintang rule, the Blue-Shirts, secret police, and brutal liquidation of opponents bare striking resemblances to the prewar regimes in Germany, Italy, and Japan. And, on the other hand, there is no refuting of the facts that some real progress toward democratic practices (i.e., the development of local self-government and popular leadership) developed in the areas under the control of Chinese Communists. What is the truth?

The test is not whether Chiang was a dictator or that the Communists are democratic. These are relative matters of the moment. The examination should be in terms of the ultimate objectives. But communism, democracy, fascism, imperialism, and socialism are just some of the vaguely observable elements in the tremendous force which is sweeping through China and Asia. It is the greatest revolt in all history—a social struggle in the broadest sense which includes basic political, economic, cultural, and ideological changes. When or how it will end—what form of political economy will evolve—no one in the world today is in a position to ascertain.

The trouble with most Americans is that they judge democracy in China by comparing it to their own system of government. On such a basis there is very little evidence of real democracy anywhere in eastern Asia. The best standard for measuring progress in a country like China is not "how close are they coming to our way of life?" but rather "how far have they advanced from the conditions that characterized their past existence?" Applying this standard, one conclusion seems clear: Regardless of the current chaos, the revolution has gone so far, no matter where it may eventually lead, that there can be no return to the past. Progress is positive.

In reply to those who charge Nationalist China with practicing fascism, it should be pointed out that Fascists and Nazis bitterly opposed all forms of democracy, whereas the Kuomintang was pledged to the creation of a fully democratic system of government. Granted that many of the reprehensible acts of Chiang Kai-shek may not have been necessary, even during the war, he was carrying out the general orders of Sun Yat-sen. The founder of the republic directed that after the revolution had achieved Chinese unification the next step would be an exclusive

GREAT ISSUES

one-party tutorship (dictatorship!) of the Chinese people. The final step—a democratic constitution and a popularly elected National Assembly—was taken in 1947.

Now in a brief reply to those who claim that the Communists in China are the only elements which have the true interests of the common people at heart, let us take one established fact, not a question open to argument. The first step by the Communists, in a newly incorporated area brought under their control prior to 1948, was to institute a reign of terror. Not only were the landlords deprived of their property, and usually their lives, but all those who had been leaders (the bourgeoisie!) or who evidenced any opposition to communism were liquidated. The remaining ignorant masses were sure to be receptive, to say the least, to tutorship in Soviet "democracy" or anything else.

Looking ahead to ultimate objectives: The Communists of China (and Indo-China) are resolved Marxists. Many of their top leaders were members of the Communist International, have lived and studied in Moscow, and maintain their connections with the Communist party of Russia. It seems rather ridiculous for American apologists to deny any such relationship for them when they themselves openly proclaim their purpose to establish a Communist government in China closely associated with the Soviet Union.

The Chinese Communists

Russian communism came to China at the beginning of the second republican revolution. Nationalist-Communist coalition was natural in their common opposition to imperialism. The coöperation continued while the two revolutionary parties moved in the same direction. When, after the capital was established in Nanking (as recounted in previous pages), the Nationalists softened their positive revolutionary action by turning to a Nationalist reconstitution, the break occurred. The Communists had joined to help the revolution of Sun Yat-sen; communism now spread to fight the Nationalists because to the Communists the revolution had not gone far enough. It is obvious that the Communists had been using the Nationalist revolutionaries (and the same is true for Indo-China) as the means toward their own ideological ends and ambitions for power.

Chinese Communists were at first thrown on the defensive, but they recovered when they discarded the orthodox Marxism of promoting revolution out of labor conflict. The small and powerless proletariat in China, as elsewhere in the Orient, was far too weak a base for revolution. Turning their attention to the miserable millions tied to the land, the Communists won converts and support. They adjusted their ideology to recognize the true sources of their strength (both discredited by official Stalinism): agrarian discontent and an experienced soldiery. Allying themselves with the dissatisfied peasantry to whom they gave land, and strengthening their peasant army, China's Communists went on the offensive.

From their "capital" of Yenan, in Shensi province, the Communists spread their control over a considerable area in northwest China. Proving that they were apt students of the Moscow teachers, they applied that top priority of Lenin and Stalin, expediency, which takes precedence over any and all philosophical doctrines. After the Sian coup the Communists allied themselves again with the hated Kuomintang (visions of the Nazi-Soviet Pact!) against the greater immediate enemy, Japanese imperialism.

During the war the Chinese Communists tremendously increased the size and strength of their armies and entrenched their influence throughout North China as far south as the Yangtze Valley. The fighting was not allowed to interfere with their program of indoctrination. Schools for both peasants and soldiers were maintained, and much of the rural countryside studied and practiced Soviet communism. Even thousands of Japanese prisoners were treated well if they willingly attended these schools of Marxism. Many of the Communist party leaders in Japan today, as well as in northern Korea, are products of these wartime Chinese Communist schools.

Following the failure of reconciliation through General Marshall, the Nationalist armies activated a successful offensive against the Communists. Spearheaded by American-trained divisions and materially aided by "supplied" trucks, tanks, and planes, the Communists were driven out of their stronghold in Shensi and Shansi provinces. Withdrawing in good order the Communist forces crossed over into Manchuria. Here they received their biggest "break" in the long conflict. The Russian troops in withdrawing north from Mukden left behind, with obvious prior arrangements, the vast stores of arms and equipment captured from the Japanese Kwantung army. With these additional armaments, particularly Japanese artillery, the Chinese Communists presented a formidable military force.

At this point, regardless of our feelings, it might be well to note a significant fact. Russian forces withdrew from Manchuria before American forces withdrew from North China. The areas seized by the Kuomintang armies were taken with the assistance of the United States, directly or indirectly. The areas in Manchuria taken by the Communists were brought under control without any assistance by the Russians, in part because the Russians had withdrawn. These events had far-reaching psychological effects in Chinese politics, especially among the liberals.

If General Marshall was correct in saying that the hopes of China rested on the center parties who opposed the right and left extremists, certainly American policies were not designed to encourage them. To millions of Chinese who equally detested the excesses of both Kuomintang and Communists the United States, by aiding Chiang Kai-shek, was merely prolonging the horrors of the civil war. It was, in their eyes, intervention in the internal affairs of the nation. The implications were used most effectively in Communist propaganda, for no relatively strong countercharge could be made against the Russians.

Chiang Kai-shek, as previously noted, refused to follow the advice of Americans and attempted to dislodge the Chinese Communists in Manchuria. In so doing he lost the civil war before it reëntered China proper. With some of the best divisions annihilated and many of the better generals lost, the retreat of the defeated Nationalist armies from Manchuria turned into a rout. The Communist troops, flushed with victory and captured (American) war supplies, exploited the weaknesses of Chiang's armies and followed through, south across the Great Wall. Peiping fell to the Communists in January, 1949; Nanking in the spring; Shanghai in the summer; and Canton in the fall of 1949. In late September Mao Tse-tung proclaimed the establishment of the "People's Republic of China," which was soon thereafter recognized by Russia.

However, it is one thing to win battles over demoralized troops and quite another matter to win the support of millions of civilians including very essential, but rather independent, technicians. It is one thing to govern scattered villages of illiterate peasants in the frontier Northwest, but a very different problem to establish a workable administration over great complex cities of several millions, including many who are highly educated. The Chinese Communists now face a terrific task which will really test, not only their beliefs, but their abilities. The terribly chaotic condition in China today calls for public administrators, economists, sociologists—experts, not political fanatics.

The Chinese Communists are already finding out that directions for the myriad practical details involved in the desires of millions of individuals are not to be found in the gospel of Marx; nor can the answers be located in the writings of Lenin, Stalin, or Mao.

People have to be fed, housed, and gainfully employed. Their human wants must be satisfied by material things, not vague promises of the hereafter wrapped up in finespun doctrines. Taxes must be collected and sewage disposal provided. Regulations are essential and laws must be enforced. The Chinese people in particular have a great heritage of customs and ideas. Like other people they have ambitions for their children, if not for themselves. They, as individuals, think and feel and wish, regardless of the new forms of bondage or disciplined acceptance which may be temporarily imposed.

The Chinese Communist leadership is cognizant of the need for securing the coöperation of a number of groups in Chinese society in addition to retaining the adherence of the general populace. They must appeal to the business-men, engineers, students, and age-long influential literati. No longer can they rest their case with negative attacks upon the Kuomintang rule. A positive program of recon-struction must be presented to win converts and hold followers. Furthermore, the Communists came into power primarily through the drive of a peasant rebellion. They now confront the urban middle classes and city industrial workers with normally opposite needs and demands.

The resulting government will have to be a coalition which will include representatives—conservatives as well as liberals—from these various important groups. It will have a very different slant from the coalition that General Marshall might have succeeded in negotiating in 1946 if American aid to the Kuomintang had been suspended. Then, the balance of military power would have been on the noncommunist side and the liberal and center parties could have strongly influenced the policies propounded by either Nationalists or Communists. In the coalition of 1949, the noncommunists may exercise some moderating influence, may slow down the pace, but cannot hope to change the direction in which the Communists decide to move. However, the significance of coalition governments in cities, regions, and nationally, with noncommunist members representing extremely powerful groups, is some-thing to be reckoned with by all concerned.

The Communists recognize as imperative that for China to be politically independent it must achieve economic independence and a broad industrialization. Possibly taking a page out of Soviet Russia's experience following their early excesses of "Red terror," the Chinese Communists are seemingly adopting a "New Economic Policy" of their own. Plans recently were unfolded by General Pi-shih, the member of the Central Executive Committee and Chinese Politburo who is responsible for finances and taxes. He said that those things already nationalized by the Kuomintang—mainly railways, mines, and some banks—would be taken over by the Communist state, but that private enterprises which are "beneficial to national economy" could continue during the development period.

· Declaring that production must come first, the Communists have promised to protect and utilize private capital. The Tientsin stock market was reopened and small factories were given subsidies by the Communists without reorganization. Strikes were prohibited and the too extreme tendencies of labor unions brought remonstrance. Mao's orders to the Red armies to respect foreign property gave a hint that foreign participation in China's industry might not be excluded.

According to General Pu-shih, noted above, not only must war-damaged industry be restored within three to five years, but industry must be raised in a planned manner from about 10 percent of China's economy to 30 or 40 percent within ten to fifteen years. These grandiose plans obviously overlook the inescapable poverty of China. The Communist planners seemingly show no appreciation of the tremendous amount of capital equipment that is needed for such extensive industrialization, and no one has revealed where the correspondingly large amounts of capital funds can be obtained. Certainly the Soviet Union is not in a position to advance either, even if it were considered expedient to do so.

Actually, the United States is the only nation that has the means to furnish the degree of aid necessary for China to build a sound national economy. Yet this aid would appear to be prohibited by present policies on both sides of the Pacific. According to Mao Tse-tung, in an article last summer "On People's Democratic Dictatorship," ". . . We belong to the anti-imperialist front headed by the U.S.S.R., and we can only look for genuine friendly aid from that front. . . ." Initially for propaganda purposes, maybe now out of habit, the Communists have a phobia about American imperialism which goes so far as to include much that has always been considered normal economic relations. As a consequence they are following policies which, unless changed, will isolate them from international trade.

If Hitler, with the advanced industrialization of Germany, found autarchy difficult; indeed, if Russia finds it necessary today to maintain trade with the United States and "the West," what chance has China to establish national economic self-sufficiency? It may be predicted that if the Communists attempt it they will be driven to such violently oppressive measures that their overthrow will be only a matter of time.

China may be on the verge of emergence as a stable free nation, or it may sink deeper into the hopeless morass of recurring tyranny and revolt. The policies pursued by the Communists will be decisive, but the policies adopted by the United States toward China and eastern Asia can still be a strong contributing factor.

The above remarks might indicate that Russian influence should be summarily discounted. This was not the intention, although the opinion is held that the part played by the Soviets has been considerably exaggerated. Certain facts should be noted. China is the first and only country outside of Russia to set up a Communist government exclusively by internal revolution and reliance upon its own forces. (Communist regimes were established in the countries of eastern Europe only when Russian armies were, at the time, within those countries or on their borders prepared to move in and take over.) Russian military and material aid was incidental to the success of the Chinese Communists.

There has never been any affinity between the Russian

and Chinese people—quite the opposite. The Chinese, around the turn of the century, experienced Russian imperialism under the czars and, prior to World War II, the new aggressive expansionism in Sinkiang and Mongolia under the Soviet commissars. In spite of the thousands of miles of common boundaries there are no significant trade or cultural bonds between Russia and China. Their centers of population and economic activity are widely separated by vast deserts and sparsely settled mountainous regions. There are no links of modern transportation and communication, no direct railroad connections except by way of Manchuria.

Actually, it is much easier and more profitable, under normal conditions, to ship across the Pacific than to trade overland with the Soviet Union. Furthermore, most of Chinese and Russian surpluses for export are competitive, which is not true of China's mutually beneficial trade with the United States and Europe. Definitely, through long friendly associations and indeed even geographically in terms of bulk cargo or convenient travel, the United States and the American people are much closer to China than is Russia.

This does not mean to imply that Russian communism is not the most far-reaching force in contemporary China. The Chinese Communists look to their Russian "comrades" for help and encouragement. Obviously the Russian Politburo will bend every effort to bring Communist China within its orbit, if not under direct control, at least as a dependable ally. The Chinese at this time have nothing to gain and much to lose by breaking their close ties with Moscow. Being part of a world-wide "revolution" gives added strength and prestige. Of course the Chinese Communists can be expected to follow the world (Moscow) Communist party "line" on all international fronts.

When it comes to directing domestic affairs, the internal policies for China, that is quite another matter. It is far too early to judge whether Mao will become a Chinese Tito It may be just more wishful thinking on the part of

Westerners. Yet there is no question that if Stalin cannot effectuate his control over Yugoslavia he has little chance to dominate the present Chinese leadership against their will. China is just too big and uncontrollable for the Russians to envelop with force or to infiltrate sufficiently to seize power from within.

Chinese communism is a split personality. Being Chinese it has to be emphatically nationalistic to hold the people. At the same time, toward the Soviet Union, it heatedly promotes international communism. The struggle between these two emotional attitudes has not caused many visible tensions yet, but the basic conflict exists and could erupt violently at any time. It would be a wise man indeed who could positively state which would predominate if it came to a showdown.

The Russian Communists do not always practice what they preach about anti-imperialism. Manchuria, which looms large in Chinese nationalism, and where most vital Russian and Chinese interests meet head on, is a case in point. Many Chinese remember the looting of Manchuria by the Russian armies and the dismantling of the large percentage of Chinese industrial plants located there. Russia holds Dairen and Port Arthur and controls the railroads. The further recent concessions to the Russians in Manchuria were hard to rationalize. That an increasing number of the Chinese are questioning the motives of Russia is another weight which might be added to the balance scales.

The intervention of Communist China in the Korean War narrows the alternatives available for United States policy, while American leadership in the United Nations' attempt to preserve the Korean Republic has provided Mao with excellent opportunity for propaganda within China. But an eventual accord with China remains an important possibility.

In summary it should be stated that, regardless of the point of view or how objective one may attempt to be, the situation in China today is so fluid, so completely out of control, that any observation is at best a speculation. To further complicate an understanding, although there is no dynamic ideology competing with communism, there is great inertia in China, which obstructs change. Confucian and other ideas are so firmly rooted that more than persuasion will be required to transplant foreign substance. Communist policies conflict with potent family loyalties and with the long-established precept that government interference in people's lives should be kept to a minimum. To what extent the Communists' ideological sledge hammer can beat down the old ideas and shape Chinese thought and action only the future can tell.

Finally, some last brief conclusions on China's long struggle for self-determination. The civil war between the Kuomintang and the Communists was only one phase of the vast revolution in China which began long before the "Communist Revolution" in Russia. Neither American democracy nor Russian communism can "save" China or even materially change the course of events. The restoration of a strong, orderly China must be accomplished within China. The form of government will be eventually the choice of the Chinese people.

CHAPTER XXIII

The Background of Contemporary American Foreign Policy

International Relations

International relations in all probability originated in early prehistoric times when some primitive tribe crossed a river or mountain range and met with another (and different) group of people. No matter how crude we might consider it now, a form of diplomacy took place. Either one tribe withdrew from disputed ground, possibly compensating the other side, or a boundary line was established by amicable agreement; or one group resorted to force and a fight for supremacy resulted. War and conquest is the most plausible theory of the origin of the first organized and established state.

Tens of hundreds of years later, that is, today, war is still the primary concern of international relations; and the prevention of war is the highest objective of diplomacy. Indeed, there is actually little that is new, basically, in international relations. The earliest existing treaty was carved in stone about 3000 B.C. It records the settlement, by arbitration, of a boundary dispute between Egyptian kings. Long theses were written in ancient China and India on the principle of balance of power as the basis of foreign relations. Customs governing the exchange of diplomatic representatives were faithfully adhered to by the Hebrew kings and others.

Rome, under the republic, formed alliances, defined the processes of declaring war and negotiating peace, and codified the laws of war. Imperialism for conquest and plunder carries through all history, and the colonial empire of Athens, based on trade, is comparable to the British Empire. The machinery for the peaceful settlement of interstate disputes was developed among the Greek city-states to an advanced degree not approached again until recent decades. The Council of Delphi can be readily described as the Greek prototype of the League of Nations.

Rome, as a Universal State, had, of course, no international relations. Based on the fact that the longest period of uninterrupted peace in recorded history was under the Roman Empire, the idea has persisted that a universal state is the prerequisite for permanent peace. The Holy Roman Empire was an early and lingering manifestation; but the ideal of imperial unity, especially when motivated by insatiable ambition for power, has brought each succeeding century war, not peace. The dreams of continental and eventual world dominion are not of certainty buried with Hitler or at Hiroshima, any more than they were at Waterloo.

After the fall of the Roman Empire at least the Western world was thrown into centuries of chaos and anarchy appropriately called the "Dark Ages." What marks the transition to the "Middle Ages" is immaterial here, for there were still no international relations. There were no nations. What is considered modern diplomacy or foreign relations originated among the independent city-states of northern Italy during the thirteenth century. It was two or three centuries later that international diplomacy was really practiced in western Europe by the emerging "states system."

The development of national group identities had been resisted by: (1) the tradition of Rome—a cosmopolitan world empire; (2) the Roman Catholic Church, holding the spiritual obedience of all the Western peoples; and (3) feudalism with its rigidly stratified society and its political hierarchy based on personal vassalage, particularly preventing the growth of nationality.

However, during the sixteenth century and the first half of the seventeenth these forces were sufficiently weakened or dissipated to permit cognizance of national entity. Gunpowder rendered the armored knight and fortified castle—the symbols and strength of feudalism—obsolete. The Reformation broke the universality of the Church of Rome. And the rise to power of absolute sovereigns, with dynastic rule over definite territory, finally registered the end of medieval Europe.

The advent of the self-conscious nation-state, conceived during the religious wars, not only made foreign policies feasible but made some organization of international relations essential. The Thirty Years' War was the last of the wars of religion and also the first of the European general wars. The Peace of Westphalia (1648) founded the European states system. In its design the structural foundations were: (1) the doctrine of unrestricted state sovereignty; (2) the accepted principles of international law; and (3) the equipoise provided by a balance of power.

For the next three hundred years this last, and much maligned, principle of international politics did help keep the number of general wars to four. These, with reference by their peace settlements were: (1) the Treaty of Utrecht (1713), which ended the Wars of the Spanish Succession (actually it stopped the first great disturber of European peace, Louis XIV, who threatened the balance of power); (2) the Congress of Vienna (1815), which reconstructed the European states system after the Napoleonic Wars; (3) the Treaty of Versailles (1919), which ended European exclusiveness and constructed a world states system after World War I; and (4) World War II, for which the principal treaty settlements are in a halting process of detached negotiations.

During the last three centuries there have been many

other wars; also, certain far-reaching developments have tremendously influenced the course of international affairs. Some forces have increased interstate frictions and the reliance upon national self-help or military power; other factors have encouraged international coöperation and organization, and given promise of permanent peace under an established world law.

In brief outline the chief developments prior to World War II were: (1) modern nationalism, an outgrowth from the French Revolution (when a whole nation rose as one under common motivations and a militant public opinion), which is still the primary force in world politics; (2) modern imperialism, a by-product of the industrial revolution, which created vast overseas empires and was the chief cause of World War I; (3) world politics, promoting a world-wide balance of power, which came through the forced acceptance of non-European Japan and the United States among the great powers; (4) a League of Nations, the first general international organization, and based upon the new concept of collective security in contradiction to balance of power; and (5) international interdependence, by the time and contact shrinkage of the world through modern communication and transportation.

World War II was terrifying in its global, total character and horrible in its capacity for utter extinction. But it has made certain propositions crystal clear. The extreme sensitiveness, political as well as economic, of every nation (especially the United States) to conditions in all other nations places the recognition of interdependence within the world community beyond refutation. The United Nations, more universal and probably superior in some respects to the League of Nations, still sadly lacks the effectiveness necessary to prevent wars. Finally, the atomic bomb dictates immediate diplomatic action by statesmanship of the highest quality.

The world can no longer patiently rely on an evolutionary progress to a better world order. Time is short and the race is close. Either the world community is soon brought under a reign of law which secures peace and justice for all peoples, or civilization as we know it perishes from the earth.

Actual relations between nations—e.g., 180 million Russians and 140 million people in the United States—simply do not exist. The contacts are maintained by diplomacy, which may be best defined as "the application of intelligence and tact to the official relations between the governments of independent states." A basic test of a state's sovereignty is the right to send and receive diplomatic agents; that is, *individuals* who officially represent their own governments in the capital of a foreign government.

The multifarious details and important, sometimes critical, issues involved in the relations between the seventy-odd sovereign states require a complex, worldwide organization. National laws regulate the foreign officers and agencies of a state, but sanctions are essential to the smooth operation of interstate relations. These are found in international law and in the treaties in force among the governments of the world. Probably the longest-established and most exactly defined principles of international law are those dealing with the practices of diplomacy. Very rarely are these customary rules disregarded even by the most audacious dictator. Added respect is assured in practically all countries, as in the United States, where treaties are included as part of "the supreme law of the land" and are therefore enforceable in the courts.

Diplomacy operates chiefly by three methods: (1) the exchange of notes, that is, a carefully written dispatch on a subject of common interest (sometimes a complaint or request) sent from the Foreign Office of one government to that of the other; (2) diplomatic interviews, usually between a foreign ambassador and the Minister of Foreign Affairs; and (3) international conferences, either of ambassadors of the interested states accredited to a particular capital, or by specially appointed high officials, foreign ministers, even heads of state, who meet at some pre-arranged place to consider an extraordinary situation.

One of the great accomplishments of the League of Nations was the creation of permanent machinery for regularizing this exceedingly beneficial form of diplomacy —the international conference. Instead of waiting until a crisis develops and war threatens before calling a conference of the powers, under the United Nations the representatives of all nations, large and small, are in frequent if not almost continuous conference. Seldom, except in recent actions of irresponsible dictators, will sovereign states go to war while their diplomats are in conference. More important, when responsible government officials (that is, *human beings* authorized to speak for many other human beings) from several or many different nations sit down conscientiously to discuss matters of mutual concern, it is the big step toward international coöperation.

CONTROL OF FOREIGN RELATIONS

The preliminary diplomatic moves prior to the recent war focused attention on certain advantages of totalitarian controls, and disadvantages of democratic controls, over foreign relations. As the war progressed to final victory the strength of democracy and the weaknesses of dictatorship stood forth. By way of introduction, a brief comparison may be worth while.

A regimented society under a dictator, skillfully employing propaganda and censorship, has obvious material advantages in its foreign relations, especially with democracies. The supreme authorities can fix the ultimate objective and intermediate goals and then direct all the resources of the state toward their fulfillment. Foreign policies are coldly calculated without concern of parliament or public opinion.

In democracies, practically the opposite is true. The free election and frequent change of national administrations make long-term planning difficult, which limits a continuity in foreign policy. Democracies give an impression of muddling along at cross-purposes, with no definite aims, and at a given moment even the general direction of diplomacy is hard to perceive. This is due in part to the operation of checks within the government, but also to the delays occasioned in obtaining approval on policy, against the opposition of various interest groups and always in the view of party politics.

The dictator allows no public discussion and forbids any criticism. This inspires overconfidence based on a false sense of popular support. Totalitarian controls may assume preëminence with continuing success, but let there be serious mistakes—defeats in battle—and there are no cushions to ease the shock, no peaceful means of changing the leaders. The overthrow of authoritarianism usually results in a complete collapse of the government.

A democratic system frustrates overambitious leaders, provides information, and encourages deliberation. It has the benefit of the opinions of many. Herein lies the greatest strength of democracies. In a supreme test—war—the free people will offer any sacrifice, will fight the hardest with their backs to the wall. They are not blindly following a self-appointed messiah; they are supporting their own chosen leader. Right or wrong as the policy may have been, it is theirs and it was instituted with the approval of the majority.

In the United States there is a wide sharing of power in the control of foreign relations among the President, Congress, and the people. The very few provisions in the Constitution which directly grant powers to the Chief Executive are as follows: The President (1) "shall have power, by and with the advice and consent of the Senate, to make treaties, provided two-thirds of the Senate present concur" (Art. II, Sec. 2, Clause 2); (2) "shall nominate and by and with advice and consent of the Senate shall appoint ambassadors, other public ministers and consuls" (Art. II, Sec. 2, Clause 2); (3) "shall receive ambassadors and other public ministers" (Art. II, Sec. 3).

It is obvious that these provisions cover only a fraction of his duties in the ordinary conduct of diplomacy. The powers of the President rest more on custom and usage and upon other powers granted him in related phases and over the various departments of the national administration. For example, as Commander in Chief of the Armed Forces, the President can decidedly affect foreign relations. As head of state the President speaks for the government of the United States and is the recipient of official communications from foreign governments. In general the President probably exercises the greatest control by his leadership in the direction of foreign policies, as we shall see presently.

The constitutional powers of Congress include: "to declare war," "to raise and support armies," "to provide a Navy," and "to regulate commerce with foreign nations." More fundamental than these expressed powers, in the effectiveness of legislative checks on the executive's conduct of external affairs, is the control by Congress over appropriations. Very few foreign policies can be promoted without financial support.

The distinguishing feature in the United States (to be found in no other constitutional system) is the two-thirds vote of approval by just one chamber, the Senate, before a treaty can be ratified. This "irreparable mistake of our Constitution" is difficult to explain when all laws, even a declaration of war, require only a majority vote in both houses of Congress.

To give two examples: American entrance into the League of Nations and American adherence to the World Court protocol. Both were overwhelmingly supported in the House of Representatives; both received a comfortable majority of favorable votes in the Senate; yet both were defeated because they fell six or seven votes short of the required two-thirds consent. This ever potential deadlock on foreign policy has caused American Presidents increasingly to use Executive Agreements, which are effective without approval. Such was the exchange after the out-

break of World War II of fifty American destroyers for
United States air bases in the British West Indies.

Popular controls over foreign policies may not be written
into any Constitution, yet in the long run public opinion
in the United States, as in all true democracies, makes the
ultimate decision. While the arrangement of legislative
and executive powers check too hasty or unwarranted
actions, both the President and Congress are held accountable to the people. Election day is the most effective control and check over diplomacy which, at the time, is not
considered in the national interest.

THE FORMULATION OF FOREIGN POLICIES
IN THE UNITED STATES

The fundamental foreign policies of the United States,
as of other nations, are (1) national defense and (2) promotion of the national interests. The first, security, is the
primary duty of all governments: to preserve the independence and the acknowledged "way of life" of the nation. But how? Through reliance upon self-help (its own
military strength), through foreign alliances creating a
favorable balance of power, through collective action
under a world organization, or by some combination of
these three means?

For the second, what *is* in the national interests—say,
for example, over a tariff policy? Is a high tariff on imports in the interests of American farmer, laborer, indus-
trialist, small businessman, shipper, banker, taxpayer, consumer, and the nation as a whole? Or would it favor one
section of the country—North, South, East, or West?
Who decides? Who formulates the year-by-year details of
policy and sets the course of American diplomacy?

An easy answer for the American democracy is, of
course, the "people," and in final analysis this is true.
However, 140 million citizens with a multitude of interests and desires, disagreeing among themselves in a thousand ways, can hardly be expected to steer the ship of
state. At best, the majority expresses itself on the guid-

ing principles through the orderly processes of government.

The President of the United States, elected by all the people and representing the nation as a whole, logically assumes the greatest responsibility for "making" foreign policy. With the aid of experts in his cabinet and official family the Chief Executive is expected to compose changes or plan future policies. The President enunciates his foreign policy in such ways as: his annual message to Congress on the state of our Union; special messages, proclamations, published notes to foreign governments, presidential addresses, and frequent interviews with the press. As titular head of his political party, especially if the party enjoys a majority in both houses of Congress, he has added influence.

Washington's Neutrality Proclamation, Jefferson's purchase of Louisiana, the Monroe Doctrine, Theodore Roosevelt's "I took the Canal zone," Wilson's "Fourteen Points," the "Good Neighbor," and the Truman Doctrine are a few illustrations of foreign policies formulated by Presidents. Not all were approved by Congress or the people, but all have decidedly affected our foreign relations.

The various executive departments of the federal government frequently exert influence on external affairs, especially War and Navy; also Commerce, Treasury, and others. But the chief burden for supervising the myriad of details connected with carrying out foreign policies naturally is carried by the Department of State. Through its experts and their advice, by its instructions to diplomats (and in terms of popular support, its public information service) the American "foreign office" is predominant in steady influence.

United States ministers abroad, when called upon to act in some decisive situation, have materially shaped our diplomacy. Strong secretaries of state, especially when under weak presidents, have often "made" policies. John Q. Adams was most instrumental in framing the Monroe Doctrine. Other examples are the Webster-Ashburton

Treaty, Secretary Seward's purchase of Alaska, the Hay "open door" notes, James G. Blaine and Pan-Americanism, Secretary Hughes in the Washington Conference, the Kellogg-Briand Peace Pact, the "Stimson Doctrine," the Hull trade treaties, and, currently, the Marshall Plan.

Congress often appears in a negative role, which is not quite fair. As a sounding board for public opinion and by acting as an agency of review it performs a highly important function in the democratic process. Congressional investigations, hearings in Washington, and foreign observations help broaden the considerations. A bright light, even though sometimes accompanied by emotional or political heat, is often turned on dubious issues.

Positive Congressional actions, either legislation or resolutions, concerning foreign affairs are exemplified in the Neutrality acts, Oriental Exclusion and other immigration laws, the Smoot-Hawley Tariff, the Spanish embargo, and the Tydings-McDuffie Act (Philippine independence). But the obstructionist activity of Congress, particularly the Senate, "not only disgraces us before the nations, but in some future world crises may ruin us."[1] Such tactics as pigeonholing presidential recommendations in the Foreign Relations Committee, filibusters, refusal to appropriate funds or approve appointments may sometimes be decisive. As Lindsay Rogers expresses it: "American foreign policy is determined not by the President and two-thirds of the Senate, but by one third of the Senate which will withhold its consent."

It is usually taken for granted that the people do not share in the formulation of American foreign policies. This is not true. The electorate expresses itself in many ways other than at the ballot box. Executives as well as Congressmen are sensitive to public opinion, especially on foreign affairs, as noted in editorials, speeches and public statements, letters, and petitions. Positive plans and proposals, frequently of a most constructive character, are

[1] R. S. Baker, *Woodrow Wilson and the World Settlement*, New York, 1922, vol. i, p. 316.

continuously being presented to Washington. Following is a sampling of organizations which make very real contributions: Americans for Democratic Action, American Bankers Association, American Bar Association, American Jewish Conference, American Federation of Labor, American Political Science Association, American Academy of Political and Social Science, Brookings Institution, Carnegie Endowment for International Peace, Council on Foreign Relations, Congress of Industrial Organizations, Foundation for Foreign Affairs, Foreign Policy Association, General Federation of Women's Clubs, League of Women Voters, National Catholic Welfare Conference, National Association of Manufacturers, National Council of Churches, World Peace Foundation, United Nations Association, and United States Chamber of Commerce.

Unfortunately there are fly-by-night organizations and many groups of selfish, misguided, or irresponsible individuals, which are very different in outlook and purpose from the associations listed above. Sometimes temporary combinations have exerted pressure out of all proportion to their numbers. Such was the America First Committee (1940), which included such strange bedfellows as the German-American Bund, Christian Front, Ku Klux Klan, and Silver Shirters, and which used every demagogic device to "Keep America Out of War" (the name of the original committee). Another previous example was the teaming up of the three super-patriots and self-appointed advisers on American foreign policy, William Randolph Hearst, Father Coughlin, and Huey Long, to prevent participation by the United States in the World Court.

By way of summary of the discussion thus far, let us paraphrase a passage from an article written by the great American statesman Elihu Root for the first issue of *Foreign Affairs* (1922): When foreign relations are ruled by democracies, the danger of war will be in mistaken beliefs. Whereas there is no way to prevent all-powerful dictators from having sinister purposes, there are ways to prevent people from having erroneous opinions. The whole people, as a part of their ordinary education, must be furnished with correct information about international relations. They should learn about other peoples and they must be taught the limitations upon their own rights as well as their duties and obligations in respect to the rights of others. Then will the people themselves have the means to test misinformation, and appeals based upon prejudice and passion.

AMERICAN DIPLOMACY

One significant factor that decidedly sways American diplomacy was omitted from the preceding discussion—that is, the policies of foreign governments, which obviously affect our policy decisions in many important ways. A change of policy, the abandonment of an established position, especially by a major power, forces the United States to reëvaluate its own policies in view of the new situation. The actions and statements of other governments may also indirectly affect American policies through their effects on American public opinion.

It is a reasonable proposition that, until recent decades, American diplomacy was predicated more on events in world politics than upon national policies or the actions of the people of the United States. American independence was won, not simply by the bravery of colonials, but by the financial, military, and naval aid of the French (supported in war against England by Spain and The Netherlands) in their desire to weaken the British Empire. The Louisiana Purchase, which made possible the dream of continental expansion, was the outcome of a diplomatic seesaw between France and Spain, capped by Napoleon's need for cash. We would have lost much more than just having our Capitol burned in 1814 if the British had not been simultaneously engaged in a death struggle with Napoleon. The pronouncement of the Monroe Doctrine, bulwark of self-determination for South America, was feasible only because it was guaranteed by the British fleet, following England's break with the Holy Alliance.

Spain's weakness enabled the United States to seize Florida, and again, at the close of the century, to take Cuba, Puerto Rico, and the Philippines.

British and French interest in an independent Texas undoubtedly hastened annexation, which in turn led to war with Mexico and expansion to the Pacific. British and French recognition of the Confederacy and their intervention in the Civil War most probably would have meant two rival states in place of the powerful union of forty-eight states. Over the years the economic and political conditions in Europe encouraged tens of millions of immigrants who have contributed so much to the greatness of America. Finally, World War I changed the United States from a debtor to a great creditor nation and established America as a power second to none in wealth, industry, and potential military strength. Today, in comparison to our past dependence on the policies of other governments, the United States is so powerful in all respects that its foreign policies are decisive in determining the direction in which the world will go in the foreseeable future.

Much of the failure of so many Americans to understand or appreciate their own government's foreign policies is due to the super-nationalistic (usually unrealistic) presentation of American history..This was particularly true in the distortions by those who sponsored isolationism. A simple example is publisher Hearst, who has repeatedly credited George Washington, to give added weight, with Thomas Jefferson's phrase "no entangling alliances." The truth is readily available in Washington's Farewell Address—in which the first President of the United States said:

It is our true policy to steer clear of permanent alliances with any portion of the foreign world. . . .

Taking care always to keep ourselves by suitable establishments on a respectable defensive posture, we may safely trust to temporary alliances for extraordinary emergencies. . . .

With me a *predominant motive* has been to endeavor to

gain time to our country to settle and mature its yet recent institutions, and to progress without interruption to that degree of strength and consistency which is necessary to give it, humanly speaking, the *command of its own fortunes.*

To the founding fathers, the keystone in the arch of American diplomacy was labeled "gain time." The newly born democracy was torn from years of war and bankrupt; its three million disunited people were scattered thinly east of the Alleghenies. There was no friendly nation that it could trust. But weak as it was, the United States had courageous and far-sighted leaders—strong men who knew war and international power politics from experience. It should be noted that from the settlement of Jamestown to the Declaration of Independence—one hundred and sixty-nine years—the colonists had been learning in the school of hard knocks for a period equal to from 1776 to the end of World War II.

Isolation, our oldest and most persistent policy, was never considered a permanent course even when it was the only sound decision. It was expedient to keep from becoming embroiled in the dynastic rivalries of Europe while the young republic gathered strength. Even pacifist Thomas Jefferson was ready to make an "entangling alliance" with the British, whom he disliked, if it had become necessary in order to acquire Louisiana from the French.

Isolation, like all general principles, may be applied differently toward the several geographic regions of the world. The corollary to isolation is nonintervention, and it is true that the United States refrained from interfering much in European affairs until it landed an armed force in 1917 and another in 1942. In the Far East, from the establishment of extraterritoriality in China (1844) and the forceful opening of Japan (1853), the United States has intermittently and often vigorously intervened, to the point of occupying Japan in 1945.

In Latin America the United States practiced single-handed intervention for three generations. It would be most difficult to rationalize any principle of isolation into the extreme statement of Secretary Olney (1895) that "today the United States is practically sovereign on this continent, and its fiat is law upon the subjects to which it confines its interposition"; or in President Theodore Roosevelt's interpretation (1904) that "the Monroe Doctrine may force the United States, in flagrant cases of wrong-doing or impotence, to the exercise of an international police power." Fortunately, with the support of the larger national economic interests which opposed the imperial interests of dollar diplomacy, the United States renounced unilateral intervention, and under President Franklin Roosevelt gained an unprecedented declaration of Pan-American solidarity (1938).

The American people from early colonial times have built fine ships and actively traded throughout the world. "Freedom of the seas" is the traditional expression of our policy which stood for the removal of restrictions on commerce. Under this principle, consistently followed, the United States successfully sought to guarantee the inviolability of private property on the high seas. It pushed for the opening of international rivers. The basic "open door" policy for China logically expressed this demand for equality of opportunity to trade. Probably it was an unreasonable extension of this principle when Americans further demanded the right to trade in time of war as well as in time of peace. The attempt to enforce this "right" did compose the international law on neutrality, but it involved the United States in every general European war that occurred.

The expansion of dominion by the United States began in 1803 with Louisiana and ended with that great blunder of American diplomacy, the acquisition of the Philippines about one hundred years later. It was under the usually misunderstood aegis of "manifest destiny." That the American people were destined to round out "their continent" may be rationalized, but there was no justification for the costly overseas empire. However, the main point,

often overlooked, is that the aggressive actions of this
cocky new nation were not motivated by mere land grabbing. American leaders, even before achieving independence, planned the eventual elimination of all European
powers from North America as the prime essential for
national security.

The Monroe Doctrine, in its original meaning, is still
the best simple statement of this top priority policy. In
1823 the United States said of the Holy Alliance—Austria,
France, and Russia—that for them "to extend their system
to any position of this hemisphere is dangerous to our
peace and safety." Reprehensible as were many later
American actions under the cloak of the Monroe Doctrine, a fair appraisal would include the demands of the
time for national security. This is particularly true of our
Caribbean diplomacy, which involved the security of the
vital Panama Canal and its approaches.

In recent years a far-reaching policy decision has directed
our diplomacy to one of its greatest achievements—national security based on the mutual responsibility of the
twenty-one American republics for united hemispheric defense, coupled with close Canadian-United States joint
defense operations. In addition the United States has
assumed a strategic trusteeship over the former Japanese
mandate islands of the South Pacific. Furthermore, Congress has authorized the standardization with friendly
nations of small arms and equipment. Once again American diplomacy for national security is dynamic. Seemingly we have profited by the bitter lessons of the psy-
chology of appeasement or a Maginot Line for national
defense.

Collective security has been supported by the United
States in the most inconsistent and spotty manner, but
one of the first diplomatic acts of the republic, the Jay
Treaty, was the first modern use of arbitration to settle
international disputes. American diplomacy can proudly
boast of world leadership in the development of the machinery for peaceful or legal settlements. The inclusion of

a clause in the Treaty of Guadalupe Hidalgo providing for arbitration, the settlement of the "Alabama" claims, the North Atlantic Fisheries case, and several boundary disputes are only a few examples.

The United States was active in the Hague court and in organizing the World Court. It took the leadership in setting up the Universal Postal Union, the World Public Health Organization, and numerous other beneficial international public unions. It joined the International Labor Organization. But when it came to accept membership in the League of Nations and the World Court, America repudiated over one hundred years of foreign policy. What prevented the United States from "carrying through" to a logical policy conclusion? One factor was the obstinacy of the Senate, insisting that no foreign commitments be made without their approval of each individual proposition. Another reason was that the country had come under the domination of the isolationists.

To all those who might promote a policy of isolation for the United States there is one answer: "Let's look at the record." From 1919 to 1940 the views of isolationists prevailed, not the counsel of Wilson, Hughes and Stimson, Roosevelt and Hull, or Wendell Willkie. For twenty years the isolationists, followed by a large majority of the people, were all-powerful in Congress. They vetoed administration policies or took negative actions on all crucial foreign issues during five administrations.

After a victorious war it was the isolationists who forced the United States to make a separate peace, and to withdraw from all association with other democracies to keep "the world safe for democracy." It was the isolationists who prevented any workable solution and imposed the devastating policy of collecting uncollectible reparations and debts, and who wrote the laws forbidding loans to our friends and allies. It was the isolationists who capped this obstruction to economic recovery by passing the Smoot-Hawley Tariff.

Having promoted international economic anarchy and

observed the resultant rise of revolutionary dictatorships, it was the isolationists who prompted disarmament and then put their sole reliance for security on the pious resolutions of the Kellogg Peace Pact. Never has an unrestricted policy been given such a long and fair trial as that awarded to isolationism. Never in all history has any policy proved to be such a complete and absolute failure in terms of the national interests of the American people. As Secretary of State Stimson so well said: "Isolation in the modern world is a fantastic impossibility."

The final deed of the isolationists, the Neutrality acts, did more to assure the early successes of Hitler and the Japanese than anything those international gangsters did themselves; also, it came very close to spelling the loss of our own independence. Disregarding all of history's lessons, the isolationists attempted insulation by legislation. Although neutrality had failed under Washington and Jefferson, and although President Wilson in his war address said: "Neutrality is no longer feasible or desirable where the peace of the world is involved and the freedom of its peoples," Congress acted anyway.

Neutrality had the further disastrous effect of limiting freedom of action and preventing the Executive from using the influence of the world's greatest power on the side of peace. Fortunately for all, President Roosevelt assumed responsible leadership, traded destroyers to Britain, pushed through the lifting of the arms embargo, and won passage of Lend-Lease to England and Russia. These measures (actually violations of the duties of neutrals) were decisive in keeping our "allies" from going under, and so gave us time to prepare. The Selective Service Law at least initiated preliminary training before the blow fell.

The Atlantic Charter, United Nations, and other declarations during the war, plus the acceptance of the United Nations Charter before peace came, marked the end of the isolationist counterrevolution in American foreign policy. The ship of state sailed on an even keel, and after some confusion, but no doubts, a true direction for American diplomacy was laid out. It is once more, as in the days of Washington and Adams, a sound course of action, not negative inaction or day-by-day opportunistic drift. United States leadership in and full support of the United Nations "is the keystone of American policy for the maintenance of peace and *international security.*"

The American people seemingly have learned their lessons from World Wars I and II; that is, the threat of war (which includes those economic and social conditions that breed war) *anywhere in the world* is a threat to their national security. The United States must help prevent war from breaking out; she cannot rest content to defend the country against attack.

However, in terms of expediency again, and in thoughtful realization of our experiences and the teachings of history, we cannot yet rely entirely upon the effectiveness of the United Nations. The United States must continue, like the founding fathers, to keep their "powder dry," or, in current terms, to keep some uranium 235 in air bombs ready for use!

CONTEMPORARY AMERICAN FOREIGN POLICY

The fundamentals of present American foreign policies may be best expressed in the words of President Truman:

1. We seek no territorial expansion or selfish advantage.
2. We believe in the eventual return of sovereign rights to all peoples who have been deprived of them by force.
3. We shall approve no territorial changes in any friendly part of the world unless they accord with the freely expressed wishes of the people concerned.
4. We believe that all peoples who are prepared for self-government should be permitted to choose their own form of government by their own freely expressed choice, without interference from any foreign source.
5. By the combined and cooperative action of our war Allies, we shall help the defeated enemy states establish peaceful, democratic governments of their own free choice.

6. We shall refuse to recognize any government imposed upon any nation by the force of any foreign power.

7. We believe that all nations should have the freedom of the seas and equal rights to the navigation of boundary rivers and waterways. . . .

8. We believe that all states which are accepted in the society of nations should have access on equal terms to the trade and the raw materials of the world.

9. We believe that the sovereign states of the Western Hemisphere without interference from outside the Western Hemisphere, must work together as good neighbors in the solution of their common problems.

10. We believe that full economic collaboration between all nations, great and small, is essential to the improvement of living conditions all over the world, and to the establishment of freedom from fear and freedom from want.

11. We shall continue to strive to promote freedom of expression and freedom of religion throughout the peace-loving areas of the world.

12. We are convinced that the preservation of peace between nations requires a United Nations Organization composed of all the peace-loving nations of the world who are willing, jointly to use force if necessary to insure peace.

That is the foreign policy which guides the United States now. That is the foreign policy with which it confidently faces the future.[2]

The President of the United States was justified in his confidence for the future when he made the above statement in the fall of 1945. Triumphant in the great war, we all thought we could look forward to peace. Hope and enthusiasm were high for true international coöperation based on the declarations of the three remaining great powers: Britain, Russia, and the United States. Sadly we were to realize that victory does not necessarily mean peace. After five years, the failure to reach satisfactory peace settlements, particularly for Germany and Japan, makes the task of transition to a peaceful world immensely difficult.

---

[2] Address of President Truman at New York, October 27, 1945.

Immediately after the war ended in eastern Europe, Estonia, Latvia, and Lithuania were reabsorbed by the Soviet Union. More gradually national political regimes, either Communist controlled or under effective pressures from Moscow, were established in eight states: Albania, Bulgaria, Czechoslovakia, Finland, Hungary, Poland, Rumania, and Yugoslavia. Russia justified her actions by the necessity of having friendly neighbors. The Soviets frustrated every attempt at international supervision to assure the free elections which Stalin had pledged at Yalta. The threatened further extension of Communist domination over Greece and Turkey created a crisis which demanded a reëvaluation of American diplomacy and a more specific statement of policy.

The Truman Doctrine was such a statement. Salient excerpts from the President's message follow:

. . . Assistance is imperative if Greece is to survive as a free nation.

As a result of these tragic conditions, a militant minority, exploiting human want and misery, was able to create political chaos, which, until now, has made economic recovery impossible.

The very existence of the Greek state is today threatened by the terrorist activities of several thousand armed men, led by Communists. . . .

We have considered how the United Nations might assist in this crisis. But the situation is an urgent one requiring immediate action. . . .

Turkey now needs our support . . . for the maintenance of its national integrity. That integrity is essential to the preservation of order in the Middle East.

One of the primary objectives of the foreign policy of the United States is the creation of conditions in which we and other nations will be able to work out a way of life free from coercion.

I believe that it must be the policy of the United States to support free peoples who are resisting attempted subjugation by armed minorities or by outside pressures.

The seeds of totalitarian regimes are nurtured by misery and want. They spread and grow in the evil soil of poverty and strife.

The free peoples of the world look to us for support in maintaining their freedoms.

If we falter in our leadership, we may endanger the peace of the world—and we shall surely endanger the welfare of our own nation.

One might paraphrase the Truman Doctrine in terms of the pronouncement directed at the Holy Alliance by President Monroe over one hundred years earlier. In the present age of guided rockets and atomic bombs, for Russian communism "to extend their [totalitarian police state] system" to control the eastern Mediterranean (or to reach the Atlantic Ocean in western Europe) "is dangerous to our peace and safety."

Temporarily stopped in the Balkans by the Truman Doctrine (and the funds appropriated by Congress), the Communists concentrated on France and Italy and a new crisis developed. America's answer, the Marshall Plan, is considered in a later chapter. Only the succinct statement by the editor of *Foreign Affairs* need be given here, as follows:

"We know it involves risks. We know it will tax our wisdom, our patience, and our pocketbook. We undertake it because we must. We can draw encouragement from the outcome, spiritual as well as material, from the knowledge that Europe wants what we can give and Soviet Russia cannot—material help—and that with it we offer what Soviet Russia will not—political freedom."[3]

There was a considerable difference of opinion over the expenditure of some twenty billion dollars for United States aid to western Europe, but the Communist seizure of Czechoslovakia ended debate and Congress authorized the necessary initial appropriations. The reëstablishment of the Communist International as the "Cominform," with its pronounced purpose of sabotaging the Marshall

[3] H. F. Armstrong, *The Calculated Risk*, New York, 1947, p. 38.

Plan, strengthened American determination. The European Recovery Program proved highly successful in the economic rehabilitation of western Europe with accompanying greater political stability.

However, the large Red Armies, admittedly capable of sweeping to the English Channel in a few weeks, undermined the confidence of many peoples in Europe. The next logical step to meet the expansionist policies of the Communists was the North Atlantic Security Pact, signed by the United States and eleven European nations on April 4, 1949. Again the Soviets helped convince those hesitant American senators who questioned its feasibility by blockading Berlin.

But promises on paper mean little without implementation. Fortunately, American security was placed ahead of party politics and the bipartisan foreign policy carried through. Congress not only supported the administration in rearming the forces of the United States but authorized definite military aid and supplies to our allies across the seas.

In brief, United States foreign policy showed marked positive development during the five years following the nominal end of World War II. From an initial period of confusion which verged upon appeasement, American diplomacy—paced by Soviet obstructionist tactics and aggressive actions—passed through the stages of negative containment (the Truman Doctrine), to positive economic assistance to those countries outside the "iron curtain" (the Marshall Plan and later the Point 4 program), to regional security pacts (Rio and North Atlantic), finally supported by rearmament (the Mutual Defense Assistance Program).

United States foreign policy for the mid-twentieth century is best expressed by Secretary of State Dean Acheson as follows: "The times call for a *total diplomacy* equal to the task of building the kind of world in which our way of life can flourish. We must continue to press ahead with the building of a free world which is strong in its faith and in its material progress. The alternative is to allow the free nations to succumb one by one to the erosive and encroaching processes of Soviet expansion."

The statement calls for some brief elaboration. It indicates that the positive results already achieved by American diplomacy must be sustained and continued effort will be required by all free peoples to meet the obvious threats of communism. The American people must have confidence in their potentially overwhelming material and moral strength, but should firmly hold the conviction to use their power decisively to attain world peace consistent with national freedom and international welfare.

United States diplomacy dictates a positive posture free of uncertainty, fear, or sense of frustration, yet with full cognizance of Russian Communist imperialism. Policies must take into account our decided weakness in eastern Asia and not minimize the great physical strength of the Communists' geographic position. In answer to any Soviet propaganda peace appeal American diplomacy must emphasize that peace is not a negative condition but a dynamic affirmative force available to free peoples who are prepared to determine their own destinies in company with other like-minded peoples.

The test of America's "total diplomacy" was not long delayed. On Sunday, June 25, 1950, without warning and without provocation, the Communist army of North Korea attacked in force the Korean Republic south across the 38th parallel. In the words of President Truman: "The attack upon Korea makes it plain beyond all doubt that Communism has passed beyond the use of subversion to conquer independent nations and will now use armed invasion and war."

Far more than American security or even prestige was at stake. The future of the United Nations and the fate of the free world lay in balance. The government of the United States did not hesitate to accept the clear challenge. Acting under the United Nations Security Council's resolution, calling upon all UN members to "render every assistance," the President ordered "United States air and sea forces to give the Korean Government troops cover and support." In the weeks and months following, substantial American ground forces and token ground, air, and sea forces of many nations joined, under the banner of the UN, in defense of freedom under law. When the UN victory was denied by the massive intervention of Red China, it was no longer possible for free men anywhere to doubt that ruthless aggression was the dominant motive underlying the Communist slogans of peace.

CHAPTER XXIV

American Foreign Policy
Before World War II

ESTABLISHING SECURE SOVEREIGNTY

IT IS A SIMPLE TRUTH all too often forgotten that what a nation can and does do is determined by its position and resources at any given time. As a nation's position and resources change from one period to another the appropriate policy, tactics, and strategy which it should follow must shift similarly.

The history of American foreign policy helps illustrate this basic truth. The United States in the year 1790 was a small, militarily weak country. Its population and resources were few indeed compared to those of Britain, Spain, Russia, Austria, and France of that era. In this setting one type of policy was appropriate. Today the United States is at the other end of the spectrum from its position 160 years ago. It is the wealthiest and most powerful single nation on earth. The decisions and actions taken by the United States affect not only the people of our country but hundreds of millions of others throughout the world. It is clear that the strategy and tactics required today must be far different from those of 1790, even though basically the ends of national security and national prosperity are essentially unchanged.

Because it has so often been misrepresented, it is interesting to present first the foreign policy suggestions made by George Washington in his famous "Farewell Address."

This is a policy obviously framed against the background of his times. And against that background its reasonableness and wisdom are beyond question. The first President of the United States said then:

It is our true policy to steer clear of permanent alliances with any portion of the foreign world. . . .

Taking care always to keep ourselves by suitable establishments on a respectable defensive posture, we may safely trust to temporary alliances for extraordinary emergencies. . . .

With me a *predominant* motive has been to endeavor to gain time to our country to settle and mature its yet recent institutions, and to progress without interruption to that degree of strength and consistency which is necessary to give it, humanly speaking, the command of its own fortunes.

To the founding fathers, the keystone in the arch of American diplomacy in their time was labeled "gain time." The newly born democracy was torn from years of war. It was bankrupt, and its three million disunited people were scattered thinly east of the Alleghenies. There was no friendly nation that it could trust. Isolation was the only sound decision then. But it was never considered a permanent course of action. It was expedient in 1790 to keep from becoming embroiled in the dynastic rivalries of Europe, while the young republic gathered strength. Yet even pacifist Thomas Jefferson, the first isolationist, was ready to make an "entangling alliance" with the British, whom he disliked, if it had become necessary in order to acquire Louisiana from the French.

The makers of foreign policy during the first century of this republic's existence were largely concerned with two facets of this country's problems. On the one hand they sought to assure the independence and territorial integrity of the United States against foreign intervention or the possibility of such intervention. The War of 1812, for example, confirmed the durability of American independence beyond all doubt and gave our ships on the high seas the backing of a nation whose sovereignty and future integrity were now beyond question.

Through the Monroe Doctrine the United States sought to insure that no foreign power stronger than itself would gain a foothold in this hemisphere from which its encroachment might eventually imperil our own interests.

DEVELOPING AMERICAN RESOURCES

The other major aspect of American foreign policy during these first decades of our country's existence sprang from the fact that to develop the rich resources in the continent over which we ruled we required foreign aid. The Americans of these decades sought from abroad labor, capital, and the technical "know-how" needed to convert this nation's potential wealth into actuality. To get the pounds, francs, rubles, and marks needed to pay for foreign aid, Americans sought foreign markets for their surplus food and raw materials. It was this pattern of resources and needs that determined the general nature of American foreign *economic* policy for the first century of this country's existence.

Consider the problem of labor, the problem of obtaining the millions of workers needed to till farms, to mine coal and metals, and to operate factory machinery. Until after World War I the United States welcomed eagerly and almost without government hindrance large-scale immigration into our boundaries. Seeking a better, freer, and richer life, the surplus millions of Europe—as well as others from Asia and Negro slaves from Africa came here in an ever increasing flood whose peak was reached during the decade before World War I. From 1905 to 1914 an average of a million immigrants landed here each year. During the century from 1821 to 1920 more people immigrated to the United States than were included in the total population of this country at the beginning of the Civil War.

This attitude toward immigration was an essential feature of our international economic policy during these years. It made possible the miraculously quick settlement of the heart of a continent and the accompanying mobilization of this nation's rich and varied resources for the attainment of an ever rising standard of living. The Scandinavian dairy farmers in Wisconsin; the Chinese coolies who laid the tracks for the transcontinental railroads connecting two oceans; the Russian-German sugar-beet workers of Colorado and Nebraska; the Czechs, Poles, Italians, Jews, Irishmen, Slovaks, Hungarians, and others who provided the muscles and energy for innumerable mines and factories—all these could make their contribution because this country needed and welcomed them.

No government decision brought these tens of millions of people thousands of miles across land and ocean to populate this land. The attractions were informal but powerful: the lure of cheap land; the glowing exaggerations of shipowners' agents anxious only to fill their employers' vessels with passengers; the anxious recruiting by factory owners seeking low-wage and docile laborers; the magnetism of a land in which a man could speak his mind freely; the happy accounts of successful early immigrants writing to their relatives and former village neighbors— all these varied forces played their part in bringing about the mass migration which created the United States of today.

Capital, the second essential required to develop America's resources, was also obtained in large measure from abroad before World War I, attracted to this country by the prospect of large profits and high rates of interest. The role played by foreign capital has recently been described in these terms. ·

For nearly two centuries during the earlier development of its natural resources, the United States was a borrower in international capital markets. In the colonial period, Dutch, British and other foreign capital helped build American cities, ports, roads and cotton and tobacco plantations. In the nineteenth century, large volumes of British capital helped in the construction of railroads, canals and factories. In the later years of the century, America drew more heavily on its own expanding savings, though it still continued to borrow abroad.

On the eve of World War I, America was still a net debtor. In 1913, we held about $2.6 billion of long-term investment abroad, compared with a foreign investment in the United States of $4.5 billion.[1]

But the prospective profits and interest available in this country would not have attracted such an abundance of foreign capital if the political and business climate here had not been favorable. The men who organized the new industries and railroads of the United States eagerly welcomed the investments of foreigners, and the United States government placed no obstacles to hinder this inflow of funds. Foreign investors took their chances here along with American investors, gaining when their projects were successful and losing when they had been overoptimistic. As dividends and interest were earned, and as earlier capital investments required repayment, British, French, and German investors received the money due them just as did Americans. The value of the dollar in terms of pounds, francs, and marks remained constant over long periods of time, so that international financial transactions could be conducted with almost the same certainty and safety as similar dealings between New York and Chicago. American economic policy over most of the nineteenth and early twentieth centuries provided equality for foreign investors and stability of international financial relations, fundamental prerequisites for the flow of energizing capital to these shores.

Positive government intervention in American foreign economic policy before World War I was of major significance primarily with respect to foreign trade, where our tariff had important consequences. To understand American tariff policy during this era we must comprehend the conflicting forces involved. United States foreign trade consisted largely of the export of raw materials and food to earn the foreign currency necessary to purchase foreign semimanufactured and manufactured articles, as well as

---

[1] Quoted from J. Frederic Dewhurst and Associates, *America's Needs and Resources*, New York, 1947, pp. 519-520.

to pay foreign investors the profits and interest earned by their capital in the United States. In 1850, for example, food and raw materials composed over 80 percent of our exports, while manufactured products, other than food, made up 70 percent of our imports. Even as late as 1901, food and raw materials were two-thirds of our exports. This was a time when cheap American cotton, grain, tobacco, and meat conquered virtually all foreign markets, while American industry, though growing rapidly, was not so strong compared to its competitors abroad.

Put most simply, the tariff struggle was between these opposing interests in American society. The growers of cheap food and raw materials wanted a low tariff or none at all. They wished to buy foreign manufactures at the cheapest prices possible, thus getting the most real value for their money and supplying their customers abroad with additional American dollars to buy their products. The manufacturers and those dependent upon them wanted tariffs so high that they would keep out cheaper foreign products and permit even new and inefficient American factories to survive and prosper. From the end of the Civil War to the presidency of Woodrow Wilson the high-tariff advocates were in control and American protectionism reigned supreme, even to the extent of protecting industries and commodities which needed no help. It is not surprising that since 1875 the United States each year has sold more merchandise abroad than it has imported, except for the three years of 1888, 1889, and 1893.

At various times in the nineteenth century, as we have seen earlier, the United States government took positive action abroad to facilitate the interests of its merchants and shippers. Thus, the Treaty of 1844 with China and the series of similar treaties that followed over the years gave this country extraterritorial rights there and opened Chinese ports and markets to our manufacturers and to our trading ships. Commodore Perry's visit to Japan in 1853, with a squadron of American naval vessels, and the commercial treaty which followed in 1858 opened up

Japanese markets and ports for American enterprise. In Latin America the United States intervened often to serve the economic and political interests of this country. It would be most difficult to rationalize the principle of isolation into the extreme statement of Secretary Olney in 1895 that "today the United States is practically sovereign on this continent, and its fiat is law upon the subjects to which it confines its interposition." Last but not least, of course, American insistence on freedom of the seas in the years 1914 to 1917 played no small role in bringing us into the first world war of modern times.

FOREIGN POLICY AFTER WORLD WAR I

The World War of 1914 to 1918 opened a new era characterized by the United States' strength and responsibility in the world's political and economic community. President Woodrow Wilson realized the nature and importance of our new role and took the lead in forming the League of Nations. He was repudiated by the United States Senate, however, when, by a narrow margin, it failed to ratify the League's Covenant. Much of the impotence of the League of Nations in the two decades between World Wars I and II can undoubtedly be traced to the failure of the United States to participate in its efforts. This country did seek to aid the cause of world peace by sponsoring efforts at disarmament of the major powers and by backing the Briand-Kellogg Peace Pact. But these efforts dealt with superficial factors involved rather than with fundamentals.

Even more profound, however, were the changes in this country's economic position vis-à-vis the rest of the world. The United States emerged from World War I as the world's greatest industrial and financial power. Even before the war the annual output of American manufactures far exceeded that of any other nation, and this advantage had increased during the period of the conflict. To procure American food and supplies during the war, countries like Great Britain and France liquidated appreciable portions of their investments in this country and shipped gold here. Moreover, substantial war debts were created as a result of the aid extended by the United States to the Allied powers.

The result was that, from a net debtor on capital account, this country became the major creditor of the rest of the world. In addition to 22 billion dollars of war principal and interest, private American long-term capital invested abroad was about 6.5 billion dollars. Total long-term foreign investments in the United States at the same time aggregated only 2.5 billion dollars. One sign of this revolutionary shift in international financial relationships was the fact that by 1920 the United States owned half of the world's gold stock, while many of the European countries lacked sufficient gold reserves to reëstablish gold-standard currencies.

American agriculture, however, found itself relatively at a disadvantage in the 1920's. Its former primacy in international trade was falling before the rivalry of cheaper cotton from India and Egypt, cheaper beef from Argentina, and cheaper grain from Australia and Canada. America's comparative advantage—i.e., its relative superiority in production—had shifted from farm products to factory goods. By 1920 more than half of our exports were manufactured products, a major change indeed.

From the point of view of pure economic advantage alone, the wisest policy for the United States in the 1920's might have consisted of these elements: first, continued rapid shift from food and raw material production, in which nineteenth-century American advantages had greatly lessened or vanished, to industrial and service production, where our domestic superiority over foreign producers was greatest; second, elimination of tariffs and other trade barriers with a view to maximizing American imports of foreign foods, raw materials, and certain types of manufactured goods which could be most cheaply manufactured abroad. The aim of this policy should have been an excess of imports over exports so as to give other nations a surplus of dollars.[2] Only if they had such a dollar surplus, or if they owned gold, could foreign nations pay us the principal and interest on the debts, governmental and private, they owed us.

But advocates of such a policy had to contend with the realities which actually prevailed, particularly the nationalism which dominated the policies not only of the United States but also of other countries, in the years following 1918. For one thing, adoption of such a policy would have meant tremendous and difficult readjustments and losses for millions of American citizens forced to shift their occupations from comparatively inefficient to comparatively efficient fields of work. Moreover, even if desired, such occupational shifts would have required much time. These factors made adoption of a "correct" foreign economic policy most difficult politically. Moreover, no nation can base its policy only upon purely economic considerations. Even Adam Smith agreed that defense is better than opulence, i.e., that a policy of free trade must be tempered by considerations of a military and strategic nature against the exigencies of the unpredictable future. To have wiped out the American watch industry, for example, because Swiss watches can be sold here more cheaply might have proved of questionable wisdom when World War II required large-scale production of precision instruments for military needs.

The actual policy adopted by the United States with respect to its participation in the international economy differed quite sharply from that just outlined. American policy during the 1920's sought to collect dividends and interest on private investments abroad plus war debt payments to the United States government. Simultaneously, the high Fordney-McCumber (1920) and Smoot-Hawley (1929) tariff acts worked to reduce foreign exports to us.

---

[2] In more general terms the policy suggested here would have to be phrased in terms of balance-of-payments considerations, taking into account also such items as shipping and other services, immigrants' remittances, etc.

American economic nationalism also expressed itself in the sharp reversal of our traditional immigration policy. Legislation passed in the early 1920's cut the former flood of immigrants to a comparative trickle. These victories for particular domestic pressure groups hindered required international economic adjustments and helped set the stage for the cataclysm of the 1930's.

Extensive American loans abroad during the 1920's made it appear for a time that the United States might succeed in its international financial juggling. The billions of dollars lent to South America, Europe, and elsewhere provided the surplus dollars foreign countries required. Other nations were enabled to pay returns to investors and the United States government, while simultaneously buying more goods from this country than they sold here. But this happy state of affairs could continue only so long as American investors poured out their billions; when that golden stream slackened and ceased the whole financial house of cards built upon it collapsed.

At their peak, toward the end of 1930, private American long-term investments abroad totaled 15.2 billion dollars as against 5.7 billion dollars of similar foreign investments in the United States, giving this country a net balance of almost 10 billion dollars. But enthusiastic American investment abroad which marked the 1920's came to an end after the stock market crash of October, 1929. The ensuing financial difficulties abroad resulted in default on payments to and repudiation of many loans obtained from American investors. During the 1930's not only did the flow of new lending decrease sharply, but a sizable portion of American loans abroad were liquidated. By the end of the 1930's, therefore, though the United States was still a net creditor on capital account, its favorable balance on long-term investments was only about half as great as at the peak of 1930.

Although many forces were involved, the sudden and sharp decline of American loans abroad was clearly a key factor producing the chaotic breakdown of international economic relations during the 1930's. The sharp drops in commodity prices, particularly of foodstuffs and raw materials, also played key roles in producing the catastrophe.

The early 1930's witnessed, in consequence: the collapse of the gold standard, the repudiation of almost all reparations and inter-Allied war debts, and the building of higher and higher tariff or quota barriers to trade between nations. International trade became more and more contracted as the flood of restrictions mounted. The total volume of American foreign trade declined sharply, going from over nine billion dollars in 1928 to less than three billion in 1932. American receipts of interest and dividends from abroad declined from almost one billion dollars in 1929 to about half that amount in 1933. More important, the world-wide economic collapse of this time brought Hitler to power in Germany and helped lay the foundation for World War II.

Except for the high tariffs adopted in 1922 and 1929, those features of American economic policy which conditioned the sequence of events in 1920 and the beginning of the 1930's were the result of decisions by private individuals, partnerships, and corporations. They were decisions motivated by the usual desire to maximize return on investments and to safeguard capital. With the advent of Franklin D. Roosevelt to the presidency, however, virtually all aspects of American foreign economic policy were directly determined by or profoundly affected by governmental actions and decisions.

New Deal Foreign Economic Policy

President Roosevelt and his advisers were preoccupied from the very beginning with efforts to end the depression. They wanted to raise prices and stimulate exports as means of reviving production, increasing employment, and improving the condition of American farmers.

One of President Roosevelt's first acts, in March, 1933, during the banking crisis, was to take the United States off the gold standard by ending the free convertibility of the dollar into a specified amount of gold. Although this action came more than a year after most of the world had left the gold standard, it was an important psychological blow at the efforts then being made to reinstate the gold standard and to establish once again stable exchange rates among different national currencies. Later the gold content of the dollar was reduced to lower its value in relation to foreign currencies.

The New Deal farm price policy reacted sharply on the United States' foreign economic position. Our government sought to increase domestic and world prices for farm products sharply by reducing domestic production. Also, where necessary, government loans were offered farmers to keep substantial portions of our production in warehouses and off the market so long as prices remained below government loan values. This may have tended to raise prices somewhat, but it had less advantageous long-run results. In the case of cotton, Dr. C. T. Schmidt has commented:

Formerly the United States dominated the world cotton markets. Thus in the 1920's we produced more than half of the world supply. And about 60 percent of this was exported. During the period 1925-29, almost 44 percent of all cotton used by foreign mills was of American origin. Contrast this with the record of recent years. During the 1934-38 growing seasons . . . our cotton exports averaged only 5,300,000 bales, a drop of more than one-third from the level of the 'twenties, and we produced only about 26 percent of the cotton used by foreign mills.[3]

In the late 1930's, American farm exports continued to dwindle in the face of rising production from cheaper, competitive areas. The United States resorted in desperation to export subsidies for cotton, wheat, and corn. The government paid exporters the difference between the artificially maintained high domestic price and the much lower world market price so as to enable the American

[3] *American Farmers in the World Crisis*, New York, 1941, chap. 4.

products to meet foreign competition abroad. From the point of view of our foreign competitors, this was economic warfare of the worst sort.

The silver program inaugurated in 1934 represents another example of a policy adopted because of strong domestic pressures but having great international significance. Since passage of the Silver Purchase Act of 1934 and later legislation, the United States government has tried to increase the price of silver by buying large quantities at prices above the world market level. But this effort to aid domestic silver miners and mine owners had unfortunate effects upon the large silver-using nations of the world. These countries found that they were losing large quantities of the metal underlying their money because owners of silver abroad naturally sent it here for sale at an artificially high price. This drain finally forced Mexico and China off the silver standard.

But not all American policy was unfortunate in its impact upon world economic coöperation. The most important American constructive contribution to world economic relations during the 1930's was the Trade Agreements program initiated by the Reciprocal Trade Act of June, 1934. This act sought to lower barriers to world trade. Agreements were reached with other countries to lower tariffs and other barriers to trade between the United States and those countries. To implement this policy, the President was given the power to lower or raise tariff duties up to 50 percent and to make reciprocal trade agreements legally binding without Senate ratification. Concessions granted a particular country under a trade agreement usually were automatically extended to other countries as well because of the so-called "most favored nation" clause in American commercial agreements. This clause provides that imports from France, for example, will receive the same treatment in the United States as those from the most favored nation. Therefore, if some particular country's imports receive tariff concessions, all other countries having most favored nation agreements with the United States must receive equal tariff reductions. Similarly, American exports to foreign countries often benefit from application of the same most favored nation clause. By finding increased markets abroad for American commodities, the agreements have aided industry and labor here, while the increased flow of cheaper foreign commodities here has tended to enrich our standard of living and increase the purchasing power of the dollar. On the other hand, relatively less efficient American industries, hurt by increased imports of cheaper foreign merchandise, have complained bitterly against this policy and fought it with every means at their disposal.

The broader significance of the Reciprocal Trade Agreements program stemmed from the fact that in a period when higher tariffs, import quotas, exchange restrictions, and other barriers to international trade were multiplying throughout the world, this program represented a major effort in the opposite direction, toward renewed health for trade and division of labor among nations. In addition, Congressional adoption and readoption of this program represented a significant victory for enlightened citizenship in the battle against the lobbying of minority interests adversely affected by the program. This victory was in heartening contrast to the defeats in other areas, such as with respect to the silver purchase program.

In at least one important area of international economic relations the failure of the United States government to intervene decisively during the 1920's and 1930's was to have serious results during World War II. This area was that of cartels, i.e., of agreements between the producers of one commodity in different nations to reduce competition among themselves. Thus, while American domestic policy, as expressed in the Sherman and Clayton Antitrust acts, opposed collusion and monopolistic practices, American legislative enactment facilitated such actions in the foreign field. The Webb-Pomerene Act of 1918 specifically permits American firms to combine with each other as well as with foreigners in order to facilitate exports.

Cartels seek to increase the profits of their members by means of practices such as the following: agreements to prevent price cutting; allocation of world markets among cartel members so as to avoid competition; efforts to curb the rise of new competitors or to bankrupt competitors who refuse to join cartel arrangements, etc. The range of commodities covered by cartel agreements in which American firms participated is quite large, including aluminum, magnesium, light bulbs, copper, chemicals, bismuth, and many others.

During the Second World War it was discovered that part of the price paid by the United States for these private arrangements included retarded development of key production facilities and scarcity of some commodities essential for military use. As a result, the United States government has looked with disfavor upon the activities of cartels in the postwar era.

THE ISOLATIONIST ROAD TO WAR

In any effort to trace the political origins of World War II the role of American official and popular isolationism during the 1930's cannot be ignored. There were many reasons for this isolationist attitude. The depression, with its consequent unemployment and other economic difficulties, helped focus popular attention more than ever on our domestic problems. The Nye investigation and other attacks upon the so-called "merchants of death" led many people to believe that wars were essentially the results of the intrigues and machinations of munitions makers. Pacifist sentiment was widespread and tens of thousands of American students took the so-called "Oxford Oath," pledging themselves never to fight for their country. Many of our people and our public officials seemed to think, apparently, that by ignoring the troubles of Europe and Asia we could hope to be spared the consequences of the rise of Mussolini in Italy, of Hitler in Germany, and of Japan's unchecked aggression against China.

In the political arena President Roosevelt sought to

counter this popular isolationism and provide leadership based upon a realization of the nature and gravity of the events of the 1930's. His recognition of the Soviet Union in 1933 was an effort to take account of the reality of that country's existence and importance. Together with Secretary of State Cordell Hull he sponsored the "Good Neighbor" policy and sought to build up good will and prestige for this country in Latin America. In his famous speech of October, 1937, the President called upon the world to "quarantine" the aggressor, thereby seeking to warn Germany, Italy, and Japan that continuance of their military expansion might bring them into eventual conflict with the United States. From the military point of view, most important probably was President Roosevelt's sponsorship of a program to build up the United States Navy from the low state to which it had fallen.

Congress, however, expressed a different attitude in 1935 by passing the "Neutrality Act," in order to show its determination that this country should not be drawn into the Italo-Ethiopian War then raging. By giving the President power to lay embargoes on war materials for combatants and by permitting him to prohibit American citizens from traveling on the vessels of belligerents, this act sought to avoid the provocations to war which it was widely believed had drawn us into the conflict of 1914-18.

The most important application of the Neutrality Act, however, was during the Spanish Civil War, when its provisions were applied to both the Republican and the Franco side in that conflict. It was clear even in 1937 to every intelligent observer that the struggle between these two sides in Spain was really the struggle between democracy and Nazi-Fascist totalitarianism. However, the United States did not intervene to help the Republican government and saw it go down to defeat. Hitler and Mussolini, who had used the Spanish Civil War as a training and testing ground for their own armies, were thus encouraged in the belief that, come what might, the United States would not go to war to save democracy anywhere abroad.

In view of the climate of public opinion and the actual policy this government followed at the time, it must be granted that these two dictators had ample ground for their belief.

Even before President Roosevelt's tenure of office, in 1932, the failure of the United States or the League of Nations to take effective action against Japanese aggression in Manchuria had given that aggressor a sense of confidence in his ability to move unchecked. The road to Pearl Harbor, it is now clear, led in the 1930's from the seizure of Manchuria to the conquest of Ethiopia and the destruction of the democratically elected government of Spain.

An influential element in this failure of the United States to act effectively to stop the catastrophe was the division among our people. Some influential groups in the United States actually looked toward Hitler and Mussolini with favor, regarding them as the saviors of Europe and Western civilization from communism. Such people did not understand that Hitler and Mussolini essentially had much more kinship with Stalin's totalitarianism than they had with democracy. They ignored the fact that these dictators had already ended in their own lands the chief distinguishing characteristic of Western civilization, its emphasis upon the dignity and freedom of the individual. Others, like Charles Lindbergh and his wife, spoke of the "wave of the future" and were convinced that the cause of the European democracies, at least, was hopeless in face of the supposed invincibility of German arms. The efforts of the Soviet Union to achieve collective security by joining with the western democracies against Hitler and Mussolini came to naught in the middle of the 1930's. The fear of helping communism and the Soviet Union, unfortunately, played a significant role in preventing the creation of an effective coalition against the Berlin-Rome-Tokyo Axis. In 1939, when England and France were finally ready to make an agreement with the Soviet Union against Hitler, they found that the dictators of Berlin and Moscow had gotten together. World War II followed immediately. Democracy had moved too little and too late. And American failure to participate actively in efforts for collective security against aggression cannot escape part of the blame for the catastrophe which followed.

CHAPTER XXV

American Foreign Policy During World War II

THE BACKGROUND OF PEARL HARBOR

To EXPLAIN THE ENTRANCE of the United States into World War II more is needed than mere reference to the Japanese attack upon Pearl Harbor. Even before that treacherous blow had been struck, the American people and the American government had traveled a long way from the spirit and the policies of the Neutrality Act of 1935. In March, 1941, the United States had shown whom it was "neutral for and neutral against" when Congress passed the Lend-Lease Act giving the President authority to turn over without immediate payment all types of military equipment and other supplies needed by England and France and their allies. Trade with Japan and other countries capable of supplying Germany was restricted months before Pearl Harbor. Not long after the German attack upon the Soviet Union in June, 1941, American Lend-Lease supplies were offered to the victim and goods were soon streaming toward the Soviet Union.

Why and how had this change in policy taken place? Many factors were involved but a few of the most important may be listed here. First, the Soviet-Nazi nonaggression pact of August, 1939, shocked many who had previously been either pro-Soviet or pro-German, making them realize the essential identity of the totalitarian states involved and magnifying their appreciation of the menace

518

this alliance presented to the democratic world. Second, and perhaps even more important, the whirlwind successes of the German blitzkrieg in late 1939 and early 1940 stunned the American people. The fall of France, Belgium, and Poland; the invasion and occupation of Norway and Denmark; the "blitz" air attack against England—all these shocked the United States and made it realize that if Great Britain should fall our security too would be threatened and threatened dangerously. Yet, even so, it was only after a bitter struggle that selective service was introduced in 1940 so as to permit the building up of the American army. Nor was the passage of the Lend-Lease Bill accomplished without overcoming the bitter opposition of those who still felt confident in the isolation and security afforded the United States by the oceans on its eastern and western shores.

Foreign Policy and the Military Struggle

World War II cost millions of lives and tens of billions of dollars' worth of property. Yet it was also the most important and largest-scale experience in international affairs ever thrust upon the United States. The conduct of the war required that our civilian and military leaders coöperate with the corresponding officials of more than a dozen other nations allied with us. At the climax of the war General Eisenhower commanded a mighty force of millions of soldiers, including not only Americans but Englishmen, Frenchmen, Canadians, Australians, New Zealanders, Indians, and men from other nations, all working together for the accomplishment of a common victory. Most important, perhaps, was the fact that for millions of Americans the terms "Europe," "Asia," "Africa," "Australia," and "South America" were translated from unreal abstractions in geography books into real areas inhabited by real people. Millions of Americans during the war lived and worked in London, Paris, Algiers, Bombay, Sidney, Manila, Kunming, as well as thousands of other smaller communities throughout the world. Today these same

Americans are back home and form an important portion of our citizenry. They know that the problems of these foreign areas must be reckoned with if we are to have peace.

Our foreign policy during the war was directed entirely toward the achievement of victory, in the shortest time and with the smallest cost. To assist our allies economically we shipped them many billions of dollars' worth of armaments, food, raw materials, machinery, and other essentials required by them. Conversely, our foreign economic policy during the war was aimed at cutting off the Axis powers from all outside commodity shipments that might aid them. Foreign merchants suspected of selling to the enemy were blacklisted so they could not receive American goods. Strategic raw materials produced in neutral countries were bought up so as to prevent their reaching the enemy, even if we had no need of them ourselves. In our relations with the neutral countries such as Sweden, Spain, and Turkey our efforts were directed at the same objective, to minimize or cut off entirely any aid they were giving our enemy economically or politically. We sought to induce them to join our side, or at least to assure that they would not go over to that of Hitler, Mussolini, and Tojo. Economic and military pressure aided our diplomats in these efforts.

Many of the most complex and difficult diplomatic tasks of the war, however, concerned problems of coöperation among the Allies. All the United Nations were allied for the objective of defeating the enemy. But in the area of strategy and tactics they often differed sharply, since each sought usually to further the end it considered most important. Against whom should the main Allied strength be directed, for example? China and Australia naturally regarded Japan as the paramount enemy. Great Britain and France looked at Germany and Italy. To the Soviet Union in 1942 and 1943, locked in death struggle with the Nazi armies, nothing was of more importance than that the western Allies should mount a second front against

the coasts of France and Belgium regardless of the cost
that might be inflicted upon them. And if a second front
were to be launched in Europe, against what part of the
continent should it be aimed? Up through the Balkans?
Into Sicily and Italy? North through the Riviera and south
France? Or east along the western shores of Europe opposite Great Britain? The answers to these questions favored
by each of the major Allies depended not only upon their
evaluation of the best steps to insure victory but also upon
the political objectives they wished to obtain and the
shape of postwar Europe they sought.

Even the distribution of Lend-Lease supplies caused
friction among the Allies, for there was not, and could
never be, enough to satisfy fully the desires of all the
claimants for this aid. How many planes should go to
England, and how many to the Soviet Union? To what
degree should we share our knowledge of radar and other
newly developed military devices with one or the other or
all of our Allies? These and similar questions caused disputes and created frictions. But under the pressure of the
war and the stimulus it gave to unity, the coalition against
the Axis survived these quarrels over resources and their
division. Of the more than 47 billion dollars' worth of
Lend-Lease aid given during the war, over 31 billion went
to the British Empire and over 11 billion to the Soviet
Union. The war might have taken a much different course
if it had not been for this aid.

In the midst of the bloody struggle on many fronts
throughout the world, the question of the fundamental
objectives sought from the war was paramount. It was important both as a means of arousing men's enthusiasm for
the struggle and for reaching decisions which would shape
the nature of the postwar world. From the perspective of
the present, Mr. Roosevelt's statement in June, 1943,
seems perhaps naïve: "Our ultimate objective can be
simply stated: It is to build for ourselves, for all men, a
world in which each individual human being shall have
the opportunity to live out his life in peace; to work pro-

ductively, earning at least enough for his actual needs and those of his family; to associate with the friends of his choice; to think and worship freely; and to die secure in the knowledge that his children and their children shall have the same opportunities."

These were fine and brave words but they did not mean the same things to Joseph Stalin or to Winston Churchill as they did to Franklin D. Roosevelt. They did not take account of the fact that France had the war objective of ending forever the possibility of new German aggression in the future. They ignored Great Britain's concern with preserving such parts of her empire as she could. And, perhaps most important, they ignored the partially concealed fact that the Soviet Union would never for a single moment forget her abiding hatred of free society and her ultimate objective of world communist revolution under her leadership.

Shaping the Postwar World

Millions of people have been bitterly disillusioned in the past few years by the sharp contrast between the harsh realities of the postwar world and the high hopes held for the future while the last struggle was on. In no country has this disillusionment been more widespread than in the United States. It will help us better to understand the current situation if we look first at the kind of world American policy makers sought in their negotiations during the war. These negotiations took place most crucially at four major meetings: the conference of the foreign secretaries of the United States, Great Britain, and the Soviet Union in Moscow in October, 1943; The Teheran Conference in Iran of Messrs. Roosevelt, Churchill, and Stalin in late November, 1943; the Yalta Conference in the Crimea of the same top leaders of the three major Allied nations in February, 1945; and the final Potsdam Conference in Germany of President Truman, Generalissimo Stalin, and Prime Ministers Churchill and Attlee of Great Britain in July and August, 1945.

What were the American objectives for a better postwar world, and how did we seek to attain them?

First, it was a paramount objective of United States diplomacy during the war against Germany to induce the Soviet Union to declare war against Japan. Our leaders believed that Soviet help in the struggle against Japan would materially lessen the time required for victory in the Asiatic theater and would thus greatly reduce the loss of American lives in that struggle. As matters turned out, Japan was already on the verge of surrender before the Soviet Union actually did enter the conflict, both because of Anglo-American successes in the long years of Pacific island victories from Guadalcanal on and because of the disastrous impact of the atomic bombs unleashed upon Hiroshima and Nagasaki.

Failure to appreciate Japan's actual weakness made us pay a heavy price, or rather bribe, to the Russians. At the Yalta Conference, February, 1945, the Soviet Union agreed to enter the war against Japan within two or three months after Germany's surrender. In return, Great Britain and the United States recognized the independence of the Soviet satellite state called the Mongolian People's Republic and practically made permanent its severance from China. They assured the Soviet Union that the former rights of czarist Russia in China before it lost the War of 1904 against Japan would be restored. The USSR was promised that its special interest in the Chinese port of Dairen would be recognized, and it was also guaranteed the lease of another Chinese port, Port Arthur, as a naval base. The Soviet Union was further guaranteed that the Chinese Eastern Railroad and the South Manchurian Railroad would be operated in the future as a joint Soviet-Chinese company. The Kurile Islands and southern Sakhalin, it was agreed, would be taken from Japan and given to the Soviet Union.

Our ally, China, whom all these provisions affected most vitally, did not participate in the conference. But it was in no position to resist the later pressure brought by the

United States and Great Britain to induce it to accede to these conditions. In return, the USSR expressed its readiness merely to conclude a pact of friendship and alliance with the Chinese government. The value of the pact, we shall later see, was small indeed.

Second, it was recognized that one of the primary problems after the liberation of occupied areas in both Europe and Asia would be the need for food, clothing, medicines, and other material relief. The United States government took the lead in securing the organization of the United Nations Relief and Rehabilitation Administration (UNRRA) to perform this emergency transitional relief function. UNRRA was proposed by the United States as early as June 10, 1943. It came into being on November 9, 1943, when representatives of forty-four united and associated nations signed the agreement establishing it at the White House in Washington, D.C. From the beginning of UNRRA's work the United States showed its willingness to and did shoulder the major part of the burden of providing the funds and the commodities required to permit it to perform its relief function.

Third, the United States sought to assure that the war should end in such a way as to maintain the continued coöperation of the three great powers which made victory possible. In addition, it sought to lay the groundwork for assuring that fascist threats to the peace should never rise again. In pursuance of these aims, the United States refused to accept German offers to surrender to it or the western Allies alone. We, along with Great Britain, pursued a policy of demanding and finally securing unconditional surrender from Italy, Germany, and Japan to all the powers, including the Soviet Union, who had participated in the victorious side of the war. Nevertheless, the USSR maintained an only partially concealed suspicion that we intended to desert her and make a separate peace.

It was recognized from the beginning that more than military surrender alone would be required to achieve a durable future peace. There would have to be a period of occupation for the defeated countries until new democratic governments could be formed in them. In addition, it was realized that, for Germany and Japan at least, these occupations might have to be long in order to permit an extensive process of reëducation and retraining to overcome the effects of long years of Fascist and totalitarian ideology. Finally, peace treaties would have to be concluded between all the defeated countries and all the victorious countries so that the world might start out again fresh, with a clean slate. The pattern of military occupation established in defeated countries was both the result of explicit decisions taken at the Yalta and Potsdam conferences and the result of the pattern of military campaigns actually conducted. In countries such as Italy or Hungary, which were occupied entirely either by the western Allies alone or by the Soviet Union alone, military governments were staffed by officers and troops of the occupying power or powers. Allied Control Commissions were set up in each of these countries in an effort to achieve inter-Allied coöperation and unity in the direction of each of the occupied countries.

In Germany and Austria the problems were more complex. These two countries were occupied simultaneously by troops from both the western Allies and the Soviet Union. The solution finally agreed upon after negotiations at Yalta and Potsdam was to divide both Germany and Austria into four zones, occupied exclusively by American, British, French, or Soviet troops as the case might be. Austria's position as a victim of Nazi aggression was recognized by giving her the right to have a national government, though occupied by Allied troops. Germany was to be governed by a supreme group termed "the Allied Control Council," consisting of the commanders in chief of the occupation forces of the four powers. In general, the Russians occupied the eastern portions of Germany and Austria while the three western powers shared the western areas of those countries. Both Berlin and Vienna are in the Soviet zones of occupation, but it was agreed that these cities would be regarded as having special status. Each has been divided into four zones, one occupied by each of the powers.

At Potsdam, in August, 1945, Truman, Stalin, and Churchill joined in announcing a list of guiding principles for Allied occupation and reconstruction of Germany. These provided for: (1) the complete demilitarization of Germany and the destruction of all facilities for producing arms; (2) an attempt to convince the German people that they had been defeated completely and that they alone were responsible for the war; (3) abolition of the Nazi party and its related groups, accompanied by a complete purge from public office of all persons who had been more than nominal Nazis; and (4) a policy of attempting to retrain the German people so as to make them democratic and suitable for trust in the future community of nations. It was envisaged that the formation once again of a central German government would be far in the future. Before then democratic governments would have to be constructed in Germany from the ground up, beginning at the local level and working up toward the district, regional, and provincial levels as the Germans proved themselves able to utilize democratic processes effectively in governing themselves.

Economically Germany was to be treated as a single unit and though no central government was to exist, the Allied Control Council was to set up common policies regarding the most important areas of production and distribution. The chief intention in the economic field was to assure that the future development of Germany's economy would stress consumers' goods production and agriculture. This conception, often known as the "Morgenthau Plan," was aimed at preventing the future resurgence of German military-economic strength. In addition the Potsdam Declaration provided that the power of cartels, trusts, and other monopolistic groups within Germany should be wiped out. The average standard of living in Germany was not to be permitted to exceed the average

standard of living of all European countries, excluding
Great Britain and the Soviet Union.

At the Potsdam meeting, too, a declaration was issued
by the United States, China, and Great Britain laying
down terms on which the surrender of Japan was demanded. This declaration made clear that while the Allied
governments did not wish to enslave the Japanese or destroy their nation, it was intended to wipe out the power
of the militarists who had brought their country into war.
The three powers made plain their intention of establishing democratic processes and freedom in Japan and of
reorganizing her industries so as to prevent her from
rearming for war in the future. The Japanese were warned
that their islands would be occupied until such time as
the objectives of the occupation, i.e., the formation of a
peaceful and responsible government, which would assure
democratic life in the future, had been secured.

Fourth, though the United States itself expected to get
no major territorial gain or reparations for its part in the
war, it recognized that many of the nations allied with it
had been grievously devastated by the conflict and were
entitled to compensation. In addition, these nations
sought other territorial or population adjustments which
they believed would strengthen their position in the future. All these matters had to be provided for through
agreement among the three great powers.

As regards reparations from Germany, the Potsdam
Conference decided that the USSR should obtain such
compensation by removing capital equipment from the
Soviet zone of that country. The USSR also received title
to all German assets in eastern Europe, i.e., Bulgaria, Finland, Hungary, Rumania, and eastern Austria. Similarly,
the western powers were to take their reparations from
Germany through capital removals from their zones of that
country and by seizure of German assets in other countries
than those where German assets were reserved for the
USSR. However, 25 percent of the capital equipment to
be removed from the western zones of Germany was to

go to the Soviet Union as additional reparations. Of this 25 percent, three-fifths was to be paid for by the Soviet Union by shipment of an equivalent value of food, coal, timber, petroleum products, and such other commodities as would be agreed upon. The remaining two-fifths was to go to the USSR without payment of any kind.

The Potsdam Conference decided that Poland, Czechoslovakia, and Hungary would be permitted to expel the German minorities living there. These minorities had aided Hitler in taking over those countries and were regarded by them as forming a threat to their future peace and internal security. The Conference provided, however, that such transfers of Germans from those countries to Germany itself "should be effected in an orderly and humane manner." Moreover, the Allied Control Council in Germany was instructed to examine the problem in order to insure the equitable distribution of these Germans among the several zones of occupation.

Two major territorial decisions were reached at Potsdam. First, the city of Königsberg and the adjacent area of German East Prussia were awarded to the Soviet Union, Great Britain and the United States promising that they would support this proposal at the forthcoming German Peace Settlement. Second, the western border of Poland was fixed so as to include a large section of what had formerly been eastern Germany. The Oder and Neisse rivers, which had formerly been well inside Germany, now became the western frontier of Poland and the eastern boundary of Germany. The cession of German territory to Poland was intended to compensate that country for the loss of its eastern territories. These had been occupied by the Soviet Union at the time Germany invaded Poland in September, 1939, and had been permanently incorporated into the USSR thereafter. From a legal point of view, these territorial decisions of the Potsdam Conference were merely recommendations and interim measures until a final peace settlement could be worked out. It was obvious, however, even at the time, that any future deviation from these territorial decisions would be most difficult, if not impossible.

Fifth, a most complex group of problems faced during the negotiations of World War II concerned the new governments to be created in the liberated areas of Europe and Asia. The problem was simple where a legally constituted government had continued to exist and act throughout the war, as in the case of China. The freed Chinese territories were turned over to Chinese rule. In the colonial areas of Asia, such as the Dutch East Indies and British Malaya, it was apparently assumed that the old ways of government could be resumed after victory over the Japanese. Little account was taken of the tremendous changes wrought in those areas after their conquest by the Japanese within the year after Pearl Harbor, particularly those resulting from Japan's anti-Occidental propaganda. In the case of Korea, whose freedom was to be achieved after decades of Japanese rule, it was agreed that the United States and the Soviet Union would jointly occupy the country. The United States was to have all of Korea south of the 38th parallel and the Soviet Union all of the area north. The ultimate objective envisoned was withdrawal of the occupation forces of both powers and the formation of a single democratic Korean government representing the will of the Korean people.

Even before the war against Germany had ended, however, it was apparent that there would be trouble in eastern Europe. Poland was the first case. For here the occupying Soviet troops installed a so-called Polish Committee of National Liberation, composed of individuals representing no one but their Soviet masters. This new regime assailed the Polish government-in-exile which had directed a Polish underground struggle against the Germans during the war from its London headquarters. In Poland itself, civil war broke out as Polish partisans fought both Soviet troops and Polish units loyal to the new provisional regime. At the Yalta Conference the three major powers agreed that the original provisional government installed by the Red Army should be broadened so as to include democratic elements from the London government-in-exile. This was actually done in the early months of 1945, and at Potsdam the three governments declared themselves satisfied with the broadened composition of the new Polish government. This new regime was recognized by all three powers as the actual Polish government and the legal owner of Polish state properties located in their territories. In addition, they noted that this new government had agreed to hold free elections as soon as possible on the basis of universal suffrage and secret ballot. All democratic, anti-Nazis parties would have the right to participate.

Sixth, the most important long-range goal of American diplomatic efforts during the war was the creation of an international community of nations governed by law. This, it was hoped, not only would prevent the outbreak of new wars in the future, but also would act to remove the underlying causes of such wars. The first necessity for such international coöperation, it was realized, was coöperation between the major powers which had fought and won the war. To secure such coöperation the Yalta agreement provided that the foreign secretaries of the United States, Great Britain, and the Soviet Union should hold regular meetings, usually every three or four months, at the capitals of these countries in rotation, to discuss major problems as they arose. In this way, it was hoped, the three major powers would be able to iron out their differences and reach amicable agreement. Such agreement was viewed as a fundamental prerequisite of a peaceful postwar world.

The central conception for the organization of a new world community was an organization to succeed the League of Nations and, it was hoped, to be much more effective than the League. The present United Nations is the fruit of that wartime conception. The fundamental principles of the United Nations were agreed upon at a conference of the United States, the Soviet Union, Great

Britain, and China held at Dumbarton Oaks in Washington, D.C., during the late summer and early fall of 1944. There the fundamental purpose of the United Nations was declared to be to maintain international peace and security and "to that end to take effective collective measures for the prevention and removal of threats to the peace and the suppression of acts of aggression or other breaches of the peace, and to bring about by peaceful means adjustment or settlement of international disputes which may lead to a breach of the peace." Membership in the United Nations was to be open to all peace-loving states. The United Nations, it was envisaged, would become a focal point for arrangements to secure international economic and social coöperation aimed at creating stable conditions and prosperity necessary for peaceful relations among peoples. The United Nations Charter was actually drafted at the San Francisco Conference held in the spring of 1945. The organization came formally into existence on October 24, 1945, after ratification by the major powers and a majority of the fifty states which had participated in the Conference.

In viewing the organization set up for the United Nations, it must be kept in mind that the fundamental premise assumed by those who framed the Charter was that the victors in the war, the United States, Great Britain, and the Soviet Union primarily, would work together honestly and sincerely in the postwar period. In consequence the Charter was so drafted as to protect the world against disturbances of peace which might arise because of the action of nations other than the great powers. This, postwar history has shown, was not only an unsound assumption but also the greatest obstacle to the effective working of the United Nations in the conditions which have actually existed.

The chief component parts of the United Nations organization are the General Assembly, the Security Council, the Economic and Social Council, the Trusteeship Council, the International Court of Justice, and the Secretariat. Other organizations have been formed as the General Assembly has seen fit to form them.

The General Assembly was originally only a body for discussion of international issues. It had no real powers to order action. All member nations of the United Nations are represented in the General Assembly by individuals who have diplomatic status. Most of the work of the General Assembly is performed by its six main committees, on each of which all the member states are represented. Decisions of the General Assembly are in the form of recommendations. Because of this organization and limitation of its powers, the General Assembly was important mainly as a forum in which the different sides on major issues were presented to world public opinion. Citizens of a democracy were thus enabled to learn all sides of controversial issues; experience showed that in totalitarian states opinion at variance with the rulers of such states could effectively be kept from the people despite this forum. As we shall see below, the powers of the General Assembly were increased in the fall of 1950.

The General Assembly had, however, several accomplishments to its credit as a result of the activities of groups subordinate to it. The partition of Palestine and other activities in that area brought about by the group headed by Dr. Ralph Bunche are illustrative. In addition, investigating commissions of the General Assembly have been active in both the Balkans and Korea, though their activities were hampered by Soviet satellites.

The Security Council is the most important single body of the United Nations. It consists of five permanent members, China, the Soviet Union, France, Great Britain, and the United States, as well as six nonpermanent members who are elected by the General Assembly for a term of two years. The Security Council is theoretically in continuous session, and a representative of each of its members must always be available at the seat of the United Nations for this purpose. The Security Council's powers are extensive. The weapons available to it in considering any dispute or other threat to world peace are peaceful mediation, nonmilitary sanctions, and the employment of military force. It must exhaust the first two methods before using the third. The Security Council may suggest that members of the United Nations apply economic or diplomatic sanctions against countries threatening world peace, or it may authorize the use of United Nations forces against an aggressor. At the time the United Nations was formed it was believed that it would have available such troops. For this purpose a military staff committee consisting of the chiefs of staff of the permanent members of the Security Council was formed to organize and direct this force. For the Security Council to reach a binding decision on any matter other than a procedural question all five permanent members must vote together. This is the origin of the so-called "veto" problem. If all members of the Security Council except one of the permanent members should support a decision that failure of one permanent member to support it prevents its passage.

Events in the postwar period showed that it could not cope with many problems because of paralysis induced by frequent Soviet use of the veto. In line with suggestions made by United States Secretary of State Acheson in September, 1950, several important changes were made in the powers of the General Assembly to cope with this and related problems. Now, if the Security Council is blocked by a veto, the problem automatically goes to the General Assembly for consideration and possible action. A fourteen-nation peace patrol has been established to provide first-hand observation and information on events in any part of the world which threaten peace. Moreover a beginning has been made toward making available to the United Nations national contingents of armed forces for action against aggression. The first of these units were employed in Korea. All these moves were aimed at remedying important weaknesses which had shown themselves during 1946-1950.

The other organs of the United Nations are important but must be treated briefly here. The Economic and Social Council consists of eighteen members elected by the General Assembly. Its function is to seek the betterment of living conditions and the protection of human rights. It has only powers of recommendation to the General Assembly but may investigate particular matters. Among the issues its committees consider are such matters as human rights, employment, social conditions, statistical reporting, the status of women, and narcotics. The Trusteeship Council was set up to replace the former Mandate Organization of the League of Nations. This Council consists of states which hold trusts over particular areas of the world as well as an equal number of states which do not hold such trusteeship rights. The Trusteeship Council in general supervises the execution of the trusteeship by individual states, but it may also under the United Nations Charter exercise the trusteeship function itself directly, if so desired by a trustee state. The International Court of Justice replaces the former World Court of the League of Nations. All members of the United Nations also belong to the Court. Its justices sit continuously at The Hague to try such international cases as may be presented to it for adjudication. Some member states have agreed to submit all their international disputes to the Court for decision, but others submit only cases they wish to have so decided.

Also attached to the United Nations are various international organizations whose functions are primarily in the economic field. Thus, the Food and Agricultural Organization (FAO) was created in order to help improve conditions of production and living among farmers and peasants throughout the world. The International Bank for Reconstruction and Development was set up to provide loans for member nations requiring capital either to repair the damages of the war or to expand their own economy. The International Monetary Fund was set up in order to provide a means for securing stability in the relations between the currencies of different countries. The Fund provides means by which the countries may correct temporary disequilibrium; i.e., if a currency falls in value in relation to another currency because of temporary factors the Fund can provide money to permit the strengthening of the weakened currency for the temporary period, so that international exchange ratios between currencies shall not fluctuate unduly. The International Labor Office, which was created long before World War II, has now been attached to the United Nations. It provides a meeting place for representatives of governments, workers, and employers to consider and act on matters of common interest with regard to conditions of employment of industrial workers in the countries of the world. The Universal Postal Union, the International Civil Aviation Organization, the World Health Organization, and a variety of similar international organizations are also related to the United Nations, though each one is itself a specialized agency.

CHAPTER XXVI

American Foreign Policy Since World War II

WHAT WENT WRONG?

IT IS OBVIOUS that the world of the 1950's is a far different one from that sought by American policy and diplomacy during World War II. Instead of a peaceful community united for reconstruction and peace, the world today is divided into two hostile armed camps. The "cold war" of the late 1940's became a shooting war in Korea when the North Korean satellite of the USSR sent its army to invade South Korea in June, 1950. Throughout the world the forces of communism and democracy are arrayed against each other, sometimes engaged in armed warfare, more often fighting with psychological weapons. Every major nation of the world maintains large armed forces which exert a heavy drain upon the standard of living of its people. The fear of war dominates the thinking of tens of millions. What went wrong?

Put most simply, the answer is that we had built our conception of a postwar world upon a completely false premise. We had assumed that the Soviet Union would wish to participate with the United States, Great Britain, France, and other democratic nations in building a peaceful and stable world community. Instead, it became evident very quickly after war's end that the Soviet Union had an entirely different objective: the domination of the world. It sought to obtain this domination by setting up

Communist regimes in those countries occupied by the Red Army, and by aiding Communist parties in other countries to gain power, either by peaceful ballot, where that seemed likely, or by armed revolt.

The above is not meant to imply, of course, that American policy has been perfect. Nor can one deny that some Americans have given the Soviet Union cause for suspicion and distrust. Some persons, for example, spent a portion of the early postwar period attempting to convince the American people that we should declare atomic war against the Soviet Union. Other similarly irresponsible statements came from various quarters. But by both word and act, the United States government attempted in the early postwar years to reassure the Soviet Union, to keep the bargains it had made, and to overcome the long heritage of suspicion and distrust between the two great countries. The effort was in vain. More recently, of course, the United States has been actively defending itself against Soviet aggression, direct and indirect. In that process we have done much that can be pointed to as antagonistic toward Russia. But a study of the chronological record involved shows clearly that the American attitudes and actions of recent years have been in reply to and as counters toward Soviet actions and attitudes, rather than the initiators of the Soviet campaign. The Moscow radio, for example, conducted anti-American propaganda in many different languages long before the "Voice of America" began replying in the same vein and over the same medium.

Soviet Aggression

How did Soviet aggression show itself? Here are a few typical examples:

1. In eastern Europe, all of which was occupied by the Red Army during and after the war, the USSR was pledged to the restoration of democratic regimes. Instead, each of these countries today is governed by a purely Communist group. All these countries have become satellites of the

Soviet Union, with the sole exception of Yugoslavia, which will be discussed separately below. The process of seizure of power has varied only in details in all these countries. Protected by the Red Army, the local Communists took over more and more power and crowded out such non-Communist elements as had been permitted to share governmental functions at the beginning. Even in countries such as Hungary, where the Communist party polled less than 20 percent of the vote in a relatively free election held shortly after the war, the non-Communist President of Hungary had to flee the country to save his life and the Communist party reigns supreme. In Poland, the commitments given by the Soviet-sponsored Polish provisional government, in order to gain recognition from the United States and Great Britain, were blithely ignored soon after the Potsdam Conference. Non-Communist leaders in Poland either had to flee the country or were imprisoned. In Czechoslovakia armed Communist bands seized power in February, 1948, while democratic forces representing the majority of popular sentiment were paralyzed by fear of Red Army intervention if they opposed the Communist seizure of power. As a result, all of eastern Europe today, with the exception of Yugoslavia, consists of a series of small-scale models of the Soviet Union. In each, industry has been nationalized, agriculture has begun to be collectivized, and free expression of opinion has been ended. The totalitarian Soviet-type state rules.

2. In Greece, armed Communist rebels fought to overthrow the democratically elected government through the late 1940's. Time and again the Greek army smashed the rebels and forced them to flee, only to find they had been saved by retreating into the Soviet satellites on Greece's borders from whence they received supplies and new recruits. Efforts to use the United Nations to halt the outside aid to these Communist rebels were frustrated time and again by Soviet and satellite action in the United Nations. American aid finally enabled the legal Greek government to overcome the rebels.

3. The old Communist International, an avowed weapon for world communist domination, has been revived in the postwar period, after its formal dissolution during the wartime period of Soviet-Allied coöperation. It was recreated in late 1947 in the guise of an organization called the Communist Information Bureau, more usually known as the Cominform. This organization includes all of the major Communist parties of Europe, and its publications show its close contacts with Communist parties in other parts of the world. Through the Cominform, Russian and non-Russian Communist leaders coördinate their activities and funnel out their propaganda line against the western democracies, particularly the United States. The Cominform has also been the Soviet Union's chief weapon in its fight against Marshal Tito. Tito, one of the most loyal Communist satellite chiefs in the period immediately after the war, revolted against Soviet domination and refused to subordinate the interests of Yugoslavia to those of the Soviet Union. As a result, the USSR, its satellite countries, and the world communist movement have been conducting a virulent propaganda campaign aimed at ousting Marshal Tito's regime and replacing it with a subservient government which will obey Moscow's wishes.

4. In the United Nations the Soviet Union time and again has refused to permit that organization to work effectively by vetoing measures passed by overwhelming vote of the other member nations. By the end of 1950, the USSR had used the veto about fifty times. This Soviet obstructionism has been the major reason for the United Nations' ineffectiveness in most of the major problems it has tried to deal with in the postwar period. The aggressor, in short, has paralyzed the organization set up to curb aggression. The Soviet Union, it should also be noted, has failed to join any of the major postwar economic organizations such as the Food and Agriculture Organization (FAO), the International Bank for Reconstruction and Development, the International Monetary Fund, and others. In the case of the first three organizations just

named, the USSR participated actively in the initial negotiations and conferences aimed at setting them up but
then refused to join. Soviet obstruction and inaction have
prevented the military Staff Committee of the Security
Council from discharging its assignment to organize an
effective military force for the United Nations. Only the
absence of the Soviet delegate from the Security Council
in June, 1950, enabled the UN to take effective action
against aggression in Korea.

5. Most flagrant has been the use of the Soviet army to
aid the establishment of Communist regimes. Such events
in eastern Europe have been noted before. In China the
Red Army withdrew from Manchuria in such a way as to
make it possible for the Chinese Communist armies to
take over as the Russians left, and to seize a large stock of
Japanese munitions and armaments which had been captured with the Japanese surrender. This placed the Chinese Communists in a most advantageous position for
future activities and played a not inconsiderable role in
making possible the communization of China that has
taken place since. In Iran, Soviet troops remained in the
north of that country beyond the date they had promised.
A Soviet-encouraged Communist government ruled northern Iran for a time until the legitimate Iranian government was able to send troops against them without fear of
turning the matter into a war between Iran and the Soviet
Union. In Soviet-occupied North Korea a similar satellite
Communist regime has been set up. A large North Korean
army was trained and equipped for the day when it struck
against South Korea. When that army had been destroyed,
the Chinese Communist government sent hundreds of
thousands of troops masquerading as "volunteers" into the
country to snatch victory from the grasp of United Nations forces. All this was done with the open support of
the Soviet Union.

Other examples could be cited of Soviet aggression and
unwillingness to coöperate, but the above are fully illustrative.

AMERICAN STRATEGY AND TACTICS

In the unexpected postwar setting created by this Soviet attitude and menace, how has the United States reacted? The strategy and tactics of the United States have two objectives. We still seek the positive goal of a better world in which peace and stability rule. In addition we seek to counter Soviet aggression by strengthening the defenses of the non-Soviet world.

American efforts to further international coöperation and to create the prerequisites for world peace and prosperity have taken many forms. The United States has participated in all the international organizations created to improve coöperation among nations with regard to particular problems or particular areas of work. Thus the United States contributed most of the three billion dollars required to finance UNRRA's major relief activities during the war and postwar periods. United States generosity made possible the work of the International Refugee Organization which did so much to help displaced persons during and after World War II.

An outstanding example of constructive American effort to create the prerequisites for a stable and peaceful future life has been our atomic energy policy. The United States at the end of the war was the only country in possession of atomic bombs and the knowledge and equipment to make additional atomic bombs. Instead of using these weapons and this knowledge in an effort to terrorize and dominate the rest of the world, the United States came forward with a broad plan for international control of the use of atomic energy. This plan would have taken away our monopoly position in this field and have given an international organization control of atomic energy. Our plan had the objective of preventing the use of this energy for military purposes while permitting its use for the great variety of peaceful purposes to which atomic energy and its by-products can be put. But in this case, as in so many others, Soviet intransigence and unwillingness to coöperate

have prevented to this date the adoption of the American
or any other effective plan of control of atomic energy.

As the menace of Soviet aggression became more evident to larger numbers of our people, the emphasis of
American policy turned more and more toward countering
the USSR. A policy based upon the assumption of "One
World" was obviously not appropriate in a situation where
two worlds exist. American strategy in countering the
Soviet threat may be summarized in the one word "containment." Put another way, the United States has sought
consistently in the last several years to prevent successful
Communist aggression. We have sought to buttress the
governments and economies of the non-Communist states
which were most dangerously threatened by external or
internal Communist aggression. The "Truman Doctrine"
announced in 1947 when it seemed Greece might succumb to a Communist revolution was the formal enun-
ciation of this policy. This has been based upon the hope
that if we could successfully prevent any further extension
of Communist power and influence, there might come a
time when either the Soviet leaders would change their
ultimate objectives or, for one reason or another, they
might be swept out of power in the Soviet Union. Nevertheless, substantial Communist success has been obtained,
especially in China, since the adoption of this "containment" policy. As a result more and more voices have been
raised to inquire whether this essentially defensive strategy
is adequate. Can't we do something to take the initiative
and the offensive away from the Communist powers? This
is one of the major unsolved problems to which we shall
have reference later in this chapter. American tactics in
the battle of "containment" have been economic, political, and military. Let us survey each of these areas separately:

The military tactics used by the United States did not
at first involve direct use of American troops to combat
Soviet or Soviet-allied troops. Until direct American military intervention became necessary in South Korea to back

up United Nations policy, we merely attempted to supply American military instructors and advisers, as in the case of Greece, to help countries fighting Communist forces. In addition, we have recently begun to supply western Europe with more than a billion dollars' worth of arms in order to permit western Europe to equip new armies which can be used to combat any possible Soviet invasion of that area. American troops have been maintained in Germany and Austria, in the American zones of occupation there. In part, this has presumably been intended as a warning to the USSR that any effort at direct military invasion of western Europe would mean conflict with the United States. It must be remembered that ever since the end of the war the people of western Europe have been in fear of a Soviet invasion, which, it has been commonly believed, could easily sweep to the English Channel within a week or two. Only the threat of America's might, particularly American atomic bombs, many people believe, has prevented this Soviet invasion. Even in 1950, western Europe had little in the way of substantial military strength to counter any Soviet military thrust. In early 1951, General Dwight Eisenhower had been named head of a joint American-Western European defense force, but actual building of this force to necessary size remained for the future.

Political tactics followed by the United States have aimed both at unifying the anti-Soviet nations and at encouraging the growth of democracy. On the score of unification, one of the most important accomplishments was the negotiation and ratification of the North Atlantic Pact. Under the terms of the North Atlantic Pact the United States, Canada, and the nations of western Europe which are signatory to this agreement have, in effect, combined in a collective security league. They undertake to act to help each other, presumably by military means, in the event of aggression against one or all of them. Among other objectives, this pact is intended to give more formal assurance of American aid to western Europe in the event

of Soviet attack than was available before. The terms of
the North Atlantic Pact, it should be pointed out, provide
only for action in the event of aggression against one of
the signatory members. It is not and cannot be an aggressive weapon, though Soviet and Communist propaganda
have attempted to depict it as such. Along a similar line
have been American efforts to secure greater unity of western Europe, looking perhaps finally to a single western
European state, though that seems a distant objective. In
the area of political unity, however, American policy
makers have consistently rejected a world government approach despite demands for this type of action from some
groups of Americans. American policy makers have apparently regarded the world government dream as perhaps a
desirable ideal for the distant future, but as one incapable
of realization amidst the hard realities of the present.

Among the most important areas of American political
activity have been the regions occupied by American
troops, i.e., the American zones of Germany and Austria,
South Korea, and Japan. In each of these areas the United
States has sought to foster the creation of democratic
governments selected in free elections based upon universal suffrage. Active Communist parties exist, for example, in the American zones of Germany and Austria and
in Japan, but no anti-Communist parties exist openly in
the Soviet zone of Germany or in any of the satellite
states. American policy in these areas has been predicated
upon the belief that only by helping the people resident
there to create their own democratic institutions could we
expect their democracy to be stable and to last beyond the
period of American occupation. American troops had already evacuated South Korea prior to June, 1950.

Germany, of course, has been the central area in this
political struggle. The German people are still the most
numerous single group between the English Channel and
the Soviet border. Their economic resources and technical
ability make them one of the most important groups in
any effort at European economic union. The initial Amer-

ican program for Germany, we recall, looked not only toward demilitarization of Germany, but also toward stripping it of most heavy industry and reducing it to a country dominated by agriculture and the manufacture of consumers' goods. But this was a plan worked out in a period when it was assumed that the United States and the Soviet Union would coöperate with other nations to prevent the recurrence of German militarism. In the actual postwar setting it became more and more evident that the Soviet Union was attempting to appeal to the nationalistic sentiments of Germans and to offer them a partnership with the USSR in the future rule of the world. Such a notion was actually made almost fully explicit in Generalissimo Stalin's greeting to the new East German Republic formed in late 1949. The United States, Great Britain, and France found after 1945 that coöperation with the Soviet Union was impossible as regards Germany, because of Soviet sabotage of Allied agreements and Soviet refusal to abide by any kind of majority rule. The USSR went so far as to blockade all surface transportation to the western zones of Berlin for a year. The three countries were finally forced to foster the creation of a western German state, comprised of the former American, British, and French zones of occupation. One of the decisive political questions of the postwar period is whether the future independent German state will be formed around the present western European government (usually called the Bonn government after the name of its capital) or around the puppet eastern German government set up by the Soviet Union. Both sides in the present struggle, in short, are striving desperately to gain the support of the German people and the future German state, a situation far removed from that anticipated during and immediately after World War II.

Some of the most thorny political problems of the postwar period have involved Asia. In general, postwar Asia has been swept by a fever of nationalism, and country after country has been freed from the shackles of colonial rule. The United States was, of course, fortunate in having agreed to give the Philippine Islands their independence long before the outbreak of World War II. The British left India and Burma peacefully and more or less voluntarily. But in French Indo-China, the Dutch East Indies, Malaya, and elsewhere in the Far East, bloody struggles have taken place. The natives, inflamed by Japanese propaganda against whites, and equipped often with Japanese arms, have struggled effectively for their freedom. Events in Korea have been discussed earlier.

In this situation the United States has been caught between two fires. On the one hand, the traditional American sympathy for countries seeking their freedom has played an important role. On the other hand, Great Britain, France and The Netherlands, the chief colonial powers, are the bulwarks of American opposition to communism in western Europe. The United States has therefore been caught in a difficult position: whatever it did it would displease a group with which it wished to be friendly. Making this problem more urgent has been the fact that Communist propagandists have been active in seeking to utilize this postwar nationalism as a means for displacing Western colonial imperialism by the new-type Soviet rule, masked as the formation of an independent state. In French Indo-China, for example, the Viet Nam revolutionary movement is headed by a Communist trained in Moscow. In China, of course, American policy suffered a complete debacle as the Chiang Kai-shek regime was routed militarily and finally forced completely off the mainland of China. In the former Dutch East Indies the issue has been somewhat happier. With the help of American negotiators, the Dutch and the Indonesians, who for many months were engaged in a bloody struggle against each other, were finally brought to agree. An independent United States of Indonesia (USI) has been formed linked to Holland by the Dutch crown. More and more it has become evident that American policy in the Far East must be aimed toward helping non-Communist native nationalists to attain and retain their sovereignty, protecting it against threat of both former colonial overseers and the new Soviet-backed Asiatic Communists. With the disappearance of China into the network of Communist states the position of India as a possible central bastion of the anti-Communist coalition of the Far East has come more and more to the fore. The visit of Pandit Nehru to the United States in late 1949 was one indication of the importance attached to the future role of India in American strategy and tactics in the Far East. Conversely, Soviet policy has been aimed at splitting India from the West, as in the UN debate over recognition of Communist China.

For obvious reasons, the foreign economic policy of the United States has been one of the outstanding facets of American diplomacy in the postwar period. World War II greatly impoverished almost all of its major participants, both because of the direct cost of waging the conflict and because of the vast amount of physical destruction of factories, transportation equipment, raw materials, and other commodities it caused. The United States did not suffer any of this direct physical destruction, though the cost of the war was, of course, enormous to this country as well as to others. American productive capacity increased substantially during the conflict. In 1945 the United States was in a far more favorable position economically speaking, compared with the impoverished other major powers, than it had been before World War II. It is not surprising, therefore, that our wealth, i.e., the abundance of goods we produce, has given us one of our strongest weapons in this struggle against Soviet aggression.

From the beginning of the postwar period the United States pursued a very generous policy toward its former allies. We canceled most Lend-Lease debts, regarding the supplies given our allies under this arrangement as part of the common war effort, rather than as a commercial loan to be repaid. In this way we sought to avoid the same burden of inter-Allied debts which so complicated and aggravated international economic relations during the 1920's and early 1930's.

The United States also regarded it as part of its obligation toward its former allies to assist them in rehabilitating their war-destroyed economies. We have already mentioned the relief functions of UNRRA. In addition, the United States provided a very sizable portion of the capital funds of the International Bank for Reconstruction and Development, set up to provide loans for repairing the damage caused by the war, among other purposes. The special position of Great Britain was recognized by the United States. We granted the British a loan of $3,750,-000,000 which was calculated at that time to meet British needs for American products in excess of what the British could pay for during the period 1946-51. The loan is to be paid in fifty annual installments, beginning December 31, 1951, and will carry annual interest of 2 percent. Loans in smaller amounts were also made to other nations in the beginning of the postwar period. From 1945 to early 1951, the total assistance abroad given or authorized by this country amounted to about thirty billion dollars, including loans and gifts to various countries, American contributions to UNRRA relief work and to the capital of other international agencies, and other miscellaneous expenditures.

Despite this American assistance and the efforts of the western European countries themselves, it had become apparent in early 1947 that these countries could not recover from the economic setbacks of the war without still further additional aid. The essence of the problem was simply that Europe lacked sufficient dollars and the goods to pay for all the food, raw materials, and machinery it required from the United States. This famous "dollar deficit" was the product of many factors. These factors included not only the destruction of productive equipment during the war but also the lowered productivity of European workers resulting from the great food shortage of the war and postwar periods. Important too was the diminution in European countries' receipts of dollars from the exports of their Asiatic colonies' raw materials such as rubber to the United States. Technical progress which made possible nylon and synthetic rubber production thus played an important role in creating postwar international economic difficulties.

American policy makers feared that this dollar deficit would lead to disastrous consequences both for Europe and for the United States. Europeans would be forced to shut down their factories because of lack of raw materials, and their people would go hungry. The resultant political dissatisfaction, it was feared, would be exploited fully by the Communists and raised the specter of Communist victories in western Europe as a result of the economic chaos it brought on. From the American point of view, for Europe to readjust, i.e., to cut its purchases from the United States in line with the small supply of dollars available to it, would have reduced American exports to Europe substantially, raising the threat of serious dislocation in at least some industries in this country. It must be remembered, however, that at the time, in mid-1947, American industry and agriculture were at or near their postwar peak of prosperity. There was not then any very urgent need for European exports to keep American prosperity going, as is often charged by Moscow spokesmen. It cannot be denied, however, that American statesmen feared the effect of a reduction of European purchases from this country at some later date, when the postwar prosperity might have diminished somewhat.

To meet this situation, Secretary of State George C. Marshall suggested in his famous speech at Harvard University in June, 1947, that the countries of Europe get together, see what they could accomplish toward their reconstruction by means of their own efforts and resources, and then turn to the United States with a request for such aid as would be required to meet the goals of postwar reconstruction. It should be emphasized that Secretary Marshall included the whole of Europe, with the Soviet Union and its eastern European satellites, in his invitation. The Soviet Union and its satellites were also included in the invitation to the first conference on the Marshall Plan, called by Foreign Secretaries Bevin and Bidault of Great Britain and France in the early summer of 1947. The Soviet Union, through its then Foreign Minister, Mr. Molotov, refused to participate in the Marshall Plan efforts. It abruptly ordered its satellite states of eastern Europe not to participate, although Poland, Hungary, and Czechoslovakia had either accepted the invitation to participate or already selected their delegates to represent them in the forthcoming conference.

Sixteen western European nations—if the term "western European" is extended to include Italy, Greece, and Turkey —did follow Mr. Marshall's suggestion to draw up a plan for their future rehabilitation and ask the United States to supply them with funds to meet the needs beyond their own resources. In the spring of 1948 Congress passed the Economic Cooperation Act of 1948, which authorized the practical realization of the Marshall Plan, and appropriated money to finance it over the first year. In April, 1949, legislation was passed providing for extension of the European Recovery Program, as the Marshall Plan has come to be called, through the fiscal year ending June 30, 1950. Most of the funds appropriated under the Economic Co-operation Act are given to the participating European countries in the form of direct grants for which no return is expected. Some of the money, however, is given in the form of loans or in the form of aid which requires certain conditions to be met. From April, 1948, to June, 1949, a total of almost six billion dollars in aid had been allotted to the sixteen participating areas. Of this over $4,200,-000,000 was in the form of direct grants. Almost half of the approximately six billion dollars allotted by ECA in this period has gone to the United Kingdom and to France. Italy has received almost 700 million dollars, The Netherlands almost 600 million and the Anglo-American bi-zonal area of Germany almost 500 million, and other regions receiving smaller amounts. By October 31, 1950, almost $11,000,000,000 worth of aid had been given or authorized by the Economic Cooperation Administration. Of the goods shipped to Europe from April, 1948, to June, 1949, the largest single item was grain for bread, the total value being almost one billion dollars. Petroleum and petroleum products made up the second largest item in value, exceeding 500 million dollars. Machinery and equipment made up the third item, only slightly less in value, and cotton, fourth, was only slightly less than petroleum and petroleum products. The Marshall Plan expenditures, in short, have enabled the people of Europe to be much better fed than they would have been otherwise. It has given them the raw materials with which to keep their factories working and their people employed, and it is increasingly giving them the machinery they require to replace that destroyed during the war and, equally important, to bring up to date production processes made obsolete and exorbitantly expensive by modern technological progress.

The consequences of the Marshall Plan have been all that we could hope for, both politically and economically. Production in the Marshall Plan countries has increased greatly, and many of them have passed their 1938 prewar peaks. Politically, Communist influence in western Europe has declined perceptibly as measured in votes received at elections or in membership. In early 1951 there seemed to be no immediate danger of Communist seizure of power, either legally or illegally, in any part of western Europe. Two or three years before, it had not seemed improbable that in France and Italy at least the Communists might soon be masters.

Yet the more the Marshall Plan accomplished its objective of permitting the increase of the physical volume of production of western Europe, the more it became apparent that certain other fundamental problems still required solution. For one thing, the currencies of European countries were overvalued in relation to the American dollar. This served to increase the dollar deficit. It made European goods excessively expensive to Americans, thus reducing European sales to this country, while tending to make American goods relatively cheap for Europeans, thus encouraging sales there. The evil economic effects of this disproportionate relationship between the currencies of the world could not last indefinitely. In the summer of 1949 there occurred a general devaluation of European and other non-American currencies, led by the British devaluation of the pound sterling by 30 percent. The result of this was that European goods became cheaper for American purchasers so long as they were stated in the same number of pounds or francs or marks or other European currency. Conversely, American goods became more expensive for Europeans. In this way the natural tendency of devaluation would be to reduce American exports to Europe to essentials, while tending to increase American imports from Europe. In both ways, therefore, devaluation of European currencies will tend to close the dollar deficit.

The necessity for devaluation further showed that the basic problem of the European economy was not only that of physical reconstruction, the phase of the matter most directly approached by the Marshall Plan. There is also the problem of finding markets for European goods abroad, so that Europe can ultimately pay for its own imports through its own exports. Once this phase of the problem began to receive attention it became apparent that major structural changes are required both in the European economy and in the relationships between the European economy and the United States. For one thing, American tariffs still tend to keep out many European goods which can be produced more cheaply in Europe than in this country. American customs procedure also often tends toward the same end, though there is nothing in law to justify much of this customs procedure. In part, therefore, it is no exaggeration to say that our need to give money to Europe to help it is simply the result of our refusal to accept the goods Europe is now willing and able to sell us to pay for what it requires. But this problem was greatly alleviated by the sharp upsurge in the American demand for foreign products after the outbreak of war in Korea.

A second phase of the problem arises from the fact that the many small nations in Europe have themselves been guilty in the past and in the present of the most virulent forms of economic nationalism. Each country has tended to build up its own industrial production, even when this industry has been costly and inefficient, in preference to buying from its neighbors those goods they could produce most cheaply, and selling them the goods it could produce most cheaply. This had led to much unnecessary duplication of productive facilities throughout western Europe and to a general increase in the cost of production, as well as waste of resources. Since this practice has impeded European recovery, the United States, through the Economic Cooperation Administration, has sought vigorously to persuade the European countries to unify themselves economically, i.e., to lower or abolish their customs barriers, their quota requirements, and the other obstacles they have set up to free exchange of goods among themselves.

This American-sponsored effort for economic unity has met with powerful resistance from various European groups. High-cost producers in different countries have no liking for the notion that they must give up their comfortable, tariff-protected domestic markets and meet the rigors of free international competition. Putting their own selfish interests ahead of the national and international good, they have put up a vigorous and, to this point, still highly effective resistance. On the other hand, it must be remembered that sudden introduction of free trade into these economies which have been so badly distorted by protectionism in the past would require enormous and painful adjustments. Desirable as the adjustments may seem to an outsider, we cannot and should not wonder that those who will have to bear the pain and discomfort of those adjustments hesitate to undergo them.

Rivalry between different European countries has also played a role in complicating the recovery efforts aimed at by the Economic Cooperation Act. Too many nations, seeking to further their own economic interest, have acted at times as though their only goal were to obtain the maximum share of the limited Marshall Plan funds available, regardless of the impact upon other nations. At times the American officials of the Economic Cooperation Administration have been forced to point out to the member nations that if they did not move in a coöperative fashion to eradicate the obstacles they themselves set up to their own recovery, Congress might refuse in the future to renew Marshall Plan appropriations and they would get no additional American aid at all. The Schuman Plan proposed by France in early 1950 called for integration of industry in western Europe, opening the way, if adopted, to overcoming many of the difficulties arising from the economic nationalism described above.

The Marshall Plan, it will be noted, was concerned only with western Europe, but obviously western Europe is not the only area that has required economic aid. The victory of the Chinese Communists in particular has focused attention upon the fact that it is precisely in the most backward nations of the world that communism is at present most threatening. The lowest standard of living in the world is to be found in the predominantly rural overpopulated nations in Asia, including not only China but also India, the Dutch East Indies, and neighboring areas. Here hunger is ever present, and the length of life on the average is short indeed by western European or American standards. These people, it is clear, offer tempting material for Communist propaganda and Communist victory. How are we to act there?

The problem is made most difficult by the fact that the poverty of these areas is so great that even if the United States were to pour in aid equivalent to that given by the Marshall Plan to western Europe it would probably have little effect. In particular, the rate of population growth in some of these countries is so great that all the benefits of such American aid in the form of food and other immediate necessities might soon be consumed by the increased population.

To meet the need of these areas not only in Asia but also in Africa and South America, President Truman, in his inaugural address of January, 1949, suggested what has come to be known as his "Point 4" program. This suggestion is aimed at increasing the production and the wealth of these backward areas by assisting them to industrialize at a maximally rapid rate. For this purpose the President suggested not only that should the United States government help provide capital, technicians, and technical knowledge but that private American investors be encouraged to go in to build new factories, new railroad lines, new transportation, new electric power installations, and the other capital structures of modern industrialization. This is obviously a long-range project. One cannot industrialize a nation of any size in one month or one year or even five years. It is still too early to judge conclusively whether this "Point 4" program will succeed in meeting its aims, or even to judge what volume of capital investment in backward countries will result from it.

It must be remembered that there are enormous economic and political obstacles in the way of this program. In the first place, the total amount of capital required to make any great amount of industrialization progress in the backward countries of the world is tremendous, and raising it is no easy task. Second, private American investors have a great and not unjustified fear that any investments they make in these backward countries may be lost because of arbitrary action on the part of the governments of the countries where that money is invested. The long history of defaults on American loans during the late 1920's and 1930's is still far from forgotten. Third, in many countries private American investment, or any American investment at all, is viewed with serious suspicion, even in non-Communist areas. Communist propaganda regarding the evil intent of American "imperialists" has made its impress felt. As a result, many countries place obstacles in the way of American investors or foreign investors generally, particularly if these threaten or promise to create new producing units which will compete with those already in existence and owned by native interests.

The United States government is cognizant of these and related difficulties and is making attempts to overcome them. Countries requiring American investment are being persuaded, wherever possible, to offer guarantees to American investors that they will be treated fairly, will be protected from arbitrary confiscation of their funds, and will receive equal treatment with native investors or producers. The United States Congress has been asked to create legal protection for foreign investment, i.e., to guarantee that foreign investors sending their money abroad in consonance with the Point 4 policy will be compensated by this government should they suffer loss because of arbitrary action.

Even before President Truman announced his Point 4 program there had been some substantial private investment abroad. Outstanding, of course, has been the tremendous program of American oil companies, which have invested large sums in prospecting and opening up huge oil resources of the Near East, particularly in Saudi Arabia. Another American corporation has been very active in developing the resources of the Negro republic of Liberia in Africa. But on the whole, American private investment abroad in the postwar era has been far below the levels of two decades ago. Whether the Point 4 program can cause it to expand sharply is one of the crucial issues of our time, for it seems unlikely that Congress will authorize the government to embark upon the huge expenditures required if it alone were to finance this endeavor. No large appropriations had been made by mid-1950 for this Point 4 program.

CONCLUSIONS

As the 1950's begin, the United States still stands as the strongest, wealthiest, and most powerful single nation in the world. It is the head of a group of nations comprising well over half of the human race. Yet it would be folly to close our eyes to the dangers and defeats of the past. At the end of World War II in 1945 the 400 or 500 million people of China were largely under the rule of the National government friendly to us. Today they are part of the Red Soviet-dominated system of nations. At the end of 1945, we alone in all the world had atomic bombs and knowledge and equipment required to make them. Today the Soviet Union apparently has atomic bombs and is turning them out as rapidly as possible. The threat that communism would take over western Europe has been stopped, for the time being at least. But the hungry, disease-ridden, and poverty-stricken masses of Asia, Africa, and South America still offer tempting targets for Communist propaganda. The outbreak of war in Korea has raised the specter of World War III in horrible proximity.

In these circumstances what can the intelligent citizen do? How can he contribute to the well-being of his nation in this important area of international relations? To a large extent the problems here are no different from those that face the citizen in other areas of social action. He must keep himself informed. He must make up his mind intelligently on the important issues and seek to communicate his views to his representatives in Congress and to the leaders of the organizations to which he belongs, so that those organizations may reflect his own opinions. The importance of proper understanding of the issues simply cannot be overestimated in this field. If he is not careful, the citizen will find himself exposed to the specious plausibility of Communist and quasi-Communist propaganda which seeks to paint the United States as a nation of "warmongers" busily engaged in trying to destroy the "democratic" societies of the Soviet Union and its satellites. Not only must the good citizen be himself able to resist this type of propaganda, he must participate actively in fighting it and exposing it wherever it appears. And while combating this propaganda, he must protect the right of those who differ with him to express their views.

In another respect, understanding is vital in this area for proper citizenship. The program for combating communism outlined above is an expensive one. It requires the expenditure of tens of billions of dollars, both for continued high military preparedness and for economic and military aid to our allies. These expenditures must be paid for by taxes. None of us likes to pay taxes, yet we must realize the reason for these expenditures and therefore for the taxes they involve. We must comprehend that if we abandon our allies abroad, if we permit the Soviet Union and its Communist underlings to conquer the areas of the world outside the Western Hemisphere, the cost to this country, not only in money but in lives, will far, far exceed the highest taxes we pay today.

The citizen must realize that the domestic issues and attitudes are closely related with foreign policy and its problems. If the United States were to have a severe depression, purchases of foreign goods would contract so sharply that much or all of the gains of the Marshall Plan would be destroyed, with the resulting evil consequences for the objectives of recovery. We must remember that since far more than one-half the world's population belongs to groups other than the white race, every lynching, every case of discrimination in this country against others because of the color of their skin or other reasons, boomerangs against us abroad. After all, can we blame the people of China, India, Africa, or South America if they are suspicious of our good intentions when some among us regard American citizens of dark skin as inferior creatures, unworthy of the rights accorded human beings? Communist propaganda has been most active in making rich capital out of this basic violation of our democratic concepts, even though this violation is the result of only a portion of our citizenry's attitudes and activities and is being combated by the United States government.

At the end of 1950 and the beginning of 1951, the people of the United States were concerned with an historic debate over future foreign policy. Initially this debate arose from the bitter defeat suffered by American and other United Nations troops in Korea, but the implications and ramifications of the issues involved far transcended that battlefield alone.

One point of view, advanced by such men as former President Herbert Hoover, Senator Robert A. Taft, and former Ambassador to Great Britain Joseph P. Kennedy represented a type of neo-isolationism. Though differing on some points, these men and those who sided with them believed essentially that Korea had proved we could not defend the great Eurasian land mass because of the vast superiority of military manpower which the Communist world, led by the Soviet Union and China, could put into the field. They argued implicitly that nowhere from the English Channel to the Pacific was there adequate will to fight or adequate force to fight with. The best policy for the United States, they believed, would be to conserve its resources rather than waste them by pouring large quantities of troops or material into these areas. Instead they urged that the United States become an armed bastion prepared to defend the Western Hemisphere and perhaps also peripheral areas such as Great Britain, Japan, and the Philippines. The United States' main reliance, this school of thought reasoned, should be upon air and sea power, recognizing what they asserted was the hopelessness of trying to meet the land power of the Communist world. The proponents of this view obviously believed that the policy of containment has failed and a major retreat is required in American foreign policy.

Against this view was arrayed the official policy of the United States government, a policy supported essentially also by such outstanding republicans as Governor Thomas E. Dewey and former Governor Harold Stassen. Proponents of this view argued that the retreat proposed by the Hoover-Taft-Kennedy school of thought would be suicidal, ensuring eventual world victory of communism. This was supported by pointing out that if Moscow's domain should extend over the vast Eurasian continent the existing balance of forces, still greatly in favor of the democratic world at the beginning of 1951, would be altered sharply in favor of communism. Control of the Eurasian land mass would give the Kremlin mastery over more than half the world's people, almost half of the world's industrial productive capacity, and over a vastly increased quantity of strategic raw materials, including the oil of the Near and Middle East, the iron and coal of Germany, France, and Luxemburg, and the like. In addition, in western Europe the Kremlin would obtain a vast number of highly skilled scientists and technicians to supplement its own grossly inadequate resources. With this vast reservoir of productive capacity, raw materials, and human beings at its disposal, the Kremlin could then go to work to so develop its industrial production and military power that within a relatively few years it would have overwhelming strength in the face of which the United States would have the alternative only of surrendering or being destroyed.

Instead of the Hoover-Taft-Kennedy proposal, the administration urged that the democratic world attempt to build up its strength, militarily and economically, so as to thwart Communist imperialism. High on the list of the measures it proposed was the rearmament of western Europe, including Western Germany, accompanied by the dispatch there of substantial American forces to buttress the military strength of those countries. President Truman and his advisers implicitly argued too that Western Germany, Italy, and Japan, the former enemies during World War II, must be readmitted to the family of nations and permitted to rearm for their own defense and for the defense of the anti-Communist world. Along with purely military measures, they urged that economic

aid be continued so as to ensure that the cost of increasing the military strength of our Allies would not be so
great as to create conditions favorable for internal Communist subversion.

While the pros and cons of this debate were being
argued over the length of the land, the rest of the world
looked on anxiously for the fateful decision which
United States citizens had to make. In western Europe,
Japan, the Philippines, and elsewhere in the world free of
the Communist yoke, statesmen and ordinary citizens
alike asked themselves anxiously what the United States
would do. In the Kremlin, as the Soviet press made clear,
the masters of the Communist world looked on gleefully
at the spectacle of confusion and division in the United
States. All over the world it was clear that the future of
the world hinged on the decision made by the people of
this country. Freedom would live or perish depending
upon the wisdom, courage, and self-sacrifice that would
be shown by the 150,000,000 persons of the United States
in the months and years ahead.

Index

Absolutism, 156, 284
Acheson, Dean, 497-498, 533
Adams, John, 39
Adams, John Quincy, 43 ff., 483
Aden, 325
Adenauer, Konrad, 353, 355, 356
Adkins vs. Children's Hospital, 65
Agrarian reforms, Russia, 153-154
Agricultural Adjustment Act, 1933, 88-89
  1938, 89-90
Agriculture, 56
  China, 405-408
  Great Britain, 288-289
  United States, characteristics of farm group, 92-94
    depression, 87-88, 507
    development of West, 78-85
    First World War, 87
    parity prices and crop control, 89-91
    prices and price levels, 86
    prosperity, 122-123
    railroad controversy, 84-85
    Roosevelt administration, 88-90, 511-512
    special interest groups, 68-69, 71-72
    technical advances, 82-84
Aiken, George D., 37
Albania, 388
Albany Plan, 16
Alexander III (Rus. czar), 169
Alexandra (Rus. empress), 172-173
All-China Congress of Soviets, 419-420, 421

Allen, William, 291
Allied Control Commission, 343, 525
Allied High Commission, 352
Allied Supreme Council, 258
America First Committee, 485
American Federation of Labor (A.F.L.), 71, 101-102
Anglican Church (Church of England), 4, 7, 30 ff., 299-300
Anglo-Chinese Wars, 428, 429
Anglo-Japanese Alliance, 434, 437
Annam, 452
Anti-Comintern Pact, 266
Antifederalist party, 40 n.
Antitrust legislation, 111-112
April Theses, 177, 184
Arabia, 426
Arkwright, Sir Richard, 286
Armenia, 259
Armour, Philip D., 105
Armstrong, H. F., 496
Articles of Confederation, 14-15, 16
Ash, Joseph, 306
Atlantic and Pacific Stores, 108
Atlantic Charter, 492
Atomic bomb, 477, 493, 496, 523, 543, 557
Atomic energy, control of, 541-542
Attlee, Clement, 313 ff., 325-326, 522
Auriol, Vincent, 370
Auschwitz extermination camp, 341-342
Australia, 285, 321, 323, 332
Austria, 135, 525-526, 544
Azerbaijan, 259

Badoglio, Marshal Pietro, 388-389
Balkans, 160, 496, 532
Baltimore, Lord, 7
Bank of England, 312
Bank of the United States, 81
Baptist Church, 31, 32, 34
Beard, Charles A., 76
Bell, John, 48
Beloff, Max, 269
Bentham, Jeremy, 290, 294, 321
Benton, Thomas Hart, 80
Beria, Lavrenti, 225-226, 242, 276
Berlin blockade, 349-350, 497
Berlin-Rome-Tokyo Axis, 516-517
Bermuda, 325
Besant, Annie, 294
Bevin, Ernest, 313, 550
Bidault, Georges, 369-370, 372, 373, 550
Bill of Rights, England, 283-284
United States, 19-22
Bismarck, Prince Otto von, 335
Blaine, James G., 484
Blatchford, Robert, 293, 306
Blitzkrieg, 519
Bloodless Revolution, 297
Blum, Léon, 364
Boer War, 321
Boguc, Dr. David, 291
Bolshevik Revolution, 142, 156-157, 177-178, 184, 257
Bonn assembly, 351-353
Bor, General, 276
Bourgeoisie, 166
Boxer Rebellion, 432-433, 451
Brand, Carl, 313-314
Breckenridge, John C., 48
Brest-Litovsk Treaty, 256-257
Bricker, John W., 37
British West Indies, 318, 319, 329
Brotherhood, universal, 157-158
Buddhism, 404
Budget, federal, 115-116
Bunche, Ralph, 532
Bundestag, 351
Burke, Edmund, 285

Burma, 312, 325-326, 328, 448, 452
Burns, John, 306
Butler, Charles, 321
Byelorussians, 149, 255

Campbell, Lord, 298
Canada, 312, 318, 319, 321, 323
Capitalism, and communism, 163-168, 195, 252, 254
and fascism, 267-268, 271
and Puritanism, 62-65
defined, 57-58
institutional elements, 58-60
corporate form of business, 67-68
economic competition, 68-74
free enterprise, 61-66
freedom of contract, 65-66
property rights, 66
Carlile, Richard, 293
Carnegie, Andrew, 105
Carpetbagging, 26
Cartels, 513-514
Cartwright, Edmund, 286
Cartwright, Maj. John, 320
Catholic Center party, 337, 338
Catholic Church, see Roman Catholic Church
Cavour, Conte di, 378, 379
Censorate, China, 412
Central Auditing Commission, 244
Central Committee, 240, 249, 256
Central People's Government, China, 421-422
Ceylon, 312, 325
Champion, H. H., 293
Chang Hsueh-liang, 454
Chang Tso-lin, 454
Charles I (Eng. k.), 5, 282-283
Charles II (Eng. k.), 31, 283
Chartism, 297-298
Cheka, 178
Chiang Kai-shek, 265, 416, 417, 419, 441-447, 453-456, 462-463, 466-467, 546
Child labor, 302
Chin Dynasty, 403

China, 126, 135, 160, 259, 261, 265-266, 523-524, 529
American relations, 440-448, 505
and imperialism, 456-461
communism, 464-473, 499, 540
and democracy, 461-464
European relations, 424-431
geography, 395-397
government, development, 416-419
future, 419-423
history, 397-404
national economy, 404-409
nationalism, 449-456
political foundations, 409-416
wars and diplomacy, 431-440
Chinese Eastern Railway, 265-266, 454, 523
Chinese Revolution (1910-11), 451
Chou Dynasty, 397-403
Christian Democrats, Germany, 351, 353
Italy, 390 ff.
Church of England, 4, 7, 30 ff., 299-300
Churchill, Winston S., 300, 311, 314-316, 522
Civil liberties, 223-227
Civil War, 25, 48, 79, 108-109, 487
Clapham Sect, 290
Clay, Henry, 43 ff.
Clay, Gen. Lucius D., 352
Clayton Act, 112, 513
Cleveland, Grover, 111
Cobbett, William, 293
Cole, G. D. H., 294, 295
Collective bargaining, 123
Collective farms, 219-221, 246
Collectivism, 151-153
Colonial Development and Welfare Acts, 312
Colonial Development Corporation, 330
Cominform, 496-497, 539
Comintern, 259-260, 261-262, 266, 270
Committee of Public Safety, 360

Committees of the Poor, 189, 191
Commonwealth, British, 312, 323-328
Commonwealth and Protectorate, 283
Communism, 124, 126, 135, 141, 452
and capitalism, 163-168, 195, 252, 254
and socialism, 312-314
China, 419-423, 444-448, 452-456, 464-473
and democracy, 461-464
France, 363-364, 366, 367-375
Germany, 334, 337, 338, 340, 345 ff., 353-356
Italy, 390, 391-393
Russia, see Soviet Union, Communist Party
Competition, 61
Compromise of 1850, 46
Confédération Générale du Travail (CGT), 370
Confucianism, 403, 405, 409-410, 415
Congregationalist Church, 5, 6, 30 ff.
Congress, U. S., 16-18, 35-36, 37, 40, 68, 85, 105, 112, 124, 480-484, 497, 556
Congress of Industrial Organizations (C.I.O.), 71, 101-102
Congress of Vienna, 476
Connecticut Colony, 6-7, 8
Constitutional Union party, 48
Constituent Assembly, France, 367-369
Italy, 389-390
Constitutions, China, 416-419
Great Britain, 9-11
Russia, 155, 194-195, 206, 210, 211, 228, 229, 237
United States, 2, 65, 76-77, 210, 283
drafting, 15-18
federal Bill of Rights, 19-22
foreign relations, 480-482
interpretations, 35-36, 40
Negro rights, 24-27

Constitutions—Continued
  United States—Continued
    ratification, 20-21
    separation of church and
      state, 30-35
    states, limitation of powers,
      22
    voting rights, 23-24
    women's rights, 28-30
Consumers Cooperative, Russia,
  208
Continental Congress, 12, 14,
  16
Contract, freedom of, 65-66
Coolidge, Calvin, 87
Coöperative societies (Gt. Br.),
  304
Coöperatives, farmers', 85, 92,
  112
Corn laws, 289, 302
Cornwallis, Lord, 320
Corporations, 56, 67-68, 96, 97
Cotton, Rev. John, 30
Cotton gin, 82
Coughlin, Fr. Charles E., 381,
  485
Council of Delphi, 475
Council of Economic Advisers,
  President's, 131-132
Courts, 278
Cressey, G. B., 396
Cripps, Sir Stafford, 313
Crop control, 91
Cushing, Caleb, 428
Cyprus, 329
Czechoslovakia, 257, 265, 272,
  452, 496, 538, 550

Dallin, David, 223
Dark Ages, 475
Darlan, Adm. Jean, 366
Dawes Plan, 339
Debt, national, 38
Declaration of Independence,
  12-13, 19-20, 24
Declaration of the Rights of
  Man, 359-360
Deere and Company, 82-83
De Gaulle, Gen. Charles, 365-
  369, 371-372, 374-375, 385
Delaware Colony, 7

Democracy, 1, 19, 20, 23, 36,
  64, 100, 126, 292, 337-338
  and communism, 461-464
  and foreign relations, 479-480
Democratic Federation, 305-306
Democratic party, 26-27, 37, 50,
  52-54, 73, 86, 88, 103, 112,
  124
  and Republicans, 45-49
  and Whigs, 42-45
Democratic-Republican party, 43
Denikin, Anton I., 258
Depressions, 87-88, 110, 113,
  114, 116, 271, 339, 509
Devaluation, currency, 136, 552
Dewey, Thomas E., 37, 51, 103,
  559-560
Dewhurst, J. Frederic, 503-504
Dilke, Sir Charles, 321
Dimitrov, G., 267-268, 271
Diplomacy, see International re-
  lations
Directory, 360-361
Disarmament, 262-263
Discrimination, 182
Dixiecrat party, 53
Doherty, John, 303
Dollar deficit, 548-549, 551-552
Dollfuss, Engelbert, 381
Domesday Book, 278
Douglas, Stephen A., 48
Draft, 118
Duma, 155, 173
Dumbarton Oaks Conference,
  531

East African groundnuts project,
  331-332
East German State, 353-356,
  545
Eastland, James O., 37
Economic Cooperation Administration, 550-551, 553-554
Economics, capitalism, see Capitalism
  concepts, 55-57
  defined, 57
Economy, planned, 182-183
Eden, Anthony, 314
Education, Great Britain, 300
  and religion, 33-35

Education—*Continued*
China, 413-415
Russia, 193-194, 247-249
Edward I (Eng. k.), 280
Edward II (Eng. k.), 281
Edward VIII (Eng. k.), 324
Eire, 312, 323, 324, 326-327, 328
Eisenhower, Gen. Dwight D., 519, 543
Elizabeth (Eng. princess), 324
Elizabeth (Eng. q.), 281-282
Employment, 113, 114, 117-118, 210-214
Engels, Friedrich, 158, 160, 162
  theories, 162-171, 178-179
Episcopal Church, 34
Estonia, 252, 254, 255, 265, 273
Ethiopia, 388, 516
European Consultative Assembly, 138
European Recovery Program (Marshall Plan), 349, 371, 373, 391, 484, 496-497, 558
  beginnings, 125-127
  Council of Economic Advisers report, 131-132
  Harriman report, 132-134
  implications, 138-140
  Krug report, 129-131
  Paris conference, 127-129, 550
  results, 135-138, 550-554
Exclusion Act (1638), 425
Export-Import Bank, 134
Extraterritoriality, 428-429, 442, 505

Fabian Society, 294-295, 306
Factory Act (1844), 303
Fair Deal, 94, 104
Fair Labor Standards Act, 65, 114
Family Code (Russia), 192
Famines, 220
Far Eastern Republic, 259
Farm bloc, 68-69
Fascism, 363-364
  and capitalism, 267-268, 271
  and China, 462-464
  Italy, 381-389

Federalism, 13-18, 344
Federalist party, 39-42, 105
Feudalism, 279, 476
Fiji Islands, 332
Finland, 254, 255, 258, 264, 273, 274
First World War, *see* World War I
Fisher Act (1918), 300
Five-Year Plans, Russia, 200-201, 207-209, 220-221
Food and Agricultural Organization, 534
Forced labor, 212-214
Ford Motor Company, 108
Fordney-McCumber Tariff, 508
Foreign relations, *see* International relations
Formosa, 425, 432, 447
Four-Power Treaty, 437
Fourteen Points, 452
Fox, George, 291
France, 135, 138, 171, 173, 174, 258, 265, 266, 291, 357-358, 433, 439, 486 ff., 550
  Communist problem, 369-372
  Fourth Republic, 366-369
  monarchy and First Republic, 358-360
  Napoleon Bonaparte, 361-362
  Revolution, 285, 477
  Second and Third Republics, 362-364
  Third Force, 372-375
  World War II, 364-366
France, Anatole, 105
Franchise, *see* Suffrage
Franco, Gen. Francisco, 266, 381
Franco-Prussian War, 362, 379
Franklin, Benjamin, 16
Frederick the Great, 335
Free enterprise, 61-66, 92
Free ports, 319
Free Soil party, 46
Free trade, 76, 300-302, 319
Freemen, 6
Friendly Society of Agricultural Laborers, 289
Frontier movement, 23
Froude, James A., 321

Fundamental Laws, Russia, 155, 194-195, 206, 210, 211
Fundamental Orders, 6, 13

Gambian egg-production project, 330-331
Gandhi, Mohandas K., 325
Garibaldi, Giuseppe, 377-378, 379
Gasperi, Alcide de, 390-393
Gauss, Clarence E., 444
General Electric Company, 124
General Motors Corporation, 124
Geneva Conference, 263
Genoa Conference, 260, 262
George III (Eng. k.), 13, 284, 298
George V (Eng. k.), 324
George VI (Eng. k.), 328
Georgia, USSR, 254, 255, 259
Germany, 125, 134, 314, 334-335, 433
  Allied occupation, 342-344, 544-545
  and Russia, 146, 171 ff., 176, 183, 251, 252-253, 255-257, 260-261, 265, 272-276
  Berlin crisis, 348-350, 497
  Communist government, 353-356
  monarchy, 335-336
  Potsdam agreement, 344-348, 525-530
  Weimar Republic, 336-339
  West German State, 350-353
Gestapo, 341
Gibraltar, 319, 329
Giraud, Gen. Henri, 366
Glorious Revolution, 7, 11, 13, 283
Goering, Hermann, 342
Gold standard, 510-511
Goldsmith, Oliver, 288-289
Good Neighbor policy, 483, 515
Gosplan, 208-209
Gouin, Felix, 368, 370
Gould, Jay, 105
Grand British League and Confederacy, 320
Grange movement, 71, 85

Grant, Ulysses S., 49
Gray, Earl, 297
Gray, Thomas, 289
Great Britain, 42, 141, 146, 171, 183, 258, 259, 261, 266, 274 ff., 550
  and China, 426-429, 433-434
  colonial policy, changes, 320-322
  Commonwealth, 323-328
  development plans, 329-333
  Dominions, 321-323, 325
  North America, 1, 2, 8-13, 76, 317-320
  economic situation, 125-126, 136-138
  historical development, agrarian revolution, 288-289
  American and French Revolutions, 284-286
  Industrial Revolution, 286-288
  labor movement, see Labour party
  reforms, 289-291, 296-304
  Saxons and Normans, 277-280
  Stuarts, 282-284
  Tudors, 281-282
Great Compromise, 18
Great Elector, 335
Great Russians, 148, 149, 225-226
Greece, 388, 475, 495, 538
Greeley, Horace, 45
Greenbacks, 86
Grey, Sir George, 321
Grote, George, 321
Grotewohl, Otto, 354
Guild system, 61-62

Habeas corpus, 17, 280, 285
Hague, The, 491, 534
Hainan, 433, 439
Hamilton, Alexander, 38-41, 43, 48, 105
Hammond, J. L. and B., 289
Hampden Clubs, 296
Han Dynasty, 403
Hanna, Mark, 86
Hardie, Keir, 293, 306

Hargreaves, James, 286
Harriman report (W. Averell Harriman), 132-134
Harrison, Benjamin, 111
Harvester, mechanical, 83
Haxthausen, Baron August von, 153
Hay, John M., 433, 437, 485
Healey, Dennis, 270
Hearst, W. R., 485, 487
Henderson, Arthur, 313, 314
Henry III (Eng. k.), 280
Henry, Patrick, 20
Hess, Moses, 162
Heuss, Theodor, 353
Hillman, Sidney, 101-102
Hindenburg, Paul von, 339, 340
Hitler, Adolf, 266, 268, 274, 339 ff., 388, 439, 450, 462, 470, 492, 510, 514 ff.
Hoess, Rudolf, 341-342
Holdsworth, W. S., 292
Holland, 126, 425-426
Holy Alliance, 490, 496
Hong Kong, 319, 325, 428, 433
Hoover, Herbert C., 87, 559-560
House of Commons, 280-282, 296-298, 305 ff.
House of Lords, 298, 308
House of Representatives, U. S., 17, 18
Hughes, Charles Evans, 484
Hull, Cordell, 484, 515
Humbert (It. k.), 389
Hungary, 259, 452, 538, 550
Hurley, Patrick J., 444
Huskisson, William, 301, 303
Hussey reaper, 83
Hyndman, Henry M., 293, 305

Immigration, 502-503
Imperial Conferences, 322
Imperial Council (Russia), 173
Imperial Federation League, 322
Imperial War Cabinet, 322
Imperialism, 167-168, 456-461
Income, national, United States, 115, 120
Income tax, 36
Independent Labour party, 306

India, 312, 319, 325, 327-328, 424, 448, 450-451, 452
Indians, American, 14 ff.
Individualism, 62-65, 77, 140, 151
Indo-China, 448, 465, 546
Indonesia, 448, 452, 546
Industrial Revolution, 286-288
Industry, China, 407-408
nationalization, 184-185, 310-311, 312, 346
United States, 104-115
Inquest, 278-279
Instrument of Government, 283
International Bank for Reconstruction and Development, 534, 548
International Court of Justice, 534
International Economic Conference, 259
International Labor Organization, 491, 535
International Ladies Garment Workers, 97
International Military Tribunal, 342
International Monetary Fund, 534-535
International Refugee Organization, 541
International relations, 474-479
control of, 479-482
United States, see United States, foreign policy
International Working Men's Association, 166, 295
Interstate Commerce Act, 85, 110
Iran, 540
Ireland Bill, 326-327
Isolationism, 487, 491-492, 514-517, 559-560
Italy, 126, 135, 183, 266, 376-377, 550
church and state problems, 378-381, 385-387
Communist party, 391-394
fascism, 381-387
nineteenth century, 377-378
Republic, 388-391

Jackson, Andrew, 43, 80-81, 103, 111
James I (Eng. k.), 282
James II (Eng. k.), 283
Japan, 146, 265-266, 274, 492, 505-506, 523, 544
and China, 410, 420, 425, 432-440, 444, 454-456, 465-466
imperialism, 457-458, 516
Jefferson, Thomas, 13, 17, 20, 24, 28, 32-33, 40-42, 78, 80, 82, 108, 483, 487, 488, 492, 501
Jews, 34, 182, 226, 340, 341-342
Jinnah, Mohammed Ali, 325
John (Eng. k.), 279
John of Montecorvino, 425
Johnson, Very Rev. Hewlett, 203, 209, 223
July Revolution, 362
Junkers, 336, 337, 340, 345
Jury, 278-279

Kaganovich, Lazar M., 242
Kalinin, Mikhail I., 267
Kamenev, Lev B., 199
Kansas-Nebraska Act, 46
Kay, John, 286
Kellogg-Briand Pact, 263, 484, 492, 506
Kennedy, Joseph P., 559-560
Kent, James, 24
Kenya, 329
Khaki election, 307
King's Council, 280
Knights of Labor, 100-101
Know-Nothing party, 47
Kolchak, Aleksandr V., 258
Komsomol, 236
Korea, 135, 432, 434, 435, 452, 529, 544
Korean War, 136, 472, 498-499, 532, 533, 536, 540, 553, 557, 559
Kronstadt Mutiny, 190
Krug report (Julius A. Krug), 129-131
Kublai Khan, 425
Kulaks, 185, 220

Kun, Béla, 259
Kuomintang, 416, 419, 421, 441 ff., 452-455, 462-463, 465 ff.
Kwantung army, 454, 466

Labor, Italy, 384-385
Russia, 210-214
United States, and agriculture, 71-72
growth of union movement, 97-104
postwar strike situation, 123-125
World War II, 117-120
Labour party (Great Britain), genesis, 305-307
historical background, 287-290, 292-305
program, 308-316
Labour Representation League, 305
Labour Representative Committee, 306
Laender, 351
La Follette, Robert M., 88, 93
Laissez faire, 300-301, 319
Lao-tse, 403
Laski, H. J., 292
Lateran Accord, 386-387
Latin America, 488-489, 515
Latvia, 254, 255, 265, 273
Laval, Pierre, 364
League of Nations, 263-264, 266, 388, 438-439, 475, 477, 479, 481, 491, 506, 534
Lecky, W. E., 295
Lee, Richard Henry, 20
Lend-Lease, 123, 276, 441, 492, 518-519, 521, 547
Lenin, Nikolai, 145, 154, 156, 189, 190-191, 198, 199, 218, 220, 235, 241, 244, 256 ff., 260, 261, 275, 314
and Marxism, 167-171, 175-179, 184-185
Leo XIII, Pope, 380
Lewis, John L., 53, 101-102
Libel Act, 298-299
Liberal party, 305, 308, 315

Liberalism, defined, 277
development, see Great Britain, historical development
Liberia, 556
Liberty party, 46
Lincoln, Abraham, 25, 36, 45, 48, 53
Lindbergh, Charles A. and Anne M., 516
Linebarger, P. M. A., 409, 416, 462
Lithuania, 254, 255, 265, 273
Little Octobrists, 236
Litvinov, M. M., 263, 264
Locke, John, 5, 11, 13, 17, 28, 141, 358
London Conference, 348
London Labour Representative Committee, 306
London Working Man's Association, 305
Long, Huey P., 485
Louis XIV (Fr. k.), 476
Louis XVI (Fr. k.), 359, 360
Louis Philippe (Fr. k.), 362
Louisiana Purchase, 40, 41, 78, 108, 483, 486, 489
Luddite riots, 287
Lysenko-Michurin doctrine, 249
Lytton Report, 438-439

Macao, 425
McCloy, John J., 352
McCormick reaper, 83
MacDonald, Ramsay, 306, 307
McKinley, William, 111
Madison, James, 21
Magna Charta, 141, 279-280
Maisky, Ivan, 273
Malaya, 332
Malenkov, G. M., 245
Malta, 329
Malthus, Thomas, 287
Manchu dynasty, 403, 416, 430-431
Manchukuo, 438-440
Manchuria, 265-266, 395, 396, 433, 434, 436, 438, 446, 454, 466-467, 472, 516, 540

Mao Tse-tung, 420-421, 422, 444, 467, 469-470, 471, 472
March Revolution, 175
Marie, André, 373
Marie Antoinette (Fr. q.), 360
Maritain, Jacques, 381
Marshall, George C., 127, 348, 392, 444-445, 466, 468, 549
Marshall Plan, see European Recovery Program
Marx, Karl, 158, 160, 161-162
theories, 162-171, 178-179, 249, 294-295, 305
Marx-Engels-Lenin Institute, 161
Maryland Colony, 7
Mason, George, 20
Massachusetts colonies, 4-7, 15
Matteotti, Giacomo, 384
Mayflower Compact, 4-5, 13
Maynard, Sir John, 185, 186-187, 220
Mazzini, Giuseppe, 377, 379
Melbourne, Lord, 289
Mencius, 403
Mendelian-Morgan theories, 249
Mercantilism, 76
Methodist Church, 32, 34, 299
Mexican War, 46
Middle Ages, 57, 62, 279, 296
Militant communism, 183-190
Mill, John Stuart, 295, 321
Mine and Collieries Bill (1842), 302-303
Minimum wage laws, 65-66
Minority groups, 182, 225-227
Mir, 154
Molotov, Vyacheslav M., 264, 273, 274, 550
Mongols, 413, 425
Monnet Plan, 370
Monopoly, 112, 139
Monroe, James, 20, 42, 50, 496
Monroe Doctrine, 483, 486, 489, 490, 502
Montesquieu, Baron de, 18, 358
Morgenthau Plan, 526
Morris, William, 294, 305-306
Morse, Wayne, 37
Munich agreement, 268 ff.

Muraviev-Amurski, Count, 141-142
Murray, R. H., 295
Muscovite dynasty, 142, 152
Mussolini, Benito, 268, 382-389, 462, 514 ff.
Mutual-assistance pacts, 265
Mutual Defense Assistance Program, 497

Napoleon Bonaparte, 78, 361-362, 450, 486
Napoleon III, 362, 379
Napoleonic Wars, 285, 291, 476
National Assembly, 359-360
National Association of Manufacturers, 71-72
National Bank, 38, 40-41, 42-43, 44
National debt, 38
National Grange, 71, 85
National Industrial Recovery Act, 102
National Labor Relations Act, 102
National Labor Relations Board, 124
National Recovery Administration (NRA), 113
National Republicans, 43-45
National War Labor Board, 119
Nationalism, 279, 449-452, 508-509
growth, China, 452-456
Nationalist party, 340
Nationalization, 184-185, 310-311, 312, 346
Natural rights, 11-13
Navigation acts, 301, 319
Nazi party, 338, 339-342, 345, 463, 526
Needle Trades Unions, 98
Negro rights, 24-27, 35, 223
Nehru, Jawaharlal, 325, 547
Nepmen, 192
Nerchinsk, Treaty of, 426
Netherlands, 126
Neutrality acts, 484, 492, 515, 518
New Deal, 53, 88-90, 94, 101-102, 103, 183

New Deal—Continued
foreign economic policy, 510-514
New Economic Policy (Russia), 191-201, 259, 260
New England colonies, 4-7
New England Confederation, 15
New Zealand, 319, 321, 323
Newcomen, Thomas, 286
Newfoundland, 312
Newton, William, 305
Nicholas I (Rus. czar), 159
Nicholas II (Rus. czar), 155, 172 ff.
Nine-Power Treaty, 437 ff.
Nonaggression pacts, 264-265, 518
Norris, George W., 93
North Africa, 366-367
North Atlantic Security Pact, 497, 543-544
North Carolina, constitution, 14
Northern Ireland, 326-327
Northern Rhodesia, 331-332
Nuremberg trials, 341
Nye, Gerald P., 514

Office of Economic Stabilization, 121
Office of Price Administration, 114, 120-121
Office of War Mobilization, 121
Olney, Richard, 489, 506
Open door policy, 433, 437, 484, 489
Opium War, 428
Organization for European Economic Cooperation, 138
Orgburo, 240, 241
Oriental Exclusion Act, 484
Outer Mongolia, 265, 266
Overseas Food Corporation, 330-331
Overseas Resources Development Bill, 330
Owen, Robert, 303-304, 305
Oxford Oath, 514

Paine, Thomas, 285, 293
Pakistan, 312, 325, 448
Palestine, 532

Panama Canal, 490
Pan-Americanism, 484
Papacy, 377, 379-381, 385-387
Pares, Sir Bernard, 154
Paris Commune, 194
Paris conference, Marshall Plan, 127-129
Paris Peace Conference, 258, 381, 436
Paris Peace Pact, 438
Parity prices, 89-91
Parliament (Gt. Br.), 2, 8-11, 13, 141, 280 ff.
  Labour party, 305-307
  reforms, 296-304
Parliament Act (1911), 308
Party Conferences and Congresses, 240, 241
Party Control Commission, 244
Patel, V. J., 325
Pauker, Ana, 276
Peace of Westphalia, 476
Pearl Harbor, 439-440, 455
  background, 518-519
Peel, Sir Robert, 301-302
Pegler, Westbrook, 224
Penn, William, 7, 31, 291
Pennsylvania Colony, 7
People's Bloc, Italy, 390-391, 392
People's Republic of China, 467
Perry, Commo. Matthew C., 141, 505
Perry, Ralph Barton, 60, 62
Persia, 160
Pétain, Henri Philippe, 364
Peterloo Massacre, 287-288
Petition of Right, 282-283
Philadelphia Convention, 15-18, 20
Philippine Islands, 425, 433, 451, 452, 458, 461, 489, 546
Pieck, Wilhelm, 354
Pilgrim Fathers, 4-5
Pioneers, Young, 236
Pi-shih, Gen., 469
Pitt, William, 285
Pius IX, Pope, 379-380
Pius XI, Pope, 387
Place, Francis, 290, 293, 303

Planned economy, 182-183
Plekhanov, George, 169-170
Plow, improvement of, 82
Plymouth Colony, 4-5, 6
Point 4 program, 448, 459-461, 497, 555-556
Poland, 160, 258, 262, 265, 273, 452, 529-530, 538, 550
Politburo, 207 ff., 239, 471
  operations, 241-244, 245, 247
Polo, Marco, 424-425
Pope, Jacob, 83
Popular Front, 364
Popular Republicans, 367 ff.
Populist movement, 86
Portsmouth, Treaty of, 434-435
Potugal, 425-426
Potsdam Declaration, 343-344, 525-530
  breakdown, 344-348
Powell, Adam C., 37
Presbyterian Church, 32, 34
President's Council of Economic Advisers, 131-132
Presidium, 230, 233, 245
Price controls, 120-121
Primary Party Organs, 239-240, 244
Privy Council (Gt. Br.), 8
Production, Soviet Union, 221-222
  United States, farm, 91
  World War II, 118-120
Progressive party, 51, 87-88
Proletariat, 166
Provisional Government, Russia, 155-156, 175, 177, 185, 186, 189
Public schools, 33-35
Puritanism, 5, 13, 30-31
  and capitalism, 62-65

Quakers, 31, 32, 291
Queuille, Henri, 373-374
Quincy, Josiah, 78

Radical Socialists, France, 364, 372 ff.
Raffles, Sir Stamford, 427
Railroads, 84-85, 409
Ramadier, Paul, 370 ff.

Rankin, John E., 27, 37
Rapallo, Treaty of, 260-261
Rasputin, Grigori E., 173
Rationing, 120-121
Reaper, mechanical, 83
Reciprocal Trade Act (1934), 512-513
Red Army, 258, 261, 497, 537-538
Red Guards, 178
Reform Act (1832), 297
Reformation, 476
Reichstag, 335-336, 337, 340
Reichswehr, 261
Religion, China, 403, 405, 409-410, 415
    colonial America, 4-7
    Great Britain, 299-300
    Italy, 378-381
    Russia, 158-159, 192-193
    separation of church and state, 30-35
Reparations, 347
Representation of the People Act, 312
Republican party, 25-26, 37, 50, 52-54, 72-73, 86, 88
    and Democrats, 47-49
    Antifederalist, 40-42
    Nationalist, 42-45
Rerum Novarum, 380-381
Restoration, English, 7
Revolutionary War, 8, 12, 13, 76, 284, 317-320
Rhineland, 266, 343
Rhode Island Colony, 6-7, 8
Rhodes, Cecil, 321
Rhodesia, Northern, 331-332
Ricardo, David, 287, 289
Richard II (Eng. k.), 281
Riga, Treaty of, 258
Risorgimento, 377-378
Rochdale Pioneers, 304
Rockefeller, John D., 105
Rogers, Lindsay, 484
Roman Catholic Church, 31, 32, 34, 62, 299, 358, 360, 425, 475-476
    Italy, 378-381, 385-387, 392
Roman Empire, 475
Romanov dynasty, 142

Rome-Berlin Axis, 266
Romilly, Sir Samuel, 290-291
Roosevelt, Franklin D., 53, 80, 88 ff., 101-102, 103, 111, 113-114, 443, 489, 492, 510, 514-516, 521-522
Roosevelt, Franklin D., Jr., 50
Roosevelt, Theodore, 51, 111, 435, 483, 489
Root, Elihu, 485
Rousseau, Jean Jacques, 358, 359
Royal Colonial Institute, 321
Ruhr, 346, 348-349, 352, 355
Rumania, 258
Russia, see Union of Soviet Socialist Republics
Russian Socialist Democratic Labor party, 170
Russo-Japanese War, 434
Ryan, Msgr. John A., 381
Rykov, Alexis, 198

San Francisco Conference, 531
Saudi Arabia, 556
Savery, Thomas, 286
Scheinman, Mr., 197
Schlesinger, Arthur M., 81
Schmidt, C. T., 511
Schuman, Robert, 356, 372, 554
Schuschnigg, Kurt von, 381
Schwartz, Harry, 222-223
Scientific socialism, 163
Scottish Labour party, 306
Secburo, 240, 241
Secret police, 157
Seeley, Sir John, 321
Selective Service Law, 492
Self-determination, 254, 449
Seneca Falls convention, 28
Separatists, 4-5
Seward, William H., 484
Sharecroppers, 87
Shaw, George Bernard, 294, 306
Sherman Antitrust Act, 110-111, 513
Shimonoseki Peace Treaty, 432
Siam, 450
Siberia, 143, 145, 147, 153, 254, 257, 258, 436-437
Silver, free, 86
Silver Purchase Act (1934), 512

Singapore, 427
Sinkiang, 395
Sino-Soviet Treaty, 448
Slave labor, 212-214
Slavery, 19, 24-25, 46 ff., 291
Slavic groups, 148-151
Smith, Adam, 287, 300-301, 319, 320, 508
Smith-Connally Act, 124
Smoot-Hawley Tariff, 484, 491, 508
Social Democratic Association, 305
Social Democratic Federation, 294
Social Democrats, Germany, 337, 338, 351, 353
Socialism, 140, 183, 191, 195, 294-295, 304, 380
and communism, 312-314
Labour party program, 308-316
scientific, 163
Socialist League, 305-306
Socialist party, France, 364, 367 ff.
Germany, 337, 340
Italy, 382-383
Socialist Unity party, 346-347
Societies, humanitarian, 290-291
Soil Conservation Act, 89
Soil Erosion Act, 89
South Africa, 321, 323, 324
Soviet Union, see Union of Soviet Socialist Republics
Spain, 266, 381, 486-487, 515, 516
Special interest groups, 68-74, 77
Spoils system, 44
Squeeze, 415
Stakhanovites, 214, 215
Stalin, Joseph, 145, 147, 155, 169, 177, 207, 218, 220, 224, 234-235, 273, 275, 472, 522, 545
and capitalism, 268
and Politburo, 242-244
Constitution, 229, 237
feud with Trotsky, 199-201, 261-262
Stalinism, 168-169, 179, 465

Standard Oil Company, 111
Stassen, Harold E., 559-560
State Bank (Russia), 197-198
State Labor Reserve Schools, Russia, 212
State Planning Commission (Gosplan), 208-209
State service and ownership, 151-153, 206-207
Statute of Westminster, 323, 326, 327
Stevens, B. S. B., 323-324
Stilwell, Gen. Joseph W., 442-443, 446
Stimson, Henry L., 492
Stimson Doctrine, 440, 484
Stolypin reforms, 171
Strachey, John, 333
Strikes, 119-120, 123-124
Strong, Anna Louise, 195-197
Sudan, 321, 328
Suffrage, female, 28-30
Great Britain, 296-298
male, 23-24
Negro, 25-27, 223
Soviet Union, 223-224
Sun Yat-sen, 416, 417, 451-453, 454, 461-462, 463-464
Supreme Economic Council (Russia), 198-199
Supreme Judicature Act, 298
Supreme Soviet, 230-233, 245
Sweden, 136

Taft, Robert A., 135, 559-560
Taft-Hartley Act, 68, 102, 104, 124-125
Taiping rebellion, 431, 451
Talmadge, Herman, 27
Tanaka Memorial, 438
Tanganyika, 329, 331-332
Tariffs, 38, 42, 43, 45, 72-73, 79-80, 106, 482, 504-505, 508, 512-513
Tatar empire, 152
Taxation, 4, 8, 36, 89, 281, 558
internal, 9-11, 16
Teheran Conference, 522
Thailand, 448
Theory of the Third Rome, 158
Third Force, 372-375

Third International, 259
Thirty Years' War, 476
Thorez, Maurice, 276
Thresher, mechanical, 83
Thurmond, J. Strom, 53
Tito, Marshal, 539
Togliatti, Palmiro, 392
Tory party, 307-308, 315
Toynbee, Arnold, 449
Trade Disputes Act, 308
Trade unions, see Unions
Trades Union Congress, 303, 313
Transportation, 84-85, 408-409
Tripartite Pact, 274
Triple Alliance, 171
Triple Entente, 171
Trotsky, Leon, 178, 256, 258
    feud with Stalin, 199-201,
    261-262
Truman, Harry S., 37, 103-104,
    134-135, 224, 392, 444,
    447-448, 493-494, 498-499,
    522, 560-561
    Point 4 program, 448, 459-
    461, 497, 555-556
Truman Doctrine, 483, 495-496,
    497, 542
Trusts, Soviet Union, 198-199
    United States, 111-112
Tsetse fly, 332
Tucker, Josiah, 320
Tukhachevsky, Marshal M. N.,
    261
Turkey, 495
Twenty-one Demands, 436
Tydings-McDuffie Act, 484
Tzu Hsi, 431, 432, 435

Uganda, 329, 332
Ukraine, 149-150, 254, 255, 258
Ulyanov, V. I., see Lenin,
    Nikolai
Unemployment, 113, 117-118
Union of Soviet Socialist Repub-
    lics, 1, 125 ff., 133, 140,
    426, 432, 440, 448, 515 ff.
    and civil liberties, 223-227
    Bolshevik Revolution, 142,
    156-157, 175-178
    claims of accomplishment,
    203-206

Union of Soviet Socialist Re-
    publics—Continued
    collective farms, 219-221, 246
    Communist Party, and world
    revolution, 253-254, 259-
    260, 262, 495-499, 536-
    561
    characteristics, 234-235
    control methods, 244-250
    membership, 235-237
    organization, 237-244
    Constitutions, 155, 194-195,
    206, 210, 211, 228, 229,
    237
    Five-Year Plans, 200-203,
    207-209, 220-221
    foreign policy, aims, 253-255,
    259-262, 275-276
    Allied occupation, 257-258
    and fascism, 266-268
    and Munich agreement,
    268-272
    and World War II,
    274-276
    Brest-Litovsk Treaty,
    256-257
    disarmament proposals,
    262-263
    Far East, 265-266
    German alliance, 272-274
    League of Nations, 263-264
    nonaggression and mutual-
    assistance pacts, 264-265
    Rapallo Treaty, 260-261
    Spanish Civil War, 266
    World War I, 251-255
    World War II, 523-530
    geography and climate, 142-
    147
    government, administrative
    structure, 228-232
    controls, 195-199
    elections, 232-234
    functions of soviets, 234
    labor, 210-214
    Marx-Engels-Leninism, 161-
    171, 178-179
    New Economic Policy, 191-
    201, 259, 260
    population, 148-150

Union of Soviet Socialist Republics—*Continued*
production, 221-222
Russian Empire, 151-160,
171-175
unions, 218-219
wages and living standards,
214-218
war-communism period, 183-
190
World War I, 173-175
Unions, 67-68, 71, 112, 370,
385
and Taft-Hartley Act, 124-125
development, 97-104
Great Britain, 303
Soviet Union, 218-219
United front, 268
United Mine Workers, 98
United Nations, 213, 418, 459,
460, 477, 479, 492-493,
498-499, 538, 539-540
inception, 530-531
organizations, 531-535
UNRRA, 125, 128, 524, 541
United States, 262, 263, 266,
274 ff., 335
China, 440-448
colonial government, 2-8
legislative powers, 8
taxation controversy, 8-11
Constitution, *see* Constitutions
contemporary, 459-461, 493-
499
control of foreign relations,
479-482
Declaration of Independence,
12-13
diplomacy, 486-493
economic development, 75-77,
95-96
agriculture, *see* Agriculture
and foreign policy, 502-514
industry, 104-115
labor, 97-104
economic system, *see* Capitalism
European aid, *see* European
Recovery Program
federalism, 13-18

United States—*Continued*
foreign policy, and American
resources, 502-506
formulation, 482-486
and international relations,
474-479
and isolationism, 514-517
New Deal, 510-514
organizations, civic, 485
party system, characteristics,
49-54
Democrats and Republicans, 45-49
Democrats and Whigs,
42-45
Federalists and Republicans, 37-42
postwar strike situation, 123-
125
post-World War I, 506-510
Presidency, 16-18, 20, 36,
480-481, 483
Senate, 17-18, 36, 480-481,
506
and sovereignty, 500-502
and Soviet aggression, 537-
561
Supreme Court, 17, 27, 36,
66-67, 85, 89, 111-112
World War II, 117-123, 518-
535
United States Chamber of
Commerce, 71-72
United States Steel Corporation, 108
Utilitarians, 290
Utrecht, Treaty of, 476

Van Buren, Martin, 45
Vanderbilt, Cornelius, 105
Vatican, 379, 386, 390, 392
Veblen, Thorstein, 55
Versailles Treaty, 257, 261, 266,
322, 339, 341, 343, 435-
436, 452, 476
Veto, 533
Vichy government, 364-365, 366
Victor Emmanuel II (It. k.),
378, 380, 383, 388, 389
Viet Nam, 546
Virginia Company, 3-4

Virginia Statute for Religious Freedom, 32-33
Voltaire, 358
Voting, see Suffrage

Wabash, St. Louis and Pacific Railroad Company vs. Illinois, 85
Wages, Soviet Union, 214-217
United States, World War II, 118-120
Wagner, Robert F., 37
Wagner Act, 102
Wakefield, Edward G., 321
Wallace, Henry A., 51, 123
War communism, 183-190
War Labor Disputes Act, 124
War Manpower Commission, 119, 121
War of 1812, 40, 42, 78, 501
War Production Board, 121
Wars of the Spanish Succession, 476
Washington, George, 37, 39, 40, 50, 82, 483, 487-488, 492, 500-501
Washington Conference, 258, 436-437, 439-440, 484
Watt, James, 286
Webb, Sidney and Beatrice, 294
Webb-Pomerene Act (1918), 513
Webster, Daniel, 45, 80, 82
Webster-Ashburton Treaty, 483-484
Wedemeyer, Gen. Albert C., 444
Weimar Republic, 336-339, 340
Wentworth, Peter, 281-282
West Indies, 318, 319, 329
Westphalia, Peace of, 476
Wherry, Kenneth S., 37
Whig party, England, 284, 297
United States, 45-47, 50
Whiskey Rebellion, 39
Whitney, Eli, 82
Wilberforce, William, 291

William I (Eng. k.), 278
William and Mary (Eng. k. and q.), 7, 283
Williams, Roger, 30-31
Wilson, Havelock, 306
Wilson, James, 11
Wilson, Woodrow, 51, 112, 452, 483, 492, 506
Women's rights, 28-30, 65-66
Wood, Jethro, 82
Workers' Food Requisitioning Squads, 189, 191
World Bank, 134
World Court, 481, 485, 491
World Soviet Socialist Union, 195
World War I, 87, 171, 321, 322, 336, 381, 452, 487, 506
Japan, 435-436
Soviet Union, 173-175, 251, 252-253, 255-257
World War II, 90, 113, 114, 128, 274-276, 324, 357, 376, 458, 476, 477
American foreign policy, 519-522
objectives, 522-535
China, 441-444, 455
economic aspects, 117-123
France, 364-366
isolationism, 514-517
Italy, 388-389
Wycliffe, John, 291

Yalta Conference, 440, 495, 523, 525, 529-530
Young Communist League, 236, 244
Youth Labor Draft, Russia, 212
Yuan Shi-kai, 416, 452
Yugoslavia, 392, 452, 538, 539

Zaslavsky, David, 224
Zhebrak, Anton, 249
Zinoviev, Grigori E., 199
Zionism, 226